Second Nature Urban Agriculture

This book is the long-awaited sequel to *Continuous Productive Urban Landscapes (CPULs): Designing urban agriculture for sustainable cities*.

Second Nature Urban Agriculture updates and extends the authors' concept for introducing productive urban landscapes, including urban agriculture, into cities as essential elements of sustainable urban infrastructure. Since 2004, when the concept was first put into the public realm, it has had a profound effect on thinking about urban design and the nature of the contemporary city. Driven by the imperatives of climate change mitigation, changing economics, demographics, lifestyle expectations and resource supply, the ideas embodied within the CPUL concept have entered the international urban design discourse.

This new book reviews recent research and projects on the subject and presents a toolkit of actions aimed at making urban agriculture happen. Referencing an international body of work, it addresses issues associated with particular urban locations and their contexts while drawing out transferable lessons and knowledge. As pioneering thinkers in this area, the authors bring a unique overview to contemporary developments in the field and have the experience to judge opportunities and challenges facing those who wish to create more equitable, resilient and beautiful cities.

The book has three parts: the first develops and contextualises the *CPUL City* theory, the second formulates *CPUL City Actions*, and the third presents a repository of contemporary design and subject references underpinning the CPUL concept and case for urban agriculture. Expert chapters by international authorities support particular themes and thoughts throughout the book.

Prompted by demand from cities, practitioners, activists, designers and planners, *Second Nature Urban Agriculture* is aimed at all those with an interest in developing quality urban spaces for the sustainable city of tomorrow.

André Viljoen is an architect and principal lecturer in architecture at the University of Brighton and, with Katrin Bohn, contributes to the work of *Bohn&Viljoen Architects*.

Katrin Bohn is an architect and visiting professor at the Technical University of Berlin. For the past 12 years, she has also taught architecture and urban design, mainly as a senior lecturer at the University of Brighton. Together with André Viljoen, she runs *Bohn&Viljoen Architects*, a small architectural practice and environmental consultancy based in London.

Second Nature Urban Agriculture

DESIGNING PRODUCTIVE CITIES

EDITED BY

André Viljoen and Katrin Bohn

Routledge
Taylor & Francis Group

LONDON AND NEW YORK

First published 2014
by Routledge
2 Park Square, Milton Park, Abingdon, Oxon
OX14 4RN

and by Routledge
711 Third Avenue, New York, NY 10017

*Routledge is an imprint of the Taylor & Francis
Group, an informa business*

*British Library Cataloguing in
Publication Data*
A catalogue record for this book is available from
the British Library

*Library of Congress Cataloging
in Publication Data*
Second nature urban agriculture : designing
productive cities / edited by Katrin Bohn and
Andre Viljoen.
     pages cm
Includes bibliographical references and index.
1. Urban agriculture. I. Bohn, Katrin, editor of
compilation. II. Viljoen, André (André M.) editor
of compilation.
  S494.5.U72S43 2014
  635.09173'2–dc23
  2013048263

ISBN: 978-0-415-54057-5 (hbk)
ISBN: 978-0-415-54058-2 (pbk)
ISBN: 978-1-315-77114-4 (ebk)

Typeset by Alex Lazarou

Printed and bound in India by Replika Press Pvt. Ltd.

Second Nature Urban Agriculture
DESIGNING PRODUCTIVE CITIES

EDITORS
André Viljoen
Katrin Bohn

MAIN AUTHORS
Katrin Bohn
André Viljoen

CONTRIBUTORS
Nishat Awan
Gianluca Brunori
Nevin Cohen
Victor Coleman
David Crouch
Gillean Denny
Francesco Di Iacovo
Ken Elkes
James Godsil
Mark Gorgolewski
Yrjö Haila
Stefan Jordan
June Komisar
Howard Lee
Elisabeth Meyer-Renschhausen
Kevin Morgan
Joe Nasr
Philipp Oswalt
Jorge Peña Diaz
Marit Rosol
Graeme Sherriff
Mikey Tomkins
Urbaniahoeve
Yuneikys Villalonga
Sabine Voggenreiter
Richard Wiltshire

EDITORIAL ASSISTANCE
Nishat Awan

INITIAL GRAPHIC DESIGN
Bohn&Viljoen, Nishat Awan, Susanne Hausstein,
Stephen Moylan

TRANSLATIONS (INTERVIEWS)
Lisa O'Connor, Katrin Bohn

Contents

CPUL City Actions

CPUL Repository

Foreword

William McDonough, co-author of the highly influential book *Cradle to Cradle: Remaking the way we make things* and of the recent book *The Upcycle: Beyond sustainability – designing for abundance.*

...we sow cereals and plant trees; we irrigate our lands to fertilize them. We fortify river-banks, and straighten or divert the courses of rivers. In short, by the work of our hands we strive to create a sort of second nature within the world of nature.

(Cicero, *De Natura Deorum (The Nature of the Gods), ca. 45 BC*)

Just across the East River from Manhattan, in industrial Queens, there's a one-acre farm atop an old shipping warehouse that produces some of the most prized fruits and vegetables in New York City. On a mid-summer day, while the N train rumbles by a few blocks away and the Chrysler Building glitters in the sun, an astonishing variety of crops grow in dozens of orderly rows six stories above bustling Northern Boulevard. There are Red Mizuna Greens, Black Krim Tomatoes, Bull's Blood Beets, Masai Bush Haricot Verts, Shisito Peppers, Thai Basil, and Purple Haze Carrots as well as numerous varieties of watermelon, cucumber, cantaloupe, and kale. Honeybees hum around stacked hives and egg-laying hens peck and preen and shuffle in their nests. Farm workers sell the morning's harvest to a crowd of shoppers and pack boxes of tomatoes and greens for nearby restaurants. In every sense, this urban rooftop is a working farm: a cultivated, productive, socially vital landscape embedded in the natural world. Second nature.

Anomalous as it may seem today, urban agriculture was our second nature for thousands of years. Tilling soil and sowing seeds were the *ur*-gestures of civilization, acts that inscribed human hopes on the land, entwined nature and culture, and transformed unsettled terrain into human places where *we* belonged. Mesopotamian and Egyptian cities were intensely agricultural, as were the Greek city states and Cicero's Rome. In each, tilling and irrigation constructed beneficent second natures within densely populated settlements, while agricultural knowledge and custom – the domestication of seeds; mathematics, engineering, and ethics; the preparation and sharing of food – nourished dynamic urban

cultures. Cities and agriculture co-evolved spectacularly. Empire drove them apart, but when I was growing up in Tokyo, farm and city were still engaged, nearby neighbors; farmers led poop carts through the streets every night, picking up nutrients for the soil. The true anomaly is the perceived dualism between nature and culture, food production and city life.

Keenly aware of the history and generative potential of urban agriculture, André Viljoen and Katrin Bohn are devoted to making it commonplace. With *Second Nature Urban Agriculture*, they offer a thorough exploration of the field from an architectural and urban planning perspective, drawing on research, fieldwork and case studies to present a framework for integrating agriculture into cities. Like Cicero, they see second nature as a productive landscape embedded in the natural processes of "first nature" and recognize the interdependence of first and second natures as the foundation of robust, resilient food systems.

Fine essays on the theory and practice of Continuous Productive Urban Landscapes make the important case for agriculture as an essential element of urban infrastructure and economies, while an informative collection of project-oriented stories from Berlin, London, New York and Detroit evokes the energy and creativity animating today's leading food-growing cities. Together, Katrin, André, and their contributors have achieved the lofty goal of producing a full-bodied repository of ideas, principles and actions that support long-term, well-financed, ecologically intelligent, superbly designed spatial responses to the challenge and opportunity of feeding people that live in cities. They have taken a giant step toward renewing the civilizing legacy of urban agriculture.

That is very good news. The long separation of city life and natural systems was good for neither. 'Nature, in the common sense', Emerson said, 'refers to essences unchanged by man; space, the air, the river, the leaf.' But surely we have changed them. We inherited a food system and a way of building cities that devalued the essences of each – soil, water, plants, people – making second nature an erasure of natural assets rather than a generative, supportive landscape for the well-being of living things. While industrial farming decimated the world's topsoil, planners misread the nature of urban form. Ebenezer Howard's *Garden Cities*, Corbusier's *Ville Radieuse* and Frank Lloyd Wright's *Broadacre City* all sought to reconcile urban and rural, but betrayed the stark divide between the city and the soil.

In the last 20 years, however, the parallel movements of organic agriculture and ecological design have been thoroughly reimagining second nature, dramatically improving the generative capacity of buildings, landscapes, urban farms and city food systems.

A few design questions have been influential: How do we become native to our place? In other words, how does nature work right *here* and what does the land tell us about what thrives in *this* soil? If we recognize the laws of nature as a model for good design, and the health of the soil as a measure of productivity and wealth, how do we develop positive, supportive interactions between natural systems and human communities? And, from an urban design perspective: What if buildings, like trees, were soil-makers and photosynthetic actors, living organisms participating productively in their surroundings?

Those questions set the course for the upcycling of second nature. A building like a tree is designed to fit in an ecosystem, not overpower nature or limit human impact. Enmeshed in local energy flows, it harvests solar income, makes food from sunlight, filters water and creates a supportive habitat for people and other living things. Offices, factories and schools with solar collectors, greenhouses and water filtration systems accrue energy and provide organic food, clean water and good jobs. They leave a beneficial ecological and social footprint.

Green roofs, like the rooftop farms profiled in these pages, take high-performance second nature to the landscape level. Not all green roofs grow food for people, but the ways in which they preserve soil nutrients, support plants and generate urban photosynthesis provide a bridge to large-scale urban farming. The living roof atop Ford Motor Company's River Rouge plant in Dearborn, Michigan – a ten-acre urban garden – is only the most visible element of a living, landscape-scale stormwater filtration system, which includes porous paving and underground basins, as well as constructed wetlands, swales and wooded meadows. A scientifically cultivated network, it dramatically reduces the rate of flow of stormwater into the Rouge River while also absorbing carbon dioxide, making oxygen, purifying the soil and providing habitat for birds, butterflies and insects.

With insights from the evolution of green roofs and from the work of brilliant farmers developing permaculture, hydroponics and rooftop soils, architecture and agriculture are no longer estranged. In Neemrana, India, when we designed a 62,500 square metre "Garden Factory" for Hero Moto, the nation's largest manufacturer of motorcycles, our leading design question was: What if a factory could be a garden of health and productivity?

It can. With a solar array, vegetated air-purification wall, rooftop greenhouses, daylighting, and ductless air delivery, the factory will generate or harvest nearly all of its needs: oxygen and fresh air for people, carbon dioxide for plants, irrigation water and hot water, electricity, cooling, food and both factory and food production jobs. Farm follows function. The building is not simply "a machine in the garden" nor "a garden in the machine." It's alive; the machine *is* a garden.

Can urban agriculture again become an embedded habit and cultural norm? Along with André Viljoen and Katrin Bohn, I believe it will. Reading their study, one begins to appreciate the energy and intelligence driving today's urban farming enterprises. In New York City, for example, urban food production is booming and the agricultural network is rooted and strong. There are commercial farms and farms focused on community engagement; farms that practice intensive, open air, soil-based cultivation and those devoted to greenhouse hydroponics. There are rooftop, building-integrated and land-based farms, as well as 700 food-producing gardens and 50 schools that incorporate student-grown food in school lunches. The network includes commercial apiaries, composters, seed banks, farmers' markets, restaurants, soil doctors and farm design services, as well as, of course, those Mizuna Greens, Black Krim Tomatoes and Masai Bush Haricot Verts.

Food has a future – we have a future – when cities build second nature from the soil up.

Preface

We started thinking about this book in 2008 in Brighton when discussing with John Thakara the legacy of the DOTT07 *Urban Farming Project* in Middlesbrough and the need for a guiding set of *actions* for implementing productive landscapes; to which John simply and dryly said, 'you need to write another book.'

Second Nature Urban Agriculture continues our exploration of how urban agriculture can be coherently integrated into cities. However, working on the book did not quite become our "second nature", and too many worthwhile events, often related in one way or the other to the urban agriculture theme, distracted us, but also broadened and enriched our perspective.

For some time we called the book to be written "CPUL 2", marking it as a direct sequel to our 2005 book which formulated the Continuous Productive Urban Landscapes (CPUL) concept. While *Second Nature Urban Agriculture* remains a companion volume, it also became clear to us that now, more than 10 years after the *CPUL City* concept's inception, this new book will be less singularly about CPUL and much more about the production of urban space in a wider, productive sense.

The concept of *second nature* began to interest us. It seemed to complement strategies and desires behind the current practices of urban agriculture in towns and cities of the world.

The term "second nature" has a double meaning: on the one hand it describes embedded, normalised habits and customs that take place without a thought, and on the other it refers to the manmade, *cultivated* space surrounding us in a similar way to (first) nature. Can urban agriculture be part of a second nature to both people and cities in the 21st century? Or has it started to be so already? Why should it, and how? Can or should planners, architects and designers play a role in making urban agriculture a true second nature, given that their profession is engaged with the production of space and hence also influences people's habits and behaviour?

It was only in the early 19th century that the term "second nature" was thoroughly developed in both senses to mean normalised habits and to define the manmade, the cultured, as a development of the natural, thereby suggesting that culture represents a somewhat higher, but different entity. Norbert Rath describes how the contraposition of "nature" and "culture", as it was still sustained in philosophy at the beginning of the 20th century, could no longer be upheld towards the century's end. However, human action will always be part of second nature, because it is subject to cultural conditions, as much as it produces them (Rath 1996).

Henri Lefebvre's interpretation of "second nature" is helpful when envisioning a sustainable urban future and questioning methods for its design. For Lefebvre, urban environments are socially productive environments, and become second nature. According to Erik Swyngedouw and Nikolas Heynen, it is this notion that 'paves the way to understanding the complex mix of political, economic and social processes that shape, reshape and reshape again urban landscapes' (Swyngedouw and Heynen 2003). Regarding the social production of urban environments, Lefebvre suggests:

Nature, destroyed as such, has already had to be reconstructed at another level, the level of "second nature" i.e. the town and the urban. The town, anti-nature or non-nature and yet second nature, heralds the future world, the world of the generalised urban. Nature, as the sum of particularities which are external to each other and dispersed in space, dies. It gives way to produced space, to the urban. The urban, defined as assemblies and encounters, is therefore the simultaneity (or centrality) of all that exists socially.

(Lefebvre 1976: 15)

Thinking about these interpretations in relation to urban agriculture, there seems to be a great opportunity here for the 'town heralding the future world' – that second nature – and its inhabitants to make a sustaining production their own, their second nature. At the same time, such new ownership reintroduces experiences of first nature into the urban, producing a new type of urban space that has the potential to lead to a greater unity with nature.

It is this interdependence of first and second nature that most significantly influences our thinking about productive urban landscapes. The term "productive" establishes a link between the urban and the landscape, both of which are still often considered opposites in the people's perception of the city. The link has already started to be made by those urban inhabitants that produce food. It has become their second nature.

So much has been written about urban agriculture, and much has been grown, built and experimented with during the last ten years marking the time between the press date of *CPUL 1* and this book. Our 2005 *CPUL* book had to make the case for urban agriculture in the first place; the new book aims to make the case for planned and desired action in order to more permanently establish urban agriculture in cities. Both times we apply an architectural and urban design perspective. And whilst our 2005 *CPUL* book collated diverse arguments which until then had not been related into a spatial understanding of urban food systems, the new book is already able to present not only written arguments, but also experience that has emerged from actual realised projects.

With the number of built projects expanding, and a long-standing international group of research friends and colleagues creating substantial repositories of case studies and practice, we drew our boundaries tightly: the focus is on *project initiation* and *design strategies* for productive urban landscapes. To that end, we opted for direct experience, so the book, in the main, refers to projects that we visited or were involved with from Germany, the UK and the USA. This is not to suggest that the ideas voiced are only relevant to these places. As if to confirm this, while finishing off this book, it has been agreed to translate *CPUL 1* into Chinese.

As with the 2005 *CPUL* book, we follow the practice of entering a critical dialogue with invited specialists to contextualise our concept and to develop and deepen themes where we as architects remain generalists. We hope that the resulting varied and critical voices will help readers to understand urban agriculture as second nature in the full meaning of the term.

The book starts by engaging a series of urban design thoughts and theories that may hold keys to the successful implementation of a food-productive city and that contextualise the subject area from a variety of expert viewpoints. At the same time, this part of the book contributes to the refining of the *CPUL City* concept based on practice, research and observations since 2005.

The second part of the book presents the *CPUL City Actions*, our planning and design guide for implementing more localised urban food systems based on urban agriculture. These four actions have been formulated during our work and practice, and with them we aim to propose a framework spanning between community food gardeners, commercial urban farmers, academic researchers, architects, planners and, above all, local residents.

We conclude with a CPUL-relevant Repository of resources that has been compiled by bringing together all the references from proceding chapters, presenting a snapshot from the time of writing. The intention is two-fold: one is to visualise the *CPUL City* concept in relation to significant urban agriculture texts and projects, the other is to provide an applied canon of important works that will remain useful to practitioners, professionals, academics, policy makers and the public for quite some time.

In a nutshell: a lot has changed since 2005, but still, when we imagine a "desirable future", we see more experience with less consumption.

André Viljoen & Katrin Bohn
BOHN&VILJOEN ARCHITECTS

CPUL

CITY

THEORY

An introduction

Katrin Bohn and André Viljoen

Food is a sustaining and enduring necessity. Yet among the basic essentials for life – air, water, shelter, and food – only food has been absent over the years as a focus of serious professional planning interest. This is a puzzling omission because, as a discipline, planning marks its distinctiveness by being comprehensive in scope and attentive to the temporal dimensions and spatial interconnections among important facets of community life.

(APA 2007)

In 2007, a US-American team of urban planners led by Jerry Kaufman formulated this now familiar pivotal thought as part of their substantial work on relationships between the food system of an urban entity, its spatial design and development planning. Published and adopted by the American Planning Association (APA), the resulting *Policy Guide on Community and Regional Food Planning* is widely accepted as marking the beginning of a new era which had been carefully and tirelessly prepared for by its protagonists over many years: food has finally entered the public and professional consciousness to the extent that the systematic designing and planning of food-related urban spaces can begin.

This does not mean that issues around urban food production, distribution, retailing, consumption and waste recycling had not been discussed before. Neither does it mean that the design professions were unaware of the influence food-related issues can have on product, space, event or process design or had not worked with these issues. Both subjects – let's bundle them under the headings 'urban food system' and 'designing for Urban Agriculture' – had been investigated for between 20 and 30 years by a variety of players worldwide. But, the APA report took this early activist-like work to a new level: it urged its legislative recognition, thereby paving the way for legally grounded, longer term, better financed, environmentally conscious and designed spatial responses at urban, rural and regional levels addressing *one* overriding issue: feeding people that live in cities. Which is half of the world's population (WHO 2012).

One might ask what the significance of these points – and hence this entire book – is for the other half of the world's population; those that live in rural areas. Additionally, the frame of reference of this book and of this subject area as contextualised by the APA report concentrates on the Global North, whilst the main urban population growth is happening in the developing countries of the Global South (WHO 2012). Who and what are we aiming for with this work?

Durable change will occur through small steps, but steps that thoroughly engage the imagination of all (or most) people for a fair, healthy and desirable future. Such durable change is needed everywhere, and the imagination of a fair future is no further developed in the Global North than it is in the Global South, and no more in cities than in villages. The challenge is to start. Addressing the problems which one is a part of is one way of starting. It may indeed only produce a small step, a small change, but – for us – these are the problems that surround us, concern us and hence require our attention.

Nowadays there is tangible evidence emerging of insights that urban food-growing protagonists intuitively always spoke about, for example: urban agriculture will augment the appreciation of rural agriculture (we speak of urban–rural linkages); it will encourage people to reward the effort that goes into producing good fresh or exotic food (think farmers' markets or fair trade); it will change the way we live in our cities (we speak of space production, participation and lifestyle choices). With our type of work, we may not immediately solve the problems of rural populations in the Global North or South, but we can create practical and conceptual conditions that – in small steps – contribute to changing the unsustainable way cities in the Global North feed themselves today. Achieving this, would really change a *great* deal...

In this first part of the book, we would like to highlight some of the theoretical discourses which provide the current academic context for work on productive urban landscapes and urban agriculture and therefore also of our work on the *CPUL City* concept. It may be worth noting that most of these 'theoretical discourses' are actually very practical, reflecting the fact that the generation of knowledge in this subject area often happens via the experiment, the empirical and its subsequent observation and evaluation.

Urban Agriculture on the map

It is undeniable that urban agriculture practice and discourse have increased dramatically over the last ten or so years. On a practical level, the frequent first scepticism has usually converted into passive acceptance with the next step being to turn this into active support, which, in many cases, has already started. At the same time, on an academic level, the relationship between urban agriculture and local urban food systems has become much clearer, and their interdependencies with peri-urban and regional supply and demand have been articulated in much greater detail. The question now is how, in the future, urban agriculture should sit *on the map*, literally spatially, but equally in terms of environmental, social and economic durability.

In the chapter *Growth and challenges since 2005*, we are taking stock, trying to summarise how and why urban agriculture has moved from a marginal subject to the centre of attention in a comparatively short time and on a global scale. The chapter loosely concentrates on the book's three case study countries – Germany, the United Kingdom and the USA – and it starts its observations around 2005, the publication year of our book *CPULs Continuous Productive Urban Landscapes*. The following chapter *The CPUL City concept* then looks specifically at the Continuous Productive Urban Landscape work as an example for how the subject area has been embedded into the international urban design discourse.

Whilst, at the end, the CPUL work focuses on the urban and architectural design implications of urban agriculture, Kevin Morgan, who researches innovations in governance and development, places a goal post by highlighting in his chapter *The new urban foodscape: Planning, politics and power* the necessity for supportive food policy and its incorporation specifically into municipal planning in order to facilitate any substantial urban food-growing activities. He describes examples of first moves in this direction and concludes that a successful alliance between the local state and its civil society could 'begin to foster rather than frustrate ecological integrity, public health and social justice'.

Joe Nasr, June Komisar and Mark Gorgolewski reinforce in their chapter *Urban Agriculture as ordinary urban practice: Trends and lessons* the need for broader strategic action when arguing that there is nowadays so much evidence of interest in and practice of urban agriculture that it has become a 'commonly recognized activity within the urban context'. The architect authors suggest a spatial typology based on a variety of case studies underpinning their contention that urban agriculture has started to transform 'from a theoretical concept with occasional, exceptional, experimental manifestations to a common phenomenon'.

Utilitarian Dreams

The year 2005 marked for us the beginning of a further working direction after about seven years of data collection and of architectural and urban design studies as contributed to the urban design discourse around this time. We began to broaden our design research into the qualitative aspects of urban agriculture space by discussing its visual and social perception with various artists, curators and filmmakers. British artist Tom Phillips devised the name 'Utilitarian Dreams' for a collaborative exhibition between Cuban and British architects and artists held in Brighton at the end of 2005 (UoB 2006). The interplay between the poetics of a working landscape and the hands-on necessities for its success are still – and always have been – the drivers for our work.

The chapter *Food growing in urban landscapes* therefore describes the spatial qualities that we, as architects, envisage for productive urban landscapes and that we see many others envisaging too, as these spaces are starting to emerge in cities around us. In the following chapter, *Productive life in the citiy*, we discuss emerging economic and socio-cultural characteristics of *CPUL-City*-like space during the early stages of its integration into European and North American cities. The chapter also addresses the rising desire of those involved with urban development and governance to find ways of measuring urban agriculture's social and environmental benefits so as to aid and underpin policy development supporting sustainable and healthy food plans.

Yrjö Haila's chapter *The city in the fabric of eco-social interdependence* reinforces yet another way of thinking about the utilitarian and the dream. Haila, a philosopher and environmental policy researcher, sees

contemporary cities as part of a historic environmental continuum and understands them as 'ecological formations in a metabolic or physiological sense' and believes that as such 'they create novel types of ecological communities' with human action being 'an integral element in the dynamics of such communities'. Much in the 'Utilitarian Dreams' sense, he concludes that 'not every urbanite needs to become a gardener, but every urbanite needs food'.

In her chapter, *Sueños Utilitarios: La Habana*, Yuneikys Villalonga questions how 'the landscape and the city update, in response to the new realities and necessities of society'. Villalonga, curator of the second part of the 'Utilitarian Dreams' project, a multidisciplinary exhibition in the Cuban capital in 2006, describes the different interpretations of productive urban landscapes by the participating artists and architects. These highlight the closeness of the utilitarian to the dreamlike, of the poetic to the prosaic, of the landscapes in our imagination to those that can be created in our cities in the future. But, as Villalonga says, 'beyond the cities referred to, "Utilitarian Dreams" reflects upon a global urban awareness, which concerns every place and everyone'.

Environmental impact and Urban Agriculture

In our 2005 *CPUL* book, we discussed the environmental impact of industrialised food production in an overarching way and, from a sustainability, suggested urban agriculture as part of an alternative solution. Now with the increased practical and academic experience of about ten years, we can re-discuss urban agriculture in a similarly overarching way. The advantage of the fast and sometimes overwhelming increase in urban agriculture activity in the Global North now allows us to take stock for the first time, both of its quantifiable and qualitative aspects. Is it possible to practically assess urban agriculture's environmental impact on the city, or the other way round; the city's impact on urban agriculture?

The two chapters *Diversity* and *Water, soil and air* aim to take account of this duality: whilst the former attempts to scope out the mostly positive environmental impact urban agriculture can have on urban diversity in a wide sense, the latter addresses the challenges urban agriculture faces when its practices could have negative results. The chapter *Diversity* argues that urban agriculture responds to more than concerns about food miles and relates it to issues such as biodiversity, local diversity or diverse food cultures and open space uses. *Water, soil and air* presents a review of concerns about the impact of pollution on urban agriculture, especially on soil, followed by a section on alternatives to soil as a growing medium.

In her chapter *Economies of scale: Urban Agriculture and densification*, Gillean Denny argues that different scales of food production need to be taken into account when discussing the potential environmental impact of urban agriculture. Through a life-cycle analysis of specific fruit and vegetables, Denny, an architect, can show how, 'through increasing local opportunity for production and procurement, emissions for specific produce can be reduced across the entire life of the produce'. She concludes that 'in the end, fresh produce emissions reveal that it is not only what we eat, but also how it is procured that will make the greatest difference in this interconnected food world'.

Mikey Tomkins, an urban beekeeper and urban agriculture researcher, discusses in his chapter *Bricks and nectar: Urban beekeeping with specific reference to London* the environmental importance of the honeybee for all human life and the ability of urban agriculture to help retain bees in cities. According to Tomkins, 'urban beekeeping is largely a cultural practice' – hence of second nature – and his chapter lays out its 'interconnecting components' relating them to spatial concerns. Bees, so Tomkins argues, 'already think about landscape as continuous, extending our concept of the CPUL as essential infrastructure beyond superstructure and into the atmosphere that ultimately connects us all'.

Green theory in practice and urban design

As mentioned earlier, urban agriculture is a primarily practical movement. Theoretical ideas about 'green' lifestyles, sustainable urban or architectural design, and participatory uses of urban space or local food

production are immediately mirrored in actual projects and prototypes. Protagonists of these types of contemporary urban space production draw from socio-cultural, ecological or design history and theory and, at the same time, theorists learn from the practical experience of commercial or communal food-growing projects.

The first two chapters developing this direction of thought look more closely at Germany and the United Kingdom to explain their current state of urban agriculture and the food-related interdependencies found within particular case studies. Great Britain and Germany are certainly not the only European countries that have seen a dramatic increase in urban agriculture activities during the last ten or twenty years. The Netherlands must be mentioned as a place where urban food-growing research and practice has helped to shape the subject in Europe and worldwide. Other countries with a 'green' approach to urban living are also often found among those where people engage in urban agriculture, often in connection with educational programmes. There are also a number of regions in countries all over Europe where urban food growing supports daily food needs.

Nishat Awan, in her chapter *Agential exchanges: Thinking the empirical in relation to productivity*, investigates philosophical and historical examples in order to ask 'what type of activity urban agriculture is, or could become'. She argues that, as urban agriculture is 'on the verge of becoming mainstream', the extreme pressure on land is an important factor necessitating redefinitions of the notions of productivity, value and agency. Awan, an architect and urban practitioner, uses built projects, many from the UK, to illustrate some of the interrelations which, when addressed, would allow 'for a more nuanced understanding of what could be considered a "success": how much production is productive enough?'

In his chapter *Shrinking cities and productive landscapes*, architect and writer Philipp Oswalt relates the contemporary urban land use debate to economic, ownership and urban development theories. Oswalt suggests that 'urban agriculture can play an important role in creating spatial and social cohesion within the European city', but that there are different degrees of urgency when implementing urban agriculture depending on the specific spatial and economic situation of the city in question. Referencing situations in Germany and the USA, he concludes that 'it will always be important to reserve space for uses such as urban agriculture in order to improve the quality of urban life'.

Laboratories for Urban Agriculture: the USA

The range of new projects in the USA is staggering, and if Cuba's urban agriculture, as studied by us about ten years ago (Viljoen 2005), revealed spatial possibilities and the effectiveness of systematic support systems, the current US initiatives are now testing different spatial, technical, organisational and financial models of production. We have started a new design research project under the above title – some of whose outcomes are presented throughout this book – which we understand as a continuation of our earlier project *Laboratories for Urban Agriculture: Cuba* that featured in the 2005 *CPUL* book.

Baltimore, Milwaukee, Detroit, New York and Chicago are amongst a vanguard of North American cities actively encouraging urban agriculture. In this section of the book, we are looking at the US-American situation with a focus on *New York* and *Detroit*. Detroit's well-publicised situation is resulting in numerous small-scale urban agriculture initiatives and some very ambitious urban agriculture proposals for commercial and social enterprises. Urban space is truly transformed. In New York it is the range of building-integrated urban agriculture projects, now complementing the city's vibrant community garden scene, that is of particular interest to us, because of its internationally pioneering role and, again, its relation to the *CPUL City* concept.

Whilst our observations of the situations in Detroit and New York often are of a personal nature, Nevin Cohen looks at 'case profiles' from the same cities in an attempt to draw conclusions about the planning and policy frameworks that can support 'emerging forms of urban agriculture'. In his chapter *Policies to support Urban Agriculture: Lessons from New York and Detroit*, Cohen, an urban and environmental planner, contends that such frameworks 'should evolve from a focus on zoning to support the existing networks of gardens and farms in cities to a more comprehensive assessment of emerging forms, scales, and configurations of urban agriculture'.

STOP PRESS: Because of the considerable changes that recently happened in Detroit, this chapter was updated in Spring 2013.

Elisabeth Meyer-Renschhausen in her chapter *Community gardening in Berlin and New York: A new eco-social movement* zooms in again to the scale of one such form of urban agriculture: the community gardens. Looking at the political, social and environmental history and context of community gardening in two exemplary cities in Germany and the USA, Meyer-Renschhausen investigates why and how 'this kind of new urban agriculture … has become a symbol and a form of positive protest'. Meyer-Renschhausen, a freelance researcher, author and political campaigner, concludes that 'community gardens are no longer utopia', but that they 'belong to the future of cities'.

We are aware that this excursion into thoughts and theory only broadly outlines the complexity of issues at stake when planning and designing productive urban landscapes. It hopefully also emphasises the pleasures, challenges and big positive benefits of engaging in the building of urban agriculture, be it practically in the city or theoretically in people's minds – or both, which would take us the furthest. Because it is so practice-based and because its practitioners are so active and inventive, this field of research and design research moves fast. The insights and knowledge assembled here were collected up to the end of 2012, with a few earlier or later exceptions. They will change and develop over time. However, their message will remain: The future of a city lies in the way its people are being fed. And the future of a desirable city lies in the way its urban space provides for food.

Urban Agriculture on the map: Growth and challenges since 2005

Katrin Bohn and André Viljoen

Undeniably, during the last twenty or so years, urban agriculture has become an increasingly common feature of many urban areas in the Global North and – responding to social, environmental and economic concerns – has long been practised in the Global South. It is now widely understood as a movement and as an urban space-use typology.

Because of its rapid development, several interpretations of the term 'urban agriculture' exist, capturing nuances within different contexts. Amongst those, two definitions stand out: one, from the seminal publication *Urban agriculture: Food, jobs and sustainable cities* authored and edited in 1996 for the United Nations Development Programme (UNDP) by Jac Smit with Annu Ratta and Joe Nasr, and the other, by Luc Mougeot who, in 2001, provides an extension of the former stressing that it is 'its integration into the urban economic and ecological system' (Mougeot 2001: 9) that distinguishes urban from rural agriculture rather than its urban location only:

Urban agriculture is an industry that produces, processes and markets food and fuel, largely in response to the daily demand of consumers within a town, city or metropolis, on land and water dispersed throughout the urban and peri-urban area, applying intensive production methods, using and reusing natural resources and urban wastes, to yield a diversity of crops and livestock.

(Smit *et al.* 1996)

Urban agriculture is an industry located within (intra-urban) or on the fringe (peri-urban) of a town, a city or a metropolis, which grows and raises, processes and distributes a diversity of food and non-food products, (re-) using largely human and material resources, products and services found in and around that urban area, and in turn supplying human and material resources, products and services largely to that urban area.

(Mougeot 2001: 10)

Smit's and Mougeot's definitions are nowadays the most commonly used ones, and we value them for their simplicity, openness and implicit inclusion of a cradle-to-cradle approach.

The boundaries of both definitions for 'urban agriculture' as a primarily output-driven and ecological approach to food growing have none the less raised their own challenges as more people from diverse backgrounds engage with the practice. New practitioners have increased the range of locations, qualitative and quantitative goals, economic approaches, activities and produce types included in urban food-growing projects, and this has, for example, resulted in the need for a broad understanding of the word 'industry'. For an open and public discourse this is a good sign, testifying not only to the concept, but also to a general will and interest in making it useful for different international urban contexts.

Urban and peri-urban agriculture (UPA) is currently the most commonly used alternative term, even though the 'peri-urban' is already contained in the original UNDP definition. This term denotes the food growing activity more precisely by location, highlighting that it is often the areas at the edges of cities that are utilised because of the availability of larger sites and their proximity to existing agricultural infrastructure. It is easier to use this term today than it was 10 or 20 years ago, when it was of paramount importance to make the case that food production should be brought back to the centre of urban consciousness and fabric, rather than pushed to its edge.

Many urban areas in Europe and North America – where our case study countries are located – and elsewhere, are actually conglomerations of one or more smaller cities, suburban and land-locked open, often formerly agricultural, areas. In these metropolitan regions, the distinction between urban and peri-urban may no longer be useful. Moreover, any urban food system for a city region doesn't exist in isolation, but interacts with its rural surroundings to a degree that the better these interactions are, the better the available food will be. Some researchers therefore speak not of 'urban', but of 'metropolitan agriculture' (REOS 2011).

It is neither possible nor desirable to feed a city solely through urban agriculture, but coordinated and well-managed interrelationships between urban, rural and international agriculture can lead to an environmentally optimal and equitable urban food system. In the 2005 *CPUL* book, we argued for a mix: a mix of open urban space uses around urban agriculture, as well as a mix of foods from various origins for the urban consumer. There, we presented estimates for potential self-sufficiency in fruit and vegetables of about 30%. Subsequently, similar figures have been calculated by other planners and researchers, e.g. Michael Sorkin (Sorkin 2012, see chapter *New York City*, p. 122), Mikey Tomkins (Tomkins 2009) or architect Joe Lobko who presented such findings for a housing development at the 2011 Ontario Association of Architects conference in Toronto (personal communication May 2011). It appears that the terms 'urban farming' and 'urban food growing' most directly take account of this interest in absolute yield. Here, the action of cultivation has priority over spatial or territorial consideration, and the terms are frequently found in community and allotment gardening literature, as well as in education programmes.

In Germany, the term 'urban gardening' has become very popular since 2011, when a book of the same name was published combining articles by a range of authors focusing on the 'return of productive gardens into cities' (Müller 2011). According to Frauke Hehl, a Berlin-based community garden activist, the term circulated informally in Berlin prior to 2011 (personal communication Jun 2012). It was first used in English, and only now enters the German discourse in its German translation as 'urbanes Gärtnern', a detail that offers yet another angle on the subject of local appropriation. Either way, a conscious distinction from the food growing focus of urban agriculture can be observed in Germany, where the wide spectrum of community gardening's social benefits are brought to the foreground influencing the public discourse on and perception of what urban agriculture is.

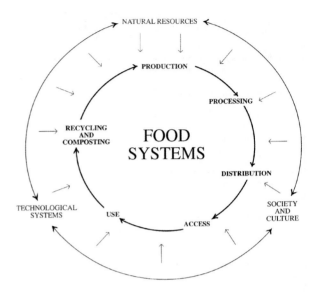

Fig 1: What are local food systems? This early graphic representation by Dahlberg of the principles of how food impacts on the city is one of a series of diagrams each showing a food system at a different scale: household, neighbourhood, municipal and regional food system (Dahlberg 2002).
(image: Kenneth A. Dahlberg, 1993)

Another group of researchers and practitioners refers to their activities under the heading 'urban horticulture'. Numerous universities and research centres, especially in the USA and Germany, run courses and research in this subject, and the International Society for Horticultural Science (ISHS *n.d.*) offers an international knowledge exchange network. Technically speaking, this term might be more correct for the growing of what are mainly vegetables, herbs and fruit within the urban realm. However, it has established itself to encompass work focusing on horticultural practice and sciences rather than the integration of agriculture into urban spaces.

It is probably simply the stark contrast between the words 'urban' and 'agriculture' – picture them both individually – that triggered the imagination and creativity of those who used the term and sent it out into to the world with a question mark – and with an exclamation mark attached. Above all, it expresses the duality of a spatial observation – the adjacency and immediacy of the urban and the field ('agri') – and a direct action – to grow ('culture').

The growing practice of Urban Agriculture

Irrespective of definitions, over the last ten years, design research and academic explorations of urban agriculture and its spatial effects have significantly increased in the Global North. From an architectural and urban design point of view, concepts such as *Agrarian Urbanism* (Waldheim 2010) and *Transition Towns* (Hopkins 2008), as well as our *CPUL City* (Viljoen *et al.* 2004), are examples of thinking holistically about the origin, current practise and/or future of spatially integrated urban food production.

The contemporary and new forms of urban agriculture in the North have, in the main, originated in North America and, looking eastwards, spread from there around the early 2000s to the UK and Europe. The establishment of economically viable schemes for various types of urban agriculture during the past five, or even ten to fifteen years, is new on both sides of the Atlantic, complimenting older, more leisure based and communal practices, such as the European allotments or the North American community gardens.

Urban agriculture brings many advantages to a city – social, health, environmental, local, educational – and can be (and sometimes is) practised not with the primary goal of food production, but of achieving outcomes in these wider fields. However, international experience from the previous years shows that more and more projects are being set up explicitly to produce food in larger quantities and/or that existing practice is being optimised. The increasing emergence of projects that are demonstrably successful enterprises – traditionally economic or social – provides proof of (and a reality check for) the acceptance of productive urban landscapes as a desired and planned urban land use.

In Germany since about 2005, urban food growers have steadily gained ground, especially, but not only, in more socially oriented urban agriculture activities. The number of community gardens in Berlin has doubled during that time and is now about 90 (Rosol 2006; TUB 2011), Leipzig, Munich and Cologne have also become important food-growing hubs and, since 2010, the 'edible town' Andernach frequently creates headlines in the news (Andernach *n.d.*). Since 2012, the facilitation of 'productive landscapes' has been laid down as

a development aim in Berlin's open space planning strategy (SenStadt 2012).

In the UK, the *Capital Growth* project gave the London community gardening scene an important boost in 2009 with the goal of creating 2,212 new projects in the three years to the 2012 Olympics. Several British cities, such as Brighton (Brighton and Hove Food Partnership [BHFP] 2012), Bristol (Bristol Food Network 2010), Leeds (Leeds Permaculture Network *n.d.*) and London (Sustain *n.d.*) have developed strong dedicated food-growing networks and programmes since at least 1999 (which is when Sustain was founded). The first farmers' market was set up in Bath in 1997 (BFM 2009), followed by the nationwide establishment of the National Association of Farmers' Markets in 1998 (Pavitt 2005), and policy interest is evident in several places, for example in London with the *Cultivating the Capital* report (London Assembly 2010) or in Brighton and Hove where the local council requires a statement about food growing for every new-built planning application (Devereux 2012).

Amongst our case study countries, the USA has pursued urban agriculture practice and research for the longest. In close cooperation with activities in Canada, urban agriculture research and dissemination began here in the late 1970s – mainly through the Canadian *Cityfarmer* newsletter (started in 1978) and later website (started in 1994) (City Farmer *n.d.*; Levenston *n.d.*). Since the 1970s, the USA community gardening scene has steadily and significantly grown in its exploration of alternative space production at a spatially, socially and politically larger scale and at least two seminal publications originate from here: Smit *et al.*'s UNDP publication, referred to above (1996), and the American Planning Association's Policy Guide on Food Planning, referred to below (2007). It is now the commercially viable urban agriculture projects that set the pace for the future.

Since the wave of literature on urban agriculture from around the turn of the century, much has been discussed and written about the various benefits of (re)accommodating food growing in urban centres. The 2005 *CPUL* book gives an account of these from what was known around the years 2003 and 2004 (Viljoen 2005). Equally, the interest in productive urban landscapes has spread, and several urban planning reports

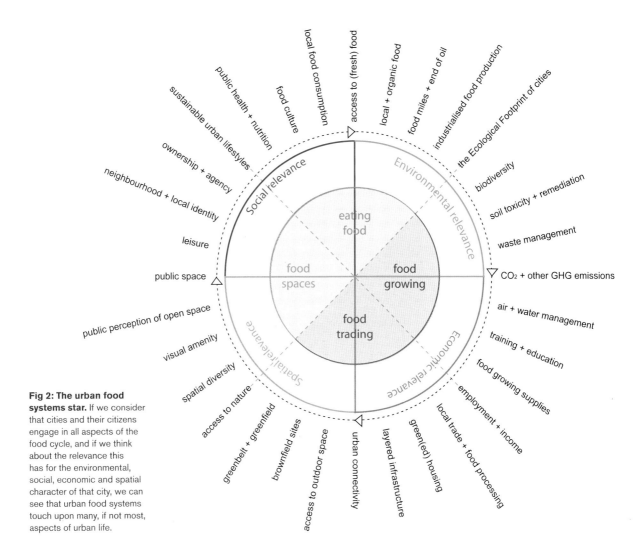

Fig 2: The urban food systems star. If we consider that cities and their citizens engage in all aspects of the food cycle, and if we think about the relevance this has for the environmental, social, economic and spatial character of that city, we can see that urban food systems touch upon many, if not most, aspects of urban life.

now recommend their introduction or support in cities such as Detroit, with the *Detroit Future City* report (Detroit Works *n.d.*), Berlin, with the above mentioned *Strategie Stadtlandschaft* (SenStadt 2012), and Leeds, through the *TRUG/Urbal* project (LMU *n.d.*).

Taking all these facts as signs of a public willingness to address urban food systems, the question now is how best to support the development of urban agriculture and productive urban landscapes so that they can reach both their full food-growing potential and move beyond niche activism to become part of integrated urban food systems, consequently gaining spatial significance within the urban fabric.

Four main challenges can be identified:

1. In order to coherently embed urban agriculture spatially into urban areas and local contexts – both temporarily and permanently – research- and planning-led urban design and architectural concepts are needed. *Keyword: productive urban landscape.*
2. Despite the great accumulated knowledge about and the huge social capital invested in urban agriculture, clear applicable guidance and best practice dissemination are essential to enable and augment the capacity of urban food growers, their projects and their sites. *Keyword: toolkit / actions.*

3. Recognised regulations or agreements with public decision makers (i.e. planning, trading, land rights) and other food-related entities (i.e. rural, markets, accreditation bodies) are needed to support and safeguard urban agriculture practice and sites. *Keyword: food policy*.
4. To become widespread and maximise its associated social, public health and environmental benefits, urban agriculture needs to be integrated into the mainstream food production and procurement systems. *Keyword: urban food systems*.

These four challenges need to be developed in parallel within a city's particular local, regional and international urban food system(s).

Urban Agriculture and urban food systems

Urban agriculture is always part of something. As a space use type, it may be part of more strategic concepts, such as *CPUL City* or *Agrarian Urbanism* or other development concepts adopted by a municipality. As a food growing activity of individuals or groups, it is part of a network of processes aiming to sustain urban life – either directly by the produce grown or by the commercial exchanges it generates. Additionally, supportive policy frameworks – food policies – generally do not target productive urban landscapes or urban agriculture alone, but wider and often very complex networks of food provision supplying city dwellers, called urban food systems.

In the 1990s, mainly researchers in the USA, for example those around Kenneth A. Dahlberg, Mustafa Koc, Kameshwari Pothukuchi and Jerome Kaufman, laid the foundations for an understanding of urban food systems that is still used and referred to today. Dahlberg's work, for example, aimed at developing food-related policy as a basis to devise specific strategies for food planning in particular urban contexts (Dahlberg *et al.* 1997) emphasising the need for understanding food systems as local systems (Dahlberg and Koc 1999). Around the same time, Pothukuchi and Kaufman began urging for food systems to be placed on the urban agenda in order to fully address the quality of life in urban localities (Pothukuchi and Kaufman 1999). Both researchers

later key-authored the now seminal 2007 APA *Policy Guide on Food Planning* which crosses the divide between food systems planning and urban spatial design (APA 2007). We see urban agriculture and productive urban landscapes as ways to contribute to this vision of a more sustainable and equitable provision of food for cities.

The concept of food sovereignty has been important in raising another significant issue: it is not just access to food that is important, but also the control a community exercises over what that food is. Initially defined during the late 1990s under that banner of *La Via Campesina* [Peasants Way] (Via Campesina n.d.), the concept is now widely discussed in urbanised environments and within urban agriculture movements. It fits well with strategies to creatively combine top-down and bottom-up initiatives. Food safety, the complex web of health and equity, also plays into the political concerns regarding the feeding of our cities and the type(s) of urban food system(s) needed.

Food systems can helpfully be broken down into smaller components – such as household or neighbourhood food systems (Dahlberg 2002) – which makes it easier to tackle more local challenges, provided that the bigger picture stays in focus. Urban agriculture and productive urban landscapes are – or should be – part of both scales of urban food systems.

To achieve this multi-scale integration requires a specific dialogue between planners and designers, and, before this can happen, a shared language needs to be developed, built on the knowledge that has already been generated around urban food systems. For example, comparing Dahlberg's 1993 food systems diagram (*Fig 1*) with one that we created in 2009 from an architectural and urban design perspective (*Fig 2*) shows one of the gaps that need bridging between urban food system planning and designing for urban agriculture, namely the consideration of 'space'.

At a spatial level, the necessary planner–designer–practitioner dialogue is just beginning. In Europe, the Sustainable Food Planning Group within the Association of European Schools of Planning (AESOP), set up in Almere (NL) in 2008, provides at the moment the most active networking and research platform for such dialogues. Since its foundation in 2008, the group has held annual international conferences progressing work on many fronts of the urban food systems and urban agriculture discourse (AESOP *n.d.*). The publication *Sustainable food planning: Evolving theory and practice* (Viljoen and Wiskerke 2012) brings together selected papers from the 2nd AESOP Sustainable Food Group Conference in Brighton in 2010, demonstrating an overriding aim to get people from diverse disciplinary backgrounds to 'talk to each other'.

Designing for Urban Agriculture and the next steps

For the planning and design professions, competitions, conferences, consultancy, campaigning, live building projects, publications, exhibitions and teaching are all ways of contributing to the dialogue about more resilient and sustainable local, urban and regional food systems. We will be looking at some of these in the chapter *The CPUL City concept* (p. 12) from a CPUL perspective.

In summary, we can say that *designing* for urban agriculture actively and consciously started around the year 2000 with some, but few, earlier individual projects. Whilst urban theoreticians discussed the subject area, especially in the USA, design practitioners began to visualise the qualities and necessities of urban food growing on either side of the Atlantic. Interestingly, in theory and design practice, the architectural and artistic professions have led the way in developing propositions.

Just one year prior to the first AESOP conference on sustainable food planning in Almere in 2008, the Netherlands' Architecture Institute in Maastricht held the first urban agriculture exhibition, an art and architecture exhibition *De Eedbare Stad* [The Edible City] (Solomon 2007). This brought together an international group of leading architects, artists and designers all, at that time, testing urban food growing within their work. Even though both milestones happened in the Netherlands, their agendas and participants only marginally overlapped pointing again to the challenge of improving communication between the various practitioners in this subject area.

In the USA, the multidisciplinary work on *Landscape Urbanism* (Waldheim 2006) and on *Agricultural Urbanism* (Salle and Holland 2010) stands out, because both concepts not only encompass the idea of productive urban landscapes, but also underpin them with grounded theoretical arguments drawn from a variety of backgrounds.

The immediate challenge for the design professions remains twofold: to communicate the qualities and possibilities of food growing architecture and landscape to all audiences, both at a theoretical/planning level and at a hands-on/practical level. However, recent discussions with planners and activists in all three case study countries confirm our observation that practice is outstripping policy, as individuals take forward urban agriculture projects at a range of scales and aims.

So, whilst historic models of urban agriculture evolved out of necessity, in the contemporary city, we now have a window of opportunity to *plan* coherent strategies for its introduction.

As urban agriculture, in all its different forms appears and grows within cities, the next critical step is to get it 'written into' planning documents and legislation as one proactive way of improving current urban food systems and providing value beyond direct financial return. In doing so, as cities like New York, Berlin and London have, a rich public discourse develops, articulating urban agriculture's many benefits – from environmental motivation to ornament to behaviour change – and challenging current measures of success. The other action required – and here architects, planners and designers have a lot to do – is to knowingly bring forth the designing and building of processes, landscapes, buildings and infrastructure which the new urban farmers and the wider urban population need and desire.

Finally, the biggest challenge is to transition from the current narrowly focused agri-food business model to one that redefines the urban–agricultural relationship. At the end, it is about understanding that the Earth is our limit and that there are others coming behind us (some of whom we might personally know). In order to work with 'limit earth' and not against it, urban design and urban practice need to include an action's total environmental impact, and urban agriculture has proven to be one way of accounting for this.

Urban Agriculture on the map:
The *CPUL CITY* concept

Katrin Bohn and André Viljoen

Our own work aims to contribute to the challenges set out in the previous chapter by proposing design strategies and prototypes that can make urban space more productive for cities and towns and more desirable for their citizens. We start from our experience of the dense European/Western urban area and attempt to enrich the qualities of urban life whilst, at the same time, reducing the negative environmental impact of current urban food systems. We have developed the *CPUL City* concept to address this.

Fig 1: The CPUL concept. Green corridors provide a continuous network of productive open space containing routes for non-vehicular movement. Variable fields for urban agriculture and other outdoor work/leisure activities are located within the network and serve adjacent built-up areas.

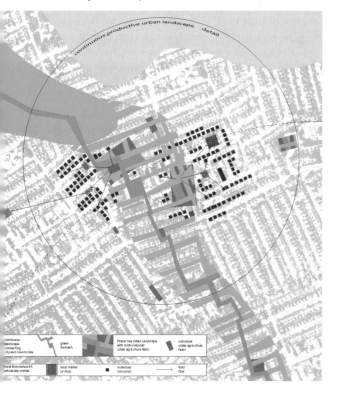

CPUL City describes an urban future based on the planned and designed introduction of what we call 'Continuous Productive Urban Landscape' – landscapes defined by urban agriculture – into existing and emerging cities (Viljoen 2005). *CPUL City* has fundamental physical and social implications. It follows a systematic approach and proposes that urban agriculture can contribute to more sustainable and resilient food systems while also adding beneficially to the spatial quality of the urban realm. It is an environmental design strategy and provides a strategic framework for the theoretical and practical exploration of ways to implement such landscapes within contemporary urban design (Bohn and Viljoen 2010a).

Central to the *Continuous Productive Urban Landscape* concept is the creation of open urban space networks providing a coherent and designed multifunctional – productive – landscape that complements and supports the built environment. CPUL's physical manifestation will fundamentally change the urban landscape and implies an equally fundamental change to the way societies and individuals experience, value and interact with that landscape. Within the *CPUL City* concept, urban agriculture refers in the main to fruit and vegetable production, as this provides the highest yields per square metre of urban ground. Key features of CPUL are outdoor spaces for food growing, leisure, movement and commerce shared by people, natural habitats, non-vehicular circulation routes and ecological corridors. Its network connects existing open urban spaces, maintaining and, in some cases, modifying their current uses (Viljoen *et al.* 2004).

Designing a CPUL (or an individual CPUL space later to become part of a CPUL) therefore means the creation of a qualitatively rich urban landscape which, above all, strives to incorporate the growing of local and organic food. The food-productive use is overlaid with and interconnected to other urban uses on the same site

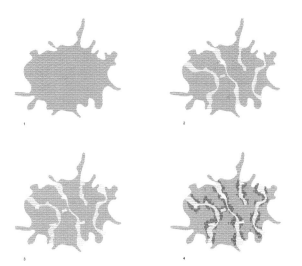

Fig 2: How to make a *CPUL City*.
1. Bring your own city.
2. Map all your existing open spaces and connect them through green infrastructure.
3. Insert agriculturally productive land. (Note: you may wish to alternate between 2 and 3.)
4. Feed your city!

Broadly speaking, commercial-scale production will be necessary if urban agriculture is to have a quantifiable impact on food production, whilst personalised production is very significant from a social and behavioural change perspective. As the previous chapter makes clear, urban agriculture will not meet all of a city's food needs, and any in-depth review of urban food systems must consider relationships between a city, its local region and beyond.

All of these arguments were formally presented in our 2005 book *Continuous Productive Urban Landscapes: Designing urban agriculture for sustainable cities*. Various environmental, economic and socio-cultural arguments confirm that the benefits of such a landscape are significant enough to consider it an essential element of sustainable urban infrastructure in future cities (Viljoen and Bohn 2005).

The CPUL concept grew out of our design research exploring the role of urban agriculture within urban design during the 1990s and was first designed in 1998 as part of Bohn&Viljoen's competition entry to the European architecture and urban design competition *Europan 5*. At this time, in the UK, increasing density as solely measured by numbers of people per square kilometre was being used as a crude shorthand for sustainable development. This unthinking acceptance of density has resulted in the loss of significant areas of open urban space and represents a misreading of the UK's *Urban Task Force* report which called for increased density and mixed use as part of a wider sustainable strategy (The Urban Task Force 1999). We argue that an intensively treated open urban landscape can compensate for the potentially lower building density which it requires and call this strategy 'Ecological Intensification' by which the aim is to reduce the entire environmental footprint of each new development. Further architectural and urban design studies, as well as the research of statistical, mostly UK-centred data, resulted in the *CPUL City* concept being underpinned by a number of interrelated social, environmental and economic arguments, as well as design arguments, for what would amount to a radical change in the configuration and programming of open urban space within an overarching desire to find more self-sustaining ways of living (Viljoen and Bohn 2000).

suggesting physical and visual access to nature everywhere in the city or town as an important step towards emerging urban lifestyles and new ways of producing space and place.

A systemic approach needs to be taken to integrate the physical CPUL/CPUL space into existing or new local urban food systems or their components, such as a stakeholder network or waste recycling or water system. These webs of complex interdependencies spun around urban food systems constitute the *CPUL City*. Of major importance for the success of *CPUL City* is the simultaneous design, planning and establishment of 'mini' interdependencies enabling the recurring sequence of successful food growing: *preparing the soil – planting – growing/caring – harvesting – eating/processing/preserving/selling – composting/seed production*.

The *CPUL City* concept recognises that each city and each site will present a unique set of conditions and competing pressures informing the final shape and extent of its productive landscapes. It envisages a 'mixed economy' of growers practising urban agriculture: projects for the community and by the community, small-scale and large-scale, commercial and communal, low technology and appropriate high technology.

Urban Agriculture within the current urban planning and design discourse: A CPUL perspective

Addressing the complexities of the urban food system, the *CPUL City* concept touches on many current discourses of very different natures. Three of these stand out in that they require the expertise of the urban designer, planner and architect and would benefit from their input: the discourse on urban agriculture, the discourse on urban landscape – in particular productive urban landscape – and the discourse on participatory design.

In relation to the Global North, the urban agriculture discourse was originally an 'English-speaking' discourse originating in Canada in the late 1970s (City Farmer *n.d.*). A solid body of literature exists since the early 1990s with publications from Canada, the USA and Great Britain being at the forefront of the debate. This 'earlier' literature concentrates on urban agriculture's positive impact with respect to food security, public health and income generation in places with high levels of social and economic deprivation. Often the research projects feeding into publications were conducted with or for internationally acting NGOs, such as the UN, and often concerned urban food systems in the Global South, as exemplified by the Canadian book *Cities feeding people: An examination of Urban Agriculture in East Africa* (Egziabher *et al.* 1994). The publication in 1996 of the book *Urban agriculture: Food, jobs and sustainable cities* (Smit *et al.* 1996) was a landmark in defining an international role for urban agriculture and may be considered seminal to a sequence of publications, academic and popular. The main author, Jac Smit, who in 2004 wrote the forward for *CPUL 1*, is considered by many as the 'father of urban agriculture' referring to both his pioneering work in putting the subject on the table and the dissemination of the term 'urban agriculture' itself.

After this book, the engagement with the subject rapidly increased globally, probably fuelled by the sudden and efficient integration of urban agriculture into Cuban cities during the 1990s and the widespread digestion of findings and agreements of the *Earth Summit* in Rio de Janeiro in 1992. Academics and practitioners in the Global South and North now looked at urban food growing from a variety of interdependent angles, beginning

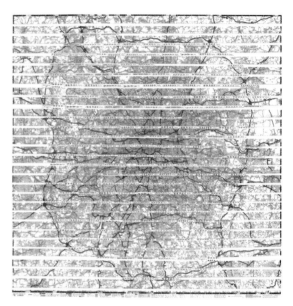

Fig 3: Exploded London. One of our earliest spatial visualisations: Adding an extra 30% to London's surface area would allow London to cultivate all its fruit and vegetable requirements without changing any existing open space.

to draw strands of research together and to transfer generated knowledge across the hemispheres. In North America and the UK, themes such as food security (Koc *et al.* 1999), sustainability in urban food production (Caridad Cruz and Sánchez Medina 2003) or the evaluation of urban agriculture field research (Mougeot 2005a) were discussed, as well as economic aspects of urban agriculture (Petts 2001a), the preservation of open space (Petts 2001b) or public procurement (Morgan and Morley 2004). German researchers at that time disseminated work on socio-political subjects such as small-scale urban agriculture (Meyer-Renschhausen *et al.* 2002) and the encouragement of local food markets (Bechstein and Kabbert 2004).

During the first years of the new millennium, empirical attempts began in the Global North to formulate coherent urban farming positions with the aim of adapting planning frameworks to the emerging needs of urban agriculture. These culminated around 2005 in our three case study countries, for example, in exemplary projects describing the different planning issues at stake within each local context:

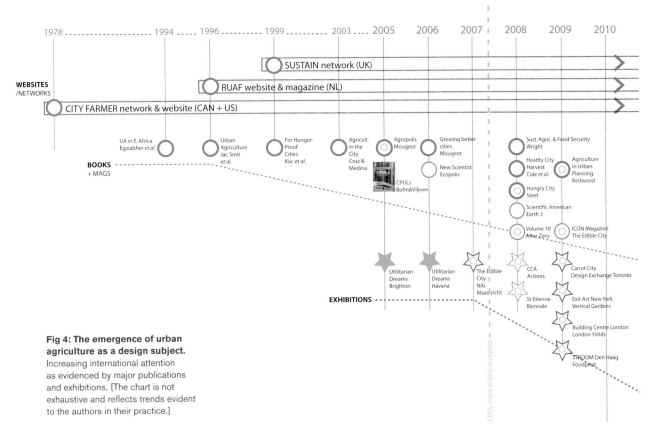

Fig 4: The emergence of urban agriculture as a design subject. Increasing international attention as evidenced by major publications and exhibitions. [The chart is not exhaustive and reflects trends evident to the authors in their practice.]

- A team of academic and student researchers of the School of Urban Studies and Planning at Portland State University, commissioned by their local city council, completed in 2005 *The Diggable City*, an in-depth spatial inventory of all potential council-owned food growing sites in Portland (Balmer *et al.* 2005).

- The agronomists behind Berlin-based social enterprise Agrarbörse organised a think-tank meeting in 2006, *Neue Felder für die Stadt* [New fields for the city], between urban food growing activists, local farmers and council representatives to discuss potential mutual benefits from integrating urban agriculture into local space use strategies (Berliner GALK 2006).

- In London, the non-governmental organisation Sustain initiated a whole range of food-awareness campaigns and achieved, amongst others, getting food on the political agenda at a Mayoral level. Since 2001, it runs *London Food Link* and was instrumental in establishing the *London Food Board* and the *Food Strategy Unit* at the London Development Agency in 2004 (Sustain *n.d.*).

While planning for urban agriculture had therefore been on the development agenda for about 15 years, the publication of *CPUL* in early 2005 was the first time that a book was devoted to presenting a coherent strategy for designing contemporary cities by 'putting questions of productive land use into the centre of urban design' (Hopkins 2006). The need for and relevance of such concepts may be seen in the international interest the *CPUL City* concept has received during the last ten years: Since 2005, the authors have lectured on their work to public and professional audiences in Austria, Belgium, Canada, Cuba, Denmark, France, Germany, India, Italy, Ireland, the Netherlands, Norway, Portugal, Spain, Sweden, Switzerland, the UK and the US.[1] Invited articles about the concept have been published widely in architectural/urban design magazines in the above named countries and additionally in China, Korea, Russia and Iran[1]. The CPUL concept has benefited from favourable comments by activists including Rob Hopkins, founder of the *Transition Towns* network (Hopkins 2006), and is cited by academics and practitioners such as Luc Mougeot (Mougeot 2005b: 12), Jac Smit (Smit 2005), Carolyn

Steel (Steel 2008: 314), Sarah Taylor Lovell and Douglas Johnston (Taylor Lovell and Johnston 2009: 44), Hodgson et al. (Hodgson et al. 2011: 56), the non-profit organisation Cultivate Kansas City (CKC 2011) and Goodbun et al. (Goodbun et al. 2012: 12).

If it is at all possible to chronologically map such a short history, we may say that during the last five years research interest in the subject has been extended noticeably beyond the prevalence of Anglo-American writing on practice and planning to wider-spread studies emerging, for example, in a greater number of European countries. This body of 'younger' literature continues to reflect on the ecological and economic characteristics or types of urban agriculture, but also concentrates on the many interrelations of urban agriculture to other urban phenomena, especially community development, as exemplified by publications about public engagement and community gardens (Rosol 2006), social benefits of communal gardening in general (Müller 2011) or community health in its wider sense (Campbell and Wiesen 2011).

Architectural and design research has equally diversified with CPUL City today being complemented by other urban design concepts for integrating urban agriculture into contemporary Western cities. Often these start from an interest different to CPUL and result in a different set of proposals, but all explore the design possibilities of growing food within the urban realm. Most notably, these are Carolyn Steel's Sitopia (Steel 2008), Vertical Farms by Dickson Despommier (Despommier 2010) and C.J. Lim and Ed Liu's Smartcities (Lim and Liu 2010).

Within design disciplines, the dissemination of new ideas takes place as much through the medium of exhibitions and events as through the publication of academic papers. In these disciplines, a rapid increase in interest, exploration and dissemination of ideas about the qualities of spaces for productive urban landscapes/ urban agriculture has been evident during the last decade. In Europe, the breakthrough in the discussion of design consequences and possibilities arising from urban agriculture was reached in 2007 when the Netherlands Architecture Institute (NAi) in Maastricht curated an exhibition titled De Eedbare Stad (Solomon 2007) (see previous chapter). Since then, the number

of similar exhibitions and 'public works' crossing the thin boundaries of urban design, art and architecture and hosted by leading international design institutions has continued to increase. These include the UK Design Council-led DOTT 07 Urban Farming Project in Middlesbrough (2006/07) (Design Council 2008), The Canadian Centre for Architecture's exhibition Actions: What you can do with the city (2008) (Borasi and Zardini 2008), the Vertical Farming exhibition at Exit Art, New York (2009) (Exit Art 2009), Urban Agriculture: London Yields at the Building Centre London (2009) (The Building Centre 2009) and the Dutch art organisation STROOM's three-year Foodprint programme (2009+) (Stroom 2009). The Canadian Carrot City project (2009+), which, one of its authors, Mark Gorgolewski, tells took its name from chapters in CPUL 1, embraces urban agriculture as a design and urban planning subject for the architectural professions in the as yet most complex constellation of international travelling exhibitions, online resources and accompanying book (Gorgolewski et al. 2011). The travelling exhibition has been shown in many places worldwide with various companion exhibitions developed around it. The CPUL City concept was invited into all of these exhibitions and features in the Carrot City online resource and book.

Have we got closer to the CPUL City?

The closeness of the urban food subject to the low-energy and sustainability discussion, the ability of architects to synthesise seemingly unconnected issues and the fascination with scenarios for urban futures all provide reasons for the notable presence of the architectural profession in the early moments of the 'movement'.

However, in order to establish whether urban agriculture and productive urban landscapes – or indeed the CPUL City concept – are beginning to gain a foothold in today's world, we also have to study how they have impacted on the very real spaces, food cultures, lives and livelihoods of their buzzing – or shrinking – cities.

Whilst the CPUL concept was seen as interesting though utopian in 2005, the situation has changed dramatically since then, to the extent, for example, that in 2011 commentators have defined the Dutch City of Almere's future plans for *Agromere* in Almere Oosterwold as a CPUL (Jansma and Visser 2011). In Agromere, the objective was to explore opportunities to reintegrate agriculture into modern city life. Through a combined stakeholder and design process, a virtual city district on 250 hectares was designed to blend living space for 5,000 inhabitants with urban agriculture (Wageningen UR 2011). This concept design highlighted urban agriculture and contributed to the municipality of Almere's own development plan. In January 2010, the Dutch government decided on the execution of this development plan, which is a 'unique system innovation in Dutch urban planning' (Jansma and Visser 2011).

In terms of disseminating new ideas on urban productivity, food systems, agriculture and their spatial qualities to the next generation, *CPUL 1* is used as a textbook in various university courses internationally covering a range of planning and architectural studies including Universities in Europe, North America, Cuba, China and probably others elsewhere. The number of student projects exploring urban agriculture issues has increased during the last five years. That the subject can stand up well amongst other architectural and urban design themes is best shown by recent competition winners, such as the *The Ark: Continuous Productive Urban Landscape Market* by Stavros Zachariades, University of Bath, UK, winning the EU-wide competition EDUCATE in 2012 (Wood 2012), or the explicitly CPUL-inspired *Adventure Farm* by Robert Hankey, Southbank University, submitted in 2008 to the RIBA Bronze Medal competition (RIBA President's Medals 2008). Within our own academic environments in Brighton and Berlin, students are now able to engage in urban agriculture projects – live projects, design projects and design research[2] – offering a new student experience that is paralleled in a growing number of institutions forming a new community of practice, including: The Academy of Architecture Amsterdam, University of Brighton, University of Cardiff in Wales, Ryerson University Toronto, TU Berlin, Sheffield University in the UK, McGill University Montreal, the New School New York and Wageningen University in the Netherlands. However, their number has still to grow, a desire and request which has been most clearly formulated by students and young researchers in 2012

during the 4th AESOP Sustainable Food Planning Conference held in Berlin and directed towards AESOP, the Association of the European Schools of Planning (AESOP *n.d.*).

In 2009 and 2010, Bohn&Viljoen Architects was one of about 160 'urban food experts' consulted by the London Assembly's Planning and Housing Committee as part of their investigation into the role of the planning system in supporting commercial food growing in the British capital. The result of this investigation process, published in 2010, is typical of international trends: 'Our report *Cultivating the Capital* calls for changes to the planning system to ... encourage food growing in London' (London Assembly 2010). Now, that is promising!

Notes
1 For details, please see <www.bohnandviljoen.co.uk>.
2 For details, please see <http://arts.brighton.ac.uk/study/ architecture/architecture-m-arch/student-work/march-studio-1-fields-and-floors-fabricating-interdependent-architectures> and <http://www.planen-bauen-umwelt.tu-berlin.de/ institut_fuer_landschaftsarchitektur_und_umweltplanung/ stadt_ernaehrung/menue/city_nutrition_home>.

The new urban foodscape: Planning, politics and power

Kevin Morgan

One of the most remarkable criticisms ever levelled at the planning community actually came from within the profession itself. The criticism was triggered by the fact that planners had addressed all the essentials of human life – land, shelter, air and water – with the conspicuous exception of food. That was the damning indictment that the American Planning Association (APA) cast on planners when it launched its seminal guide on community and regional food planning in 2007, a belated attempt to compensate for its neglect of the food system (APA 2007). The APA's epiphany was brought about by the work of two innovative US planning academics who had concluded that the food system was *'a stranger to the planning field'* (Pothukuchi and Kaufman 2000).

The planning community – academics and professionals alike – needs to engage more consciously with the food system because, with burgeoning urbanisation, cities are looming larger and larger in the food system and the food system is becoming ever more important to the health and well-being of the urban population. Feeding the city in a sustainable fashion – that is to say in a manner that is economically efficient, socially just and ecologically sound – is one of the quintessential challenges of the 21st century, particularly in Asia and Africa, where chronic hunger and malnutrition are most acute. With a majority of the world's population now deemed to be urbanised, the *urban foodscape* will assume ever more significance in food security debates (Morgan 2009; FAO 2011). To explore these issues in more depth, this chapter addresses the following questions:

1. Why has the *food system* assumed such political significance in recent years?
2. How and why are city governments embracing *food policy*?
3. What *local powers* do cities have at their disposal to reform their foodscapes?
4. How can cities become more effective *political actors* in a food system that is increasingly in thrall to corporate power?

From the margins to the mainstream: the political significance of food

It is not too much to say that, until recently, the food system barely registered on the mainstream political agenda in the Global North because of the widely held belief that it had delivered all that was asked of it. Slowly but surely, however, the hidden costs of the conventional food system began to resonate in the public domain. While there is no single reason why the food system has moved from the margins to the mainstream, the escalating costs of diet-related diseases and environmental degradation loom large in any explanation (Morgan *et al.* 2006; Lang *et al.* 2009).

If anything, it is the *multifunctional* character of food that makes it such a unique political phenomenon, because the food system is heavily implicated in so many public policy arenas. In other words, the political significance of the food system stems from the combined effect of the following trends:

- Food security is now perceived as a *national security* issue following the urban riots that erupted in many countries after the food price hikes of 2007/08.
- The food chain accounts for some 31% of *greenhouse gas emissions* in the European Union, making the food system a crucial target of policies to counter climate change.
- The epidemic of obesity and other *diet-related diseases* makes the food system a prime target of campaigners who want to transform the National Health System from a treatment service to a health-promoting and prevention service.
- *Food poverty* is increasingly visible in the cities of the Global North, as we can see from the explosive growth of food banks, making food a social justice issue as well as a human health issue.
- The food system is now perceived as a prism through which planners seek to promote more

sustainable *natural resource management* and ecosystem services.

* A *quality food revolution* is underway as people rediscover the pleasures of good food and its associations with place and provenance (Morgan and Sonnino 2010).

Taken together, these factors have fashioned a *new food equation* with the result that food is no longer a marginal issue in mainstream political discourse (Morgan and Sonnino 2010). From the global to the local level, the food system has acquired a visibility and a salience that it has not known in generations. Globally, this was most apparent when the G8 group of countries convened its first-ever meeting on food security in 2008, a priority that has been reinforced by the more important G20 group of countries. Locally, food policy is now being addressed at the *sub-national* level as local and regional governments are no longer prepared to take their cues from remote national governments, many of whom confuse food policy with agricultural policy.[1]

Cultivating connections:
how and why cities are embracing food policy

The multifunctional character of food creates challenges as well as opportunities in policy circles. While it helps to raise the profile of food across multiple policy agendas, multifunctionality also compounds the problem of where to locate a policy that straddles so many different domains. Over the past decade, municipalities in many countries have struggled with the question of how to incorporate food policy into their strategies and structures. In political terms this question generates two intensely practical issues – who should assume the leadership role for food policy and in which department should this role be located?

The experience of municipal food politics in Europe, North America and Africa suggests that the answer to this question very much depends on the way food policy is framed; that is to say, it depends on the prism through which the urban food question is viewed and valued by politicians and their civil society interlocutors. Take the Toronto Food Policy Council (TFPC) for example. Created in 1991 as a sub-committee of the city's

Board of Health, and widely regarded as one of the most effective food policy councils in North America, the TFPC has framed its mandate in such a capacious way that it has been able to make a significant contribution to a broad array of municipal policies, including urban agriculture, community gardening, environmental planning, official land use planning, nutritional education and anti-hunger initiatives, where it has sought to highlight the connections between food policy and other policy domains (Roberts 2001; Blay-Palmer 2009; Toronto Public Health 2010).

Municipal food policy in Vancouver offers another instructive example. Local food policy officially began in 2003, when the city council approved a motion supporting the development of a 'just and sustainable food system', the twin frames of a subsequent *Food Action Plan*. A notable feature of the food governance debate in Vancouver concerned the balance of power between city government and the community-based Vancouver Food Policy Council (VFPC). The *Food Action Plan* had originally recommended that food policy staff should report to the city government, specifically to the Director of Social Planning, a decision contested by community members of the VFPC, who felt that this city-centric arrangement would compromise their status and their voice in the new food governance system. This tension 'reflects the risk of governmental actors remaining powerfully determinant in partnership processes and outcomes in spite of claims of equal participation and input' (Mendes 2008: 955).

In both Toronto and Vancouver, the success of the food policy councils is seen to depend not on a zero-sum power struggle between city government and civil society, but rather on a judicious combination of 'top-down' support from the key institutions of the city government allied to the 'bottom-up' energies of civil society. This has been aptly described as 'sharing the burden of reform', where municipal food policy is concerned (Mendes 2008: 953).

Although food policy councils have not (yet) taken off in Europe as they have in North America, municipal food policy is taking off in other ways, partly in response to top-down global initiatives like *Local Agenda 21*, which encouraged locally based initiatives to promote sustainable development; partly in response to bottom-up pressures like the locavore movement, which champions the pleasures and benefits of fresh, locally produced food in and around the city; and partly in response to the burgeoning costs of treating diet-related diseases. To appreciate the common themes running through municipal food policies, it is worth looking at three urban food pioneers in the UK, beginning with Brighton and Hove, home to the first Green MP in the country and one of the first British cities to design an urban food policy.[2]

Originally conceived in 2003, the Brighton and Hove Food Partnership (BHFP) owes its origins to the combined efforts of three distinct actors – civil society groups that wanted to see a more localised and sustainable food system, the health promotion unit of the Primary Care Trust and the city council's Sustainability Commission. Following a series of public engagement exercises, the *Spade to Spoon* food strategy was launched in the summer of 2006. Its opening sentence refers to 'our health and our environment', and these are the two dominant themes that are used to frame the local food strategy. Equally significant, the audience to which it is addressed is broad and inclusive and in no way confined to the stereotype of middle-class locavores. *Spade to Spoon*, it announced, 'aims to develop an integrated, cross-sectoral approach to food policy, which links initiatives within public health, environmental sustainability, community development, education, agriculture, cultural and economic development, waste management, urban planning/land use, and tourism' (BHFP 2006: 4). A key milestone occurred in 2007, when BHFP signed a contract with the NHS to deliver a healthy food programme, a move that carried both new funding and more staff, putting the partnership on a more secure footing. As we will see in the following section, Brighton and Hove has also led the way in rewriting planning policy to render it more supportive of urban agriculture, community growing and green infrastructure.

In the same year that the BHFP was conceived, an informal partnership was being forged between the City Council and the National Health Service (NHS) in Manchester. In 2003, the NHS in the city decided to develop a public health strategy for food and nutrition at the same time as the City Council took the decision to enhance its school meals service and its wholesale and retail markets to improve access to healthy food. These joint endeavours formed the basis of the *Food Futures Programme*, an urban

food strategy that was formally launched in 2007 to improve the health of the urban population, protect the environment, strengthen the local food economy, build more sustainable communities, and promote culinary diversity and access to good food across the city. In addition to a core budget of £86,000 per annum, the programme utilises a wide array of local and national grants, like the grant funding for a community salt reduction project from the Food Standards Agency and a carbon reduction grant from the City Council to support sustainable food projects. The programme is managed by a partnership board that is chaired by an executive member of the City Council, with the membership drawn from heads of service within the council and community nutrition services in the NHS. A recent review of the programme found that it needed to secure higher-level political commitment from the city and the NHS if service priorities and budget allocation were to better reflect the goals of the food strategy (Raiswell and Cox 2012). The devolution of public health services to local government in England presents Manchester with a new opportunity to integrate food and health in a community-based strategy for sustainable development, a fitting reunion because, historically, public health was originally part of the repertoire of municipal government when the latter sought to regulate the noxious effects of the industrial revolution.

Another urban food pioneer is Bristol, the first city in the UK to formally create a Food Policy Council (FPC). The FPC was the culmination of many years of local food activity in a city that boasts a very active civil society and an environmentally conscious city government. The civil society groups actually organised themselves under the banner of the Bristol Food Network to enhance their profile and their voice in urban politics. The City Council and the NHS also played an innovative role by making joint appointments to develop a food and health strategy for the city. Within the City Council, a cross-departmental network called the Food Interest Group took on an important role in raising the profile of food across all council policy domains. It was against this background, that the Bristol Food Policy Council (FPC) was formed in 2011 to take the urban food agenda to a higher level. In its first year, the Bristol FPC decided to focus on three priorities:

1. public sector food procurement in the city, especially in schools and hospitals;

2. community growing schemes to inspire and enable popular participation; and
3. a campaign to support independent traders and preserve retail diversity in the face of the ubiquitous supermarket.

Alongside the creation of the FPC, Bristol City Council and its partners commissioned a comprehensive urban food audit, the result of which was an innovative report called *Who feeds Bristol?* (Carey 2011). One of the distinctive features of this food audit was the fact that it embodied and championed a *food systems planning* approach that sought to treat food as an integrated system.

In addition to these three cities, many others could have been added to this list of urban food pioneers, like Sandwell, Sheffield, Plymouth and London, all of which have designed distinctive urban food policies in recent years. Whatever their nuances, these food policies have two things in common. First, health and the environment tend to be the most important themes for framing food policy, even though many other themes are invoked as well. Second, every city has sought to design and deliver its food policy in partnership with its local civil society groups, whether this takes the form of an independently constituted partnership organisation (as in Bristol and Brighton) or a city-government vehicle that has strong community involvement as in Manchester. These partnerships constitute *spaces of deliberation* in which local state and local civil society collaborate for mutually beneficial purposes and seek to fashion joint solutions to common problems (Derkzen and Morgan 2012).

Reforming the urban foodscape: procurement, planning and partnering

Food policy has been dominated for so long by national and international levels of policy-making, it is sometimes suggested that cities have little or no capacity to shape the food system, because they lack the powers to do so. But, as the Toronto Food Policy Council argues, while cities lack 'the full toolkit' of policies, they are not without powers to reform the food system (TPH 2010: 16).

Within the urban food policy repertoire, three powers merit special attention because, taken together, they can help to reform the urban foodscape. This section will briefly highlight these three powers and show how they can be deployed to fashion more sustainable urban foodscapes.

Perhaps the most powerful food policy that cities have at their disposal is their very own *procurement policy*. The power of purchase has been shown to be very effective when it is part of a healthy public food provisioning programme (Morgan and Sonnino 2010). One of the most impressive examples of an urban procurement policy is Malmö, the third biggest city in Sweden, which plans to provide 100% organic food in all its public catering services, including public nurseries, school canteens and residential care homes (Malmö City 2010). Originally designed as a climate-friendly food experiment, the urban procurement policy in Malmö is also used to promote the city's public health agenda. Significantly, the extra cost of organic ingredients has been offset by reducing the amount of meat in the diet and by using more seasonal fruit and vegetables, making the organic transition a cost-neutral exercise. Although public canteens are an important part of the urban foodscape in many countries, they tend to be a forgotten foodscape because they lack the visibility of the globally branded fast food industry. Malmö merits our attention because it is using the power of purchase to convey two very important messages: (i) that public canteens are a vital part of the new urban foodscape and (ii) that city governments are far from powerless to shape these new foodscapes.

Another power that cities could deploy in more imaginative ways is *planning policy*, which is often used to frustrate development rather than foster it. Although planners have neglected the food system in the past, they are now beginning to address the urban foodscape so as to: (i) protect and increase the diversity of food retail outlets so that they are accessible by foot or public transport; (ii) promote urban agriculture in and around the city by expanding access to allotments, community growing spaces and a range of other underutilised public and private space; (iii) discourage food waste and promote more socially and ecologically benign ways of recycling it; and (iv) create jobs and income for producers who need access to the 'footfall' of urban consumers (White and Natelson 2011).

Local planning powers are now being used to re-regulate all aspects of the urban foodscape. For example, Waltham Forest in East London is believed to be the first local authority in the UK to use its planning powers to prevent new hot food takeaways opening up in close proximity to schools, fuelling a new urban planning trend across the UK. Meanwhile, Brighton and Hove is using supplementary planning guidance to incorporate food into the planning system and encourage more food growing spaces in the city. These examples have a powerful demonstration effect, enabling other urban areas to reimagine themselves through their local foodscapes.

Finally, there is the *power of partnering*, where city governments enter into mutually beneficial collaborative partnerships with local businesses, social enterprises and civil society groups to achieve in concert what they could not hope to achieve alone. New forms of partnering are being forced on municipal governments throughout Europe and North America by the advent of austerity capitalism. In the face of unprecedented public expenditure cuts and the deepest recession since the 1930s, large swaths of the urban population are unable to meet basic human needs, including the need for food, fuel and shelter. If these needs are to be met in a dignified way, city governments will have to enter into 'co-production' partnerships because they no longer have the resources to do it alone. While austerity capitalism threatens the integrity of the public realm in every country, a crisis also presents opportunities to radically rethink the way we meet our basic human needs, especially the production and consumption of food, which could be rendered more sustainable and more localised if the bottom-up potential of community-based social enterprise was allied to the top-down support of a smart state (Morgan and Price 2011).

Sustainable cities: the politics of the new urban foodscape

For all the attention it has garnered in the middle-class media, the 'alternative food movement' remains small, fragmented and politically ineffectual, if indeed it can be called a movement at all. Although it could have a broader, more popular appeal, this 'movement' is currently fractured into single-issue campaigns for local food, organic food, fair trade food and ethical labels that together command less than 5% of the grocery market in most countries. If a serious food movement is ever to be fashioned in the UK, food activists of different persuasions would do well to examine the history of the Community Food Security Coalition (CFSC) in North America, where the social justice and sustainability wings eventually decided that they could achieve more by working in concert than by working alone, forming a *common* front that respected the *diversity* of their mandates and their interests (Allen 2004; Winne 2008). The fact that the CFSC decided to disband in 2012 in no way detracts from the argument here; indeed it underscores the point that sustainable food movements need to sustain themselves politically.

Although no single actor can ever hope to challenge the corporate power of the mainstream food system, the *collective power* of cities could change the character of the urban foodscape, rendering it less obesogenic and more of a health-promoting environment where a diverse and nutritious food offer is readily available and affordable.

The Sustainable Food Cities Network (SFCN) was launched in the UK in 2011 to help cities to realise their collective power in the food system. Organised by the Soil Association and hosted by Bristol City Council, the launch was attended by many of the urban food pioneers that feature in this chapter. The SFCN has attracted a great deal of interest from more than 20 cities in the UK because it aims to give their urban food programmes a national profile and a political voice, both of which will help other cities to rethink their roles and responsibilities in the food system.

The SFCN has endorsed a set of five principles for a sustainable urban foodscape, namely: (i) health and well-being for all; (ii) environmental sustainability; (iii) local economic prosperity; (iv) empowered and resilient communities; and (v) fairness throughout the food chain. Although these principles are clearly aspirational at present, they nevertheless constitute a compelling vision for a food system that puts *people* before *profit*, a system in which the urban foodscape is fashioned by *design* rather than *default*, the result of democratic deliberation rather than the deadly duo of corporate power and pusillanimous planning.

The SFCN is one of the most hopeful expressions of an emergent urban food movement in the UK. Although there is currently no organisational equivalent to the CFSC, there is clearly enough social and political activity in the UK to justify the creation of an organisational umbrella under which disparate food groups could forge a common front. A food-based social movement is difficult to conceive in the UK today because so much of its activity consists of local action and single-issue campaigns, with the result that it lacks organisational coherence and political voice.

Conclusion: from alternatives to alliances

This chapter has sought to document the prosaic first steps of an emergent urban food movement by highlighting how and why municipal food strategies are emerging throughout the UK as a consequence of a new alliance between the local state and its civil society interlocutors, a compelling testament to the convening power of food (Morgan 2009). New trends in urban food policy – like food partnerships and food policy councils for example – suggest that a new urban politics is beginning to emerge around urban food security in the broadest sense of the term. One of the distinguishing features of this new urban politics is the stance of civil society organisations (CSOs) to mainstream political activity: where they once saw themselves as an 'alternative' movement, in the sense that they were instinctively inclined to contest rather than collaborate with the local state, they are now much more likely to forge alliances with receptive local politicians and planners to help the latter to reimagine their roles and responsibilities in the food system. This is especially true of Sustain and the Soil Association, the most influential CSOs in the UK food sector.

Although CSOs can help to reshape the food policy agenda, they need the support of a smart local state to share 'the burden of reform'. For its part, the state needs the local knowledge and the civic energy of CSOs to redesign public services, creating radically new opportunities for what Robin Murray calls public–social partnerships (Murray 2012). Food system planners will need to draw on such partnerships, because urban design concepts, such as *CPUL City*, need support from the whole community, not just the planning community, if they are to be successfully realised as an integral part of a health-promoting foodscape for the many and not the few. Without community support and participation, the CPUL concept could find itself assimilated into the wealth-generating repertoires of the rich, furnishing a green veneer to the gentrification of urban areas designed for the few not the many, a strategy that is already apparent in cities like Phoenix, Arizona (Ross 2011).

With burgeoning urbanisation, cities are now one of the key arenas in which the future of food policy will be decided. If the future is anything like the past, the urban foodscape will remain essentially what it is today: a profoundly obesogenic environment that is increasingly in thrall to corporate interests, especially the supermarkets, many of whom are flocking back into city centres as their 'big box' out-of-town superstores have peaked as business models. Alternatively, the alliance between the local state and its civil society partners could inspire and enable cities to fashion urban foodscapes that are designed to ensure that good food is readily available and accessible to all by regulating public space more effectively and deploying the untapped powers of procurement, planning and partnering. Under this scenario, the urban foodscape could then begin to foster rather than frustrate ecological integrity, public health and social justice, the intrinsically significant goals of a sustainable foodscape.

Notes
1   The biggest influences on the food systems in the EU and the US are the Common Agricultural Policy and the Farm Bill, neither of which mentions food in their titles even though they have a huge impact on what we eat.
2   Although Brighton and Hove claims to be 'the first city in the UK to write a food strategy back in 2006', it is worth noting that the *London Food Strategy* was actually launched in May 2006.

Urban Agriculture as ordinary urban practice: Trends and lessons

Joe Nasr, June Komisar and Mark Gorgolewski

People are rediscovering urban agriculture as a strategy for supplying urban settlements with healthy fresh food, in particular as a practice that can (and should) be integrated into the ordinary urban fabric and offers great design potential. While initially proposals for such initiatives were primarily conceptual, within a few short years, realized projects have mushroomed, incorporating food production into neighbourhoods, housing and open space, using a variety of strategies, design approaches and components. Now that these experiences have started to accumulate and have a bit of history, what lessons can be drawn from the emergence and replication of such practices? Based on cases identified through our *Carrot City* initiative (Gorgolewski, Komisar and Nasr 2010 and 2011), combined with other documentation, as well as analysis of the relationships between urban agriculture, design and planning, we will draw some lessons from this first generation of actors who have sought to make urban agriculture a commonplace part of the urban landscape through project design, planning and policy.

Historical antecedents to Urban Agriculture and recent trends

Urban agriculture was once an integral part of urbanization, practised in a variety of ways in many cultures. Growing food was integral to urban development that, not surprisingly, often emerged on prime agricultural land. It was only with the advent of refrigeration and efficient long-distance transport (trains, shipping and later trucking) that cities could be severed so completely from food production. But at the same time, the importance of growing food close to where people lived was also being (re-)embraced by urban planners. At the beginning of the 20th century, several visionary designers and planners conceived of settlements that included both housing at an efficient density and residential vegetable garden plots for food production, as well as parkland. At that time, one of the most notable strategies for incorporating urban agriculture into development was Ebenezer Howard's concept, expressed in his classic book *Garden cities of to-morrow* (Howard 1902). His ideas were realized to some extent in Stockfeld, near Strasbourg, France, designed in 1910 by Edward Schimpf. Stockfeld included a central garden space divided into allotments for each resident. *Letchworth Garden City* and *Welwyn Garden City* in Hertfordshire, England, designed by architects Barry Parker and Raymond Unwin, were also influenced greatly by Howard's ideas and included spaces for food production. Similar to Howard's ideas are those of German landscape designer Leberecht Migge whose proposals for a variety of 'Siedlung' [settlement] plans attempted to integrate the functions of the dwelling and garden aiming at family food self-sufficiency (Haney 2010). Although even Le Corbusier and Frank Lloyd Wright considered food production in their early-20th-century visionary plans, in general the trend, as the century progressed, was a separation between food and the people who consumed it, even in suburbs where there was ample cultivation space.

In the West, a major exception to the trend of separating city from productive gardening was the increase in food production during the World Wars where the development of kitchen gardens, allotment and community gardens, sometimes called 'victory gardens' or 'war gardens', responded to both real and anticipated shortages. During World War I, US President Herbert Hoover administered a policy of eliminating food waste and encouraging production to enable the shipment of food to American troops and allies overseas. On the forefront were programmes in Wisconsin led by the inventor and public administrator Magnus Swenson to reduce food waste, encourage the planting of home vegetable gardens, and spread knowledge about preservation techniques such as canning. These initiatives served as a model for similar strategies practised throughout the US and Europe (Janik 2009–2010).

More recent examples of visible urban food production include the London programme to add 2,012 vegetable gardens in time for the 2012 Olympic Games (Capital Growth *n.d.* b), as well as Michelle Obama's White House garden (Obama 2012). These illustrate the way that urban agriculture is increasingly embraced as an important strategy to improve access to local, fresh food, particularly for the food insecure. It is also seen as part of a comprehensive sustainability agenda and a necessary strategy to help cope with climate change, population growth and diminishing resources. However, with an increasingly dense urban condition in part driven by sustainability concerns, contemporary urban gardeners have to contend with a lack of available land for gardening. Finding places to grow in the city requires rethinking what is planted or raised, as well as finding new opportunistic spaces for production. Designers and creative residents are responding to this through discovering new places to grow food in unused spaces from rooftops and underused paved areas to the lawns at affordable housing estates and suburban homes, once regarded as land for decorative planting only. Although acceptance for productive front-lawn gardening is not yet widespread, backyard gardening is on the increase. Some of this production is achieved through a strategy called *Small Plot Intensive (SPIN) Farming* (Satzewich and Christensen 2011) whereby professional farmers grow crops in a cluster of borrowed or leased urban or suburban backyards. The rooftops of large urban buildings, such as warehouses and office buildings, are the newest frontier, as we will discuss below.

On a regional scale, there is a growing movement to explore new ways of connecting produce from nearby farms to the city through such schemes as community-supported agriculture (CSA) where customers buy shares of local farmers' crops in exchange for weekly boxes of fresh crops, and initiatives such as neighbourhood and regional farmers' markets. The relationship of the grower to regional market opportunities, as well as restaurants and grocers who feature local, seasonal food has been the subject of studies concerned with food security, nutrition and environmental sustainability. Such food strategy studies, as well as the formation of food policy councils, are just two indicators of a trend toward an increasing recognition of the role of connections between growers and consumers.

Fig 1: *Carrot Green Roof.* This green roof in Toronto is an example of a multifunctional productive roof over a retail building.

Urban agriculture has been embraced in recent years as an important strategy to increase access to local, fresh food, particularly for the food insecure. It is also seen as part of a comprehensive sustainability agenda and a necessary strategy to cope with climate change, population growth and diminishing resources.

Many recent proposals that address space and population challenges are unorthodox and seem at first to be improbable, but creative farming solutions for waste spaces and underused areas are now being realized, although usually at a smaller scale than some of the bolder proposals. Thus early concepts for vertical farming, including MVRDV's *Pig City* skyscraper proposed for the Netherlands (MVRDV 2001) and Dickson Despommier's elaboration of the vertical farm model (Despommier 2010), working with various architects, remain unrealized. Nevertheless, smaller-scale vertical crop growing has become a reality. *Lufa Farms* in Montreal (discussed below) is a thriving CSA rooftop greenhouse farm that incorporates a vertical hydroponic growing system. Nuvege's commercial farm in Kyoto increases its growing space by using a vertical tray system for their hydroponic farm (Nuvege 2011). Others have developed window-wall growing systems, and the design firm Plantagon International is now working with Tongji University in Shanghai to research vertical growing systems (Plantagon *n.d.*). Although not skyscrapers, these projects demonstrate the viability of some creative approaches to farming vertically and expanding to new types of spaces once overlooked for producing food.

Towards Urban Agriculture as ordinary urban practice: a typology

The emergence of food production as a commonly recognized activity within the urban context has started to transform urban agriculture from a theoretical concept with occasional, exceptional, experimental manifestations to a common phenomenon. Urban food production has long existed in backyard and community gardens, but here we are referring to other situations that are more complex, multifunctional or are found in more unusual settings.

We propose here a typology of some of the main spaces in which urban agriculture is starting to become a common practice, illustrating each one with a few examples from North America.

The multipurpose rooftop

Flat roofs have long been used as a resource for urban dwellers – in some hot countries, sleeping on the roof is the natural response to oppressively hot conditions. Another common use of flat roofs has been (and in some cases, still is) cultivation in pots and, occasionally, the raising of small animals and birds (pigeons being the most common case). This allows a flexible use of a space that otherwise sits empty. Part of the flexibility is the ability to adjust to a variety of climatic conditions and to adjust the characteristics of the roof accordingly.

In recent years the rooftop, traditionally a wasted asset, has been rediscovered as a resource for food production, as well as other uses (energy and water collection, a place for leisure activities) – particularly in dense cities where available land is prohibitively expensive, unavailable or even contaminated. Not surprisingly, New York City, with expensive and scarce land, has emerged as a hotbed for rooftop food production. Rooftops (as well as balconies) there have always been common locations for container gardens. However, in the past few years, New

York City has become known for experiments in using roofs more intensively for growing; striking images of young farmers working the soil with skyscrapers in the background have attracted considerable attention.

Not-for-profit *Eagle Street Rooftop Farm* atop a warehouse in Brooklyn was a pioneer in this movement (Eagle Street *n.d.*). Exceptional for the partnership it involved, the modalities of the operation (including the way the soil mixture was brought up to the roof), and the outreach to various communities that were included from the start, *Eagle Street* was unprecedented, showing what is possible on a roof. A second New York project, *Brooklyn Grange*, soon followed aiming to show that the techniques pioneered at *Eagle Street* could be adapted and expanded for commercial purposes (Brooklyn Grange 2012). This was meant to make *Brooklyn Grange* distinctive in purpose, as well as in scale. In the end, while the setting, the mode of organizing, and the forms of marketing are quite different, the farming techniques and the multifunctionality of this project echoes the *Eagle Street Farm*. In 2012, after only two years of operation, *Brooklyn Grange* was already in the process of initiating a second site. The process of replication is an indication that commercial rooftop farming is viable in New York City.

A very different approach seems to have emerged in other large North American cities. In Toronto, one pioneering case was the *Fairmont Royal York Hotel*, which initiated a raised-bed garden on its 14th-floor roof to both train their chefs and provide fresh and unusual ingredients for its restaurant (Carrot City 2012a). After a decade or so of inconspicuous cultivation, word spread about the existence of this hidden project. This model has now been replicated globally across the luxury hotel chain as well as at many other hotels with rooftops and terraces suitable for cultivation.

Another early case in Toronto was the roof of *Carrot Common*, a low-rise retail and office centre anchored by a large food cooperative (*The Big Carrot*) with a long history of community outreach. Several years ago, part of the *Carrot Common* roof was transformed into a combination of outdoor community meeting space and space where edible plants are grown using a variety of containers. Recently, the roof was again transformed, and is now a highly multifunctional space called the

Carrot Green Roof, with shallow green planting beds for native plants, wetland plants, herbs and more, a large patio holding many different types of containers for vegetables requiring deeper beds, vertical surfaces for growing, as well as a food preparation area, solar collector panels and a meeting area for community activities including outdoor theatre (CGR *n.d.*).

Cultivation has quickly become a common rooftop use in many different contexts and forms across Toronto and several other North American cities. Examples now include: restaurants that grow vegetables and herbs (and even hops) on their roof (even using a staff farmer); several housing projects (for social housing as well as privately owned apartments) that incorporate mini-allotments on their roofs for residents; and socially oriented facilities (community health centres, YMCAs and a native population social centre) that include productive uses on their rooftops.

This practice of turning rooftops into productive spaces that include cultivation of edible plants is becoming familiar enough that some institutions are looking at their roofs more routinely now as an unused resource. One of Toronto's largest builders, Daniels Corporation, now includes urban agriculture strategies such as

rooftop and community gardens, container gardens and edible landscaping as part of its new building projects (Daniels *n.d.*). In addition, the Greater Toronto Area YMCA system is currently looking systematically across all of its facilities in the metropolitan area to envision how their roofs can be put to better use.

The urban greenhouse

While it may have emerged as a feature of rural aristocratic estates, it is in cities that the greenhouse was really developed. In France, for instance, the 18th-century *orangerie* (the formal, often fanciful, greenhouse structure that was associated with many palaces to produce exotic edibles for the wealthiest) led in the 19th century to the more commonplace *serre*, ordinary glassed structures often found close to cities or in them which were oriented to supplying fresh produce to urban residents, along with *cloches* (glass plant covers), conservatories and other season-extension techniques. The greenhouse spread in the second half of the 20th century as an extensive symbol of industrial agriculture, often located at some distance from cities, across Europe and North America. After years of decline in urban areas, the greenhouse is now being reinvented as an essential piece for the expansion of food production in cities. The

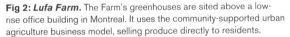

Fig 2: *Lufa Farm.* The Farm's greenhouses are sited above a low-rise office building in Montreal. It uses the community-supported urban agriculture business model, selling produce directly to residents.

modern greenhouse serves several functions: season extension, development of specialized crops, local production of seeds and seedlings, intensification of production, and housing specialized techniques such as hydroponics and aquaponics. All these are combining to raise the profile – even necessity – of urban greenhouses.

In Canada, two cases have become known as exemplary instances of a greenhouse used as a keystone for an urban food production project. In Toronto, *Artscape Wychwood Barns* serves as the perfect example of the greenhouse as a multifunctional community space where production of food is secondary to other functions: production of seedlings for distribution to various groups around the city, space for teaching about growing and preparing food, even space for special events and training meetings. This exceptional case reappropriates an abandoned industrial facility (formerly used for repairing streetcars) through the use of state-of-the-art equipment and design features to serve its multiple functions (Artscape *n.d.*).

In contrast, *Lufa Farms* was established in Montreal as an entrepreneurial operation aiming to supply a large array of fresh herbs and vegetables year-round to several hundred households by adapting the model of community-supported agriculture to the urban context. It uses modern technologies and controlled environments. The rooftop location on a low-rise office building enables proximity to customers and the use of an unused urban resource (Lufa Farms *n.d.* b).

The reason both *Wychwood Barns* and *Lufa Farms* built reputations as places worth exploring is that they represented two exemplary approaches to the urban greenhouse. Very quickly the model each of them represents is being replicated and adapted. The educational and catalytic greenhouse is becoming an essential feature of many new urban agriculture projects, whether associated with schools, community centres or community food centres.

Meanwhile, the commercial greenhouse is getting replicated in urban areas, becoming the new poster child of urban agriculture as a future-oriented movement. *Gotham Greens* and *Bright Farms* in New York City (Gotham Greens *n.d.*; Bright Farms *n.d.*) are just two of

Fig 3: *Maison Productive House.* Domestic-scaled passive solar design and urban agriculture are integrated into Montreal's *Maison Productive House*, designed by architect Rune Kongshaug.

the new projects that are entirely based on greenhouse production. While all rely on the use of greenhouses, there is much variety between them. Many occupy rooftops, some are based on or in existing buildings and they are sometimes part of cultural facilities that aim for training and rehabilitation, while others are meant as pure commercial operations. Moreover, some of these projects are being designed for replication from the start. *Gotham Greens*, *Bright Farms* and *Lufa Farms* have all been conceived from their inception as start-up sites that will be replicated in other locations in multiple cities. Thus, it appears that within a few short years, urban greenhouses may become as commonplace as they had been a century ago – though their production techniques, the materials used for them, their very nature, will be quite distinct from that earlier generation of urban greenhouses.

Productive housing

The complex relationship between home and food production has a long fluctuating history. In the past as well as today, in many parts of the world, the integration of food production (and processing) into the residence or its immediate surrounding was and still is commonly found. Whether it is containers on rooftops, pots on balconies, raised beds and chicken coops in backyards, or fruit trees and berry bushes in side-yards, the presence of food producing spaces within the residence has always been commonplace, although diminished in recent times, as discussed above.

A number of efforts have been undertaken recently with the explicit aim to reconnect home and food, using very diverse approaches in wildly different settings. For some, like the architect Fritz Haeg, such a reconnection is a political act, aimed to attack the scourge of the manicured, ecologically costly front lawn commonly found in numerous suburbs across the US, as well as suburban developments in other countries. His *Edible Estates* project is meant to serve as an artistic statement that demonstrates the possibilities of transformation from lawns into more productive spaces, simultaneously achieving aesthetic and symbolic goals (Haeg 2010).

Equally ambitious and quietly effective is the *Vacant Lot* initiative by Gareth Morris and Ulrike Steven of the architecture firm What if: projects. Its initial intervention placed attractive raised beds and containers in large grow bags on the paved or green open spaces of a couple of social housing estates in London, UK. Replication has been enabled by the success of the pilot projects, leading to expansion to over a dozen such sites across the northern part of central London (What if: projects *n.d.*).

The need to develop sustainable housing models that address density, energy, water and food has led a young Montreal-based architect, Rune Kongshaug, to propose an alternative housing model. After his early involvement in McGill University's urban agriculture initiatives, Kongshaug sought to transform the entire

three-dimensional nature of multi-unit housing to make all possible surfaces productive. In his aptly named *Maison Productive House*, a project that partly incorporates an older structure, he has created a prototype to demonstrate the possibility of such a transformation while investigating the challenges faced in integrating food, energy and water systems (produktif design studio *n.d.*). Kongshaug is already working on new projects with lessons learned from the prototype building.

The fertile neighbourhood

Along with the attention of reconceptualizing the home as a space for food production, there have been parallel efforts to reconceive the whole neighbourhood along the same lines. This greater scale adds several challenges to the expansion of urban agriculture, as it requires a high level of coordination, collaboration, planning and enabling regulations. However, it also offers additional opportunities; as the scale of production can be expanded, the potential for community building can be tapped, and the broader milieu for living and working can be approached as a space for food production.

Given the limitations of intervening at the neighbourhood scale, the examples of multi-party partnerships targeting whole neighbourhoods remain in short supply. Some outstanding examples like *Mole Hill* in Vancouver integrate food production within a single residential block (Carrot City 2012b). Less common are more ambitious attempts to address urban agriculture throughout a neighbourhood. Vancouver's *Olympic Village* illustrates some of the challenges. Initially, a very detailed and well-thought-out plan was developed for what was then called Southeast False Creek. However, the implementation has lagged behind its ambitions, as the overall development of this former industrial area ran into various financial challenges, impacting the financial capacity to integrate food production spaces throughout the new neighbourhood (Carrot City 2012c).

A very different experience can be found in Toronto's *Regent Park*, a large social housing complex, which is currently being redeveloped. *Regent Park* has long had a strong presence of gardening scattered across the open spaces between its residential buildings. While, initially, urban agriculture was not included in the new district, this has changed fundamentally: food production is

Fig 4: *Regent Park.* Rooftop growing spaces in housing settings, like this example from *Regent Park* in Toronto, provide many social benefits for a diverse demographic, in addition to fresh fruit and vegetables.

now a key feature of the neighbourhood. Several new residential buildings (including a seniors' residence) have been built with food production spaces on roofs, balconies and terraces; special community food-growing spaces are being included in the new large park and atop the new community centre. A food access coordinator enables linkages with various stakeholders and helps develop and realize a holistic vision for the neighbourhood as a place for food.

Regent Park represents a good example of how urban redevelopment can incorporate urban agriculture. Similarly, the creators of some new neighbourhoods at the urban periphery are also starting to seriously consider the place of food production in their development. Much peri-urban development takes place in 'greenfields', replacing farmland with buildings and lawns. Alternative models of development are emerging which attempt to maintain agricultural activity while creating new housing stock. Some do so by simply setting aside some farmland, but others are applying more creative approaches that combine farming and housing synergistically. *Prairie Crossing*, near Chicago, is perhaps the best example in North America of this approach, sometimes termed a 'farming subdivision' (Prairie Crossing *n.d.*).

A private company, the TSR Group, is seeking to develop a replicable model of new development that maintains significant farming activity while transforming

farming practices. Their concept, *Agriburbia* (Redmond 2010), recognizes a role for hobby gardeners as well as professional farmers who would operate on parcels distributed across a whole development, where a significant percentage of the land is maintained in farming and gardening while housing density is increased. A prototype of this concept has been proposed at *Platte River Village*, a project in Milliken, near Denver. Some of the principles in such projects share the basic tenets advocated by the New Urbanism movement – it is thus not surprising that one of the leaders of this movement, Andres, authored with his firm Duany Plater-Zyberk a short book in 2011 called *Garden cities: Theory and practice of agrarian urbanism* (Duany 2011). This builds on the experience of HB Lanarc, a Vancouver-based design and planning firm that has pioneered the focus on 'agricultural urbanism' as a principal area of practice (de la Salle and Holland 2010). All these cases indicate the emergence of agriculture in urban neighbourhoods as an increasingly recognized area of intervention by planners, designers and other professionals who work on the shaping of urban expansion through new communities at the edges of urban areas.

The examples above show four of the main areas, where urban agriculture is shifting from hypothetical to actual, and from exceptional to commonplace. While we chose to focus on these four types of space, several others could have been included here. The community garden is being transformed in many cases into polyvalent sites for communal meeting, baking, cooking, as well as for acculturation, mental health programming, and more. Large landholders (such as school boards and universities) are starting to recognize that institutional land is a major asset that can be used as a resource for the expansion of urban agriculture, so many of them are starting to facilitate access to surplus land that they own or control, and in some cases develop overall policy to expand the possibility of accessing such lands. A proliferation of school gardens as well as campus horticulture programmes are appearing to the extent that some municipalities are setting goals of 'a garden in every school'. With these types of urban agriculture and others that can be identified, a picture starts to emerge of a continuous patchwork of different spaces across a city or a metropolitan area where urban agriculture is starting to be found as an increasingly commonplace activity – moving towards the realization of continuous productive urban landscapes.

Implications for Urban Agriculture as part of ordinary urban landscapes

The examples above also show that in recent years urban agriculture in richer countries has been evolving from a few types of common low-key forms (community gardens, allotments, simple school gardens) to some outstanding innovative cases which have brought creativity, vision and recognition to the urban agriculture concept. Nowadays, the signs are that we may be moving from the exceptionalism of these cases to the ordinariness of practices (more or less) based on these pioneer cases.

As part of this shift, the stakeholders implicated in urban agriculture are being transformed and increasingly expanding. Beyond the usual actors long associated with urban food production (NGOs, gardening associations), a number of key actors are playing important new roles in the development, dissemination, replication, communication and scaling up of urban agriculture. These include developers, builders, municipal employees, employees of quasi-governmental agencies and students, among others. Moreover, the urban growers themselves are becoming more diverse and, in many instances, moving towards urban farming as a profession.

We expect this evolution to continue to expand, diversify and become more complex as it becomes more common. With this trend, urban agriculture is likely to face growing pains. Existing challenges may become more notable or more constraining as they impact a far larger number of actors and stakeholders. Choices between different approaches and sustainable practices (say, open-air vs. greenhouse cultivation on rooftops, or expanding urban foliage through tree planting vs. field cultivation that requires maximum sunshine) will become more frequent. Such conflicts would be the ultimate sign that urban agriculture is becoming a commonplace practice, an ordinary part of the urban landscape.

Utilitarian Dreams:
Food growing in urban landscapes

André Viljoen and Katrin Bohn

Three basic natural resources – sunlight, water and land – are essential for the success of plants and buildings and therefore for the well-being of people. When designing for a food-productive city, there are trade-offs to be made between the allocation of space for day-to-day urban living and for food growing. These trade-offs remind us that absolute self-sufficiency for an individual building, an open urban space or a planted vegetable patch is not a particularly desirable aim for that city and its inhabitants. Interdependencies, not isolation, make for sustainable and resilient systems. For these interdependencies to happen, urban space must be designed and laid out, so that it encourages and supports urban food-growing activities.

Land

The 2005 *CPUL* book notes the need to balance a number of factors when determining the scope and scale of urban agriculture within particular cities (Viljoen 2005: 266–8). If, as a starting point, we assumed that the *CPUL City* concept is being applied as part of a transition to cradle-to-cradle systems, then a target could be set to utilise all of a city's existing compostable waste as the nutrient input for urban agriculture. Compostable material – mainly fruit, vegetable and horticultural waste – can be boosted significantly by including safely treated general food waste and sewage. Such an approach would provide a baseline from which to estimate the amount of soil-based urban agriculture that a city can support without external nutrient supplements. The area of cultivation could then be calculated and related to potential growing sites within the city. As far as we are aware, no city has yet completed such a systematic calculation. So far, the scale of urban food production has been small enough that the supply of compostable waste far exceeds the demand (personal communication with Will Allen, Jun 2009).

Apart from compostable resources, other criteria including topography, access to sunlight and building metrics can also be set as starting points for inventorizing suitable land or surfaces for urban agriculture. However, urban land not only needs to be suitable, it also needs to be looked for creatively.

A study by Mikey Tomkins of the amount of land available for urban agriculture in a particular area of South London revealed large discrepancies between official records and the amount actually available (Tomkins 2009). Tomkins identified 21 hectares of open space compared to 14 hectares recorded by the local Council and only 5 hectares recorded by the Greater London Authority. He concludes that 'the more remote the official body, the less accurate the recorded figures for open space', warning more generally of the risk in assuming that official figures are correct. Tomkins further estimated the amount of produce that might be grown on the available land after removing open space that was actively used by residents (for example playgrounds). This resulted in a potential area of approximately 9 hectare, or 4.5% of the entire 191-hectare site. Using standard figures for efficient yields and for vegetable consumption in the UK, these 9 hectares could supply 26% of the vegetables consumed by the residents. This indicates the significant potential for ground-based urban agriculture in appropriate locations and confirms estimates published in our 2005 *CPUL* book.

Studies underway by Tomkins in more densely built parts of central London have found that residents who wish to cultivate crops often need to import soil into the city, either because open space has been paved over or due to concerns about the toxicity of soil (personal communication Jul 2012). Introducing closed-loop composting systems can go a long way towards alleviating such shortages of soil. The scarcity of soil in some areas is also one reason why soilless cultivation, such as hydroponics and aquaponics, is becoming a popular choice for urban agriculture.

What makes for a successful productive urban landscape?

In the chapters *Food in space: CPULs amongst contemporary urban space* and *Cuba: Laboratory for Urban Agriculture,* the 2005 *CPUL* book presented an overview and spatial analysis of the characteristics of individual urban agriculture sites. Since then, we have extended and tested our earlier assumptions, and this work has provided one of the sources for the *CPUL City Actions* presented in this book.

In 2006, as part of the *Utilitarian Dreams* exhibition in Havana, we developed a project to register public perception about the spatial and aesthetic qualities of urban agriculture sites. Called *Finding Parque Lenin,* the project invited comparisons between Parque Lenin on the outskirts of Havana and open spaces in the city centre and their related uses and lifestyles (Viljoen and Bohn 2009). Members of the public were surveyed with the aim of finding out if there was an unprompted correlation in the public mind between traditional spaces – such as parks, gardens, squares – and urban agriculture spaces. Parque Lenin was chosen as a reference because of its significance in people's memories as a popular leisure destination, and its extensive heath-like landscape, mixing natural and constructed, agricultural and infrastructural features. The park opened in 1972 in celebration of post-revolutionary socialism and, prior to transportation difficulties starting in the 1990s, was frequently visited by residents of all ages. Of the 268 respondents to the survey only 8 had never visited Parque Lenin, and about 80% would have liked to visit it more often (*Fig 1*). Participants in the survey described the park in terms of open natural landscape and recreation, comparing it to other parks, exhibition centres and amusement parks within Havana. While the general positive attitude to urban parks and being in open space supported the CPUL concept, it was clear that urban agriculture was not thought of as part of the city's landscape or landscape infrastructure. And whilst a 'coffee shop' (named in one questionnaire) qualified

as space of similar character to Parque Lenin, a market garden did not.

To challenge such an omission of urban agriculture from the public perception of quality open space, designers and planners need to take account of both the needs of urban farmers and those characteristics of open space that people desire.

From the *Finding Park Lenin* project, we concluded that three key issues need to be addressed prior to establishing any CPUL:

1. Utility landscape versus ornamental landscape: It is wrong to assume that exposure to urban agriculture alone will result in it being perceived as desirable, as "organic ornament".
2. Working landscape versus leisure landscape: Cultural and generational associations with agriculture and working the land, which may carry connotations of poverty and hard labour, need to be taken account of.
3. Accessibility versus inaccessibility: In Havana's case, urban agriculture sites, typified by discreetly enclosed organoponicos, do not allow access for mixed use or "adjacent" occupation.

Much of our work outlined in the *CPUL City Actions* addresses these concerns and aims to introduce a *new way of seeing* urban agriculture. Projects like *Unlocking Spaces* in Brighton and *Spiel/Feld Marzahn* in Berlin establish short- and long-term interventions providing working forums and prototypes for residents' input into a dialogue about future development, the ownership of open space and accessibility. The multi-programmed nature of many other urban agriculture sites, such as Berlin's *Prinzessinnengärten* (Clausen and Müller-Frank 2012) or London's city farms (FCFCG *n.d.*) exemplify urban agriculture's potential to include space for recreation and celebration. That said, practice on the ground is just beginning, and we need to continue investigating the inherent qualities of this new and evolving productive urban space.

FINDING PARQUE LENIN

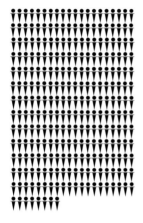 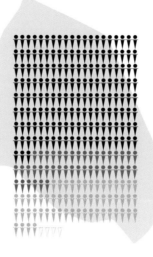 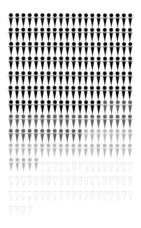

268 people surveyed
in Havana during November 2006 as part of
the project *Finding Parque Lenin.*

Parque Lenin is a vast landscape and amusement park on the southern outkirts of
Havana and has a positive presence in the
population's memory. It opened in 1972 as
recreational landscape celebrating a new
socialist lifestyle. Located in generous heath-
like open space and designed by the
country's leading architects and landscape
designers, Parque Lenin contained
numerous event spaces, a lake and its own
interconnecting railway.
The park remained a favourite destination
until the fuel crisis of 1989, when visitor
numbers dropped due to lack of
transportation.
By 2006, most attractions had seriously
deteriorated. Restoration started in 2005.

264 people visited Parque Lenin
at least once in their life (**98.5%**).

Of these, **163** people (62%) visited during
the last 6 years (since year 2000), despite
Cuba's severe economic difficulties which
also affected Parque Lenin (little transportation to + little maintenance of the park).
44 people were unclear about their last
visit, whilst **57** people definetely visited
before the year 2000.

85% of people who visited Parque Lenin
would like to go there again.

205 people who visited Parque Lenin responded to the question *"Which spaces in the
inner city remind you of Parque Lenin?"*

Of these, **135** people (**66%**) could name an
open space in Havana that offered qualities
similar to those found at Parque Lenin.
18% of people were unsure, whilst the
remaining 16% responded that no space
reminded them of Parque Lenin.

Fig 1: Finding Parque Lenin. A public survey undertaken in
Havana as part of this 2006 project asked respondents about
their perception of Parque Lenin, a large and popular park on the
outskirts of Havana. The aim was to see if people valued open
urban space and if a connection was made between the qualities
of the park and the city's urban agriculture. 268 people completed
the survey, of which 264 had visited Parque Lenin at least once in
their life. Of these, 62% had visited it in the previous six years, i.e.
since the park suffered from lack of access by public transport. 205
people responded to a question asking if they could name another
space in Havana that reminded them of Parque Lenin and 135 of
these named an open space. No respondents said that an urban
agriculture site reminded them of the park.

Urban scale: paths and fields

The network of paths and fields that make a CPUL
provides cities with more than circulation routes. As
proposed in our early work, CPUL networks facilitate
flows of food, people, primary elements such as air and
biodiversity and – in spatial terms – take account of
rural hinterland, city centre and the wider urban fabric
(Viljoen *et al.* 2004).

CPUL space is green infrastructure that can protect and
improve the functionality of ecosystems. It includes
biodiversity conservation (see chapter *Diversity*, p. 60),
contribution to human and social health and well-being,
sustainable agriculture and water management, climate

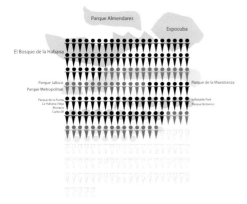

Parque Almendares

Expocuba

El Bosque de la Habana

Parque Jalisco
Parque Metropolitan

Parque de la Maestranza

Parque de la Punta
La Habana Vieja
Monaco
Carlos III

Inflatable Park
Parque Botanico

135 people who visited Parque Lenin and could name another open space in Havana that offers qualities similar to those found in Parque Lenin responded as follows:

46 votes went to the 3 most popular spaces
27 votes went to the next 3 popular spaces
43 votes went to 15 open spaces with more than 1 person voting for each of them

The remaining votes (**14%**) named various open spaces once or were unspecific.

0 people who visited Parque Lenin and could name another open space in Havana that offers qualities similar to those found in Parque Lenin considered one of the city's numerous urban agricultural sites.

"Organoponicos" are the most frequent types of urban agricultural landscape in Cuban cities and are familiar to inhabitants. They happen everywhere, i.e. right in front of your doorstep, and in lots of different sizes and shapes. Their commercial urban farmers are very visible members of the urban population. Urban agricultural sites produce significant amounts of fruit and vegetable in Havana, and people buy from them on a daily basis.

change mitigation and adaptation and support for the development of a green economy.

The *CPUL Opportunities Map* created for Middlesbrough (see *CPUL CITY Actions*, p. 188), shows one example of how such a network can be created, in this case following the lines of small streams that run through the town. The *CPUL City* concept is starting to be used to inform planning strategies aimed at creating and interconnecting open urban space for a number of ambitious new developments. As this book goes to press, the West African Municipality of Bobo-Dioulasso in Burkina Faso, working with a number of agencies including UN HABITAT, have defined as a vision and a goal the creation of 'a mosaic of connecting green spaces inside and at the

periphery of the city' explicitly using the CPUL concept as a model (Baguian 2013). The concept is also being applied within Europe as indicated by the inclusion of urban agriculture in the draft strategic vision for the Dutch city of Almere: 'The city's ambition is to develop this area towards a so-called continuous productive urban landscape producing food, energy, resources and water within and for the city (based on Viljoen, 2005)' (Jansma and Visser 2011).

The connecting routes that run between individual urban agriculture sites are an essential part of CPUL space and give spatial coherence to the entire network. These "thin productive connectors" accommodate pedestrian, cycle, wind and water flows, as well as creating

Fig 2: Madison's *Capital City Bike Loop*. Parts of this cycle route combine pedestrian and cycle ways with communal food-growing spaces adjacent to housing and wildlife planting. The ensemble of planted areas shows similar seasonal characteristics to landscape architect Piet Oudolf's 'new perennial' planting approach as found, for example, on New York's *High Line*.

wildlife corridors that encourage biodiversity. An innovative and very successful example of such a connector has been created in the North American city of Madison, in the state of Wisconsin *(Fig 2)*. Madison's *Capital City Bike Loop* provides a cycle and pedestrian route running round the city's centre, passing through large residential areas, parts of which, adjacent to St Paul Avenue, have been developed as a productive landscape, flanked by communally managed food-growing sites and areas of wildlife planting for local prairie plants.

Another example of what might be called "prototype" CPUL routes is the *Dequindre Cut Greenway* which runs from Detroit's river front on the route of a disused railway line inland towards the city's Eastern Market *(Fig 3)*. It borders both an urban farm used as a training centre by the Greening of Detroit organisation (see chapter *Detroit*, p. 130) and Mies van de Rohe's residential development *Lafayette Park*, set within a richly layered landscape by Alfred Caldwell to a master plan by Ludwig Hilberseimer. Together, these spaces demonstrate the potential for a seamless urban landscape connection between the domestic sphere, public urban space and a productive green infrastructure.

New York is already implementing a *Greenway Plan*, which proposes '350 miles of landscaped bicycle and pedestrian paths crisscrossing New York City' (NYCDCP

1993). Bringing together the *Greenway* with ground-based and building-integrated urban agriculture sites would offer the potential to create a coherent three-dimensional CPUL network integrating pleasant and health-enabling circulation with productive and socially active urban agriculture fields.

The agricultural and architectural scale within productive urban landscapes

The chapter *Food in space* in our 2005 *CPUL* book, referred to at the start of this chapter, compared European open urban space and CPUL space under the headings of *Spaciousness*, *Occupation* and *Ecology*. Today, ten years on from this conceptual start, we are applying the same three criteria to actual locations in order to assess how well, together, they inform a new dynamic productive urban landscape.

Spaciousness

If urban agriculture fields reach a certain size, their sheer dimension could negatively result in the de-urbanisation of cities, by virtue of the physical distance created between one part of the city and another. However, this concern need not prevent the integration of large fields into the city, because it is their plan form and their horizon that largely determine if they disconnect or connect built-up areas. Two examples, Berlin's disused Tempelhof Airport (approx. 370 hectares) and *Central Park* (approx. 340 hectares) in New York demonstrate this characteristic in different ways as "oasis" and "bridge".

Tempelhof's vast flat plane presents an archetypal "field" in the city. Unlike most other urban parks that use the verticality of planting or topography to animate space and create enclosure, the sheer horizontality of Tempelhof creates an oasis of tranquillity within the city. It has three distinct edge conditions: a hard urban building line, a railway line forming a low, non-permeable barrier, and a near seamless blending into adjacent park-like spaces. These characteristics are most comparable to the positive isolation of rooftop farms. Within Tempelhof, one is unaware of the city *and* "nature", it is in a positive sense "apart" from the city.

Central Park, by contrast, is embedded within the city. Its edges, defined by the city's grid, remain permeable with many points of entry, and the park provides both routes across the city and a refuge from the street. Its plan form – an elongated rectangle with proportions of roughly five (North–South) to one (East–West) – alternatively provides a sense of enclosure in nature along its long axis and sense of urbanity through views out and into the city across its short axis. This phenomenon has the unique characteristic that the park can become both a connective urban tissue within the city (you know that you are in the city, that you walk in the city) and, by just turning 90 degrees, an "escape" from the city into a constructed second nature *(Fig 4)*.

In summary: We will continue to think *"Spaciousness"*. We add: "oasis", "bridge", "field", "nature", "apart", "escape", "sense of enclosure" – all part of an urban agriculture that contributes to urbanity and food sovereignty.

Occupation

We will also continue to think "occupation" because CPUL space is productively and publicly occupied. Productive space may be separated from public space by means of level changes, gaps or visibly permeable boundaries, but the two operate as adjacent types and together create a new typology of urban place. The design vocabulary for these spaces is emerging. They may be larger fields or intimate spaces or examples of "hands-on urbanism"*(Fig 5)*. They may be located near to paths or set at vantage points *(Fig 6)*, allowing for views over the urban agriculture fields and out to the city. Some of these spaces invite informal occupation.

We can experience the sensation of adjacent occupation, when, for example, sitting under the water tower on the *Brooklyn Grange* rooftop farm or when looking across the East River in one direction and productive fields in the other from the corner of *Eagle Street Farm* (see chapter *New York City*, p. 122).

Ecology

Highly complex urban ecologies continue to be better understood as research and practice grows within a spectrum ranging from "organic" forest gardening – for example as practised by adherents to permaculture – to

industrialised techniques – as, for example, in aquaponic systems. The inclusion of urban agriculture into cities requires that the public accept and appreciate a more seasonal and formally cultivated landscape. The processes of growth, blossoming, die-back and germination will all be visible, far more so than in municipal parks that follow familiar and managed ornamental aesthetic. Closed-loop, no-waste food systems utilise the interdependencies within cycles of consumption and production, and this will be mirrored in the new urban landscape. The change is already underway as, for example, in the recognition of the need for bee habitats (see chapter *Bricks and Necter*, p. 84) or in the interest expressed in the work of plantsman Piet Oudolf and his practice of the so-called "New Perennial Movement". Oudolf's planting is found on New York's *High Line* and in London's *Potters Fields Park*, both of which celebrate a plant's entire life cycle (Oudolf and Kingsbury 2010). And both the *High Line* and *Potters Fields* place people in the centre of rich and dynamic landscapes, constantly in states of flux, seasonally with slow changes from an abundant summer growth to a frugal winter landscape. These are like agricultural landscapes, where soil, wildlife and plants are each highlighted at different times.

Fig 3: Detroit's *Dequindre Cut Greenway*. This open space network can be understood as a prototype CPUL, connecting recreational areas, like the river front, residential areas, such as Mies van de Rohe's *Lafayette Park* [to the left], the city's urban agriculture hub, Eastern Market, and Greening of Detroit's urban farm that lies ahead.

Fig 4: *Central Park* New York. Urban agriculture fields can be big without destroying a sense of urbanity. Plan form is important, and one of the best examples of how fields can contribute different characteristics to a city is found in New York's *Central Park*. Here, the long north–south axis creates a sense of enclosure within nature and a corresponding break from the city. The east–west axis, by contrast, accentuates the connections from one building to the next across the park. This dual perception is part of the richness that CPUL space can also bring to densely built cities.

Growing livelihoods in urban landscapes

A prime example of multi-use productive spaces that provide food and income can be found in the Argentinian city of Rosario, where three spatial types have been defined and implemented: large public Garden Parks 'in which recreational, productive, educational and commercial activities are developed', neighbourhood-scale Educational Productive Squares, and Productive Streets. Significantly, the Rosario project includes a supportive municipal framework, and the productive infrastructure integrates regular urban markets, product processing (vegetable boxes and cosmetic products) and skills-capacity building for participants (Dubbeling 2011). The Rosario project has developed with the support of the international network Resource Centre on Urban Agriculture and Food Security (RUAF) within a context of poverty and scarcity for the urban farmers who, by working and engaging with wealthier inhabitants as clients, generate food for themselves as well as income from the sale of produce.

Providing for urban lives is the ultimate test for productive urban landscapes. The urban contexts of such landscapes will change from city to city, but what will remain for their users is the pleasure of working the land, being in it or seeing it being worked on – combined with the pleasure of tasting the land's produce – or earning a living from that land.

Fig 5: *Allmende-Kontor* Berlin. Intimate "self-built" spaces for seating and planting constructed as part of Berlin's urban agriculture *Allmende-Kontor* [Bureau of the Commons] project on the site of former Tempelhof Airport. This arrangement of seating areas for relaxation embedded within and directly adjacent to food growing areas represents a primary configuration of small gregarious spaces set within larger productive fields.

Fig 6: *High Line* New York. Vantage points along this regenerated former railway line provide the catalyst for spaces accommodating individuals and groups, allowing for sitting and lying, looking out beyond, over and into planted areas. All of these are also characteristic of CPUL space. The popularity of New York's *High Line* demonstrates the desire for coherently designed urban landscape combining paths, planting and spaces for stopping.

Utilitarian Dreams: Productive life in the city

André Viljoen and Katrin Bohn

We have argued elsewhere that, in urban agriculture, scarcity and abundance can lie very close to one another because with few resources urban agriculture can enable abundance (Viljoen and Bohn 2012). At the same time, developments within the past few years have demonstrated that culturally and economically vibrant cities also have a great desire and ability to support ambitious urban agriculture proposals. Whilst these proposals usually originate from individual initiatives, it is also true that a supporting infrastructure is necessary to create stable and resilient urban food systems. This is one of the things that, for example, Cuba, as a nation, and New York City have in common. We can see that the food-productive life in our cities depends on and varies with social and economic conditions and these will determine the appropriateness of different types of urban agriculture.

With reference to projects already underway in Milwaukee, New York, London and Berlin, we aim to illustrate a variety and richness of approaches typical of any movement in the transition between a pioneering phase and the establishment of norms of practice.

Economic approaches

Currently, the economic models for funding new urban agriculture projects are converging towards either social enterprise or straight commercial models, with food markets often providing crucial support for both.

The organisations *Growing Power* in the USA and *Growing Communities* in the UK both demonstrate the possibilities from a long and steady growth of social enterprises, if guided by clear agendas, leadership and management. Whilst set up with somewhat different, less vigorously urban agriculture-oriented aims, *Agrarbörse Ost* in Germany, is of similar character. Established respectively in

1993 (Growing Power *n.d.* b), 1996 (Growing Communities *n.d.* a) and 1990/1996 (Agrarbörse *n.d.*) all promote sustainable and healthy local food systems with urban agriculture as a core activity. *Growing Power* also developed and now actively pursues an explicit socio-political agenda aimed at empowerment and equality, whereas *Agrarbörse* originally had – and still does to some extent – a political/economic aim and later reoriented towards more social and ecological interests.

A number of common strands for setting up urban agriculture projects become evident when analysing the business models of these social enterprises:

- All started with **access to land**. In *Growing Power*'s case, an existing 0.8 hectare [2 acre] market garden with greenhouses in Milwaukee, and in *Growing Communities'* case, a modest space within an existing London park and two small sites nearby. The sites were not ideal, and needed much work to make them productive. *Agrarbörse* acted as public agency for several charitable projects, which often involved the construction or maintenance of public sites.
- Compared to conventional enterprises, each organisation spent **a prolonged time developing** and refining their practice. Over more than ten years, *Growing Power* developed low-impact, intensive growing techniques and established vegetable markets in poor neighbourhoods as well as a second centre in Chicago, thereby extending practice beyond its base in Milwaukee. *Growing Communities* established over a similar period a sophisticated organic vegetable box scheme utilising a *Food Zone* model (Growing Communities *n.d.* b) to determine how its own produce could be combined with supplies from adjacent farmers to minimise environmental impact and offer an adequate quantity and variety of produce. Although, in detail, each organisation has different modes of operation, important common factors are their long-term persistence and clear agendas.

- To be economically viable, an urban agriculture project needs **reliable leases** for the urban space it is occupying. *Agrarbörse* is lobbying the Berlin municipality for minimum lease times of 12 to 15 years for urban agricultural uses (TUB 2011).
- Julie Brown, one of *Growing Communities'* founding members, has always been adamant that **yields and economies of production matter**, something which can get lost in arguing for the social and communal benefits delivered by urban agriculture and urban food systems projects. Annual reports published by *Growing Communities* record a consistent growth in the sale of their organic vegetable box scheme by about 30% per year between 2005 and 2009 (Growing Communities 2009). Although these percentages are high, the actual amounts remain modest when compared to more commercially oriented vegetable box schemes.
- At a time when the cost of imported food and the salaries of market gardeners are extremely low, many urban agriculture projects will **rely to some extent on grants and volunteering** in order to build economically competitive business models. It is likely that this situation will change in the future as food prices rise. *Growing Communities* are clear about their relationship to the status quo when stating that 'this approach of getting on with creating a viable alternative to the current food system is in the spirit of Buckminster Fuller who said: "You can never change things by fighting the existing reality. To change something, build a new model that makes the existing model obsolete"' (Growing Communities *n.d.* a).
- Unlike in most rural agricultural enterprises, urban agriculture often takes on **roles in environmental education**, as on economical opportunity on the one hand, and reflecting the desires for alternative urban lifestyles on the other. *Agrarbörse* is not only training gardeners, but attains a considerable amount of recognition and funding through their work with young people, especially through their project *Treibhaus* [greenhouse] a youth centre for youngsters not related to urban agriculture (Agrarbörse *n.d.*).

Once the projects stabilise, the process of growth is often constrained by, first, a lack of sufficient land and, second, a lack of trained urban farmers.

For about a decade, *Growing Communities* had access to three modest, so-called market garden sites for food growing, although, in reality, they were much smaller than traditional market gardens. To address this, post 2010, they established a network of "patchwork farms" consisting of several small private and publicly owned growing sites. At the time of writing, the amount of ground under cultivation, the number of trainee growers and the number of employment opportunities created continues to expand rapidly, including plans to set up a considerably larger 1.6 ha [4 acre] "starter farm" on a vacated council nursery plot in Dagenham, East London. The lack of trained urban farmers has been addressed by adopting a now familiar sequence of actions: first, working with volunteers to establish and, importantly, demonstrate the quality and reliability of urban agriculture produce; then bidding for project-based funding from an array of grant-giving bodies and, at the same time, the effective use of a website and social media. Alongside reliance on volunteers, a formalised *Apprentice Growers Scheme* now trains volunteers, many of whom go on to cultivate plots forming the "patchwork farm" or work on other sites. Funding for the 1.6 ha "starter farm" at Dagenham will enable the employment of a gardener for about two years after which the farm is intended to be self-funding (Growing Communities *n.d.* a).

In the 14 years between 1993 and 2007, *Growing Power* essentially followed the same business model as *Growing Communities*, but at a larger scale and with a more aggressive marketing strategy, helped both by founder Will Allen's background in business and by his drive to align food justice with social justice. Both organisations operate as not-for-profit companies with associated tax benefits. *Agrarbörse* is also a registered society, however, being originally set up with the strategic aim of helping in the transition from GDR to a capitalist food economy, it benefited from funding support and municipal cooperation early on, and its business model – until its refounding in 1996 – was a relatively secure one. Since 1996, however, they pursue a social enterprise business model. All three projects systematically spent time working on developing the financial viability of urban agriculture, incremental growth in production, recruiting volunteers, creating real jobs as turnover increased, developing training programmes, building alliances with local authorities and agencies, and taking on additional land for growing. Notwithstanding this marked success, Allen notes: 'The honest truth is that with urban agriculture, we are not there yet. We have not yet made it reliably profitable. I think we can, though.' (Allen and Wilson 2012: 226).

Will Allen describes the evolution of his ideas on urban agriculture and the establishment of *Growing Power* in his book *The Good Food Revolution* (Allen and Wilson 2012). Allen believes in the approach of economist Ernst Schumacher, articulated in his book *Small is beautiful: Economics as if people mattered* (Schumacher 1973). Contrary to *Growing Communities'* contention that an entirely new food system needs to be constructed without much engagement with the existing food industry, Allen is prepared to work with partners who are fully embedded in corporate, industrialised modes of production, distribution and marketing. During its early years, *Growing Power* had to deal with serious financial struggles, but in 2011, its continued expansion was clearly evident, as was this "catholic" approach to working with partners who, on the face of it, did not support Will Allen's belief in small-scale, intensive organic production. The late Jerry Kaufman, who many consider the founding father of food planning in the USA, was a leading member of *Growing Power*'s board of directors and described Allen's policy as one of maintaining an "open table" excluding no one from the debate and accepting financial support from unexpected sources provided that no conditions would be placed upon its use (personal communication 2011). In 2011, this was made starkly clear when Allen accepted a grant of one million dollars from the supermarket chain *Wal-Mart* to support 15 regional *Growing Power* training centres. Similarly, *Growing Power* cultivates land using organic principles adjacent to a food processing plant run by *Sysco* who purchase the crops. Sysco produce ready meals for schools in the USA, and certainly do not follow Schumacher's principle of 'small is beautiful'. Critics argue that Allen is complicit in supporting these corporations' programmes of "green wash", while Allen sees his actions in the context of an entrenched system that will take time to change. Jerry Kaufman was instrumental in developing a business plan to move *Growing Power* into financial profitability. By 2007, it turned in a modest profit with income being raised from a mixture of food sales and grants. Will Allen records that, in 2006, about one third of their gross income came from direct sales

worth about \$375,000, while a further two-thirds was raised from grants. At the point of transition to profitability, the organisation employed 12 staff, but also relied on volunteers and trainees in order to maintain production (Allen and Wilson 2012: 200).

Future plans by *Growing Power* include the construction of a modestly scaled vertical farm, which is perhaps more akin to strictly commercial aims of organisations such as *Lufa Farms* in Vancouver (Lufa Farms *n.d.* a) or *Gotham Greens* in New York (Gotham Greens *n.d.*), both of which have developed lightweight hydroponic rooftop greenhouses on existing buildings. These two new urban farms minimise the environmental impact of their hydroponic systems and use biological rather than chemical insecticides. *Gotham Greens* are reported to produce locally cultivated crops for sale in supermarkets that are no more expensive than more distantly sourced organic produce (Zeveloff 2011), while *Lufa Farms* include their produce in a vegetable box scheme supplemented with organically certified produce from local farmers, following a model very similar to *Growing Communities* (Lufa Farms *n.d.* a).

Agrarbörse who, at the time of writing, are running several projects involving urban agriculture in Berlin are planning to tackle the challenge of retail opportunities for urban farmers by setting up a "farm store" – a new building typology in the German capital – that would store, sell, process and exchange food products of even very small individual urban producers who currently face difficulties when marketing their products (Riedel, personal communication Apr 2012).

The economics of building-integrated urban farms is less easy to review at this stage of development, as their history is much shorter, with, to our knowledge, the exception of three entirely commercial rooftop greenhouses established in 1995 above the *Eli Zabar* gourmet market store in New York City (Eli Zabar *n.d.*). In *Eli Zabar's* case, it appears that the building owner runs the market and greenhouse, removing rent for the roof space from the cost equation. For hydroponic greenhouses a well-developed industry already exists and, other than questions raised by gaining access to a rooftop (see *Laboratories for Urban Agriculture: The USA: New York City*, p. 122), the economic models used for running a business are well established. In the early stages of integrating rooftop farms into cities, farmers will most likely seek out easily accessible flat roofs, strong enough to accommodate the additional load and requiring minimum alteration to a building. In the future, it is likely that existing flat roofs may be selected, even if they require structural reinforcement, or in the case of less suitable profiles, even complete rebuilding as part of a building's refurbishment.

One of the most interesting proposals for the reuse of an existing (industrial) building is the *Malzfabrik* in Berlin. Originally built in the early 20th century as a malting factory, this heavy-constructed building includes a number of accessible large water tanks and a significant area of roof space suitable, or to be made suitable, for conversion into a greenhouse. The building's developers are currently working with a team to agree on a financially viable aquaponic system as part of a much larger mixed-use commercial development (ECF *n.d.* a).

Social productivity

Not all urban agriculture projects are motivated by agricultural yield and many measure their productivity in terms of social benefit, not least of which is improved public health. In fact, most practitioners recognise benefits related to behaviour change, often brought about by the awareness-raising capacity of food growing projects. When describing *Growing Power*'s impact, Erich Schlosser comments:

...the good that Growing Power is doing in the communities it serves – the heart attacks and strokes and hospital visits it helps people to avoid, and the sense of empowerment that it gives, the families that it brings together – represent a form of social profit that it is impossible to quantify.

(Schlosser 2012)

These significant health and well-being benefits apply especially to community-based or individual urban agriculture projects and are already being consciously documented (Campbell and Wiesen 2009). However, urban agriculture's full recognition as an important driver for social improvements still has to happen amongst many civic decision makers. "Full recognition"

means that the needs of urban farmers and gardeners are treated equally seriously as those of other stakeholders who create benefits for the local community through their work. If this happens it will enable consumers to significantly and sustainably change their behaviour with regard to food.

In the UK, the allotment can be a catalyst for (behaviour) changes related to diet and health. Surveys undertaken by Gillean Denny in Cambridge and Middlesbrough reveal the allotments' continuing influence on food choices across all socio-economic ranges. Most notable are a substantial increase in the quality and quantity of fresh food being consumed by allotment growers during the growing season and a decreased dependency on grocery stores for fresh produce: 70% in growing seasons and 24% during off season. Changes in "food miles" reduce personal carbon emissions by an estimated 950 kg CO_2 per year, even while still predominantly utilising grocery stores during off-season months and maintaining an overall dependence on fossil-fuelled transport year round. Allotment tenants also surpass the recommended 30 minutes per day of exercise through time spent on the allotment and through active-commuting related to food procurement. Furthermore, allotment holders who ate less than the recommended daily intake of fruit and vegetables before they had an allotment, increased their fruit and vegetable intake once they started growing food, and this increase was reflected in an increased proportion of fruit and vegetables purchased throughout the year. If this trend is validated in further research, it will indicate the significant behaviour change impact that may be attributed to even relatively modest urban agriculture interventions (Viljoen *et al.* 2009).

Subsequent experience gained when working on student and demonstration projects, such as the *Edible Campus* at the Faculty of Arts, University of Brighton (UoB 2011), suggests that even very modest food growing activity can affect changes in food purchasing habits, resulting in increased consumption of fresh fruit and vegetables and reduced consumption of animal and processed products.

Finding the right tools for achieving large-scale and voluntary behaviour change in favour of environmentally sustainable development has long been a challenge and so the potential noted here is worth further research. It is the complexity of urban agriculture's benefits that is beginning to be appreciated: New York's deputy food policy coordinator Jordan Brackett, for example, felt that the behaviour change potential of community-based projects had been understood within his food policy team resulting in support for schools and community programmes (personal communication Aug 2011). Such "unmeasurable" benefits are increasingly directing policy makers and politicians who now want the metrics to make the case for the quite radical changes required to embed productive landscapes within cities.

The usefulness of metrics

New York City provides a good example of how metrics are being used to quantify the impact of community-based food growing. There are several drivers for this: on the one hand, for example, community gardens still do not have permanent legal protection and, therefore, such measurements can be used politically, for example by the New York City Community Garden Coalition. On the other hand, active practitioners can use this data to underpin arguments when applying for charitable or commercial funding. In addition, once the data is available it will provide evidence to inform urban policy.

The organisation Farming Concrete provides an entrepreneurial example and methodological model for collecting food production data whilst setting up a structure that allows for the continuation of data collection without the need for external funding. The project will be considered a success by its founders, if, after ten years, sufficient data has been collected to make it obsolete. Starting in 2010, three annual reports for New York City have been published online (Farming Concrete 2012). Mara Gittleman and Kelli Jordan, founders of Farming Concrete, described how they aimed to use 'citizen scientists' to record the amount of produce cultivated in community and school food gardens (personal communication 2011). They developed a practical approach recognising different levels of interest and motivations found within growers. The most accurate data is gathered by individuals who weigh their entire output using kitchen scales and record the types of crop cultivated. A second approach is to get growers to record the types

of crops cultivated, but not measure their weight. These two methods allow for an assessment of the variety and quantity of crops harvested. Farming Concrete's findings were significant: there are some real farmers in the city, and the gardens produce more food than was initially thought. For 2010, they recorded about $200,000 worth – or over 80,000 lbs – of vegetable crops produced, excluding spring crops, from 68 gardens with a net growing area of 1.7 acres (0.7 ha). They explicitly noted that not everything grown on the surveyed sites was measured or recorded (personal communication 2011). Despite this achievement, it is important not to confuse the yields logged by community growers with those that can be achieved by commercial growers.

In Farming Concrete's experience, local academics had concerns at the start about farmers measuring their own output, but now academics are also using this method. Practitioners find it 'infinitely more accurate' than other methods for estimating yield (personal communication 2011). Many community gardens are now being studied by external researchers, who are seen by gardeners as experts but also as demanding intruders. However, Farming Concrete enabled practitioners to also see the benefit of gathering data: for some, it is personal interest, for others, a means to assist with funding applications and membership recruitment or to establish which crops are the most successful in different locations.

As a replicable model, Farming Concrete's success has been based on a formal and funded public portal, represented by its website and annual reports, combined with a very active informal, but skilled and focused community of practice 'communicating over coffee and online'. Funding came from a variety of sources including New York's publicly funded Green Thumb community gardening project, a student internship at The New School and other funding from a variety of organisations promoting an improved public realm. A measure of Farming Concrete's impact is that – according to Sustain's Sarah Williams – the longer-established London-based food charity Sustain is planning to adopt the citizen scientist approach to quantify yields and encourage more intensive production from London's community food growers (personal communication 2012).

Reflecting on the project's strengths and weaknesses, Mara and Kelli thought its decentralised nature was its strength because the community is 'doing it', which needs a flexibility and willingness to find out what works. A reality, but also a frustration, is the attrition rate for participants despite the effort put into running the project. *Farming Concrete* recommends recruiting twice as many participants as required. A notable success was recorded during the project's second year, when gardeners came forward to join the project, rather than having to be recruited.

Other increasingly important metrics include recording the environmental benefits of urban agriculture, for example those relating to its potential to minimise rain and storm water runoff, especially from impervious areas of paving and rooftops. Concurrent with the foundation of *Farming Concrete*, Tyler Caruso and Erik Facteau established the organisation *Seeing Green* in New York to document the water retention potential of rooftop farms, as well as to advise more generally on their design (Seeing Green *n.d.*). Set up using crowdsourced funding and on a more commercial basis than *Farming Concrete*, their findings will help to make the case for urban agriculture's contribution to sustainable urban drainage systems.

In the future, metrics associated with the use of compostable waste and water storage can be added to those emerging for yields and reduced stormwater runoff. Recording quantifiables, such as measures of food production or water retention, are relatively straightforward tasks and may be considered a "stage one activity", not only when it comes to assessing a city's environmental performance, but also when generating the reasons for implementing productive urban landscapes.

Food policies for everyday life

Benefits and metrics need evaluation and coordination if the different parties involved in reforming urban food systems are to work together. Joint top-down and bottom-up processes can move initiatives 'from alternatives to alliances', as Kevin Morgan puts it in his chapter (p. 23). Looking once more at New York the work of the mayor's food policy coordinator and team illustrates this process very well: first, the formal establishment of such a position or body helps to facilitate coordinated food

planning by providing a single point of contact; second, food policy has been included in the city's planning documents. Both of these actions are extremely significant and they are still extremely rare.

Food policy in New York operates in a context of extreme discrepancy in wealth with near to 400,000 millionaire residents and about 1.8 million people on incomes below the official federal poverty threshold. The latter are eligible to receive benefits from federal, not city budgets, in the form of food stamps which operate like a credit card. Furthermore, 6 million of New York City's 8.5 million residents live in food deserts (Brackett, personal communication Aug 2011). Far from being a singular case, this condition is increasingly prevalent in nations that follow a neoliberal economic agenda, and to address it requires top-down commitments.

Whilst food sovereignty and food security might be the most important global political concerns for the feeding of our cities, food poverty and food deserts are the most critical socio-political contexts for local action. Access to food becomes an important factor for urban planners from a multitude of angles, and a number of widely applicable points can be noted:

- Budget: Given limited resources, an interesting **budgeting tension** was identified in food deserts between funding urban agriculture and recognising its "great" educational impact or funding new supermarkets. The idea of supermarkets in food deserts deserves further scrutiny to identify to what extent they contribute in the first place to the problems created by narrowly defined, profit-driven models.
- Food schemes: New York has developed **innovative food schemes** targeting people on low incomes. These include about 500 mobile fruit and vegetable carts generating modest incomes for vendors. The city believes that for every one dollar spent using food stamps, one-and-three-quarter dollars is spent in the local economy, further aided by a so-called *Health Bucks Initiative* offering a 40% bonus when food stamps are used to purchase fruit and vegetables (Brackett, personal communication Aug 2011).
- Nutrition standards: Direct procurement of about 250 million meals per year (school dinners, etc.) in New York City provides another avenue for **improving nutrition standards**, and initiatives

have included the banning of trans fats in procured food. Improved nutrition standards, in return, will facilitate healthier food shopping choices (Brackett, personal communication Aug 2011).

- Interdependencies: New York's innovation during Mayor Bloomberg's tenure was to recognise food and agriculture as a cross-cutting planning issue and, most significantly, its **spatial and systemic interdependencies**. The decision to revise the city's long-term sustainability strategy *PlaNYC* to include food planning in 2011, just four years after its initial publication, can be seen as part of the zeitgeist (NYC *n.d.*). From the perspective of creating a *CPUL City*, *PlaNYC* acknowledges some key features by committing to provide access to green space (that can include urban agriculture) within any ten-minute walk and by recognising the potential to create closed-loop waste systems utilising, for example, restaurant waste.

- Spatial access: Although *PlaNYC* recognises the spatial requirements of urban agriculture with respect to the need for sites, it cannot be said to be linked to a **wider productive urban space strategy** as, for example, envisaged by the *CPUL City* concept. Such a strategy, however, would not only facilitate the access to sites across a city, but also to food products by encouraging their direct distribution and exchange.

- Regional produce: When asked why New York City did not just **advocate increasing the amount of and access to regional produce**, the city's deputy food policy coordinator's answer was that they were not sure about the environmental impact of imported food compared to local produce, for example one long-distance transportation versus a number of smaller, perhaps inefficient local trucks. Furthermore, they did not know if there were local 'choke points' within food distribution pathways in the city (Brackett, personal communication Aug 2011). Such questions are now being addressed by a number of studies underway. One of the most systematic studies is being undertaken by the Urban Design Lab at New York's Columbia University as part of a *National Integrated Regional Foodshed Project* which aims to research the reintegration of regional food production into local supply chains (Urban Design Lab 2011a).

- Land ownership: Challenges to realising this integrated vision are common to many cities and include

public and private land ownership discrepancies, the silo mentality that prevents different municipal departments from communicating with one another, and the delivery of policies that are reliant on different agencies and agents to work together.

Conclusion: change!

There are several departure points for bringing together the food-productive life in our cities, such as environmental concerns; community cohesion and identity; encouraging small-scale enterprise; environmental education; improving health and individual lifestyles; creating one's own city of short ways; and encouraging local exchange, monetary and otherwise. All aim to finally agree on a coherent policy for coordinating the multiple players involved with productive urban landscapes.

The metrics for recording social, economic and environmental models of such viable urban agriculture – with all its benefits and challenges – are being developed now, and it is likely that the financial challenges for breaking even, socially and economically, will be eased as the real cost of food becomes even more evident in the future.

Having started this, developing equitable urban life requires a public platform. Public platforms for urban agriculture may take different forms, but all operate under the broad umbrella of environmentally sustainable development. Models for this do now exist, ranging from the discussed advisory strategies emerging in cities like New York to the precisely focused practice-based programmes of *Edible Rotterdam* (Graaf 2012) or the Swiss research programme *Food Urbanism Initiative* (FUI 2011) to every food growing project's own stakeholder engagement. Platforms like these can provide the framework for jointly building a new urban agriculture infrastructure, embedded in the city and recognising the multiple benefits arising from its integration.

So, the spaces envisaged in *CPUL City* are not only food-yield-productive, but their everyday use is also guided to be healthy, fair, economically stable and convivial. These spaces are green and open, and they flow out and into the countryside... and back from there... as does wildlife... and air... and people, above all... and food...

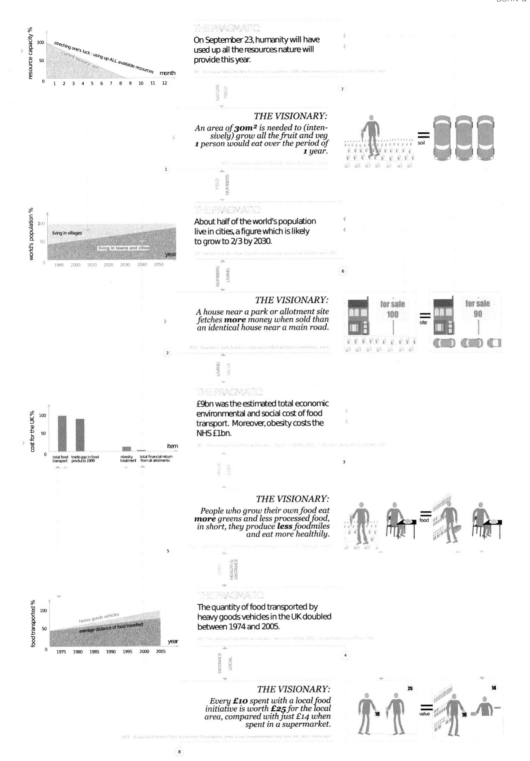

THE PRAGMATIC

On September 23, humanity will have used up all the resources nature will provide this year.

7

THE VISIONARY:

*An area of **30m²** is needed to (intensively) grow all the fruit and veg 1 person would eat over the period of 1 year.*

1

THE PRAGMATIC

About half of the world's population live in cities, a figure which is likely to grow to 2/3 by 2030.

6

THE VISIONARY:

*A house near a park or allotment site fetches **more** money when sold than an identical house near a main road.*

2

THE PRAGMATIC

£9bn was the estimated total economic environmental and social cost of food transport. Moreover, obesity costs the NHS £1bn.

3

THE VISIONARY:

*People who grow their own food eat **more** greens and less processed food, in short, they produce **less** foodmiles and eat more healthily.*

5

THE PRAGMATIC

The quantity of food transported by heavy goods vehicles in the UK doubled between 1974 and 2005.

4

THE VISIONARY:

*Every **£10** spent with a local food initiative is worth **£25** for the local area, compared with just **£14** when spent in a supermarket.*

8

Fig 1: The pragmatic and the visionary. A UK-centred dialogue on our society's relation to food, space and everyday life within the city.

The city in the fabric of eco-social interdependence

Yrjö Haila

The material success of humanity presents us with a range of perplexing questions, but the most perplexing question of all is the enormity of the success itself. Plenty of indicators are on offer; for instance population growth, the spread of the human population across the Earth, appropriation of biological productivity for human purposes (estimated at 25–40%, Smil 2002) and the diversification of economic life. The last offers what is perhaps the most dramatic single indicator; Beinhocker notes that the number of 'stock-keeping units', a measure retailers use to count types of units they sell in the economy, for the Yanomamö tribe in the Amazon numbers a few thousand at most while the corresponding number in the economy of New York City is in the order of tens of billions (Beinhocker 2006).

It is well understood, of course, that the material success has to be due to efficient utilization of what nature offers. As with all organisms, humans are dependent on metabolic exchange with the environment, that is the acquisition of necessities such as food and water and the expulsion of waste. Metabolism necessarily modifies environmental conditions at close range. Human metabolism is social in nature, embedded as it is in the division of labour among members of communities to which human individuals belong. The outline of the history of human material sustenance is known quite well. Early forms of social sustenance date back several million years, but a major transition occurred with the origin of agriculture and permanent settlements just over 10,000 years ago, and with the origin of written language some 6,000 years ago. After these transitions, human population size started to soar. Against the temporal scale of biological evolution, these transitions were very recent indeed.

It becomes easier to understand the human material success when we take account of the fact that most of the skills humans have adopted have incipient models in what other animals are able to do. It is against this

insight that the exclusively human skills rise into focus. What is specific to humans is grounded in our ability to construct symbolic worlds in which we reside: Terrence Deacon used the term 'symbolic species' to describe this speciality (Deacon 1997). Deacon talks about the ability to use symbolic language in particular, but also material environments decorated with everyday utensils, built structures, cultivated environments and social paraphernalia exert symbolic force. Historian of architecture Joseph Rykwert offers a classic description of the city as a formation laden with symbols (Rykwert 1988).

Symbols create temporal realities over and above what is immediately experienced here and now. Symbolic meanings that are projected toward the future make the future, in a sense, present in the present: such projections become a part of the reality that directs our actions. This is what normative rules, conventions and institutions do as 'second nature' (Dyke 1988). A political declaration such as, for instance, the goal set by the European Union to halt the deterioration of biodiversity first by 2010 and then, after this had failed, by 2020, is basically symbolic: the chances of reaching the goal are very small, but it has an effect on decisions made today.

Material artefacts are future-oriented as well. This is certainly true of houses that are meant to be lived in by an innumerable number of generations in the future. Similarly with material practices: tilling the land makes sense, provided labour conducted today bears fruit after a certain period of time. But whether the fruit of the labour will actually be harvestable depends on human success in persuading nature to comply and produce those fruits. In addition, success depends on coordinated action of the members of the society.

All this means that human material success is backed by an increasing dependence of humans upon ecological conditions in the surroundings; not independence as might be thought. More accurately, we are in a relation of interdependence with the surrounding ecological conditions, increasingly with the biosphere as a whole; humanity depends on environments modified by previous human labour (second nature), and such environments depend on continuous human modification and care.

Symbolically laden human imaginations quite obviously have their downside, too. We are able to construct projections that are pure myth and fantasy. This ability is particularly pronounced if we extrapolate recent experience toward the future in a straightforward linear continuum. This dilemma is at the heart of the current eco-social predicament of humanity.

The dynamics of social metabolism

The machinery of human social sustenance is analogous to the machinery maintaining the metabolism of individual organisms; what is needed is transported in and waste is expelled back out. The continuous flux of materials is driven by an external source of energy. The system is very far from thermodynamic equilibrium. The energy that maintains life on Earth is ultimately derived from the sun in the form of intensive radiation that plants and other photosynthesizing organisms can use to synthesize organic materials. Other organisms derive the energy they need from organic matter they acquire from their surroundings.

Organismal metabolism is coupled with usable sources of energy in the surroundings, as the dependence of life on solar radiation clearly shows. In addition, a broad range of different organisms is able to exploit energy flows of other types in their surroundings; Turner dubbed this phenomenon 'the extended organism' (Turner 2000). The elaborate nest structures of termites and ants are examples. A similar distinction can be applied to the social metabolism of human communities. In the terminology of economist Nicholas Georgescu-Roegen, 'endosomatic' metabolism refers to what happens inside human bodies and 'exosomatic' metabolism to the functioning of the human economic system that is driven by various external sources of energy. This distinction is pretty straightforward and has been made in variable terminology by several authors, but Georgescu-Roegen drew particularly consistent conclusions

concerning both human economic history and our present ecological predicament (Georgescu-Roegen 1971).[1]

Built structures as well as tools and other utensils are part of our exosomatic metabolic machinery. It is thus well understandable that permanent settlements and, eventually, the city opened the way for a great intensification of exosomatic metabolism. But cities are still metabolic systems, analogous with organisms, maintained far from thermodynamic equilibrium by material throughput driven by a flow of energy acquired from the outside. Cities and organisms are also vastly different, but the analogy offers valuable comparative perspectives on dynamics of change in short versus long temporal horizons (Dyke 1988; Polimeni *et al.* 2008).

In the short term, efficiency of the metabolic process is critical, indicated by what is achieved when a certain amount of material is harnessed into use with a certain amount of "work". Well-established laboratory procedures are used for measuring the efficiency of organismic metabolism. The efficiency of social metabolism is described using, for instance, Gross Domestic Product (GDP), the market value of goods and services produced within a country in a given period of time, as an indicator of efficiency of a national economy in monetary terms. GDP serves reasonably well the purposes of governmental book-keeping when the economy is running smoothly. However, indicators of current efficiency, whether of organismal or social metabolism, turn out to be deficient whenever environmental conditions change. GDP is a totally unrealistic indicator of the health of an economy on a longer temporal perspective, as it neglects the consequences of environmental deterioration.

In changing conditions, a critical feature of a metabolic machinery is its adaptability: Is the system – either an organism or an economic unit, such as a city – able to cope with the new environmental conditions in the long term? In biology, the long term is covered by evolutionary adaptability. Slobodkin and Rapoport give a phenomenological account of the dilemma using a metaphor of 'existential game' (Slobodkin and Rapoport 1974). In an existential game, there are no permanent winners. The reward consists of staying in the game. Current understanding of gene expression and of the evolutionary dynamics of individual development

("Evo-Devo") offers detailed knowledge on the mechanism, but the story is too long to take up here.

The adaptability of economic metabolic machinery is a more contentious issue. In modern societies, this is a question about the evolution of human exosomatic metabolism. A key issue is economic growth, both in a historical perspective and at present. It is quite obvious that economic growth had its origin in permanent groups and, later, settlements in which some of the members could secure their sustenance without participating in actual work. Incipient division of labour has ancient roots. The basic factors driving economic growth have remained similar all along: trade, increasing productivity of labour in agriculture and, later on, in manufacture, refinement of the division of labour, improving skills and motivations of labourers, stability of laws and institutions that provide favourable conditions for economic transactions and accumulation of property, and so on (Mokyr 1990).

A couple of further specifications are necessary. First, extensive and intensive growth need to be distinguished. The former refers to expansion into new regions without structural change, and the latter to novel structural adjustments within the economic machinery. Modern economy equals capitalism and is characterized by intensive growth. Joseph Schumpeter emphasized that capitalism is an evolutionary system and characterized the factors promoting intensive growth as follows: 'The fundamental impulse that sets and keeps the capitalist engine in motion comes from the new consumer goods, the new methods of production or transportation, the new markets, the new forms of industrial organization that capitalist enterprise creates' (Schumpeter 2005: 83).

In the course of growth of the capitalist machinery, exosomatic metabolism has increased in relative significance far over anything known before in human history. An essential part of this transformation has been a revolution in the techno-economic base of industrial production; namely, a transition from organic to mineral-based economy (Wrigley 1988). Mineral-based energy economy – dependence on fossil fuels – is basically parasitic exploitation of carbon storages produced by the biosphere in the course of several hundred million years in the geological past.

A second necessary specification is that nature is an integral element in economic productivity. This is one of the central tenets that Georgescu-Roegen held against mainstream economists. The economy does not create anything new; instead the economy brings about novel combinations of forces of nature, human labour and capital stock built up by previous economic activity. All these factors are equally necessary for economic development albeit in different forms. The modern mineral-based industrial economy marks a transition in the relative significance of exosomatic versus endosomatic metabolism, and it is deceptively easy to forget the role of nature's dynamics. However, the transition owes its success to ancient ecology that has produced fossil fuels and ancient geology that has produced exploitable mineral deposits. The natural processes humanity has to thank for these resources are way beyond the sphere of our influence. Economists have, of course, known for quite some time that particular mineral resources as well as sources of energy are exhaustible, but the standard response has been: whenever a resource is exhausted, find a substitute.

Third, a short-term increase in efficiency of resource use does not mean the amount of resources used will decrease. This phenomenon is known as the Jevons paradox, named after the analysis by 19th-century economist William Stanley Jevons of what he called 'the coal question'. Jevons noticed that an increase in the efficiency of the use of coal in steam engines leads ultimately to an increase in the quantity of coal used, not to a decrease as might be expected. This is because the original drop in demand leads to a drop in price and increasing consumption will eat up the original decline in the quantity used, usually very quickly. This phenomenological rule, also called 'rebound effect', has been vindicated over and over again (Polimeni *et al.* 2008).

The economic dynamics of human societies are deeply enmeshed in nature. Understanding this fact should become part of our cultural consciousness. This is a concrete challenge, not an abstract one. Hence, novel initiatives are needed, such that capture the imagination and creative action of people. It is within this framework that urban agriculture has to be viewed, but before getting there, we have to take note of another aspect of the historical legacy we have inherited.

Modernity: the tragedy of human material success

There is another story to be told about the stabiliza-tion of modern societies, parallel, but also alternative, to human material success, namely, the fading away of human eco-social dependence from the cultural under-standing of modern societies.

The roots of capitalism extend back in time at least to medieval cities and trading centres in the Mediterra-nean world, if not to Antiquity, but digging out the roots is not necessary for our purposes. Another part of the historical dynamics of capitalism is important, however: credit. Institutions of credit have facilitated economic transactions directed toward the future on an increasing scale. Joseph Schumpeter regarded credit as 'differentia specifica' of capitalism. Credit is obviously necessary for long-term investments, but is also laden with a conceptual quandary: credit brings about 'systematic undervaluation of the future', but '[t]his problem is being obscured by the practice of postulating that the economic engine is being maintained, or maintaining itself, as a matter of course' (Schumpeter 1944: 929).

Undervaluation of the future is a consequence of eco-nomic growth: if prosperity increases toward the future, then the monetary value of any particular ingredient of material wealth will be, relatively speaking, cheaper in the future than it is today. This explains the pervasive claim of growth optimists that it is (always) wise to accumulate riches today to get more resources for solv-ing problems tomorrow. But this, of course, is strongly constrained by what the problems are like those that accumulate towards the future. Georgescu-Roegen had a terse aphorism to the contrary: 'Given the historical uncertainty ... instead of maximising the present value of future wellfare, we should seek to minimize future regrets' (Mesner and Gowdy 1999: 63).

As recent experience has taught all too convincingly, the accumulation of credit can create huge economic problems when finances and what is called the "real economy" deviate from one another. The economic system may be transformed into a huge Ponzi scheme – as, in fact, has happened during the last few decades (Feierstein 2012).

When undervaluation of the future becomes the normal routine, another consequence follows: the real material dependencies of humanity on the conditions of nature vanish from sight. An older ideological layer, religious belief in Divine Providence, had already prepared the soil for such a misperception. From mixing together with providentialism, momentarily uplifting economic experience grew another transcendental conviction: blind trust in inevitable human progress through reason and economic growth. This received strong boost by a general increase in 'exosomatic comfort', as Georgescu-Roegen put it. In the realm of material economy, trust in progress equals to a belief in the substitutability of (almost) anything for (almost) anything else.

This ideological trajectory is a manifestation of the tragedy of material success; the prevailing inability to understand that economic growth cannot solve the problems it has created. The dominant position of industrial agriculture is as good a specific demonstra-tion of the tragedy as anybody can wish (Giampietro and Mayumi 2009).

There is no doubt that there has been a gradually emer-ging consciousness about the human biospheric depend-ence. The seeds were sown during the 19th century, basically as a reaction to wanton destruction and over-use of nature (Haila 2012). But we have to move further. The task is to unpack the elements of human biospheric interdependence. At issue is what mutual interdepend-ence means: humans should be able to construct a benign second nature under the conditions given by first nature, the biosphere (Haila and Dyke 2006).

Drawing qualitative distinctions between types of problems is a first necessity. A primary distinction to draw is between source scarcity, which refers to scarcity of resources, and sink scarcity, which refers to the filling up of places to dump waste. Mineral-based industrializa-tion has provided means to overcome source scarcities over and over again in the course of history. Mainstream economists have acquired great skills in promoting the view that such substitutability can be achieved far into the future as well. There is an underlying problem in this scheme, however, as pointed out by Georgescu-Roegen: the need for substitution arises when the most easily accessible mineral deposits are used up and exploitation moves elsewhere. This always implies increasing need of energy, as well as more extensive strain and disruption to the environment.

Sink scarcity is a different kind of problem altogether. The changing composition of the atmosphere and the concomitant warming of the climate bring this fact into focus at the moment. The capacity of the atmosphere and the biosphere to assimilate the accumulation of greenhouse gases is limited, basically due to everything we do.

The global erosion of biodiversity is essentially a manifestation of sink scarcity, too. As human material activity increases in scope and extent, this tends to produce a general deterioration of the conditions of the Earth's ecosystems. Indications are as numerous as one can wish: suburban sprawl and the concomitant expansion of traffic networks, homogenization of agricultural and silvicultural landscapes, eutrophication of waterways, open-cast mining, and so on.

A credible alternative to the dream of progress cannot build upon a total rejection of the current economy. It is unclear what a total rejection could mean in the first place. Differentiation is necessary as regards specification of the problems and finding credible responses. A promising perspective is to get back to the basics: how can a secure food economy be built up for current cities?

First of all, most cities throughout human history have actually depended on their own cultivations. The ancient city states, including the Greek *polis*, were agricultural cities as Max Weber already pointed out. Classical sources give ample support for such a view: Hesiod's *Works and Days*, Vergil's *Georgica*, and so on. Cities developing agricultural systems in their surroundings become dependent on environments that remain favourable only under the condition of constant human intervention. In well-bounded situations, the mutual coupling can be described as co-evolutionary symbiosis. Venice is an example, beginning from the interdependence of the city with the lagoon where it was established on a group of inhospitable mudflats.

Conquest and colonization offers another model probed already by the Greeks and their precursors. Conquest is hardly a sustainable option on a longer term, however:

an imperium built upon conquest runs short of regions to conquer. Soon it becomes necessary to actually form permanent economic connections with the areas conquered, but imperia aiming for stabilization face problems of diminishing returns (Tainter 1988). The fall of Rome is a good and sobering example: Western Rome collapsed after having lost its granaries in northern Africa to barbarian hordes that reached the region via the Iberian Peninsula. Eastern Rome hung around for another couple of centuries supported by its granaries closer at hand in the eastern Mediterranean.

Modern cities show huge variation in how different elements of food procurement are combined together, as analyses in different chapters in this volume demonstrate. A major point, and a major necessity is, however, to adopt a bottom-up perspective and get people involved. Urban agriculture is an important initiative in this regard. It can pave the way for a new understanding of cities, founded on material practices which may gain symbolic weight, comparable to what happened in classical cities (Rykwert 1988).

Critical capacity and informed action

To come to grips with the current eco-social predicament, global book-keeping of both waste of resources and state of sink problems is certainly necessary, but there are no straight roads from there to what can be done locally – simply because human actions do not add up in a linear way. Aggregation produces figures such as the global ecological footprint, but interpreting them is difficult. This is analogous to what is known as the fallacy of misplaced concreteness in economics: figures may be precise, but their meaning is obscure.

I'll conclude with a normative perspective. The first necessity is to open up new options for people to take up. Every new type of solution is tiny to begin with and, hence, does not play any role or obtain any visibility in macro-economic calculations. In particular, we have to focus on processes that are opened up by new initiatives and developments. Urban agriculture is clearly one such field: activity that cannot be evaluated solely by its formal weight in global food statistics.

Philosopher and social critic Cornelius Castoriadis was particularly interested in the growth of human capacity to assess critically one's conditions and prospects of life (Castoriadis 1991). Critical capacity grows out of an understanding and concern for the existing conditions and of the imagination that goes beyond them. Thus, it prepares a scheme for an alternative future. Imaginary is the other key term in Castoriadis: Imaginaries are plausible futures that grow out of the conditions at present.

According to Castoriadis, there have been two stages in the prehistory of modern society that have supported the growth of critical capacity: the *polis* of the classical world, and the medieval city state. Humanity is dependent on cities and cities are also at the apex of the current environmental predicament.

There is one more element in the historical legacy of the city that has to be taken up: cities as breeding grounds for cooperation, communality; the common good. The focus of economic concerns has to move away from obsession with material comfort. After all, as Geogescu-Roegen put it, the aim of the economic enterprise is not material flow, 'the real product of the entire activity is the mysterious immaterial flux of life enjoyment' (Bonaiuti 2011: 100). Such a move brings about a novel question: how can we support the origin and growth of a new kind of collective consciousness in existing cities? We should build up capacity for reorganizing collective activities as such that local efficiency is increased, but that the activities do not fall prey to the ghost of the Jevon's paradox – i.e., that the fruits of increasing efficiency in terms of diminishing load to the environment will not be wasted.

I believe an ecological perspective on cities offers elements for a new and more concrete perception of human eco-social interdependence. First of all, cities are ecological formations in a metabolic or physiological sense; the task is to make transparent the mutualistic versus parasitic relationships of city economies with the environment. This can be achieved with a metabolic perspective. Single numerical indicators such as 'ecological footprint' or 'carbon footprint' may help, but they provide vision only toward one narrow focus at a time.

Also, cities are ecological formations in that they create novel types of ecological communities; what humans do is an integral element in the dynamics of such communities. Differentiation between scales is an important characteristic of ecological communities, including urban areas. Cities as ecological entities can be approached starting from three spatial and temporal perspectives, namely region, landscape and site. Region refers to the (bio)geographical context; landscape refers to the mingling together of human work and activity with the environment into symbolically significant milieus; and site refers to specific locations that are meaningful for individuals through experience and affect.

Most importantly, the future of cities depends on what people do, and are empowered and entitled to do. Urban agriculture and other ecologically sound activities gather their momentum against this background. Fruitful partnering between city officials and civil society actors, a dynamic interplay of bottom-up and top-down initiatives, would provide energy for a supportive process, as Kevin Morgan points out in his essay. The team around Tjitske Akkerman evaluate this possibility from a policy research perspective (Akkerman *et al.* 2004). Let's not forget, either, that urban agriculture gives support to new thinking concerning the whole system of food production. Critical capacity is germinating in urban garden lots, together with carrots, parsnips, tomatoes, beans and whatever else people grow there. Not every urbanite needs to become a gardener, but every urbanite needs food. A new combination of needs and pleasurable activities is at issue.

Note
1. Georgescu-Roegen's main conclusions are presented in the essays in Bonaiuti 2011; for a primer on quantifying social metabolism, see Giampietro and Mayumi 2009.

Sueños Utilitarios: La Habana

Yuneikys Villalonga

Utilitarian Dreams was a multidisciplinary project examining past, present and future cityscapes. Focusing mainly on Havana and Brighton, it continued an earlier dialogue and project, commissioned for *Cinecity: The Brighton Film Festival, 2005*. The 2006 exhibition in Havana, Cuba, followed a month-long collaboration/workshop between architects, artists, art critics, and students from the Universities of Brighton and CUJAE Havana. The collaboration provided time to formulate a number of questions: How do landscape and the city update in response to new realities and necessities of society? How are the private and public landscapes of the city shaped by historical, economic, social and political circumstances? How and to what extent do citizens affect and become affected by their surroundings from psychological, aesthetic and spatial points of view? How do individual and social projects converge, and which are the visions, memories and desires people project into the future?

The exhibition space was an abandoned pedestrian crossing that passes underneath one of the most popular avenues in Havana: Carlos III. It was lent by the Vivarta Studio Theatre, for whom it serves as headquarters. Referring to the urban landscape while being placed underneath the city provided an interesting curatorial perspective. Some of the projects realized for the show observed the social meaning of individual, natural and architectural borders. Others looked at the aesthetics, the memory and the traces of the cityscape. There were questions related to freedom of choice and contrasts in the "desire lines" found in different parts of Brighton and Havana.

The *CPUL City* concept developed by Katrin Bohn and André Viljoen was employed to speculate on the possible future growth of Dublin, London and Havana. The same concept was applied to realize *Carlos III Micro-Organopónico*, a structure of organoponicos (urban market gardens) that inserted the project into the city of Havana, as it ran upstairs from the exhibition spaces below ground to their entrance at street level. The project *T.error* by T10 (Fidel García) interfered with less visible boundaries. Using a system of antennas, a laptop and sensors, it prevented citizens who live in the area from listening to official radio stations. These became interfered with whenever a person approached the work, creating around the show, as García describes it, 'a territory free from the ideological contamination of the news'.

Historical photographs from London's Imperial War Museum showed green alternative projects in the devastated post-war city. They were in dialogue with Tom Phillips' piece titled *A Century of Continuity Within Change*, which presented a chronological collection of one hundred postcards depicting the ongoing continuity of ornamental planting between 1900 and 2000 at the Eastbourne Carpet Gardens in England. Alejandro González and Pavel Acosta's photographs examined the current conditions of venues in the city that had a different significance in the past.

Altogether, *Utilitarian Dreams* was full of hybrids going beyond traditional architectural and artistic forms of expression into what could be better described as "Cultural Manifestations": probably the only way to bring into dialogue so many different aspects of the past, present and future spaces of the cities that we live in.

Utilitarian Dreams was possible due to the joint efforts of the architecture programs of the University of Brighton, UK and CUJAE Havana, The British Council in Cuba, and the Batiscafo Residency, Gasworks/Triangle Arts Trust, England, UK.

Fig 1: "Drumflowers"/*We can make tomorrow better*.
Inkjet and silkscreen on paper, 50x85cm. Tom Phillips, 2006.

The title I devised for our project, Utilitarian Dreams, was well endorsed by my eventual visit to Cuba itself. As a child born into a wartime Britain bombed into austerity, I knew of the pride of struggle, and saw its peaceful side in Cuba and its people. Our study of organoponicos was a lesson not only in urban regeneration, but in the poetics of small-scale agriculture reinvading the urban construct (as I had seen in the wartime *Dig For Victory* allotments of my childhood in London). Here and there, travelling through Cuba, I saw written up the inspiring slogan from Che Guevara, 'Today we can start to make tomorrow better'. This has an ever more universal value as we begin to fight climate change, uniting to save the environment from degradation; we will find ourselves in the first global continuous revolution as each nation recognises the imperative.

TOM PHILLIPS
London, 2006

In my childhood, I often heard people speak about the "Man of the Future". This would have been at the age of five or six. I belonged to the generation who enjoyed staying at the students' summer camp *Tarará* and going for visits to Parque Lenin. These places were emblematic at those times when the future of my generation was being set. We were called "The 2000 Generation"; the date sounded really far and promissory to me. *Havana City; Future* is a return to these places today (20–25 years later) to discover their new condition, in a journey to the promised future. My generation, the one before, and the present one meet in a "reflexive picnic" to repeat to ourselves over and over again, that our future is every moment. Anyhow, the future of 20–25 years ago is today, right?

ALEJANDRO GONZÁLEZ
Havana, 2006

I have been very interested lately in the way people fulfil and materialise their needs, wishes and utopias, especially when this implies a reformulation of spaces that people share in the city. In the Series *Out*, I photograph street versions of popular sports that take place in spaces full of "architectural barriers", but where the determination of participants (poses, style, outfit) paradoxically make them closer to the ideal of the professional player. The game actually happens in people's heads: only there, the structure of a football field is superposed on a terrace roof, a garage entrance or a garden.

PAVEL ACOSTA
Havana, 2006

The word *organopónico* is familiar to all Cubans and refers to market gardens located in the city centre which supply urban residents with locally produced fruit and vegetables. Although initially introduced as an emergency measure during the "special period", they provide a model for how cities can reduce their environmental impact, while adding a new dimension to their experience. For Utilitarian Dreams, we constructed a working *Micro-Organoponico* within the exhibition space's entrance area, utilizing materials supplied by the adjacent Calle Retiro Organoponico. The installation allowed one-to-one contact with some of the basic elements of an *organopónico* – plants, soil, raised beds, water flow – and introduced Bohn&Viljoen's propositions for a *Continuous Productive Urban Landscape* in Havana (Havana CPUL).

BOHN & VILJOEN
Havana, 2006

Fig 2: Alrededores de la Ciudad Escolar "Tarará".
12 de junio de 2005, La Habana, Cuba. Alejandro González, 2006.

Fig 3: Football (from the Series "Stolen Spaces").
4 photographs, light jet print, 100x66cm. Pavel Acosta, 2006.

Fig 4: Carlos III Micro-Organopónico. Installation (assisted by
L. Frómenta and R. Martínez). André Viljoen and Katrin Bohn, 2006.

Environmental impact and Urban Agriculture: Diversity

Katrin Bohn and André Viljoen

Minimising the environmental impact of food production has always been central to the *CPUL City* concept, as has the cradle-to-cradle approach proposed by Michael Braungart and William McDonough (Braungart and McDonough 2002). To extend our understanding of the positive environmental contribution of urban agriculture remains important, taking account of the complex web of its quantifiable and qualitative potentials, including those measurable, such as closed-loop systems, and those less measurable, such as cultural diversity. Therefore, we will review the figures for the environmental impact of contemporary urban food systems presented in the 2005 *CPUL* book. Using the UK as an example, we will relate the *CPUL City* concept more directly to its role in enhancing urban biodiversity as a basis for more diverse cities.

Food production and consumption

Prior to 2005, when testing the argument that organic urban agriculture could make a worthwhile contribution to environmental improvement, we first concentrated on establishing to what extent the prevailing food system in the UK contributed to greenhouse gas emissions. Against this, we set the reductions organic agriculture might achieve, argued for seasonal consumption (Viljoen 2005: 19–31) and applied worst-case scenario reductions in yield. At that time, it was necessary to go back to energy intensity studies from the 1970s to estimate energy inputs for food production due to a lack of more recent data. Since then, comprehensive studies have taken place and, overall, the figures presented in 2005 are now confirmed by more recent studies. A direct

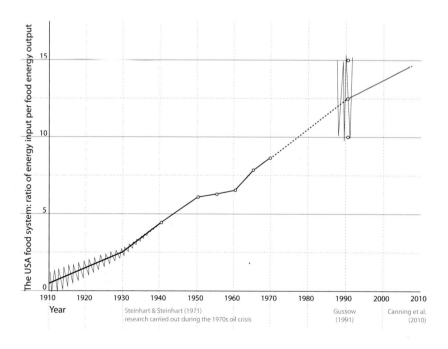

Fig 1: Food production and ecological footprint. This chart combines figures from several researchers showing the increasing ecological footprint of food produced in the USA, using embodied energy as a measure.

comparison between different studies remains challenging though, because of the different parameters used in their calculations. One of the earliest studies showing the increasing embodied energy of food was produced by John Steinhart and Carol Steinhart addressing the agribusiness approach to farming in the USA (Steinhart and Steinhart 1974). It was included in the original *CPUL* book, and its update is included again showing that the trend still continues.

To establish the significance of food-related greenhouse gas (GHG) emissions, we focused on those generated by a household and concluded that, taking an average of the available data, the impact of food-related GHG emissions was similar to that from household private car use or general household energy use. More recent detailed studies of UK household GHG emissions by Angela Druckman and Tim Jackson (Druckman and Jackson 2010) have concluded that food and catering together account for about 22% of a household's total GHG emissions. They also record that space heating and other household GHG emissions (resulting from energy used in the house, but not for cooking) account for 24%, while commuting only accounts for 8% of a household's total GHG emissions. Exact comparisons cannot be made with our earlier figures, because Druckman and Jackson use a different, but likely more accurate, methodology than that used for the study we referred to in 2005 (DETR 1998). They additionally include recreation

and leisure as a household activity, accounting for 25% of a household's GHG emissions. But, if anything, Druckman and Jackson's figures suggest that food-related GHG emissions now are at least as significant as we had recorded in 2005. It is also worth pointing out that Druckman and Jackson have calculated UK household GHG emissions based on so-called "consumption figures" which include GHG emissions that have been produced outside of the UK due to, for example, growing food overseas. Some GHG emissions studies for the UK only include emissions actually produced within the UK – so-called "production figures" – and these will artificially deflate total GHG emissions. Furthermore, Druckman and Jackson show that household consumption was, on average, responsible for 76% of the UK's GHG emissions, and that the UK is increasingly "offshoring" its emissions, i.e. the GHG emissions due to goods and services consumed are being produced in other countries. Including offshore emissions shows that the UK's total GHG emissions are increasing (Druckman and Jackson 2010).

A study produced by The Carbon Trust (Carbon Trust 2006) and further analysed by Robin Roy (Roy 2012) also confirms that food-related emissions are at least as significant as we had recorded in 2005, but its figures, like those used in the above-mentioned 1998 DETR study, are based only on CO_2 emissions and do not take account of other gases with global warming

Ecological Footprint: CO_2 emission and current urban lifestyles

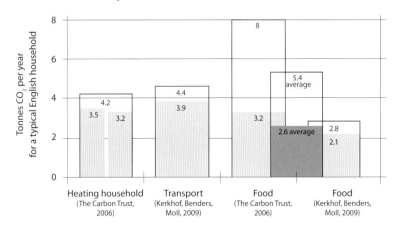

Fig 2: CO_2 emissions and current urban lifestyles. A comparative study of CO_2 emissions associated with energy use by a typical household highlights two facts: one, food consumption accounts for emissions that roughly equate to those for overall household energy use or overall transport emissions, and two, the emissions have not reduced very much during the first decade of this century.

potential. The Carbon Trust study uses consumption figures when calculating CO_2 emissions and so includes emissions produced outside of the UK. It does not break down emissions per person or per household, but concludes that – for the UK as a whole – food and catering together account for about 22.4 million tonnes of carbon per annum [MtC], space heating and other household energy (resulting from energy used in the house, but not for cooking) for 46 MtC, and that commuting accounts for 13 MtC of total CO_2 emissions from UK households. Roy has used UK figures from the Carbon Trust study to estimate an individual's CO_2 emissions due to food and drink are approximately 1.07 t per year per person (Roy 2012), and Bohn&Viljoen, in a separate unpublished analysis, valued typical UK household CO_2 emissions due to food and drink at about 3.2 t per year per household in 2006.

Urban agriculture has the capacity to reduce food and catering emissions when adopting strategies that maximise local and seasonal consumption and minimise food processing and car dependency for trips related to small-scale food shopping or growing. The scenarios for such reductions are complex, and some are addressed in Gillean Denny's chapter (p. 76) of this book. Denny suggests that urban agriculture can, in a UK context, result in a reduction in fruit-and-vegetable-related GHG emissions of 43% – and up to 57% if food purchasing integrates urban agriculture products with non-urban crops that have the lowest embodied GHG emissions. We assume that these results will be similar in northern Europe and America, and, where growing seasons are longer – i.e. closer to the equator – urban agriculture has the potential for an even greater impact.

Diversifying our food cultures

A study from the USA showed that GHG emissions are especially concentrated in conventional meat and dairy production, to such an extent that avoiding red meat and dairy products for one day a week would save as

Fig 3: Diverse urban agriculture yields. Fruit and vegetable yields – and hence required urban areas – can be very different due to cities' specific contexts.

	Yield [kg/m²yr] (units standardised by Bohn&Viljoen Architects)	Area for 1 person consuming 600 g fresh fruit & veg per day	Reference
Family vegetable plot in a self-sufficient community (Germany, early 20th century)	Yield not specified, 400 m² for a family of five	80 m²	Haney 2010 (quoting Migge)
Allotment plot tended by an experienced grower (UK, 1970s)	4–11	55 m²	Leach 1976
Allotment plot (UK, 1917, end of First World War)	4–11	55 m²	Crouch and Ward 1998
"Marais System" using night soil as fertiliser and professional grower (Paris, 19th century)	8–27 NB: comparable to Cuban community gardens	27 m²	Stanhill 1977
Intensive organic market garden (UK, 2000s)	12–34	18 m²	pers. comm. – Soil Association Conference 2007
Organoponicos – high-yield market gardens (Cuba, 2000)	25–68 NB: continuous growing season	9 m²	Caridad Cruz and Sánchez Medina 2003

much in GHG emissions as would a theoretical elimi-nation of all food miles (Weber and Scott Matthews 2008). This study also showed that fruit and vegetable consumption in the USA has the second highest GHG emissions impact per household. Increasing people's involvement in food production (i.e. through urban agriculture) can contribute to food-choice behaviour changes (i.e. reduced meat consumption), as well as to more local food produce (i.e. reducing food miles). Reduced meat consumption and in increased consump-tion of fruit and vegetables produced using environ-mentally sustainable urban agriculture provides a resilient solution for minimising our food-related GHG emissions.

Organic agriculture

In 2005, when presenting our results for potential reduced energy inputs to organic agriculture, little pub-lished data existed quantifying the energy benefits of organic agriculture. Since then, much has been written and, in 2012, a large meta-analysis of research papers comparing organic and conventional agriculture in Europe was published. It concluded

...that organic farming in Europe has generally lower environmental impacts per unit of area than conventional farming, but, due to lower yields and the requirement to build the fertility of land, not always per product unit. The results also showed a wide variation between the impacts within both farming systems. There is not a single organic or conventional farming system, but a range of different systems, and thus, the level of many environmental impacts depend more on farmers' management choices than on the general farming systems.

(Tuomisto *et al.* 2012)

The meta-study of Hanna Tuomisto's team used ten sub-categories for comparing organic and conventional agriculture, and distinguished between impact per unit area and per unit output. It concluded that organic production was better for organic matter in the soil and biodiversity, as well as for reducing phosphorus losses and energy use. On the negative side, organic produc-tion was worse for nitrogen losses, required more land due to reduced yields and had more potential to leach

substances into groundwater (eutrophication). The over-all conclusion of the study looks at optimising agricul-ture to take the best from each system, in other words: to diversify according to the specific production context. At the time of writing, this appears to be the accepted view for many academics and is informing policy, such as that on "Sustainable Intensification" adopted by the UK government's Department of the Environment, Food and Rural Affairs (Defra 2010a), and may include nanotechnology and recombinant DNA technologies. But, as Howard Lee notes, 'scientists, such as Altieri and Rosset (1999), who support agroecology (the produc-tion of food using ecological criteria and with optimal support for smallholder farmer livelihoods) are more sceptical' (Lee 2012: 458).

In our own work, we have experimented with non-organic systems, such as hydroponics, when responding to building-integrated design tasks and to optimise yields (see prototypes *The Urban Agriculture Curtain*, p. 166, and *Growing Balconies*, p. 236). However, while ecologically optimised agricultural systems make sense, we would also caution against the dropping of organic production as a goal.

If referring to the crops most likely cultivated using urban agriculture, i.e. fruit and vegetables, then organic production scores better than conventional, with GHG emissions and acidification of soil both being less than for conventional production (Tuomisto *et al.* 2012). Furthermore, the reported yields for organically grown vegetables compared to conven-tional farming have increased noticeably from the 66% before 2005 (Viljoen 2005: 26) to a mean of 79% in 2012 (Tuomisto *et al.* 2012: 316). Additionally, there is better CO_2 sequestration in organic farming according to a team around Wijnand Sukkel quoting a paper by Annette Freibauer *et al.*, which concludes 'that organic farm management could sequester between 0 to 500 kg of organic carbon per hectare per year more than conventional agriculture' (Sukkel *et al.* 2008: 553).

Ecological Intensification in urban design

There is a sense that the term *Sustainable Intensifica-tion*, as used in the above-mentioned Defra 2010 report,

Fig 4: CPULs can support diverse ecologies. A view of our 2007 Opportunity Map for a CPUL in Middlesbrough shows the three components defined in the English review *Making Space for Nature*: large core sites, connecting corridors and smaller stepping stones (small urban agriculture sites shown in red), that together make a resilient and ecological network.

makes it too easy for non-equitable, large-scale agribusiness to claim its practice by introducing a series of token changes to their operations.

Prior to the term *Sustainable Intensification* appearing, we had proposed in 1999 at a London symposium on urban sustainability the concept of 'Ecological Intensification as an idea to test our proposals. This refers to the notion of increasing the use of renewable natural resources (sun, rain water, the soil for crops), but also to the intensification of human use, that is occupation' (Bohn and Viljoen 2001). *Ecological Intensification* prioritises organic practices, and we apply this principle within the *CPUL City* concept. The concept of *Ecological Intensification* was, it seems, "in the air": Agronomists Tittonell and Giller note that

...the concept of ecological intensification was coined by Cassman (1999) to define the set of principles and means necessary to increase primary productivity in the major cereal agroecosystems of the world [...] Ecological intensification is now understood as a means of increasing agricultural outputs (food, fibre, agro-fuels and environmental services) while reducing the use and the need for external inputs (agrochemicals, fuel and plastic), capitalising on ecological processes that support and regulate primary productivity in agroecosystems.

(Tittonell and Giller 2012)

So, around 1999 the idea of *Ecological Intensification* was emerging independently across several disciplines such as architecture, urban design, agronomy and agriculture. This potential interdependence is significant for the advancement of productive urban landscapes.

CPUL, Urban Agriculture and biodiversity

In 2010, the United Nations University Institute for Advanced Studies (UNUIAS) issued a policy report on cities and biodiversity and noted that

...as the rule of interdependent adjacencies in urban ecology has it: the more diversity, and the more collaboration 'between unlikely partners', the better the chances for biodiversity, sustainability, and resilience (Hester 2006). Linked to this idea is the concept of Continuous Productive Urban

Landscapes (CPULs), which represents a powerful urban design instrument for achieving local sustainability while reducing cities' ecological footprints (Viljoen 2005).

(UNUIAS 2010: 31–32)

The UNUIAS report notes that cities are not yet at the centre of discussions about biodiversity, nor is their role within biodiversity fully understood, although cities have a significant impact on biodiversity.

Simplifying a very complex web of interdependencies, we can say that biodiversity has gone the way of city high streets: dominated by a few big "resilient" species with a sprinkling of different and unique species surviving in niche locations. The lack and accelerated loss of diversity is a major concern, as all human activity is dependent upon the ecological services provided by the natural environment. At the broadest level, ecosystem services provide support for life, health, economy and culture, more specifically directly affecting water, food and material supply. They are fundamental to human well-being. Critically, ecosystems moderate climate, for example by changing the ways in which solar radiation is absorbed or reflected. A wide diversity of plant and animal species supplies us with a form of insurance or natural capital. Insurance is meant in two senses: one, that a diversity of species enables different plants to thrive under different climatic conditions – an important consideration in times of uncertainty about climate change – and two, farming and medicine still rely on new sources of plants and organisms for improving yields and treatments. This dependency is recognised in the original United Nations' *Convention on Biodiversity* (UN 1993), and captured in the European Commission's strategy document *Our life insurance, our natural capital: An EU biodiversity strategy to 2020* (European Commission 2011).

A *CPUL City* would provide the ideal context for a biodiverse city. Organic urban agriculture, as shown earlier, increases biodiversity compared to conventional agriculture. CPUL space would run between, in, over and on buildings; ecological corridors connect larger parcels of land and include independent island sites.

This structure matches what is called for in the recent review of England's wildlife and ecological networks, *Making Space for Nature* (Lawton *et al.* 2010). The authors' team, led by John Lawton, recommends the creation of a suite of high-quality sites of different size and type. Their strategy envisages an ecological network made up of core sites, connected by buffer zones, wildlife corridors and smaller stepping-stone sites. A key concept within it is the need for 'coherence and resilience' (Lawton *et al.* 2010: 32), matching the *CPUL City* aim for a coherent and sustainable introduction of urban agriculture within a continuous spatial network. Lawton's report confirms the UNUIAS report's contention that cities are not (yet) at the core of the biodiversity debate. Open urban space and new ecological sites will now be important in building urban biodiversity. The UNUIAS report, for example, goes on to encourage the 'provision of a good network of urban green spaces and functional aquatic habitats' as well as 'local sustainable production methods for biodiversity in urban areas' (UNUIAS 2010: 29–31). It also makes the case for the agroecological management of urban food systems as a means to enhance biodiversity conservation (UNUIAS 2010: 31–32).

A white paper on the future of the UK's natural environment published by the Department for Environment, Food and Rural Affairs outlines the government's vision for the next 50 years, along with practical action to deliver that ambition (Defra 2011b). It states that 'valuing nature properly holds the key to a green and growing economy, one which invests in nature – not just for us but for our children's children' (Defra 2011b: 2). This fits well with the economic understanding of productive urban landscapes. The white paper also recognises the need for a cross-sector approach, devolved local action and – introducing a key reform – 'ecologically coherent planning, retaining the protection and improvement of the natural environment as core objectives of the planning system' (Defra 2011b: 15).

Separate to any business opportunities arising from productive urban landscapes or their natural capital, access to open space has its own financial benefit. Lawton's team notes that

...people who live within 500 metres of accessible green space are 24 per cent more likely to meet recommended levels of physical activity, while reducing the numbers of sedentary individuals in the population by just 1 per cent

could reduce morbidity and mortality rates valued at £1.44 billion for the UK.

(Lawton *et al.* 2010: 6)

When compared to the estimated cost of between £600m and £1.1b for establishing a coherent and resilient green network (Lawton *et al.* 2010: ix), the long-term financial argument looks promising. And given the concentration of people in cities, the need for such urban networks is made ever more convincing. We may conclude that biodiversity delivers or supports much-needed ecosystems services and that it can be achieved by creating 'more, bigger, better and joined' (Lawton *et al.* 2010: 3) resilient and coherent ecological networks... CPULs.

Challenges and actions for implementation

The challenges for achieving coherent and sustainable urban networks, i.e. implementing *Making Space for Nature,* by following a multi-stakeholder approach should not be underestimated. They include rethinking the way in which space is given economic value within the urban realm, including in and on buildings. Culturally, it requires a shift in our understanding of the city, the citizen, the farm and the country.

In the UK, cities are starting to develop biodiversity plans. Brighton and Hove City Council's *Biodiversity Plan* provides a good example of how a medium-sized city goes about this. The plan notes that 'parks, open spaces and biodiversity' was ranked third (behind transport and sustainability) by respondents in their list of priorities for a new 'spatial vision' for the city (BHCC 2013: 6). Whilst gaps can be identified in the plan – for example woodland pasture, woodland, traditional orchards and organic urban agriculture are not included – it does acknowledge a thriving food-growing sector with strong community involvement. Intensive agriculture is recognised as a threat, while agri-environmental schemes represent an opportunity. The next step will be to join up these first observations and to produce a spatial plan.

The *CPUL City Actions* presented in this book attempt, with reference to the European Union's *Biodiversity Strategy,* to map out a way to 'encourage collaboration between researchers and other stakeholders involved in spatial planning and land use management in implementing biodiversity strategies at all levels, ensuring coherence with relevant recommendations set out in the European Territorial Agenda' (European Commission 2011: 8). Brighton and Hove's *Biodiversity Action Plan* can be seen as addressing two CPUL Actions: undertaking an *Inventory of Spatial Capacity* and applying the *Top-Down and Bottom-Up* principle.

Following the lines of thought presented here and adopting an environmentally sensitive approach – i.e. addressing resource use, ecological footprint, environmental legacy – can create an enriched and more enriching city. In such a city, biodiversity, energy diversity, diverse infrastructures, cultural diversity, yield and spatial diversity all have parts to play in building sustainability and resilience, and they meet in the realisation of diverse food cultures.

Environmental impact and Urban Agriculture: Water, soil and air

André Viljoen and Katrin Bohn

It is probably not entirely true that, as Lefebvre describes, nature dies with the establishment of the town or city, the second nature (Lefebvre 1976). Many natural elements remain integral to the urban environment and sometimes, as in the case of bees or particular plant societies, they may flourish better here than in their rural habitat.

All of these "natures" are important for urban agriculture practice: edible plants rely on healthy ecologies including other plants, sun, air, rain, water, soil, minerals, insects, worms and humans. Three of the more nurturing elements are repeatedly seen as the main challenges for urban agriculture: water, soil and air.

Urban Agriculture and urban pollution

Just as the long-term health effects from the application of pesticides and the use of genetically modified crops in conventional agriculture raise concerns within the organic movement, so the potential impact of urban pollution raises concerns about where and how urban agriculture is practised.

Specific guidance on soil toxicity and urban agriculture sites is rare. In the Netherlands, a report by *Senter-Novem* (Wezenbeek 2007) provides an overview of methods for assessing the chemical quality of soil, including for urban food cultivation, and a report by the Dutch Ministry of Housing, Spatial Planning and the Environment publishes specific guidance for levels of chemical toxins acceptable for urban food growing in appendix 6 of their standards and guide on toxin levels and soil (VROM 2008). But even this Dutch report is aimed at specialists in toxicology and plant biology. It is therefore very difficult for practitioners and planners or designers to arrive at an overview of the situation or to identify robust rules of thumb.

Pollutants may be present in soil, water or air, and toxins can accumulate in plant tissue. Perhaps surprisingly, a relatively high concentration of toxins can be found on a plant's surface due to deposition from the air. When assessing toxic residues, it is important to take into consideration which parts of the plants will later be consumed. According to Christian Hoffmann, an urban planner and soil scientist based in Berlin, there are, for example, certain cereals or fruit trees that accumulate toxins in their leaves, but have comparatively clean grains and fruit (personal communication 9 Sep 2012). Also, while some plants, such as corn and potatoes, are considered "excluders", i.e. their toxin concentrations are usually lower than in the surrounding soil, other plants, such as lettuce or spinach, are accumulators, i.e. their toxin concentration is higher (Metz *et al.* 2000). To accurately assess the risk posed by pollution, it is necessary to evaluate the levels locally, and experience shows that these can be highly variable within a city and even within a given site. Attitudes to the potential impact of urban, especially airborne pollutants, vary widely, and a common response we hear from urban food growers and consumers is that if people are prepared to breathe urban air, they should be prepared to eat urban crops grown in clean soil.

One of the first studies on urban agriculture and pollution was published in 1976 in Montréal by researchers from McGill University's Minimum Cost Housing Group. This study used a rooftop farm with 250 growing containers and ancillary equipment, such as cold frames, to explore food growing ideas and develop an early reference to assist groups interested in urban agriculture. As part of this two-year study, tests were undertaken to establish lead and cadmium content in a small number of crops from the rooftop farm and in comparable crops from a conventional rural farm. Similar crops for sale from a greengrocer were analysed as a control, as well as the soil used in the rooftop containers and on the rural farm. The overall conclusion reached in 1976 is not dissimilar from findings today, namely that 'there does not appear to be a general trend emerging from the two series of tests. Perhaps the only conclusive statement to be made is that leafy vegetables should be washed before consumption to reduce contamination levels' (Alward *et al.* 1976).

In his book *Urban Agriculture: Ideas and designs for the new food revolution*, the Canadian writer and environmental designer David Tracey develops the idea that people living in cities are exposed to toxins irrespective of what food they consume (Tracey 2011). He quotes a study which assessed 141 back gardens growing food in Boston, USA. These gardens used raised beds to mitigate against garden soil contaminated with lead, probably from paint that had been used on the houses. The study found that the level of lead contamination in the beds increased over four years, due, possibly, to 'fine grained lead dust wafting up from surrounding contaminated soil' (Tracey 2011: 141). However, in this example, eating produce from the raised beds accounted for only 3% of children's daily exposure to lead.

Tracey also notes an unattributed piece of research indicating that although all Canadians have some lead present in their bloodstreams, 25% of Canadians had toxic levels of lead in their blood 30 years ago (approximately 1980) compared to only 1% by about 2010. Public health programmes targeting toxins do work, and this is very positive news for urban agriculture in the longer term.

Paul Römkens, a Dutch senior researcher at Alterra, Wageningen University supports such findings: '... in our studies, we usually conclude that, despite the elevated levels of metals like lead (100–800 ppm) or mercury (up to 3 ppm), risks are acceptable, meaning the exposure remains well below the critical threshold' (personal communication 13 Mar 2013). Römkens further points out that 'in Europe, deposition from airborne pollutants from traffic has decreased substantially and, at present, the levels in crops are largely controlled by levels in soil and variation in the properties thereof'. However, he also highlights that 'other factors than [trace metal] deposition will be more important' and these factors are discussed in the following parts of this chapter.

Polluted soil and air

If soil, air and water are clean, then crops will be healthy. Unfortunately, not all crops that look healthy have been grown in healthy conditions. Toxic soils, for example, can be found in unexpected places, and the range of soil pollutants and pollution can be large, even on small sites. Furthermore, not all crops accumulate toxins from the growing environment in the same way. Bioavailability is for example important, which depends on pH-value or humus and clay content and is organism-specific. This means that different plants in the same location can accumulate very different levels of the same trace metals (Sauerbeck and Styperek 1988). An important factor in polluted areas, according to Römkens, is also the amount of soil sticking to plants by rainfall (splash) or dust (dry weather), especially for long-standing crops and/or those with intricate and/or waxy leaves, like curly kale. This process partly explains levels in some herbs too (personal communication 13 Mar 2013). For most urban farmers, the problem remains that, due to a lack of guidelines on acceptable practice, they can only be made up for by investing in expensive testing of soil, water, air and – afterwards – produce.

There are some studies available on individual pollutants to urban crops, such as a university-led field study from Evanston, USA, on lead contamination in food grown in urban settings. The researchers around Mary Finster conclude their detailed study with practical recommendations for urban gardeners (Finster *et al.* 2004). Recommendations include using buildings and large areas of vegetation to act as barriers to traffic-related pollution, or the use of mulches or weed tarp to protect against airborne pollution. Whilst such studies are great resources of well-researched information, they can be very fragmented, hence difficult to find, and may not be applicable in other regions.

At the time of writing, European Union regulations only exist for maximum concentrations of lead, mercury and cadmium in fruit and vegetables once these have been harvested and are ready for consuming. Urban farmers can, however, look for guidance on cultivation standards set for rural farms. A useful overview of organic rules and criteria for certification within Europe was undertaken during 2009 as part of the European Union-funded research programme *CertCost* (CertCost 2009).

From the online repository created by this study, it is evident that airborne pollution has not generally been considered a major hazard for rural organic agriculture, and the primary concern is to avoid contamination by artificial pesticides and genetically modified crops. The *CertCost* repository does, however, include two references to organic standards that make specific recommendations in relation to the adjacency of planting to busy roads: one from Sweden, the *KRAV Standard* (2006), for edible crops and one from Austria, the *Bio Austria General Standard* (2006), for herbs.

A paper by Eva Mattsson in the *Cert Cost* repository summarises the *KRAV Standard* as follows:

Areas were plants are cultivated and products stored should be located so that the production is not contaminated and the value of the production is reduced as food or feed. Crop production for food shall not be situated closer than 25 meters from roads having more than 3000 vehicles per 24 hours.

(Mattsson 2006)

Mattsson goes on to note that 'there are general requirements in the EU Regulation 2092/91 about the risk of contamination of products in the inspection requirements [...], but not in the production rules' and concludes that 'there is little scientific research in this area which should be of concern not only for organic, but also for conventional produce' (Mattsson 2006).

The *Bio Austria General Standard* sets a more limiting rule for the production of organic herbs advocating that 'locations of herb production near densely populated areas (cities) are to be avoided. The distance to highly used roads (highways, high-speed road, major streets (Bundesstraßen) must be at least 50 metres. Protective hedgerows are generally recommended in such cases' (Plakolm and Fromm 2006). If applied, the Bio Austria standard would exclude all herb production from cities, taking the precautionary principle to an extreme. However, this recommendation explicitly applies to very busy roads, i.e. multi-lane highways, and this has to be seen in relation to the actual urban site in question. A study referred to below found that the herb basil grown in central Berlin, i.e. with a lesser distance to roads, had lower concentrations of heavy metals than did basil sold in Berlin supermarkets.

Inspired by a presentation on *CPUL* in 2009, plant ecologist Ina Säumel and colleagues from the Technische Universität Berlin set up a research project collecting sample vegetable produce from 28 urban food growing sites in Berlin and analysing these to record the concentration of potentially toxic trace metals in the produce. The Berlin study found that supermarket produce – in general, but not in all cases – had lower levels of toxins than the samples of urban agriculture produce analysed in the experiment. Kohlrabi, green beans and basil grown in the city, for example, generally contained lower levels of trace metals than supermarket produce, whereas the other urban crops measured – tomatoes, carrots, potatoes, white cabbage, nasturtiums, parsley, thyme and mint – could have significantly higher levels. It also found that there did not seem to be clear a correlation between certain crops that are thought of as low (legumes), moderate (root) and high (leafy) accumulators of toxins (Säumel et al. 2012). The study did not measure the toxins found in the soil in which the urban crops had been grown, so it is not possible to know if the contamination was due to soil-based or airborne pollutants.

However, the Berlin study helpfully estimated the average exposure to trace metals resulting from eating the urban agriculture produce analysed based on an average daily consumption of fruit and vegetables for adults and young children. Using figures from the World Health Organization for recommended limits to daily intakes of copper, zinc, cadmium and lead, the authors found that

an adult consuming an average of 100g each of carrots, tomatoes, kohlrabi, chard, and potatoes would be ingesting 3%, 17%, 5% and 5% of the accepted daily intake of zinc, lead, copper and cadmium, respectively. Children younger than six years consuming 50g each of the vegetables would be ingesting 6%, 35%, 11% and 10% respectively of the accepted daily intake.

(Säumel et al. 2012: 130)

It was found that crops grown in pots (with imported soil, one expects) had higher levels of contamination than did crops grown directly in the soil. Hoffmann points out that this may happen 'because the plant's roots will root more intensively in the confined space of the pot and can thereby – potentially – take up more toxins than when growing in the open' (personal communication 9 Sep 2012). According to him, in the open plants can root deeper and avoid the higher concentrations of toxins which often are encountered in topsoils. Another explanation for toxin concentrations in plants may lie in the use of earth supplemented with commercial garden soils. Compost can speed up the absorption of trace metals (Murray *et al.* 2011) or, according to Hoffman, 'may contain more pollutants in the first place'. Additionally, studies undertaken in the Netherlands indicated that high levels of compost can lower soil's pH-value: non-composted soils had a pH-value of 6.5–7, whereas heavily compost-laden soil had a pH of 5.5 resulting in a higher, but not critical, uptake of heavy metals (Römkens and Rietra 2012).

Regarding the findings from the Berlin study, Säumel and colleagues concluded as follows:

… several colleagues which are dealing with human health and ecotoxicology pointed out that there is a great lack of research on this topic and many guidelines need to be re-evaluated… They think that the levels have to be lower than actually prescribed as a precaution measure. In addition, critical levels are very individual depending on overall consumer exposure to these trace metals or other contaminants and on consumer's health and body constitution.

(personal communication 21 Nov 2012)

In Berlin, adjacency to roads was generally found to increase levels of trace metals in crops, but 'the presence of barriers between cultivation site and roads strongly reduces trace metal content' (Säumel *et al.* 2012: 130). This observation echoes the organic production recommendations on road distances mentioned above. Both have similarities: they suggest spatial solutions which, at their best, would be designed – a barrier can be a hedge, but it could also be a building. For urban farmers currently cultivating in cities with higher traffic loads, this is highly significant. Buildings acting as screens will not only reduce airborne pollution, but can also provide a degree of security for farmers. Furthermore, the courtyard – in our case, the field – bounded on its perimeter by buildings, is a well-established and successful urban typology. Where urban agriculture is practised in a more open environment, an edge of non-edible plants can provide perimeter protection.

An exact area of planting or distance required for the effective reduction of airborne urban pollution from traffic is not yet known and the sites used in the Berlin study appear to have less than the minimum 25 m zone for busy roads advocated by the KRAV standard. Hoffmann confirms that hedges as barriers have proven to work well, but advises that

these need to be planted in stepped sizes and in several rows, so as to filter particles at different heights. A dead hedge, for example, is ideal for heights up to half a metre, because traditional hedges are often bare towards the ground… Moreover, it is important not to compost foliage of such hedges because of potential contamination.

(personal communication 9 Sep 2012)

Where uncertainty exists, sound advice should be sought and, as Römkens puts it, this 'ranges from "do as you like"' to recommendations not to grow certain (e.g. leafy) crops in specific parts of a garden, 'but plant flowers or use this area as pavement between more suitable spots' (personal communication 13 Mar 2013).

Water and water quality

Looking at water provision and concentrating on our three case study countries (the UK, the USA and Germany), for most urban agriculture sites water is or can be made available. However, the World Health Organization notes that 'a lack of water to meet daily needs is a reality today for one in three people around the world. Globally, the problem is getting worse as cities and populations grow, and the needs for water increase in agriculture, industry and households' (WHO 2009). In the future, many cities are predicted to experience water scarcity and so efficient irrigation systems, water recycling and rainwater harvesting are all critical future technologies, if urban agriculture is to expand significantly.

Many outdoor urban agriculture sites rely predominantly on rain, which, other than in exceptional circumstances, will be clean. Urban farmers who require irrigation will usually (or could) collect rainwater for later use, and there is now an industry devoted to supplying rainwater-harvesting systems spanning from small-scale domestic to comprehensive large-scale installations. Expert advice might be recommended for certain rainwater storage systems, such as rainwater retention basins or trickle areas, as these may encourage the collection of pollutants. For watering edibles, the storage of rainwater should happen in containers of food-standard quality. Many city authorities and environmental agencies provide domestic or communal users with guidance on installing systems. They also identify concerns that may easily be overlooked: Some building materials may be toxic, e.g. copper-covered roofs or those treated with fungicides or herbicides (San Francisco Public Utilities Commission n.d.), or certain roof surfaces might accumulate airborne pollutants (dusts) which are then washed into the rainwater supply. Hoffmann notes the potential for toxin reconcentration within an urban agriculture site, if rainwater – collected from large polluted/polluting surfaces – is used for watering much smaller planted areas (personal communication 9 Sep 2012).

If rainwater cannot be collected or is not available in sufficient quantity, food growing projects in the UK, Germany and the USA usually revert to the location's mains water system. Here, agreement may need to be sought with the city's council authorities and/or with the neighbours of a particular site. An alternative to mains water is the use of groundwater supplied via a well. In this case, unless the groundwater's water sources and ground conditions are known, Hoffman advisesthat it is very important to establish the water quality with regard to organic and inorganic toxins, as well as its microbial quality, because of potential contamination from historic or neighbouring sources of pollution (personal communication 9 Sep 2012).

The environmental balancing of water usage and soil replacement is an aspect that has not yet been widely discussed within the urban agriculture community: Hoffmann alerts to the fact 'that the often practised growing in containers – due to polluted soil conditions – leads to higher water usage, because of a lack of moisture raised by capillary action, plus larger evaporating surfaces compared to growing the same produce in the ground'.

In many cities, storm water runoff is of concern due to its ability to cause sewers to overflow with the risk of releasing raw sewage into water courses, or becoming contaminated after running over polluted surfaces. Soil-based urban agriculture on ground or rooftops has the potential to absorb rainfall and delay and reduce excessive runoff. In many cities, this still has to be recognised. Evidence exists, for example, for the rainwater retention of green roofs with estimates of 70% water retention per annum for green roofs with a growing medium between 250 and 500 mm deep (FLL 2008). But despite this, soil-based rooftop farms are not always included in policies to encourage green roofs as part of a stormwater infrastructure plan. For example, in 2011 New York did not automatically classify rooftop farms as water absorbing, although tax relief is available for that reason to building owners who install generic 'Sedum' type green roofs (see chapter *Laboratories for Urban Agriculture: New York*, p. 1222).

The future of soil-based Urban Agriculture

The best indicators available for soil quality, apart from undertaking actual chemical analysis, will be found by reviewing a site's previous uses and by observing potential sources of airborne pollution such as the proximity to heavy traffic or chemical works. According to Hoffmann, the next step of analysis is to study the soil for admixtures of charcoal, glass or plastics: 'Building rubble, tar or slags are clear signs of contaminated soil... But not to see any toxins, does not automatically mean there are none...' (personal communication 9 Sept 2012). Where there are any concerns, soil should be analysed and a professional report commissioned. Where a food growing site has soil that is known to have been polluted from past industrial activity, the standard solution is to use raised beds containing clean soil that is isolated from the earth with a membrane. Soil can also be exchanged, but this is expensive.

In urban areas with a lack of access to soil, many practitioners – amongst them Will Allen, founder of urban agriculture enterprise *Growing Power* (Growing Power *n.d.* a) – advocate creating it from urban compost. This reduces the environmental and financial problem of transporting soil and avoids the loss of fertile soil from another place, but it needs time, space and equipment to gather and compost waste materials. The quality of the compost will depend strongly on its ingredients:

using leaves from trees that line roads, for example, can lead to heavily polluted composts (Ehrig 1992). Composting, although simple and straightforward to do, requires care in planning and implementation to ensure, first, that waste material is non-hazardous, and second, that it is undertaken correctly and potential pathogens are destroyed during the process. On-site composting enables the production of quantities appropriate to the planned scale of cultivation.

Assessing concerns over potential future risks from urban agriculture crops grown in the open, Paul Römkens comments:

In Europe deposition of airborne pollutants from traffic has decreased substantially… [Today] I would worry more about organic polycyclic aromatic hydrocarbons (PAHs) deposition from traffic than about metals. PAHs are known carcinogens and can lead to abnormalities in physical development. There is much less information available about PAHs. We demonstrated that PAH levels in soil (from polluted mine waste in this case) were far less relevant (for organics) than [airborne] deposition. PAH levels in crops are generally lower for those grown on polluted waste than those grown in clean soil in an [air-polluted] urban environment. Again, the absolute levels were low, so this is all relative, but it tells you something about the process. Ultimately, I would like to see real human exposure risk assessments undertaken for urban soils. These would include exposure to the many sources of toxins in the environment, [i.e.] for soil this would include intake from soil (by children) and crops. We recently adjusted [our] [uptake] model, since – for lead (but also for substances like DDT) – it was way too conservative (i.e. it assumed uptake at too high a rate) leading to advisory levels of 120 parts per million (ppm) in soil. This meant that more than 90% of Dutch inner city areas would pose a risk, which was nonsense. Based on data collected during 2010–2012, this level was then increased to approximately 500 ppm, which is still conservative, but reduces the unnecessary unrest among users and the waste of money spent on cleaning soil where it is not necessary. This may all sound as if I advocate very lenient soil policy, but that is not the case. I merely try to find real levels beyond which people have to worry based on data from soil, crop and exposure assessment… so far, such detailed management schemes are scarce.

(personal communication 13 Mar 2013)

Christian Hoffmann agrees that the current contamination models are conservative, but contends

that this has a good reason, as most substances are only studied in a monocausal way leaving it unclear whether it is not their combination, when being eaten, that may lead to negative consequences… guideline amounts are primarily political in nature and often related to the cost of de-contamination.

(personal communication 9 Sep 2012)

What becomes clear from all of these various points of view is that urban agriculture needs to be embedded in wider environmental strategies, for example aiming to reduce air pollution for plants and people or increase biodiversity, as well as in a more holistic provision of occupational choices, which, for example, enable people to participate in the use of their urban environment and ground. What also becomes clear is that urban agriculture could be an enabler or important part of a useful "urban clean-up": better air, better soil, better water, better food, in short – better lifestyle choices for a better future.

Alternatives to soil

Hydroponics have been developed as a means of efficiently growing fruit and vegetables in a medium other than soil – water – which allows nutrients to be supplied directly to the plants' root systems. Hydroponics use controlled technical systems where the selection and supply of nutrients optimise growing conditions. Although they cannot be considered organic, their advantages stem from their highly controlled use of water and plant feed.

Compared to traditional soil-based cultivation, the often-quoted benefits of hydroponics mainly relate to much improved yields, reduced water consumption and minimised use of insecticides for greenhouse-cultivated crops. Greenhouses will generally provide a degree of protection from airborne pollutants for any plants much in the same way as screen planting does – but in the case of hydroponics, which are often installed indoors, such "protected cropping" is the norm. From the perspective of *CPUL City*, the clear benefit of hydroponics is their low weight, making them suitable for spaces that are unable to support the weight of soil, such as certain rooftops or vertical/hung systems. This weight saving simplifies the structural requirements for building-integrated agriculture, although soil is easier and cheaper to set up and does not require a highly skilled workforce. Hydroponics may also be used in areas without access to soil, for example paved urban areas, or where toxic soil exists. Its reduced water consumption is a significant advantage if reliance is being placed on rainwater harvesting. Systems may be used domestically or commercially and extensive information resources are available for both scales as exemplified by the publications of Howard Resh (Resh 2004).

Regarding the actual food output from hydroponics, Resh is quoted as reporting yields for tomatoes that 'ranged from 5 to 10 tons per acre in soil, but 60 to 300 tons per hydroponic acre' (SoCal Aquaponics *n.d.*). Whilst more circumspect, a New-Zealand-based hydroponic suppliers' and consultants' network in principle supports this, noting that 'hydroponic crop yields and crop rotations are usually much higher than crops grown in fertile soil in the same environment. This is financially significant' (Pure Hydroponics *n.d.*).

Allied to hydroponics is the much older culture of fish farming – or aquaculture – which is judged to be 'the fastest growing animal food production sector... [that] will soon supply more than half of the world's seafood for human consumption' (Klinger and Naylor 2012).

Traditional aquaculture uses large volumes of water mainly to keep fish healthy and avoid the build-up of toxins from fish waste (e.g. ammonia). Hydroponics, on the other hand, are reliant on the constant supply of processed chemical feeds by means of irrigation. Modern aquaponics combine the characteristics of both systems with the intention of creating a near closed-loop system. In aquaponics, the intention is to utilise plants, often supported by biological filters, to absorb and harvest fish waste as nutrients for plant growth, while also cleaning water for recirculation back to the fish. Although, at the time of writing, aquaponics remain in the development phase with several improvements being explored, extensive projects have been set up, including the two well-publicised examples in Milwaukee: an installation at *Growing Power* (Growing

Power *n.d.* a) and *Sweet Water Organics*' experimental laboratory prototyping larger-scale systems in a disused railway workshop location (Sweet Water *n.d.* b). Operating at very different scale, the project *Farm:Shop* in London has converted a typical, domestic-scale terraced building into a multipurpose productive hub (Something & Son *n.d.* b).

Often, the buildings that aquaponics (or indeed any other indoor growing operations) occupy do not provide optimum growing conditions, and thus rely heavily on the use of artificial lighting and, at times, temporary thermal insulation. Technical systems are being developed and promoted aiming for building-integrated fruit and vegetable production that is entirely independent of access to daylight and natural ventilation. Proposals include the use of LED technology for electric lights in an artificial environment in which nutrient provision would similarly be controlled. Those developing these systems expect them to be very efficient, but this assumes that they know exactly what the specific requirements of plants are for optimum quality (Plant-Lab *n.d.*). Above all, such systems require electrical energy and, at the time of writing, we have not been able to identify the overall energy balance between inputs and outputs when compared to traditional organic cultivation. Architecturally, this strategy is akin to the 20th-century model of sealed, fully air-conditioned and controlled environments, which have frequently been criticised as highly energy inefficient and responsible for sick building syndrome. Independent of technical efficiency, aquaponic systems have fundamental environmental requirements that particular architectural solutions can assist or hinder. These include access to daylight for growing, utilisation of renewable energy, rainwater harvesting, thermal efficiency and structural solutions for supporting heavy water-filled fish tanks. In urban conditions, the vertical section of buildings can be used to locate plants where there is access to light, so that roof space and facades could accommodate naturally day-lit greenhouses and basements insulated fish tanks.

Practical research into and testing of aquaponics is being conducted across a broad spectrum of initiatives – some of which are described in this book – while theoretical benefits are being explored both from an academic and business perspective. A major economic study focusing on Nordic countries and Canada reviewed the potential benefits and current economic challenges of aquaponics and concluded that it offers potential as a "win/win" symbiotic closed-loop system (Karlsdottir *et al.* 2012). This study is particularly relevant to the CPUL concept, first, because it is based on actual field studies, and second, because it includes a prototype zero-discharge aquaponic system. "Zero discharge" refers to no water being lost from the system, which is significant because fish farms that utilise efficient water recirculation still renew up to 10% of the water in their tanks per day. This volume of fresh water is large, especially in an urban situation and/or one using harvested rainwater. Third, the study concludes that aquaponic systems produce better-tasting vegetables in larger quantities than conventional hydroponic systems and that 'in order to make this industry sustainable, it is necessary to have small to medium farms that produce both fish and plant fresh to local/regional markets. This means that the technology can be more "low tech" and hence more affordable for the farms' (Karlsdottir *et al.* 2012: 24). Such small- to medium-sized farms, that are economically independent or form part of a restaurant or canteen's food supply, would fit well into the *CPUL City*, especially if developed as building-integrated systems.

Aquaponic and hydroponic systems have the potential to provide a highly efficient and diverse source of nutrition that is scalable from small domestic to large commercial installations. Potentially they can come close to zero-waste systems, but, being highly controlled in their mechanical operation, they require close monitoring and are not as resilient as the less predictable, but more comprehensible soil-based organic agriculture. Additionally, living fish in aquaponics need to be kept healthy, preferably without medication.

In the future, hydroponics and aquaponics can develop along two different lines: one, following a biotechnology approach geared towards centralisation and/or maximum profitability, and two, following an approach less dominated by high technology, but more closely linked to existing natural and local biological cycles. Irrespective of which route is taken, aquaponics and hydroponics will probably always require higher mechanised and monitored systems than soil-based cultivation. For any indoor systems that demand artificial lighting or temperature controls, the overall energy balance between

input and output, and between renewables and non-renewables, will need careful assessment to judge their overall efficiency, especially if scarcity becomes a more dominant factor.

For the foreseeable future, it is likely that soil-based, hydroponic and aquaponic urban agriculture systems will develop in parallel. Given the richness and diversity of currently tested approaches, each of them will soon – if not already – be able to adapt to energy- and resource-efficient options that provide healthy and pollutant-free produce tailored to their specific growing location. Productive urban landscapes could then become truly continuous: into urban fields and streets, up building facades, onto roofs, onto decks, down building infrastructure, into urban fields again, parks, streets, up again, down, into, out of – and throughout the year...

Economies of scale: Urban Agriculture and densification

Gillean Denny

Fresh produce consumption in the UK currently generates 30% of total UK agriculture-related greenhouse gas emissions (Garnett 2008) and, currently, 40% of UK food supplies are import-dependent (Defra 2010b). Limiting the environmental impact of fresh produce consumption is not an easy task for any household, regardless of geography or economic standing. Fortunately, a life-cycle analysis of tomatoes, potatoes and apples reveals that the burden to decrease greenhouse gas emissions lies not only on the producer and consumer, but also on the urban environment.

Our integrated global food system provides out-of-season products whenever and wherever we choose. This means production method, packaging, transportation, storage and consumer procurement all have the potential to affect the foods we consume before they ever reach the kitchen table. Many approaches have been utilized over the years to reduce impacts from both the producer and consumer side of the equation, with varying degrees of success. These include creating more efficient production methods, alternative transportation and storage, and consuming local and seasonal crops. Pursuing an urban agriculture (UA) agenda not only combines many of these strategies, but also generates avenues through which the city or town itself may engage to limit overall food impacts. However, the type of UA participation and density of the urban environment will directly determine the effectiveness of such practices.

A 2012 study by the author, examining current UK fresh produce consumption, identified the potential to reduce fresh produce emissions through economies of scale in both UA practice and urban densification. For the purposes of the study, UA was subdivided into 'direct UA' and 'indirect UA'. Direct UA included allotments and garden vegetable patches where the producer was also the consumer. Indirect UA focused on larger commercial ventures where the consumer purchased UA outputs from a local urban farm, market or vegetable box scheme. Both of these consumption practices were then applied to consumers from East Anglia and Greater London within three density zones: dense urban, town and suburban. Current fresh produce consumption emissions were estimated for UA practitioners, derived from their relationships to available amenities and consumption practices unique to the residents from these three urban densities.

Based on these findings, optimal scenarios were then defined for current UA practices and for future patterns of urban consumption. The study showed that lower emissions are not only achievable through UA participation, but require UA participation. Better still, through efficient utilization of current systems, UK households could maintain their desire for out-of-season produce and still manage to reduce total yearly fresh produce emissions by 57%.

Life-cycle analysis complexities

A broad analysis of greenhouse gas (GHG) emissions associated with a product or activity is known as a life-cycle analysis (LCA). The LCA of a food product begins with the raw materials and ends with the disposal of any remaining materials at the end of a product's use (e.g. Williams et al. 2006, 2009; Audsley et al. 2009; Smith et al. 2005; Wiltshire et al. 2009). Since the majority of agriculture production's primary emissions are not carbon-based (37% methane and 53% nitrous oxide), multiple forms of GHG emissions must be included. These

Fig 1: Average monthly emissions. Emissions (g CO_2e/g) for apple, potato and tomato produce commodities available from all procurement locations, differentiated by urban household density. Total emissions include both production and consumer burdens

PRODUCE COMMODITY AVAILABLE FROM PROCUREMENT LOCATIONS WITHIN TYPOLOGIES

Legend:
- PRODUCTION BURDENS
- CONSUMER BURDENS

X-axis: AVERAGE MONTHLY EMISSIONS (g CO2e/g)

Tomato
- Urban: Supermarket (packaging), Supermarket, Local shops, Market, Farmers' market, Produce box, Direct UA
- Town: Supermarket (packaging), Supermarket, Local shops, Market, Farmers' market, Produce box, Direct UA
- Suburb: Supermarket (packaging), Supermarket, Local shops, Market, Farmers' market, Produce box, Direct UA

Potato
- Urban: Supermarket, Supermarket with packaging, Local shops, Market, Farmers' market, Produce box, Direct UA
- Town: Supermarket, Supermarket with packaging, Local shops, Market, Farmers' market, Produce box, Direct UA
- Suburb: Supermarket, Supermarket with packaging, Local shops, Market, Farmers' market, Produce box, Direct UA

Apple
- Urban: Supermarket, Supermarket with packaging, Local shops, Market, Farmers' market, Produce box, Direct UA
- Town: Supermarket, Supermarket with packaging, Local shops, Market, Farmers' market, Produce box, Direct UA
- Suburb: Supermarket, Supermarket with packaging, Local shops, Market, Farmers' market, Produce box, Direct UA

multiple GHG emissions can be expressed as a single unit of CO_2 equivalent (CO_2e) to a certain Global Warming Potential (GWP) (HM Government 2006). All food-related LCA emission burdens can be attributed to one of three stages: pre-farm gate (pre-FG), post-farm gate (post-FG), and consumption. Emissions during these stages will vary depending on the produce type, scale of operation, sourcing origin, means of procurement by the consumer and time of year. Though consumption emissions are important, production emissions (pre-FG and post-FG) comprise 73–100% of total fresh produce emissions (see Fig 1), making the type of produce consumed, source of origin, and the method of production vital to limiting household emissions (Denny 2012).

Production methods will vary depending on produce type, farming scale and geographical location. Arable farming is used for cultivation of produce, such as apples and potatoes under the open sky. More Mediterranean crops, such as tomatoes, are typically cultivated using methods of protected cropping, which utilize structures, such as glasshouses, polytunnels, or hydroponics to increase production yield and extend growing seasons. Due to additional pre-FG emission burdens from heating, lighting and the structures themselves, protective cropping produce can carry approximately 84% higher emissions (see Fig 1) than more traditionally farmed arable produce (Denny 2012). It is for these reasons that a tomato grown locally in the UK, within the shelter of a glasshouse, may incur higher emissions than that of a tomato flown from the Canary Islands that may have higher post-FG transport and storage burdens, but is grown using lower-emission pre-FG methods.

Direct Urban Agriculture versus indirect Urban Agriculture

Scales of production also play a role in affecting emissions. Intensive, extensive and organic production methods are different approaches to balancing crop yields. However, a more efficient use of space requires higher input burdens and therefore may incur greater emissions (Denny 2012; Wiltshire et al. 2009; Lynch et al. 2011; Ziesemer 2007). This is particularly important when discussing the potential advantage of limiting emissions through UA production.

Direct UA produce, where a household grows its own food, is generally believed to carry few emissions due to local proximity and a lack of dependence on mechanization. Also, being fresh from the garden, direct UA produce is unlikely to incur commercial packaging emissions, which can increase total household consumption emissions up to 50% (Denny 2012). Unfortunately, LCA studies of UK allotment produce (Carter 2011) and a community apple orchard (Denny 2012) reveal direct UA production may incur greater emissions than some commercial produce, depending on season and produce type. This can clearly be seen in Fig 1, where the average monthly emissions of direct UA are compared to fresh produce from other locally available amenities, such as a supermarket or farmers' market. These surprisingly high emissions are largely the result of frequent household car use in the maintenance of the allotment or orchard, inefficient use of maintenance materials, wider site maintenance, and the quantity of wasted produce due to spoilage from inefficient harvesting practices.

Though individual UA practitioners may choose to change their habits, it is only through economies of scale that many of these direct UA inefficiencies may be addressed. As a larger, commercial venture, such as a market garden, indirect UA is not as likely to suffer from hobbyist neglect or inefficient use of resources. As a local UA farm, indirect UA typically also benefits from the lower emission post-FG burdens of minimal transport and storage. These savings contribute to the lower emissions carried by farmers' markets, produce box schemes and local shops which are more likely to sell indirect UA produce grown locally in the same city or town (see Fig 1).

However, there are downsides to increased production capacity. The US National Center for Appropriate Technology's *ATTRA* project (ATTRA 2011) suggests that increased scale of acreage and production also necessitates higher mechanization, infrastructure and emissions burdens. Therefore, a smaller plot of less than three acres, using a hoop house or polytunnel structure and employing more traditional, less mechanized farming methods will potentially have fewer emissions. Meanwhile, a larger indirect UA operation may incur emissions identical to or above those of standard non-UA production. These higher emissions would be the result of using glasshouses and machinery to increase the efficiency of irrigation, cultivation, harvesting, storage and transportation. Though yields would be potentially greater through large indirect UA operations, to limit environmental impacts, UA practitioners may choose to rely on direct UA or smaller indirect UA farms for specific types of produce.

Urban densification

Economies of scale may also help decrease fresh produce emissions through a more thorough understanding of food-related emissions and urban densification. When comparing dense urban environments to their town and suburban counterparts, higher-density communities benefit from a greater availability of amenities, such as food sources and low-emission public transport. Promoted through principles such as *Smart Growth* and the *Proximity Principle*, these factors result in decreased dependence on household car use and an increased likelihood of purchasing food from a small, independent vendor (Reeds 2011; TSO and DfT 2005; DfT 2002). This becomes particularly important when determining the environmental impacts of transport-related food emissions.

For UA practitioners in East Anglia and Greater London, their relationship with their urban environment results not only in varying transport practices for different food locations, but also in varying dependence on those locations throughout the year. This, in turn, alters both the emissions of available produce each month and consumers' procurement transport emissions.

The author's 2012 study found that transport to markets and supermarkets accounts, on average, for the highest emissions regardless of urban density. Town residents travel the greatest distance to supermarkets and local shops, while large urban/city households travel the least. Town residents travel the shortest distance to a market location. Suburban households use a car more frequently to reach local shops and markets, while town residents use it mainly to go to the supermarket, and urban/city households to their direct UA locations. Suburban residents tend to walk the most to direct UA locations, while urban households walk the most to every other location. Town households report the highest

cycling percentage, and direct UA transport incurs the fewest emissions for town and suburban households. Urban/city residents show the most consistent reliance on local shops for fresh produce purchases, which is fortunate because these locations carry the least emissions for urban households, due to the type of produce sourced and the urban consumer's relationship with local shop locations.

Many factors may cause consumers to change their transport and food procurement practices throughout the year. For UA practitioners, the greatest change comes in the form of availability from their direct UA location. All households, whether from a suburb, town or dense urban environment, have a direct UA location approximately within a mile [1.6 km] of their house. From May to November all households show increased reliance on direct UA coinciding with the primary harvest season for many UK UA practitioners, and some of this produce then continues to be available all year through home storage. Increased direct UA usage also coincides with decreasing market purchases for suburban and town households as their desires for fresh produce begin to be met by their own garden.

Consumer emissions, however, are just one aspect of total emissions and must be put in context. In the wider scope of available produce during any given day, where that produce is obtained will determine not only the consumer transport emissions now associated with the product, but also the production emissions. Unlike the consumer transport emissions, the production emissions for a single location are subject to change throughout the year, depending on where and when the produce for that location has been sourced.

For example, though urban density increases amenity availability for most food-related locations, urban UA households experience the greatest distance and highest associated transport emissions for direct UA locations. Suburban households meanwhile, which are further away from all commercial procurement locations, experience higher associated transport emissions than urban households, yet simultaneously show greater dependency on lower emission supermarket produce. Therefore, in a particular month, even though transport emissions are high, depending on the type of produce purchased, suburban households may experience lower total fresh produce consumption emissions. This does not mean to say that UA cannot assist in limiting emissions; rather these factors suggest that the many aspects of how we relate to UA, in any scale of urban context, must be reassessed.

The same study (Denny 2012) shows that an increase in the availability and use of local shops, markets, and opportunities for both indirect UA and direct UA production, can decrease consumer burden emissions by 15–57%. Town households show the least total consumption emissions, suggesting that close proximity to a frequent market and direct UA location, but also being remote from and not reliant on a supermarket, could generate the least emissions. Therefore, to reduce fresh-produce-related emissions through urban planning, providing easily accessible, local retail and UA options

is desirable in order to limit household car dependency, reduce packaging needs, and optimise for the cultivation of low-burden emission crops.

Household consumption emissions

To determine how various scales of UA and urban density affect household fresh produce emissions, the author's surveyed production and consumption emissions for the UK (2010–2011) were applied to standard UK consumption data available through Defra's *Family Food* dataset (Defra 2011a). For the year 2010, a person was reported to consume 3,286 g/week of fresh and processed fruits and vegetables, including potatoes, in East Anglia and 3,022 g/week in Greater London.

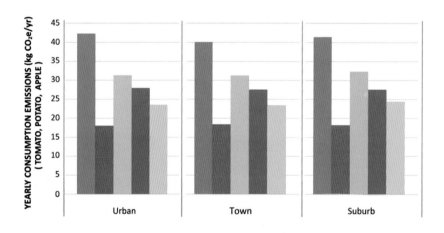

■ **SCENARIO 1:** Procurement location dependency based on recorded household practice
■ **SCENARIO 2:** Least emissions available from all procurement locations
▨ **SCENARIO 3:** Indirect UA consumption only
■ **SCENARIO 4:** Direct UA consumption only
▨ **SCENARIO 5:** Combined UA consumption only (Direct & Indirect)

Fig 2: Fresh-produce yearly consumption emissions scenarios. Total yearly produce consumption emissions (kg CO_2e/year) for combined apple, potato and tomato consumption, including reported primary packaging percentages, for each procurement typology based on reported monthly procurement location dependency for each produce type. Scenarios are based on actual reported monthly procurement location dependency for each produce type, the least possible monthly emissions available for each procurement location, complete indirect UA dependency, complete direct UA dependency and combined UA dependency. Consumption quantities are adapted from Defra's *Family Food* dataset (2011) for the year 2010 and comprise the average consumption of commodities for East Anglia and Greater London with 431 g/wk of potatoes, 112 g/wk of tomatoes and 167 g/wk of apples.

These average consumption quantities were then used to determine yearly consumption models for a single member of a household from each urban density, and were analysed for five different consumption scenarios. These scenarios reveal how seasonality and procurement typologies affect fresh produce consumption emissions, and how intensive UA involvement can actively reduce emissions. For a more detailed explanation of methodology and calculations, see the actual study (Denny 2012).

Scenario 1: Household consumption practice emissions are based on recorded food location dependency and represent the current situation for UA practitioners within each urban density.

Scenario 2: The idealized procurement model represents the least emissions possible for that month across all procurement locations for a specific urban density.

Scenario 3: Indirect-UA-only consumption expresses the emissions of reliance solely on farmers' markets and produce box schemes, though indirect UA could be available from both local shops and supermarkets.

Scenario 4: Direct-UA-only consumption expresses sole reliance on an allotment, vegetable patch, or community orchard.

Scenario 5: Combined UA dependency expresses the least emissions possible for produce utilizing both indirect and direct UA locations depending on produce type.

Total consumption emissions across the entire year reveal that recorded consumption practice emissions (scenario 1) are 57% greater than the least possible emissions achievable through utilizing all available procurement locations with the ideal emissions possible for a particular month (scenario 2). On average, the least emissions for potatoes are derived from local shops, for apples from a produce box scheme, and for tomatoes from direct UA, when in season, and from local shops or markets, when not in season.

Fig 2 suggests total yearly household consumption emissions can be reduced by up to 57% through utilizing all available procurement locations, and making selections based on the least emissions possible for available produce within that month. Dedicated UA consumption (combined direct and indirect) can reduce emissions by 43%. This suggests that, while UA can be largely beneficially, it cannot work alone to achieve the best results, particularly since for large portions of the year both direct UA and indirect UA experience gaps in produce availability. Likewise, though both show adequate capability of reducing emissions separately, when combined into one consumption model, a household is able to take advantage of the least emissions for produce suited to those scales of operation. For direct UA in particular, the level of household engagement and dependency adjusts seasonally throughout the year, from approximately 64% during warmer months of the year to only 3% in winter. This increased dependency on UA during the warmer months of the year is an encouraging statistic for UA producers since fresh produce consumption, and therefore emissions for these same households, can increase up to 49% in June from a January low.

The high May, June and July emissions are the result of several factors. Increased direct UA dependency for produce, such as potatoes, during this season means an increase of produce with inefficient input burdens for low harvest yields. Also during this time, there is greater dependence on high-emission domestic UK commercially protected cropping produce, such as tomatoes, which carry the highest burdens of any produce in the study. Finally, during the UK summer, there is a break between using up UK apples that have been stored and the arrival of the new year's harvest. To fill the gap, there are increased high-emission foreign imports from countries such as New Zealand. Meanwhile, lower December, January and February emissions are the product of opposite conditions: increased foreign import, out-of-season produce (tomatoes) and increased harvest and storage supply of low-emission domestic UK produce (potatoes and apples).

It is during this time of high summer emissions that urban density can play the largest role in helping to limit emissions. Though total yearly emissions are only seen to differ up to 2.2 kg between urban densities, when examined on a monthly basis, from July to October, monthly emissions vary 18%–28% depending on the month, as opposed to 15% in December. This strongly suggests that availability and proximity of food procurement locations on total consumption emissions of a household have the greatest influence when product availability choice is greatest and all produce types are available from all procurement locations, including UA. Therefore, an East Anglia or Greater London household with access to a full and varied range of produce procurement amenities during the peak of all produce availability (July–November) would be in the best position to actively reduce household consumption emissions.

Just as was seen with scales of UA production, urban densification appears to work through a Goldilocks principle, where low suburban densification and high-density urban planning can both result in greater emissions for UA practising households. Lower emissions by mid-density town-based households are largely due to their greater dependency on allotment and market produce, and a lower dependence on supermarket produce. Embedded within these procurement dependencies are a reduced reliance on a household car and greater reliance on domestic seasonal produce from UA sources. The reduced dependency on supermarkets is likely due to supermarkets being nearly twice the distance for town households than any other procurement typology.

Ideal consumption

Many food utopias depict a strict reliance on local and seasonal foods, wishing to create national food security and limit the time and distance between the farm and the kitchen table. Though "local" is not always better from a production emission standpoint, there is no doubt that such a utopia could be managed effectively to reduce emissions. If households chose to walk or cycle instead of taking the car, and if consumers chose to eat squash instead of tomatoes in the middle of February, then indeed, total fresh produce emissions would reduce dramatically. Unfortunately, the UK palate and nutritional requirements are both in favour of the greater variety provided through an international food system. The solution to consuming low-emission fresh produce is therefore not one of limiting, but of utilizing the current systems we already possess and understanding where and how they fit best together to generate a more efficient, prioritized fresh produce network.

From a commercial angle, reduced emissions could be achieved through increasing domestic production for produce with low pre-FG and post-FG burdens when it can be grown in season. Simultaneously, dependency on high-emission pre-FG produce should be reduced in the UK. These commodities are grown largely through protected cropping means and not suitable for the agri-climate on a commercial scale of production, though it should be noted that new innovations in combined heat and power systems are decreasing these burdens. For domestic produce with high pre-FG burdens, produce should be imported from appropriate agri-climates, subject to nutritional debates, or grown through direct UA or low-emissions indirect UA. Likewise, reducing the amount of primary packaging could reduce emission burdens up to 50%, assuming proper secondary packing is used by the industry and consumers only purchase what can be consumed before spoilage.

On an urban planning level, emissions across all households illustrated that varied availability of procurement locations and distance to those locations results in varied dependency and transportation modes. If consumers are more inclined to use non-motorized transport to reach nearby local shops and markets, and if UA participation may limit production burdens for certain produce types, then the purposeful availability and integration of these procurement locations within urban plans should be encouraged, not only from an emissions perspective, but also for the range of other benefits related to health and sustainable community development. Likewise, the procurement system itself could be redesigned, featuring local, walkable procurement locations for perishables and further, out-of-town procurement locations for non-perishables (Beecroft et al. 2003).

As a consumer, supermarket produce should be avoided with greater reliance on local procurement sources. Even if local shops and markets source similar produce items to the supermarkets, reliance on motorized transportation and greater travel distance negate any lower production burden emissions supermarket produce may carry. For the least emissions within East Anglia and Greater London (Denny 2012), potatoes should be procured from local shops (September–April) and produce box schemes (May–August). Apples should be procured from produce box schemes if produce is available, followed by local shop produce. Tomato produce should be procured from local shops or markets (December–April), Direct UA (May–October), and produce box schemes or farmers' markets (April–November). Indirect UA could easily provide produce to any local shop, market, or produce box scheme, thereby reducing the emissions of these locations even further.

When specifically addressing UA, communities should not only provide space for the integration of direct UA initiatives, such as allotment communities, but also begin to generate local spaces of 1–3 acres for the creation of indirect UA market gardens, which sell produce directly to local consumers or provide stock to neighbouring local grocers and markets. Various methods and technologies exist for maximizing UA yield with only a small physical footprint. Vertical gardens utilize wall space, while potted plants and grow bags allow for production in spatially restricted areas, such as apartment balconies. UA strategies have even been developed to combat scenarios of environmental contaminants, particularly in brownfield sites. Raised beds need never let produce growing areas mix with contaminated earth, and hydroponics have the capacity to grow food without the use of soil altogether, so needing clean ground space should not preclude UA (In Vitro 2008).

From an emissions efficiency point of view, allocation of specific UA priorities should be assigned to both direct UA and indirect UA scales of production. Direct UA is particularly useful for limiting emissions of produce with high commercial input burdens, such as tomatoes or produce typically grown under protective cropping. Therefore, households with allotments or vegetable patches should focus on soft, perishable fruits and vegetables. For all other produce, smaller indirect UA operations up to 3 acres benefit from the efficiency of commercial production and limited requirements of local distribution, making it sensible for facilitating lower consumption emissions. Therefore, households wishing to consume these items should purchase them from a local indirect UA provider.

As with everything else pertaining to fresh produce emissions, efficient management of resources is key to limiting emissions. For direct UA households who wish to grow their own food, this means not only being conscious of what is grown, but how it is grown. Carter

revealed the emission burdens associated with inefficient farming methods and spoilage (Carter 2011), but there are other ways to address direct UA emissions. In an allotment situation, tenants can buy necessary materials in bulk and coordinate shopping efforts to reduce allotment-wide maintenance emissions. With cooperation, spoilage could be avoided if particular tenants are absent, and workshops could be conducted to educate hobbyists on efficient gardening practices. Though allotments and vegetable patches are seen as individual pursuits, tenants could coordinate efforts to grow larger plots of separate crops, similar to community garden efforts. Though this would potentially reduce the individual identity and sense of ownership inherent in the allotment tradition, it could also go a long way to reducing fresh produce related emissions for all tenants.

By being aware of where food comes from and how it is produced, UA practitioners and the entire UK food industry can better tailor the whole system to actively reduce emissions through growing produce that is best suited to the scale of production. We can also better tailor our environments to reduce emissions through understanding how consumers move within these different scales of urbanism. By increasing local opportunities for production and procurement, emissions for specific produce can be reduced across its entire life. In the end, fresh produce emissions reveal that it is not only what we eat, but also how it is procured, that will make the greatest difference in this interconnected food world.

Bricks and nectar: Urban beekeeping with specific reference to London

Mikey Tomkins

'Insofar as bee-dependent plants touch human life', write Keith Delaplane and Daniel Mayer, 'whether providing us with a bountiful food supply or a pleasant walk through a city park, humans are dependent on bees' (Delaplane and Mayer 2000). However, how dependent urban agriculture is on urban beekeeping is little understood or discussed.

Urban beekeeping is largely a cultural practice with its own short history, little engaged with the broader discussion on urban agriculture despite its potential importance. Researching this subject is challenging because we currently have limited knowledge about it: on its direct harvests such as honey, its potential contribution to urban pollination and the overall limitations on density of urban honeybees. Therefore, this chapter should be read as a scoping report that reviews and discusses the disparate data and research on the phenomena with specific reference to London. Such a discussion will help extend an understanding of the cultural practice and how this might contribute to our conceptualisation of urban agriculture, mapping out the benefits, constraints and gaps in knowledge for future development.

In writing this chapter, I also reflect on my experience as a beekeeper in London since 2000, together with some insights from working as a community beekeeping officer in the capital for the charity *Sustain* (Sustain 2012). While this chapter discusses honeybees, it recognizes that there are multiple species of bees, as well as other insects, in the UK that play a vital role in floral pollination services.

The honeybee and beekeeping

Within temperate zones, when we refer to beekeeping (apiculture) we are usually referring to the management of European honeybees (*Apis mellifera*), which, as the name suggests, produce honey. Bees are kept in hives within an apiary (site or enclosure for hives) and a hive in summer will contain a colony of up to 60,000 female worker bees. Additionally, a colony will have one queen and a few hundred male bees or drones (Tautz 2008). Honeybees are valued in terms of honey production and the pollination services to large-scale agricultural crops worldwide as well as ornamental and natural landscapes (Jones 2004; Klein *et al.* 2007; Delaplane and Mayer 2000). Tom Breeze and colleagues quantify the contribution of the honeybee to pollination as providing a maximum of 34% of the UK's agricultural pollination needs (Breeze *et al.* 2012).

While there is a reported decline in managed honeybees and beekeepers across Europe, including 54% in England between 1985 and 2005 (Potts *et al.* 2010), urban beekeeping is seeing something of a renaissance. This is linked to responses ensuing from the many calls to 'save the bees' across a wide section of NGOs and within the media (Sustain 2012; FoE 2012). Urban beekeeping follows general beekeeping as being predominately a hobby, requiring no licences or registration (BFA 2011).

Beekeeping and Urban Agriculture definitions

Broadly speaking, urban beekeeping follows the urban agriculture definition as it relates to 'the growing of plants and the raising of animals for food and other uses within and around cities and towns' (Veenhuizen 2006). It is a farming practice involving the management of livestock and the harvesting of direct and indirect products for largely human and environmental benefits (Heaf 2011). The direct products of the hive are honey (produced from nectar), wax (produced from wax glands), pollen (collected and stored to feed brood) and propolis (collected from tree resin), as well as the socio-cultural benefits of beekeeping (lifestyle), while the indirect benefit is the pollination of plants. However, unlike for most farmed animals, the beekeeper is not directly responsible for the feeding of their colonies, which are reliant instead on the wider landscape for access to food in the form of floral resources. Within urban environments, this brings a potentially strong connection between residents and beekeepers still yet to be fully exploited. Arguably, bees, in developed countries at least, are the only domesticated farm animals we allow to feed "wild" in our cities.

The interactions between beekeepers and communities is worth stressing, as the direct harvest of hives remains with the beekeeper, but the indirect harvest of increased pollination interacts with all aspects of the social and environmental spheres.

The researchers around Anne Bellows write that in countries of the Global North livestock is a 'largely unknown, underground and unevenly regulated activity' (Bellows *et al.* 2000), which is certainly also applicable to certain aspects of urban beekeeping. More importantly, 'livestock encompasses multiple meanings for practitioners in the urban environments: economic buttress, tradition, cultural and/or religious endurance, and community cohesiveness' (Bellows *et al.* 2000). The cultural services of beekeeping connect with the wider urban agriculture discussion to include 'the non-material social needs such as relaxation, exercise, health, leisure and well-being' (Perez-Vazquez 2002) outside of commerce alongside its intrinsic biodiversity and ecological functions (Taylor Lovell 2010).

Beekeeping and cities

Urban bees thrive in cities such as Paris, Tokyo and New York. In 2005, the City of Vancouver published its policy on urban apiculture, writing that 'urban beekeeping can contribute to pollination, and better harvests in backyard, street, rooftop, and ... is an important complement to urban food production and to the City's sustainability goals' (Vancouver 2005).

Urban beehives often play on an architectural metaphor, as a modular, skyscraper-like addition to the urban

landscape (Ramirez 2000), with certain aspects of urbanity also working in favour of city bees, such as the warmer climate extending the foraging season (McNeil 2009). Urban areas are also potentially far richer in seasonal floral diversity compared to rural farmland (Worcester University 2010). The *National Ecosystem Assessment* reports 'some evidence that pollination levels of particular plant species are higher in gardens than in arable farmland' (Defra 2011c). Urban residents therefore play a significant role in feeding urban bees that in turn provide residents with honey and increase urban agriculture yields through pollination. Research shows that honeybee colonies in Birmingham produce more honey than nearby country bees (Memmott 2011), with Karin Alton and Mark Patterson writing that 'unless there are significant [...] changes to the way we manage our countryside... urban areas could become the last refuges for many of our native polinators' (Alton and Patterson 2013).

Bees may have found an oasis in cities, but our food security is dependent on the health of all global bees, meaning we should encourage bee-friendly, biodiverse organic agriculture everywhere. It is evident that the urban pollination footprint is huge when we take into account pollination dependence of food and other resources that are imported into cities. This has been little accounted for in research and may be difficult to sustain with declining bee numbers (Breeze *et al.* 2012; Potts *et al.* 2010).

Fig 1: Rooftop apiary in East London. The modular hives echo the "modern" architecture and the distant towers of the City of London. (image: Micha Theiner, 2011)

Urban beekeeping in the UK

Despite considerable popular attention given to urban beekeeping in the UK (Benbow 2012; Benjamin and McCallum 2011; Hughes 2010), it is a small subset of national beekeeping although most urban areas support some level of practice (Defra 2008). Officially, urban beekeeping is defined as apiaries that fall inside a 10 km square of Ordnance Survey maps and whose population is over 120,000 (Defra 2008). Urban apiaries on average contain 3–3.8 hives, while rural apiaries on average contain 6.2 hives (BBKA 2011). In England and Wales, 9.6% of the 25,220 officially recorded apiaries in 2008 are therefore urban (2,420 apiaries) (Defra 2008). In 2008, most cities in England and Wales had fewer than 100 official apiaries (each containing 3–3.8 hives), with the exception of Manchester (150 apiaries), Birmingham (450) and London (650) (Defra 2008). *Fig 2* shows the total numbers of officially registered honeybee hives per city in England and Wales in 2008, and additionally in London in 2010 and 2012 using data provided by Alan Byham at *Beebase* (personal communication Sep 2011).

It would seem straightforward to describe beekeeping practice as urban if hives are placed in urban environments, yet bees will forage across a wide terrain commonly travelling distances of 2–4 km, crossing all anthropogenic boundaries and landscapes in searching out floral resources. Therefore beekeeping expresses a duality: the ecological story of the bee and the social story of the beekeeper.

Beekeeping in London

In 1866, the London apiarian Alfred Neighbour described the phenomenon of 'metropolitan beekeeping' thus:

There are many persons now in this noisy city pent, who [...] doubt even the possibility of bees feeding themselves amidst such an 'endless meal of brick'; but we can easily prove that bees are able to produce honey, both for themselves and for their masters.

(Neighbour 1866)

Neighbour kept his bees in Holborn, and nearly 150 years later the area is still promoting urban bees (Parham 2011). Twelve hives were installed in 2011, and office employees involved with beekeeping report a greater awareness of urban agriculture and food issues through contact with bees (Parham 2011).
Also, office beekeepers report an increased morale, contact with nature and other workers, and reduced stress.

According to *Beebase*, in 2012 the capital had over 3,200 official hives, a sharp rise from 2,089 hives in 2008. However, this figure is likely to be higher; estimates suggest that only 75% of hives are registered by beekeepers (Alton and Patterson 2013). Hives, which contain a single colony, are not evenly spread, with central London having a higher density of colonies than outer areas that, one could argue, have much larger greener areas or diverse landscapes. For example, within a 3 km

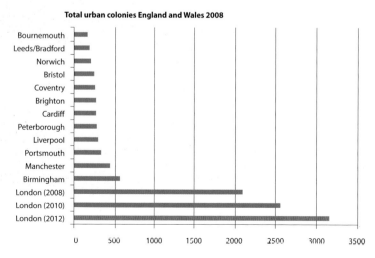

Fig 2: Urban beekeeping in England and Wales. 2008 data for exemplary UK cities and additional data for London in 2010 and 2012.

Fig 3: Golden Company Beekeeping training session.
Rooftop in the City of London 2011. (image: Micha Theiner, 2011)

radius of Trafalgar Square in central London there are 150 colonies (approximately 50 apiaries) at a density of one hive per 19 ha. By comparison, as we start to move out to 20 km from the centre, there are 3,999 colonies (1,333 apiaries) with a much lower density of one hive per 31 ha.

There is little research to substantiate what effect urban hive densities might have on honey crops and the pollination of crops (pollination services). However, I would suggest that these are probably high enough to sustain a good level of pollination when considered together with wild pollinators such as bumble bees, whose urban numbers are reportedly high (Defra 2011c). There are also

few incidents of urban residents complaining of low harvests and any that surfaced might be better explained
through other environmental issues such as weather
fluctuations. One way to consider the necessary density
of urban beekeeping is to follow Heaf's argument that
sustainable beekeeping is one that is 'low-intensity…
carried out by a larger population of beekeepers' (Heaf
2011). This suggests that urban beekeeping should
be low density, yet offer high accessibility in terms of
knowledge and practice.

While we can discuss beekeeping as a generic practice,
there are certain key differences between rural and
urban practices. For example, swarming – the moment
when a colony splits in two and a football-sized cluster
of bees leave to find a new hive – can be a nuisance in
cities if roads need to be closed. Even though finding the
space for food growing in cities can be an issue, hives
take up very little space (a few square metres), and beekeepers have adapted by using communal space, public
sites or taking to rooftop beekeeping. As Camilla God-
dard, a London beekeeper, points out: 'the city becomes
a playground […] you're in such strange places […] up
on the rooftop, in tucked away places, on top of offices
or shops. People dress for where they work and you're
like batman, but in a white space suit!' The closeness and
multiplicity of city spaces means that urban beekeeping
is intrinsically linked to a wide cross section of society.
Camilla states further: 'I see myself as an undercover
farmer because my bees feed on everyone's land […]
so you need to be interested in society because it's all
about connections […] it's a good way of bringing people
together' (personal communication Apr 2011).

The capital's beekeepers occupy all levels of the physical
and social space of the city: prisons, allotments, schools,
housing, businesses, rooftops and public parks (Corelli
Academy 2011; Sustain 2012). Regents Park in central
London is home to a commercial beekeeper with over 40
hives (Pure Food 2011), and two London prisons have
apiaries. Famous rooftop apiaries include *Fortnum and
Mason* in Piccadilly, both of the *Tate Galleries*, the *Royal
Festival Hall* and *St Ermin's Hotel* (Beecraft 2011). Kennington Park in south London supports a community
organisation called *Bee Urban*, run by Barnaby Shaw,
which describes itself as an 'environmental community project' aiming to link gardening and beekeeping
through community education (Bee Urban 2012).

In an interview with beekeeper Barnaby Shaw he contends that it is 'the community aspect of it, the shared
[…] the relationships between the joint beekeepers,
the bees, and city space' that draw him to community
beekeeping. He talks about creating a public apiary,
stating that 'for me at Kennington [Park] lodge it's more
about […] doing open days to give city people an insight
into beekeeping […] general beekeeping awareness,
pollination and pesticides for example […] 'cause here
in south London, we have such a high density of people
on the surrounding estates […] I think essentially it's
access, a wider audience…' (personal communication
2011). Cities become a hive of social interaction, where
the bees' foraging habits engage with the need to share
social and ecological resources.

Beekeeping in London is multifaceted: comprising training, education, breeding, selling of colonies, swarm collection, technical assistance and limited honey and wax
production. It is private, education-oriented or community-based. Urban beekeeping practice in the capital
has diverse entry points; in the hands of Wolff Olins,
beekeeping has become part of a local youth development project with the charity *Global Generation* (Global
Generation 2012), while the *Bee Collective* offers community honey extraction facility in the Victoria area of
London. The project offers the processing and marketing
of London honey, giving beekeepers a fair and guaranteed price, feeding profits back into promoting habitat
for honeybees and wild pollinators in the capital (Bee
Collective 2012). Specifically within a community setting, there is a high degree of awareness that beekeeping
connects to wider urban environmental aspirations,
something to be encouraged (Bradbear 2003).

Direct harvest: London honey

While the future success of urban bees will be linked to
pollination services for urban agriculture, cities can also
be productive for honeybees in terms of direct harvests
such as honey. The harvesting season for beekeeping
starts around the end of July and, in 2011, London held
both a honey show and a honey festival. Over 4,000
people attended the latter with 600 people queuing to
taste 44 London honeys (Sustain 2012). It is legal in
the UK for food producers to sell direct to shops or the

Fig 5: The variety of London honey is surprising. Honey jars from Kings Cross, London Fields, Lambeth and Dulwich in 2011.

Fig 4: Tasting honey at the London Honey Festival 2011.
44 London honeys were available for tasting.
(image: Micha Theiner, 2011)

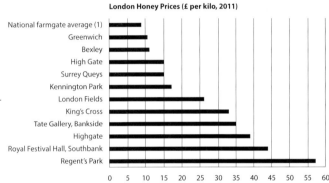

Fig 6: London honey prices per kilo. The data was collected by the author in 2011.

public so, occasionally, you will find London honey on sale in local shops, on farmers' markets or at festivals. In 2011, the author collected 66 jars of London honey direct from London's beekeepers. *Fig 4* shows that their colour and consistency varied enormously, even amongst hives that were within 250 metres of each other. While valuable as a local food product, it also encapsulates a unique ecological and social story about the human–bee relationship.

Most beekeepers extract the honey manually with no additional processing, such as heat, and in this sense it is a raw product. However, honey is heavy and the harvest needs to be driven to the place of extraction and multiple points of sale, giving it a potentially large energy footprint.

Due to the absence of consistent data, figures for honey production in London are difficult to assess. Individual beekeepers may not weigh or even take a harvest, while others report harvesting 30–70 kg a hive. According to Jane Mosley, the British Beekeepers Association surveyed 1,390 members in 2010–2011 and quotes 11.7 kg as the London average, below the national average of 14.5 kg (personal communication Sep 2011). This means that potentially London's 3,200 official hives produced approximately 37,440 kg of honey in 2011.

The British Beekeepers Association reports a national average price of £8.89 for 1 kg of honey bought directly from the producer (BBKA 2011). *Fig 6* shows that London honey prices range widely from the national average: Greenwich honey costs £10.50 per kg, while Regents Park honey costs £57 per kg. This values London's 37,440 kg of honey at between £332,841 (national price of £8.89 per kg) or £2,134,080 (local price of £57 per kg). These figures should not be taken too literally, as there are no substantive surveys of urban honey production. However, it does start to create a picture of a practice, its economy and current scale.

Beekeeping and urban pollination

Kevin Welzel writes that 'there are many studies showing the relationship between distance and pollination in commercial agriculture, but not in urban agriculture' (Welzel 2010), despite the fact that bees clearly have a supporting role to play in pollination of urban agriculture (Bates *et al.* 2011). Mark Winston notes the importance of honeybees to urban agriculture, especially where groomed cosmopolitan gardens and pesticide use prevent wild bees from thriving (Winston 1998). Kevin Matteson and Gail Langellotto report the contribution of native or wild bees in New York community food gardens noting the absence of honeybees (Matteson and Langellotto 2009). However, this could be explained by the fact that until 2010 New York City prohibited beekeeping (along with many North American and Canadian cities), classing it livestock alongside cattle and chickens.

What is important about both studies is the discussion of fragmentation, scale, and proximity of landscape types within urban areas and the effects these might have on pollination services of bees. As Johan Colding writes, 'urban ecosystems are the most complex mosaics of vegetative cover and multiple land use of any landscape... where change is the norm rather than the exception' (Colding 2007). Concomitantly, the urban agriculture landscape is not an isolated monocultural agricultural system, but more a series of 'human-modified fragmented habitats' complemented by wild growth, street trees, private gardens and parks (McFrederick and Lebuhn 2006).

In such a landscape, planning pollination services for urban agriculture is an almost impossible task because there are few studies of urban bees and, specifically, there has been little research on the effects of cities on pollinator groups (McFrederick and Lebuhn 2006; Bates *et al.* 2011). Our lack of knowledge on urban bee fauna stems from the fact that research has only just begun to document diversity, species dynamics and profusion (Hernandez *et al.* 2009). Within the fragmented urban matrix, as opposed to the monoculture of field agriculture, the importance of honeybees as a pollinator that prefers general and larger forage areas might be less significant.

Therefore, while urban pollination services need to be assessed looking at the future potential for urban agriculture as essential infrastructure (Viljoen *et al.* 2005) these pollination services need to be considered across all insect groups, requiring both planned sites for keeping bees (apiaries) and unmanaged sites, such as undisturbed patches of urban landscape, for wild pollinators.

In order to provide a good level of insect pollination, we would need to be mindful of balancing spaces with a high level of alteration, and natural, wild or fallow landscapes. Adam Bates and colleagues note that 'generalist, strong flying, species [...] [honeybee and red-tailed bumblebee] [...] usually demonstrated no negative response to urbanization' and that 'intense anthropogenic landscape alteration negatively affects rarer, more specialist species' (Bates *et al.* 2011). As P.G. Angold and team propose, 'planners can have a positive impact on urban biodiversity by slowing the pace of redevelopment and by not hurrying to tidy up and redevelop brownfield sites' (Angold *et al.* 2006). This suggests the idea of a fallow city where sections are allowed to regenerate themselves periodically, providing a variety of habitats suitable for diverse pollination groups that collectively could have a bigger impact on urban pollination services than increasing honeybee numbers alone. However, we could think about this in reverse: There are many essential supporting services required for urban agriculture – such as soil, water, fertilizer – and pollination services are one of these. While we may currently lack some of these essential support services, the existing apicultural practice is well placed to provide some aspects of pollination for any rapid increase of urban food growing. This would be hard to action if it where not already in place, but should also be balanced with the need to support wild pollinators, acknowledging their vital role in local food production.

Concluding remarks

This chapter has attempted to scope out the interconnecting components of urban beekeeping, exploring some of the current knowledge and data and their connection to urban agriculture. It is clear that honeybees and many other insects are at home amongst bricks and nectar with some reports suggesting that cities provide better habitat than rural environments.

As an urban farming practice, beekeeping is currently limited as honey is relatively expensive and scarce, and there is little in the way of a wax market. The indirect benefits of pollination – both to utility and aesthetic landscapes – cannot currently be quantified, but empirically it is easy to argue for the intrinsic necessity of all bees in cities. Overall, pollinator populations are currently being balanced by the vagaries of incremental cultural changes, such as a rapid increase in hobby beekeeping or a dramatic decrease of 12% in domestic vegetated landscape since 1998 – a loss of 3,000 ha (C. Smith 2010). Moreover, policy direction does not appear on the horizon to create pollinator-friendly cities, but if developed in conjunction with the need for urban agriculture, the social and economic returns for beekeeping could be enhanced significantly. Overall, urban bees contribute to ideas of continuous productive urban landscapes in terms of human-environmental relations (Viljoen *et al.* 2005). Bees are instinctively joining the dots between parks, gardens and wasteland, creating exemplar productive corridors. They already think about landscape as continuous, extending our concept of the CPUL as essential infrastructure, beyond superstructure and into the atmosphere that ultimately connects us all.

Acknowledgements

The author would like to thank Alan Byham, Regional Bee Inspector for South East England, for invaluable access to hive data, official beekeeping numbers and many important conversations. Dr Adam Bates (Earth Sciences, School of Geography, Earth and Environmental Sciences, The University of Birmingham, Edgbaston, Birmingham B15 2TT) and Dr Karin Alton (Research Fellow, Laboratory of Apiculture and Social Insects, School of Life Sciences, University of Sussex, Falmer, Brighton BN1 9QG) both generously provided feedback on early versions of this chapter highlighting important caveats on dates in the discussion. Also, Micha Theiner for kindly donating the images used (www.michatheiner.com).

Green theory in practice and urban design: Germany

Katrin Bohn and André Viljoen

One can trace the current national popularity of urban agriculture in Germany back to the urban communal farms of the 1970s. This movement negotiated its profile amongst the established, but not spatially or thematically connected, urban food growing in allotments [Kleingärten], private and municipal house gardens [Hausgärten], school gardens [Schulgärten, Gartenarbeitsschulen] and remaining urban farms [Stadtgüter, Stadtgärtnereien, Bauernhöfe]. Around the mid-1990s, a new generation of initiatives – not yet understood as urban agriculture – branched out into a communally oriented practice, as exemplified by the Germany-specific *Interkulturelle Gärten* [intercultural gardens] originating in Göttingen in 1995 (IGG *n.d.*), and a commercially oriented practice, as exemplified by the Berlin-based social enterprise *Agrarbörse* set up in 1996 (Agrarbörse *n.d.* a). Germany's most prolific community garden, *Prinzessinnengärten* in Berlin (Nomadisch Grün *n.d.*), also a social enterprise, can be seen as an example of the planned and designed linking of communal and commercial aims.

Today Germany has a varied and growing number of academics and practice-based researchers working from a theoretical or planning perspective to understand, develop and promote urban agriculture's spatial consequences, both nationally and internationally: landscape architect Frank Lohrberg, one of Germany's best-known experts in the field, is currently coordinating one of Germany's major international research programmes – *COST Action Urban Agriculture Europe* – from within his department *Landscape Architecture* at the RWTH Aachen University (COST *n.d.*); Philipp Stierand, a freelancer with a background in spatial planning, researches the spatial side of food systems and has disseminated his findings since 2009 via public lectures and the blog *speiseräume* (Stierand *n.d.*); in 2010, the *Leibniz-Zentrum für Agrarlandschaftsforschung (ZALF) e.V.* [Leibniz Centre for Agricultural Landscape Research], Germany's key research centre focussing on agrarian land use ecologies,

started to conduct quantitative research into urban agriculture; important urban agriculture protagonists like Felicitas Bechstein, Heide Hoffmann, Andrea von Allwörden, Thomas Aenis and Christian Ulrichs are based at the *Agrarian and Horticultural Faculty* at Humboldt University Berlin. Here, individual researchers have been engaged in urban-agriculture-related studies for a long time with publications and conferences reaching back beyond the turn of the century, such as the international conference *Urban Agriculture and Horticulture: the Linkage with Urban Planning* in 2000, coordinated by Hoffmann (HUB 2000).

From a more social perspective, the *Stiftung Interkultur* [Inter-Culture Charity] with a team around Christa Müller (see below); the department of *Gender and Nutrition* at Universität Hohenheim around Anne Bellows; Elisabeth Meyer-Renschhausen, freelancing or with the department of *Politics and Social Sciences* at Freie University Berlin (see p. 146); Gert Gröning with the department of *Garden Culture and Open Space Development* at the University of the Arts Berlin; and Marit Rosol from the department *Human Geography* at Goethe University Frankfurt (see p. 178) are leading German research into the origins, development, impact and future of urban food growing, especially community gardens and gardening.

Some urban-agriculture-related research reached and reaches out of Germany. During the mid- and late 1990s, the German Foundation for International Development [Deutsche Stiftung für Internationale Entwicklung (DSE)], for example, co-funded and/or coordinated several large-scale agri- and horticultural projects in developing countries that, at the same time, generated valuable thoughts and concepts for a broader understanding of urban agriculture. As part of this, Richter, Schnitzler and Gura, for example, whilst working on vegetable production systems in the subtropics, contributed to our current understanding of urban agriculture as being not only defined by location, but also by its interconnections to urban food systems (Richter *et al.* 1995). Together with the German Foundation for Technical Cooperation [Deutsche Gesellschaft für Technische Zusammenarbeit (GTZ)], DSE also ran the 1999 international workshop *Growing Cities, Growing Food* in Havana, Cuba, which resulted in a still significant publication of the same name in 2000 bringing together writings by some of the most important urban agriculture experts of the time (Bakker *et al.* 2000). Today, probably the best-known of these German/international projects is *Urban Agriculture Casablanca*, an eight-year project about the role of urban agriculture as facilitator of climate-optimised urban development. It has been led by Undine Giseke at the Institute for Landscape Architecture and Environmental Planning at the Technical University Berlin (TUB *n.d.*).

Overall, we may summarise that in Germany today one encounters a popular and innovative community-oriented urban agriculture practice that impacts on open urban space in many cities and towns. One can also identify the early beginnings of yield-oriented or commercial practice, especially in Berlin, where several initiatives are currently in their test or development phase. Examples of both of these practices will be presented in this chapter and elsewhere in the book. Moreover, several research teams, mainly at or connected to German universities, have started to actively observe the mechanisms and implications of urban agriculture, drawing conclusions for specific local application. Notwithstanding this activity, at the time of writing, comparatively little has been done in the country in terms of food policy, food systems planning, or design research into urban agriculture. The important results from international research projects have not (yet) significantly infused spatial planning or food systems work in Germany. However, some projects are starting to do this and have already produced promising and innovative results. Again, we will present some of these in this book.

Generally, we may conclude that those reasons which lead to the earlier or more intensely pursued establishment of urban food-growing practice and food systems work in the USA or UK were in Germany either not as strongly present or not as strongly perceived. This may be in the main due to:

- different experiences and perceptions of food security and food-related life quality
- different desires for food security and food-related quality of life
- different desires for and perceived roles of open urban space
- different competing pressures on open urban space due to differences in availability or use density, and, reciprocally, different pressures on open space in peri-urban areas
- differences in usage rights and duties when negotiating with a site's public managers
- a different understanding of civil rights and responsibilities when they concern food provision
- different desires for and involvement in the development of one's own food culture
- a different understanding of an individual's contribution to society as a whole, including charitable work and business success.

Urban Agriculture in Germany: a geographical overview

Discussions about food systems at all scales have been as absent from the German political, planning and social agenda as elsewhere in the Global North. Even though the existing food systems are comparatively well integrated into everyday life, this does not mean that they have achieved their potential with respect to fundamental environmental or sustainable food quality.

For example: on the one hand, Germany has the biggest organic food-produce market in Europe with €6.02 billion turnover in 2011 (followed by France (€3.39 billion) and the UK (€2 billion)), whereby the associated per-head expenditure is average, with €74 per year compared to other European countries (BÖLW 2012: 13). In Europe, Germany is also one of the biggest producers of organic foodstuffs (BÖLW 2012: 11). On the other hand, nearly half of this produce is being sold in large organic supermarkets [Bio-Supermärkte] even though they constitute only 17% of the total number of organic food stores (BÖLW 2012: 14). From an urban planning and design point of view, this favours food systems, as well as types of urban space use, which are usually not associated with sustainable urban lifestyles.

It may also be part of the explanation why the number of farmers' or organic food markets is relatively low; for example, seven such markets in total in Berlin (Berlin *n.d.*) is relatively lower than the 20 certified farmers' markets in London (LFM *n.d.*). This impacts on the experience and perception of food's significance within the daily routines in our 21st-century cities.

However, these associated challenges have been recognised and for about ten years Germany has been gradually developing its voice in the international food systems and (food) productive landscape discourse. Urban agriculture projects are now present in many German towns and cities with an array of production and organisational types, most of which, as in other countries, were set up as self-initiative by protagonists with diverse agendas. As described elsewhere in the book (for example chapter *Growth and challenges since 2005*, p. 6), one can currently observe a clear dominance of social drivers for urban agriculture practice.

The five towns and cities Andernach, Göttingen, Leipzig, Munich and Witzenhausen are presented here, because each has developed a distinct and innovative approach to urban food growing. We speak in greater detail about Cologne in the second part of this book, and the greatest detail we provide for Berlin at the end of this chapter.

As mentioned before, Göttingen is home to the first inter-cultural garden in Germany, the *Internationale Gärten,* set up in 1995 through the joint bottom-up top-down efforts of immigrant Bosnian women and their municipal social workers (IGG *n.d.*). Run as a registered charity since 1998, the gardens quickly became a much copied example for a new way of using public urban land in a socially and food-productive sense. Intercultural gardens are today an integral part of the German community gardens scene with more than 100 located across Germany (anstiftung *n.d.* a). Their focus on intercultural exchange makes them very accessible for people from diverse backgrounds and furthers at the same time a multifaceted food culture. Apart from the two intercultural gardens, Göttingen hosts several other urban agriculture projects, which have recently created their own common network platform, the *Göttinger Nährboden* (Janun *n.d.*).

Leipzig has the greatest number of allotments per inhabitant in Germany, maybe as a continuation of the allotment movement that was founded there in the 1860s. Additionally, since the turn of the century, bottom-up initiatives have developed some nationally innovative urban agricultural projects, most of which, whilst socially oriented, concentrate explicitly on food growing. In 2001, Germany's second intercultural garden was set up here, the *Bunte Gärten*, who found their location in an unused municipal horticultural nursery where the 50 participants now grow edibles on the 1 ha site, as well as in an existing commercial-size greenhouse (Brückenschlag *n.d.*). Since 2011, the *Initiative für Zeitgenössische Stadtentwicklung (IFZS)* [Initiative for Contemporary Urban Development] runs the community garden *Offener Garten Annalinde* as a 'creative medium' for their ambition to initiate wider discussions about the future of Leipzig (IFZS *n.d.*). Initially part-funded by the EU programme *Youth in Action, Annalinde* is today not only a food growing site that visualises a participatory use of urban space; it also offers a broad range of food-focused environmental education programmes. Apart from these two examples, there are several other urban agriculture projects running in Leipzig, including a community-supported agriculture project. Many of these are supported by *Stiftung Bürger für Leipzig*, a bottom-up residents' foundation which has engaged since 2003 in campaigning and action work to improve everyday life in the city. One of their most significant pieces of work in terms of urban agriculture is the production and online publication of an open space inventory, the *Flächendatenbank*, that shows more than 100 urban sites with relevant data, such as address, size, ownership contacts, that have fallen redundant and could be reactivated, at least on a temporary basis (Bürger für Leipzig *n.d.*).

Andernach, a town in the Rhineland, also works with its asset open space and, since 2010, has become Germany's first "edible city" by following two strategies: revitalising urban communally owned brownfield sites and – so far unique in Germany – exchanging the decorative planting in its municipal parks for edibles. Together with the town's open spaces department, Heike Boomgaarden, a horticultural engineer and gardening show TV presenter, initially started a permaculture project at the edge of town in 2009 using land provided by the municipality and with support from a social enterprise retraining the long-time unemployed (Boomgaarden *n.d.*). Based on this project, Andernach's municipality had already recognised the potential of urban agriculture as a means to improve the appearance of its green spaces, increase local biodiversity, engage the public in the shaping of its environment and – important for many German cities – lower maintenance costs for communally owned open space. With the backing of the town hall and an adapted open space planning concept [Grundkonzept der städtischen Grünraumplanung] (Andernach n.d.), Andernach began in an "approved top-down" process to convert the largely lawned town wall's moat into a growing zone for fruit, vegetables, herbs and flowers which residents can freely pick, as well as help maintain. There is a focus on biodiversity: for example, in 2010, 101 types of tomatoes were planted. The conversion of many municipal flowerbeds and schoolyards has followed and residents have supported their town's new appearance. National interest became so great that Andernach presented its approach to an international audience with a conference held in 2013 (Andernach n.d.).

As member of the German Transition Town movement, Witzenhausen, a small town near Kassel, also hosted a national conference in 2013 on the subject of "edible cities", the unvergEssbar Konferenz (TT Witzenhausen n.d.). Urban agriculture and local food initiatives play an important role within all six registered German transition towns, and in Witzenhausen, it is the combination of the shrinking city phenomena, enthusiastic agricultural students within a Kassel University campus and local residents that led in 2009 to the bottom-up foundation of a dedicated activists' network.

München [Munich] is a key location for urban agriculture practice and its initial integration into the planning system. It is home to several types of intercultural and community gardens, many allotment sites and a large number of pedagogically focused school gardens (Haide 2012). The city has developed a successful self-harvesting type, Krautgärten, following a Viennese example of the same name. Since 1989, six such gardens have been set up through a cooperation between the municipality with its own farm Stadtgut Riem and other local urban farms in the east of the city (München 2012a), and nearly ten more have followed as private initiative all over Munich (Haide 2012), often close to the city's edge, i.e. in proximity to rural land. The six municipal Krautgärten provide around 400 plots of about 60 m^2 each on nearly 20,000 m^2 of land. On average, each

gardener harvests 200 kg of vegetables and herbs per plot per growing season (Hennecke 2012), which – in weight, and spread over a year – would roughly equal their WHO-recommended daily intake of 400g of fruit and vegetables (WHO 2005). This is remarkable. The Krautgärten have become an integral part of the city's urban development planning. Whilst they are a hands-on way of responding to local desires for fresh and healthy food provision, Munich is also pursuing equally remarkable larger-scale planning strategies that include urban agriculture: since the 1990s, the city of Munich has supported about 100 urban farms in its greenbelt – the Grüngürtelbauern [greenbelt farmers] – aiming to develop an 'adapted agriculture' maintaining and developing 335 km^2 of municipal open land as productive open space (München 2012b). This strategy did not originate from concerns about food or the food system, but to safeguard and develop the city's open space. Today, more than 30 of the farmers belong to a network of producers selling their products directly to urban residents, encouraged by a municipal support programme [Modell Direktvermarktung]. Others concentrate on the farming (and processing/distributing) of cattle, the creation and maintenance of healthy biotopes and continuous biotope networks, as well as the provision of leisure facilities, all in close cooperation with the municipal planning department (München 2012c). The Agropolis project by an interdisciplinary group of two architects/urban planners and a landscape architecture practice is probably Germany's most ambitious current design project aiming to integrate food growing and an urban food strategy into the city. In 2009, the team won an urban design competition in Munich with its proposal for a new development for 20,000 people at the edge of the city in the borough of Freiham. The proposal defines itself as a 'catalyst of urbanisation' and suggests an incremental strategy of first introducing urban agriculture to the peri-urban site and later – up to 30 years later – the housing (Agropolis n.d.). The project has secured local support and enthusiasm, and, as a result, the project team has been commissioned by the city to develop a concept for temporary land use within the first building phase (Agropolis n.d.).

Urban designers tend to look at best practice in this subject area from local and spatial perspectives, because this most immediately informs their understanding of the tangible design consequences of urban agriculture.

However, there are also a number of nationwide initiatives contributing to the establishment of productive urban landscapes by setting up overarching or networked food growing projects or lending expertise or political and financial support to projects.

As an example, the privately funded charity *anstiftung & ertomis* has, since 2003, run the already-mentioned *Stiftung Interkultur* project focusing on intercultural gardens in Germany (anstiftung *n.d.* b). *Stiftung Interkultur* collects data about existing intercultural and community gardens and makes it publicly available. It researches and publishes on urban agriculture, especially its social and communal aspects, and supports many live and research projects financially and with its expertise.

Mundraub.org serves as an example for the working methods of a new generation of German urban food activists. Set up in 2009 as an online geo-tagging platform, this interactive inventory maps freely accessible and harvestable fruit trees by engaging the public as "fellow researchers". Originally started for Berlin and Brandenburg, the county around it, the project has spread very quickly across all of Germany and now has more than 8,000 registered users and includes almost 7,000 categorised fruit trees and shrubs (Terra Concordia *n.d.*).

Berlin

Currently, Berlin is the German city with the most diverse urban agricultural practice. This can be attributed to the capital's political history of the last 50 or so years as a green and left-wing stronghold, coupled with a sudden abundance of open urban (brownfield) space which fell or remained underused after the German reunification in 1990. The municipality is financially constrained. As in other German cities, space production linked with food production often has a political motive. Social productivity is also in the foreground of urban agriculture in Berlin, with most commercially oriented projects being social enterprises, usually practice-based, bottom-up and with strong relations/ negotiations to the municipality.

The Berlin-based *AG Kleinstlandwirtschaft* [Working Group for Small-scale Agriculture] is associated with the emergence of explicit urban agriculture in Germany in general. Set up in 1997 by a group of academic activists and urban gardeners, it summarises many preceding years of more dispersed discussions and actions. It has since been instrumental in developing a national theoretical platform for people who wish to use open urban space more productively in a social and ecological sense, as well as in actively supporting urban food-growing projects, mostly in the Berlin area. Since 1998, the *Working Group* has run an online information network that, since 2004, has been continued by the Berlin-based network *urbanacker* of which the *Working Group* is a founding member (AG Kleinstlandwirtschaft *n.d.*). *Urbanacker e.V.* and *AG Kleinstlandwirtschaft* make up the two strongest members of the extended and engaged Berlin grassroots network of gardening activists. Both grew out of actual conflicts over public space uses which sharpened their own, but also the council's view of urban agriculture.

The long history of communication between the Berlin Senate and the gardening activists' network has resulted in several promising experiments, one of which has been executed on the site of the former Tempelhof Airport, which closed in 2008. Having been awarded a 5,000 m^2 site at Tempelhof after a competition held by the Senate in 2010 (Sen Stadt 2010), a group of activists created in 2011 their most ambitious public and communal urban agriculture project yet, the *Allmende-Kontor*. Described by its founders as a 'platform for knowledge transfer and networking in urban agriculture' (Allmende-Kontor *n.d.*), *Allmende-Kontor* built a community garden in only three months with the help of several hundred volunteers (Meyer-Renschhausen 2012). The garden now serves as the physical base and expression of the networking platform and produces a variety of vegetables, herbs and flowers usually for consumption by the individual growers. The project attracted a lot of public and media interest and is promoted by the Senate as successful example of a series of temporary "pioneer projects" in the high-profile urban design discussions about new uses for the airfields (Tempelhofer Freiheit *n.d.*).

Community gardens [Gemeinschaftsgärten] are Berlin's most frequent form of urban agricultural activity. However, economically viable or commercially oriented schemes occupy more space than these in the city and, generally, focus more intensely on food outputs.

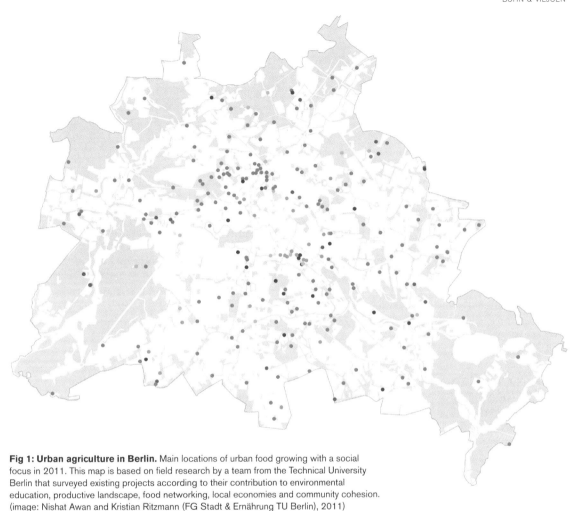

Fig 1: Urban agriculture in Berlin. Main locations of urban food growing with a social focus in 2011. This map is based on field research by a team from the Technical University Berlin that surveyed existing projects according to their contribution to environmental education, productive landscape, food networking, local economies and community cohesion. (image: Nishat Awan and Kristian Ritzmann (FG Stadt & Ernährung TU Berlin), 2011)

As mentioned before, these projects – run by about ten initiatives in total – mostly define themselves as social enterprises meaning that they pursue a social or not-for-profit goal in parallel with aiming to achieve financial independence.

Some of the most important economically viable projects in Berlin have already been described elsewhere in this book:

- *Agrarbörse Ost e.V.* who farm five sites within the city, the largest being the 100 ha *Landschaftspark Herzberge* with a focus on sheep farming (Agrarbörse *n.d.* b)
- The community garden *Prinzessinnengärten*, originally started in 2009 as *'nomadic urban agriculture'* on a temporarily-available, large inner-city site (Nomadisch Grün *n.d.*)
- *Efficient City Farming* project which, as part of a holistic environmental strategy for *Malzfabrik,* a large former industrial site, is currently proposing an extensive building-integrated aquaponic system (ECF *n.d.* b)

Additionally, as in many cities, there are various local enterprises growing, processing and marketing primary food products, mainly inside buildings, such as honey, mushrooms, herbs or mustard. The mushroom farm *Biopilze* is one example, growing organically certified oyster mushrooms in a building basement and selling them to local restaurants and individuals (Biopilzfarm *n.d.*).

Bauerngarten is a successful crossover of agricultural activity, environmental vision, commercial independence and urban lifestyles. This urban agriculture enterprise, set up in 2009 by two ecological agronomists, runs three sites in Berlin providing about 500 people with organic vegetables and herbs (Grafenstein *n.d.*). The entrepreneurs rent land from the city council, lay it out in a distinct circular pattern of individual plots and grow produce on it for Berliners who rent a plot, can participate as much as they wish and harvest crops at the end of the season.

Whilst urban agriculture initiatives in Berlin, both commercial and communal, are well networked into the city, their sites are generally not (yet). Usually, there is little spatial relationship between the food growing space and the space around it – think fence, gate or road – and no physical relation between the individual food-growing projects. Whilst this is not uncommon worldwide – urban agriculture sites usually are spatially dispersed and "fenced-in" – in Germany, this becomes especially apparent when studying the situation of the city's allotment sites within the urban fabric.

Allotments [Kleingärten] are the biggest urban food-producing entities in Berlin by number and total area. However, to non-members, these productive and green spaces in the city are often seen, but not directly experienced, because physical and invisible social boundaries prevent public access. Increasing the porosity of sites is beginning to happen and would – alongside enabling alternative infrastructures – also progress the development of their food systems potential, for example by generating more exchanges of produce.

Apart from the allotments, municipal farms [Stadtgüter] and farms within the city boundary [Stadtbauernhöfe] would have been the main urban food producers for cities in Germany before the change to today's industrialised food production which had its start in the 1950s. One such municipal farm is *Domäne Dahlem*. On 15 ha of land, it produces organically certified fruit, vegetables and animal products, sold in an on-site shop, as well as at local farmers' markets. Environmental protection and education is an important and integral part of the farm and attracts 300,000 visitors per year. Started in 1976, the project is one of the oldest in Berlin and is now run jointly by a county-owned foundation and a local interest group (Domäne Dahlem *n.d.*). *Domäne Dahlem* – about 100 years ago it was at the edge of the city – reminds Berliners of the city's geographical situation within the agriculturally active rural hinterland of Bundesland Brandenburg.

Community-supported agriculture (CSA) [Solidarische Landwirtschaft] in its original form is just emerging in Germany – around Berlin, there are now about five of these (SoLawi *n.d.*) – but, over the last 20 years, rural and urban initiatives in Berlin have developed their own linkages:

Meine ernte, a hybrid between CSA and the already described *Krautgärten* or *Bauerngarten* operates from two sites at the edge of Berlin. In these types of schemes, of which there are several in Berlin and other German cities, an external third party – here the registered association *meine ernte e.V.* – cooperates with a professional farm – here the *Gartenbaubetrieb Vogel* – and plants and manages individual vegetable plots on the farm's land. Berliners rent their plot from *meine ernte* and engage in the selection, care and harvest of the produce with the support of the association (meine ernte *n.d.*).

Ökodorf Brodowin is the best-known example in Berlin of the box-scheme type of rural–urban exchange where a local rural farm provides city dwellers with a regular supply of produce, often brought to the doorstep. About 12 such schemes exist in Berlin (FÖL *n.d.*). *Brodowin* farm produces 25 types of vegetables, potatoes, grain, milk, eggs and meat to Demeter standards on its 1300 ha farm 60 km outside of the capital (Brodowin *n.d.*). Running successfully since the mid-1990s, the farm now delivers to 1700 Berlin households and children's nurseries per week through its vegetable boxes *Brodowiner Ökokörbe*, as well as selling their produce in an on-site shop (Brodowin 2011).

An important step towards a regional food system is the *VON HIER* project, a retail and marketing initiative aiming to increase the proportion of regional food products in some of the major supermarkets in Berlin and Brandenburg. Set up in 2007 by local producers and retailers with the support of both county council's branches of Local Agenda 21 as well as other stakeholders, *VON HIER* encourages supermarkets to ensure that by 2020 about a third of sold edibles will have been procured from local producers. At the moment, about 30 regional producers sell their food products under the label *VON HIER* within this scheme (BBM *n.d.*).

Some newer commercial initiatives are equally encouraging, and the outstanding example is *Markthalle Neun* established in 2011 in one of Berlin's few remaining food market halls. Cutting out the middle man, *Markthalle Neun* gives a steadily growing number of local small-scale producers the chance to sell their fresh or freshly processed produce during market days or special events. After a year, due to demand, the regular market days were increased from one to two per week (Markthalle Neun *n.d.*).

Encouraging a more even distribution of farmers' markets is one of the aims of several Berlin-based initiatives, such as Slow Food Berlin, in order to enable more Berliners to buy fresh produce locally, both from rural and urban producers (Slow Food *n.d.*). As noted, these actions have just started to be considered in relation to planning developments. Their potential integration into a planned and designed productive urban landscape would not only physically connect people to produce and production, but also provide the spatial framework from which to envision a sustainable future for Germany's capital.

Conclusion: the promising beginnings of municipal and planning support

As is the case elsewhere in Germany, Berlin does not yet have a Food Board or Food Policy Council. However, a local "good food" campaign group is just about to emerge out of initiatives by the Berlin convivium of Slow Food Germany who, according to Pamela Dorsch, one of its leaders, is developing this with interested partners and inhabitants (personal communication Sep 2012).

Berlin's Senate Department for Urban Development and the Environment [Senatsverwaltung für Stadtentwicklung und Umwelt] publicly presented its draft "green vision" for the German capital's open space planning in September 2010. Adopting what we might call a "top-down responsive" approach, in 2009, a team of

two landscape architecture practices started working on the draft supported by a series of think tanks to which, amongst many others, urban agriculture and productive urban landscape experts contributed. Following public presentation, Berlin residents were invited to comment on the draft strategy. Comments were taken into account, and the final *Strategie Stadtlandschaft* [Urban Landscape Strategy] was adopted by the Senate and made publicly available in Spring 2012. Whilst the document's recommendations cannot be enforced, they provide a thorough and strategic orientation for any open urban space development in Berlin up to the year 2050 (SenStadt 2012). The strategy's subtitle is 'natural. urban. productive.' is mirroring the three main directions in which the city seeks to direct its future open space planning. The document's recommendations do not demand urban agriculture, but explicitly include it as a recognised land use under the heading 'productive'. 'Productive' is here described as 'an urban interpretation of the cultured landscape, of open space, that is generated not only through its designers, but equally through its users' (Giseke 2010). This inclusion of productive spaces into the planning and development strategy is significant for Berlin and Germany, and for the urban agriculture discourse in general.

Finally, the urban agriculture examples in this chapter represent *the start of a process which is specific to Germany*. All parts of this description are significant: that there is a process which has started; that this process is specific to its local context(s); that it is generating a variety of enjoyable and replicable examples; and that all of this is about urban agriculture and hence, by definition, about productive urban landscapes, and about finding ways to a sustainable urban future.

Green theory in practice and urban design: The United Kingdom

Katrin Bohn and André Viljoen

This chapter continues with an overview of how, with different approaches to those in Germany, urban agriculture is developing and being embedded within the UK. Compared to Germany, urban agriculture has been less theorised in the UK, but with respect to implementation, as for example evidenced in its wider food policy initiatives (see chapter *The new urban foodscape*, p. 18), the UK is more advanced. Both countries have many projects based around community gardening and allotment culture, but the academic and societal framework for these is different: when looking at community gardens, the German approach is more politically driven, for example with a focus on building opportunities for intercultural exchanges, whereas the UK focus is more generally directed towards environmental education and urban space production. If we compare allotments and their German equivalent, *Kleingärten*, both have national organisations representing their interests, but the political influence held by the German gardeners is far greater and probably more conservative than that held by UK allotment holders. If community gardens are excluded, the UK has a longer tradition of establishing broad-based, one-off, bottom-up, food-related initiatives, stretching back at least to the 1970s with the establishment of the rural-based *Centre for Alternative Technology* in Wales, which put food and energy production on an equal footing, and continuing with initiatives like the 1990s *Hockerton Housing* project in Nottinghamshire in the north of England. *Growing Communities* (see chapter *Productive life in the city*, p. 40) represents the social enterprise end of the scale, while more recent urban food projects include the much-publicised market town communal project *Incredible Edible Todmorden*, and the *Social Platform for Urban Agriculture* in Leeds.

With this in mind, the previous chapter records the more recent development of urban agriculture theory and practice in Germany in general, while this chapter concentrates on the specific processes leading to the establishment of two significant food-related projects in the UK's largest city, London.

London already benefits from having the *London Food Board* and the food charity *Sustain: the alliance for better food and farming*. Sustain (bottom-up) has a national remit, but is very active in London, both with respect to advocacy and delivery of food-related projects. It is a charity and limited company representing a wide alliance of food groups advocating more sustainable and socially equitable food systems within the UK, Europe and beyond (Sustain 2011). The London Food Board (top-down) is 'an advisory group of independent food policy organisations and experts which oversees the implementation of *The Mayor's Food Strategy: Healthy and Sustainable Food for London*, published in 2006, and coordinates work and leads the debate on sustainable food issues in the Capital' (Mayor of London n.d.). Both organisations are active in the policy arena and in raising municipal and institutional awareness of sustainable food systems. They are now in a position to push for the implementation of urban agriculture projects.

Of the two food-related projects we are looking at, one – *Capital Growth* – follows a creative top-down approach, and the other – *Transition Town Brixton* – is one of the most active bottom-up initiatives developed within the Transition Towns movement. Both take the individual urban agriculture project to a new level, thereby supporting and informing the beginning UK food policy discourse.

Capital Growth

Capital Growth was a programme initiated in 2008 to create 2,012 new food growing spaces in London by 2012. Although *Capital Growth* had no official connection to the London Olympics that were staged in 2012, it was generally perceived as an "Olympics" project.

There are parallel narratives as to who initiated the idea for *Capital Growth*. The official view is that it was inspired by Vancouver Food Policy Council's *2010 Challenge* aiming for 2,010 new community-shared garden plots by 2010 (Capital Growth *n.d.*). The policy report *Feeding the Olympics*, published in 2007, argued that sustainable food supply should be integral to the organisers' goal of creating 'the greenest Olympics', including a commitment to create 2,012 new food growing sites. Another inspiration came from the architect Fritz Haeg, who in 2007 issued his manifesto for 'a new extreme summer event: Olympic Farming' (Haeg and Au 2007). Haeg's proposal was first presented in Tate Modern as part of their 2007 *Global Cities* exhibition and subsequently at London's City Hall in 2008 during the *Growing Food for London* conference. Haeg's manifesto was shown as an upbeat and playful vision for London, where over 6,000 acres [2,500 hectares] would be farmed organically by so-called 'Olympic farmers' supplying all the needs of the Games, and then, 'after the summer of 2012, London residents will inherit a spectacular network of urban pleasure gardens that will feed them with the seasons, instead of empty monumental shells erected for a moment of global vanity' (Haeg and Au 2007).

The *Growing Food for London* conference presented far more than the Olympic Gardening manifesto. It included context-setting papers by Joe Nasr and June Komisar (see chapter *Urban Agriculture as ordinary urban practice*, p. 24) and covered major topics such as training, business models, access to land and future visioning. As one of London's first urban agriculture conferences, it had been initiated and hosted by London Food Link and benefited from Sustain's capacity to bring together a number of London's main sustainable food stakeholders, including Bohn&Viljoen Architects, to plan the conference.

The conference coincided with the election of Boris Johnson as Mayor of London, whereby his victory as a representative of the Conservative Party resulted in some uncertainty as to how London's food policy would be advanced. Attending the conference, Boris Johnston announced his support for its aims and for increased food growing in London. Shortly thereafter, he appointed Rosie Boycott, well known as a feminist and journalist, as chairperson of the London Food Board, the previously mentioned advisory board for The Mayor's food policy.

At about the same time, *Capital Growth* was announced, the title being a playful twist on London's role as a centre for global capital, its conservative business agenda and a call for urban food growing. *Capital Growth* took a less radical approach than that advocated by Fritz Haeg, but none the less now benefited from a back-story to which he contributed. This back-story includes a very active local charity, the *Bankside Open Spaces Trust (BOST)*, that had established a number of successful food-centred community gardens in the area surrounding London's City Hall and Tate Modern. Working in conjunction with Tate Modern and the Architecture Foundation for their 2007 *Global Cities* exhibition, Fritz Haeg was commissioned to create, jointly with local residents, an edible landscape on a site chosen by BOST: the *Brockwood Edible Estate*. This project on a formerly underutilised lawn in front of the Brockwood Housing Estate, south of Tate Modern, gave additional legitimacy to the concept of urban food gardens although the estate's residents took some time to accept that it would be realised and not suffer from vandalism. Its new landscape now forms part of Haeg's *Edible Estates* project, that transforms domestic lawns into productive fields for urban agriculture. Until then *Edible Estates* had been based solely in the USA and the *Brockwood Edible Estate* became a precedent for the *Capital Growth* projects to follow.

While the Mayor of London provided the visible figurehead and initial funding to promote *Capital Growth*, it was delivered as a project by *Sustain: the alliance for better food and farming*. Working with support from the London Development Agency, the Mayor and several other food-related organisations, *Sustain*, via its London Food Link network, won funding from the UK National Lottery's Local Food Fund to facilitate a comprehensive support structure for inviting Londoners to apply for small grants to establish new community food growing initiatives. Salaried staff, interns and volunteers worked with Sustain/London Food Link to advertise the *Capital Growth* project, invite applications for funding, review all applications for viability, provide guidance and basic training, and later monitor the successful applicants' performance. Curiously, this creative top-down approach followed – with less external pressures and more modestly – processes that were similarly seen in Cuba when,

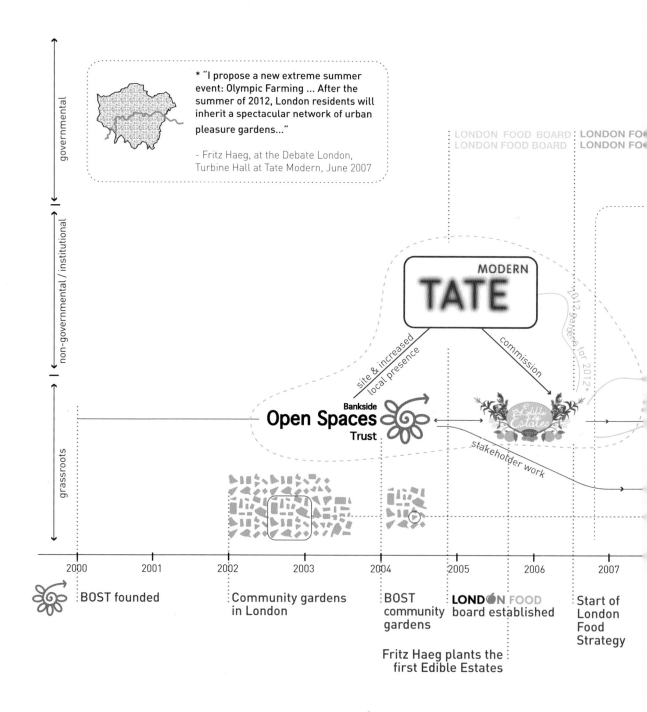

* "I propose a new extreme summer
event: Olympic Farming ... After the
summer of 2012, London residents will
inherit a spectacular network of urban
pleasure gardens..."

- Fritz Haeg, at the Debate London,
Turbine Hall at Tate Modern, June 2007

LONDON FOOD BOARD   LONDON FOO
LONDON FOOD BOARD   LONDON FO

governmental

non-governmental / institutional

grassroots

MODERN
TATE

site & increased
local presence

commission

2012 gardens for 2012 *

Bankside
Open Spaces
Trust

Edible
Estates

stakeholder work

2000   2001   2002   2003   2004   2005   2006   2007

BOST founded

Community gardens
in London

BOST
community
gardens

LONDON FOOD
board established

Start of
London
Food
Strategy

Fritz Haeg plants the
first Edible Estates

102

**Fig 1: A process diagram
for *Capital Growth*.**
Design research analysing
and visualising the multiple
interdependencies that lead
to the establishment of Urban
Agriculture Berlin projects.
Undertaken jointly with the
department City and Nutrition
at the Technical University.
(image: Bohn&Viljoen and
Nishat Awan (FG Stadt &
Ernährung TU Berlin), 2012)

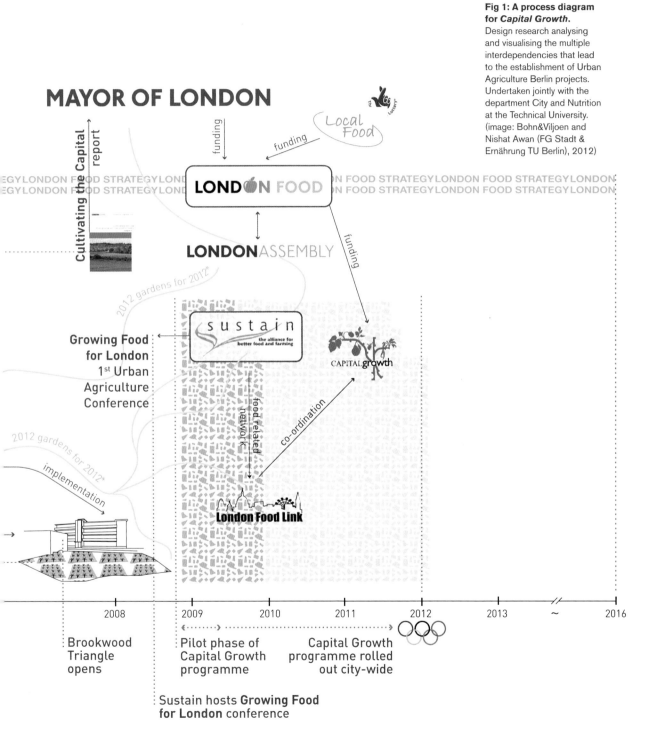

after the collapse of the Soviet Union, the country initiated a coordinated urban agriculture programme.

During 2012, *Capital Growth* achieved its target of 2,012 new food growing sites and was extremely effective in raising the profile of urban agriculture in London. Whilst it appears to sometimes have been difficult to maintain consistency of output from individual food growing sites, enough projects have succeeded to, in our view, judge it a worthwhile programme. In addition to supporting community food growing and community building, it also promoted experimentation, for example by means of prototype installations, such as our *Growing Balconies* project (see the second part of this book).

As a legacy, *Capital Growth* continues post-2012 with a now far greater emphasis on promoting yields from sites. To do this, it has borrowed the citizen scientist approach piloted by the New-York-based project *Farming Concrete* (see chapter *Productive life in the city*, p. 40). Several *Capital Growth* projects, such as *Blenheim Gardens Edible Estate* in Brixton, referred to below, continue as successful urban food-producing spaces. Regarding food growing and the Olympics' site, we and contributing author Dr Howard Lee, in 2012 – following an invitation by Jenny Jones, representing the Green Party in the London Assembly and a former Deputy Mayor of London – have been briefing the London Legacy Development Corporation on strategies for integrating urban agriculture into the former Olympic site.

Transition Town Brixton

Benefiting from *Capital Growth*, but older and independent, *Transition Town Brixton* was established in 2008, it has a longer history that closely tracks the development of the Transition Towns movement, of which it is a part. The movement owes its origins in 2005 to a permaculture course run by Rob Hopkins in Kinsale, Ireland, which resulted in the development of an Energy Decent Plan for the local council. Soon after, in 2006, the establishment of *Transition Town Totnes* in the UK led to the formation of the Transition Town Network, 'To support community-led responses to peak oil and climate change, building resilience and happiness' (Transition Network 2012). Food security and food sovereignty are

common starting points for community action when Transition Town groups are established, and reference is frequently made to urban agriculture in Cuba. By 2009 over 120 Transition initiatives had been identified in the UK and beyond, including the one in Brixton (Transition Network 2012).

Brixton is a district in the South London borough of Lambeth. It has a rich and diverse history that ranges from having London's first street with electric lighting, Electric Avenue, to less benign memories of the 1981 Brixton Riots, driven by racial tension, overlaid with economic, social and political inequalities. It is an area with great variations in wealth, ethnic and cultural diversity.

In 2007, shortly after the founding of the Transition Network, the Lambeth Climate Action Group was established, which led to the founding of *Transition Town Brixton* during 2008. During the intervening period between 2007 and 2008, projects by academics, artists and residents took different approaches to establishing localised and ecological approaches to food production.

One of the most important urban agriculture initiatives explicitly working to build capacity in *Transition Town Brixton* was initiated by Robert Biel and Yves Cabannes, academics from University College London's (UCL) Development Planning Unit. Called *ABUNDANCE* (Activating Blighted Urban Niches for Daring Agricultural Networks of Creativity and Endeavour), this project was funded for one year by UCL's knowledge transfer initiative *Urban Buzz*. It was set up as a top-down/ bottom-up initiative between UCL, *Transition Town Brixton* activists and the resident's association of a Guinness Trust Housing Estate in Brixton, the chosen site for the food growing. Three aims had been set for its year-long funding period: mapping potential urban agriculture sites; growing food and; demonstrating urban agriculture in action. Four legacy goals were set: to influence local authority policy; build community knowledge; reappraise city living; and provide a live example of transition. The launch in late 2007 was well advertised and upbeat in its projections for future growing on the selected estate and beyond (UCL Development Planning Unit 2007). While over 300 people attended the launch and the project has had a long-term impact on food growing and sustainable food practice in Brixton, it is also true to say that not all of its envisaged aims and goals were met. This is not unusual in pioneering projects, and a very useful and reflective post-project evaluation provides good guidance on lessons learnt for future projects (Noy 2009). Headline conclusions are that one year is a very short period in which to set up an ambitious urban agriculture project – this is just one growing season in the UK – but even more important is the need to establish strong community buy-in at the planning stage, prior to any launch. Noy recommends undertaking a needs assessment with residents in the area as well as clearly identifying existing resources and capacities with which to work.

Although *ABUNDANCE* did not produce as much food as envisaged, it did lead to the later establishment of two growing sites with support from *Capital Growth* at Blenheim Gardens and the Tulse Hill estate. Additionally *Transition Town Brixton* established a database of growing initiatives in the area. It has also influenced local policy development, such as whenLambeth Council produced a "Credit Crunch Report" advocating that 'The council should promote and expand food growing groups and networks in the Borough'. The council also mentioned food growing in its regeneration master plan, *Future Brixton*. Beyond these achievements the feedback from those residents who did start to grow food is positive (Noy 2009).

As well as projects with explicit urban agriculture agendas, ones with a more diffuse arts-based urban food focus, such as one called "Invisible Food", alerted people to wild and edible plants already growing within the city (Buck 2009).

Alongside these and other non-food-related actions, *Transition Town Brixton* established a number of sub-groups dealing with specific issues, such as transport, recycling and energy use. The introduction of a local currency, the Brixton Pound, followed to encourage trade within the borough (The Brixton Pound *n.d.*). During 2010 *Transition Town Brixton* continued to consolidate its position within, by becoming a community interest company with the objective of furthering and supporting its members' aims and objectives.

As this book goes to print, *Transition Town Brixton* remains very active within the borough, new community growing areas have been established and its food group pursues a number of activities to promote sustainable local food. By using a well organised and structured approach that values networking open to participation by all and is willing to work with the local council, *Transition Town Brixton* has managed to embed, make visible and raise a dialogue about food and energy transition within a large London borough. In the future, as with many alternative movements, the question will be how these many Transition Towns transition to the mainstream.

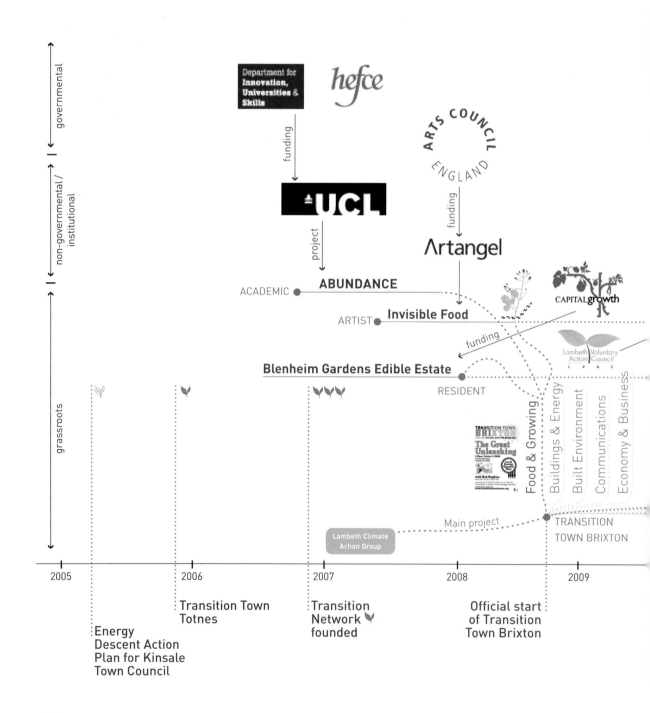

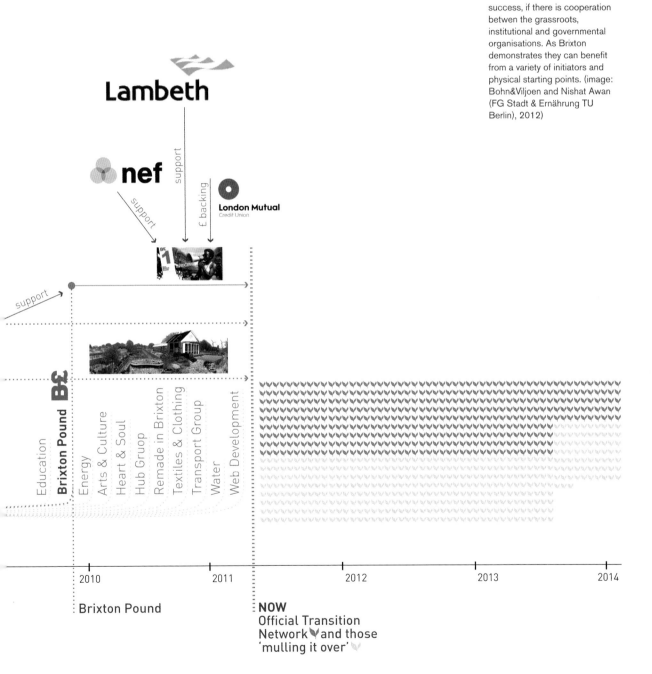

Fig 2: A process diagram for Transition Town Brixton.
Urban agriculture projects increase their chances of success, if there is cooperation betwen the grassroots, institutional and governmental organisations. As Brixton demonstrates they can benefit from a variety of initiators and physical starting points. (image: Bohn&Viljoen and Nishat Awan (FG Stadt & Ernährung TU Berlin), 2012)

Agential exchanges: Thinking the empirical in relation to productivity

Nishat Awan

From a peripheral activity, urban agriculture seems to be on the verge of becoming mainstream. This could be due to a raised awareness of the environmental crisis, economic pressures, as well as the looming health crisis of higher global obesity rates (James *et al.* 2001). At this important moment, it may be useful to revisit certain assumptions related to what type of activity urban agriculture is, or could become. Through a close reading of historical examples initiated in response to the last major crisis, the 1970s oil crisis, and other more recent examples, this essay will explore questions of productivity, the artificial separation of nature and culture, notions of the empirical and the question of agency. It will also speculate on the role of design in making socio-spatial interventions within urban food-growing practices. In particular, the essay will make the point that due to the combined pressures of the multiple crises we face today, and the desire to make change quickly, certain important aspects of earlier responses are now in danger of being overlooked. These include notions of self-provisioning, inventiveness, the use of technology as a social and situated practice, and an economy based on use value.

Productivity

For large cities, such as London, an important factor is the extreme pressure on land and the need to secure areas for food growing. This can easily translate to questions of productivity: how many tomatoes can be produced in a given space; how much water do they need? A more nuanced definition of productivity would not simply equate to quantifiables, such as yields, but would also refer to social productivity, or changes in behaviour and health. Unpacking the notion of productivity also raises questions, such as who produces and for whom, and asks what types of value this production embodies. How to define productivity is an especially problematic

endeavour in relation to modes of capitalist exchange. As Marx's analysis revealed, the accumulation of wealth is based on the production of surplus value produced through workers' labour; yet it is the same system that does not value reproductive labour, or those exchanges that occur within the domestic sphere. In Marxist analysis, the distinction being made here is that between 'exchange value', that is, whether something can be quantified according to how many of this is the equivalent to that, and 'use value', which is about qualitative judgement and encompasses different ways of using and placing value on things (Goodbun 2001).

Whilst urban agriculture includes a whole spectrum of initiatives – from the market garden run as an enterprise to community gardens that are less about food production than about the production of social space – in relation to urban food growing, the distinction between exchange value and use value is important, as it marks the radical edge of such initiatives. As urban agriculture in its new popular mode is looking to become more mainstream, it seems in some cases to be shifting from use value to exchange value. Many of the new projects are beginning to think in terms of economies of scale, surplus value and the creation of commodities. It is also often thought that this is only correct in times of crisis: in order to make real change, urban agriculture needs to become part of the wider economy and to therefore be able to produce value in terms of exchange. But the real battle lies in deciding what that value is. As the proponents of ecological thinking have often repeated, processes of commodification that are at the basis of capitalist exchange rely on those things that capital does not value, such as air and water, considered to be both infinite and free. So, it would seem important for urban agriculture to work within a system that *does* place value on the air, on water, on the quality of soil, etc., but that this should not be measured in terms of monetary value. Whilst initiatives such as the carbon tax do try to place non-monetary value on our common pool resources, what is required is a more radical approach which, rather than working within a system that has proven to be so completely flawed, tries instead to imagine another way. Considering such resources through an understanding of their use value reveals the need for a very different system of valuation, one that is both communal and able to make connections on a planetary scale. Here, the contemporary discourse on the commons (Hardt and Negri 2009) provides a way of thinking about the air, water, etc. not just as resources, but as relations. How we manage and place value on these has to be considered as a series of dynamic and negotiated relations between communities and places, in particular as trans-local relations that connect diverse localities and communities across distances (Atelier d'Architecture Autogerée 2012a).

It is interesting to note that the last major crisis in the so-called developed world, the 1970s oil crisis, resulted in a set of propositions also trying to work with the notion of what could be common, particularly in terms of knowledge and know-how. Many saw this as an opportunity to reset our relations to the planet and to each other. In these responses, the change in lifestyle required to be less dependent on oil was intimately linked to new economic models based on use value over exchange value. One of the most famous of these was the *Whole Earth Catalog*, published regularly between 1968 and 1972 and later carrying on in various guises (Brand 1968–72). The *Catalog* embraced systems theory; it was a manual and an address book for self-provisioning. There was nothing for sale in the *Catalog*, instead they were a repository of information, giving contact details of retailers, prices for items, facilitating access. Its DIY approach valorised the amateur through providing what the *Catalog*'s strap line called 'access to tools'. Through making this information available at a nominal price, the *Catalog* anticipated the creative commons movement through democratising access to knowledge. For this reason, it has been referred to as a conceptual forerunner to the internet. The scope of the *Catalog* is demonstrated by the range of information in the 1968 edition, which, on one page, included a review of a comprehensive book on organic gardening, instructions on how to grow mushrooms intensively in a stacked system, and ideas on how to start beekeeping. Another page gave detailed instructions on making a Chinese horizontal windmill and another on how to make a

simple and inexpensive solar water heater (Brand 1968: 22, 29, 31). As these examples illustrate, the emphasis of the *Whole Earth Catalog* was on inventiveness and making do. However, being a product of its time and emerging from the US context of individualisation, what the *Whole Earth Catalog* and the counter-cultural movement that it was a part of failed to do was think how these individual efforts might become common. Beyond the idea of a commune or a self-sufficient community, what was not addressed was how these could also make relations across diverse communities. Here, the discourse on the commons and the importance of making trans-local connections again provides a useful starting point.

Natures–cultures

The period of the late 1960s and early 1970s produced many other projects that dealt with questions of food growing, ecology and our relations to the planet. These projects, alongside the *Whole Earth Catalog*, are useful to refer to today for the very specific ways in which they mobilised new technologies and in how they addressed the crucial question of production. Etymologically, 'to produce' is defined as 'to develop, be extended', or 'lead or bring forth, draw out' (Harper 2001–12). It is only later that the meaning of the word shifts towards 'bring into being' (Harper 2001–12). This is an important evolution: whereas 'developing' or 'bringing forth' are expressions embedded in the world around us, 'bringing into being' has all the tendencies of the God-like human subject; creating food, taming nature, but remaining separate in the sphere of culture that encompasses human activity.

This separation of nature from culture is the basis of Bruno Latour's critique of the modern condition, which could also be described as separating the human from the environment or the subject from the object. For Latour, this edifice is constructed through two sets of interlocking practices, which are named 'the work of translation' and 'the work of purification' (Latour 1993: 49–90). The work of translation creates hybrids of nature and culture, while the work of purification separates them – the two practices working in tandem to create the modern illusion of the total separation of nature from culture, whilst producing lots of amalgamations of the two in the form of 'natures–cultures'. What this process does not take into account is 'the work of mediation' that takes place between the two poles of nature and culture, a role Latour assigns to what he calls 'quasi-objects/quasi-subjects'. He claims that the modern condition turns 'full-blown mediators into mere intermediaries. An intermediary, although recognised as necessary, simply transports, transfers, transmits energy [...] A mediator, however, is an original event and creates what it translates as well as the entities between which it plays the mediating role' (Latour 1993: 77–78). This means that the practice of mediation is a knowledge-making practice embedded in the world around us.

One of the most inspiring practices of the late 1960s acted in the role of mediator that Latour has described through acknowledging that productivity in the context of ecological practices has to always be in the mode of the production of natures–cultures. The *New Alchemy Institute* was a research centre founded in 1969 by two marine biologists, John Todd and William McLarney, and an artist, Nancy Jack Todd. It is perhaps this combination of interests that led to their unique approach of combining detailed scientific knowledge with farming practices, design and architecture. In the context of the newly flourishing environmental movement, their approach was based on a critique of modern industrial agricultural processes in order to find energy-efficient, integrated systems of living that could operate in harmony with the planet. They produced a series of 'living machines' that took their inspiration from wetland ecologies, but were reproduced using the latest technology.

The New Alchemists pioneered a number of intensive farming techniques that worked through creating cycles of use and reuse and they developed a viable practice of aquaculture; fish farming in a system that both housed the fish and also fed them. They chose to use the African fish Tilapia, now available readily but barely known at the time. Tilapia was chosen as it is a hardy fish, and when it was farmed using the aquacultures developed at the *New Alchemy Institute*, it dramatically increased the amount of protein in the system. Aquaculture was developed specifically with this goal: to be used in areas that suffered from malnutrition. In a recent lecture, Nancy Todd stated that a number of countries in Africa

are considering installing aquaculture systems similar to those developed at the *New Alchemy Institute* (Todd 2005). In fact, many of the ideas first researched and practised there are now seen as standard ecological design practice, such as the use of composting toilets, the purification of water using plants, solar collectors, or composting greenhouses, which were a modern adaptation of the centuries-old French method of heating glass cloches with horse manure.

What is apparent from these examples is an easy relationship to the technological, without any of the hesitations that arise from separating disciplines and approaches. There was also a generosity to these acts, as all the information and techniques developed were readily available and described in detail in the *Journal of the New Alchemists* in the hope that others would replicate and extend their experiments.

The empirical

Approaches to urban agriculture are often also polarised between the qualitative and the quantitative, but the edge between what is quantitatively determined and what is qualitatively determined is often fraught. Aspects such as yields, soil quality, etc. are important topics of research, both academic and practised, but how they intersect with more qualitative information about who looks after the plants, how often and in what circumstances is difficult to encapsulate. Whilst there are exceptions, such as the CPUL concept, often on one side of the debate are those that advocate the making of social spaces of exchange that change the way we think and our relations to the environment, and on the other are those that try to maximise yields and integrate food growing into urban planning. In addressing this dichotomy, it is useful to refer to recent research in the social sciences on the inventive capacity of numbers (Guyer 2010). Often in architectural research and practice, the empirical is equated with the quantifiable; that is, the practice of ordering but, as Helen Verran amongst many others claims, numbers not only have the capacity to order, but also to value. Verran argues this, for her numbers embody 'materialised relations', forming 'an inventive frontier in social, cultural, political and moral life' (Verran 2010: 171). Thus the process of enumeration itself is a transformative activity, and numbers have an impact on that which they address.

Verran identifies two different ways numbers are mobilised: as icons or as representation. As representation, numbers can be used by gardeners to quantify harvests of fruit and vegetables of a given area, what is commonly referred to as yield. In other circumstances, those same numbers can perform very differently as they shift into iconic mode: the data on yields, perhaps collected informally by growers, could be mobilised to inform a market for the trading of fruit and vegetables as commodity. The much-vaunted *Capital Growth* programme in London uses numbers exactly as icons: 2,012 gardens were to be established for the year 2012, coinciding with the Olympics in London (Capital Growth *n.d.* b). Once again, what is removed from such uses of number is the crucial question of value, which in this case is related to the important issue of how to sustain those 2,012 gardens. How many people will be required to look after them, and will they carry on doing so once the funding and interest runs out?

For Verran, the main difference in the way numbers perform are the types of relations they embody, taking the form of one/many or whole/parts. These relations are a 'way of asking whether a number is a cardinal number and works to conserve value by working the one/many form, or an ordinal number working to conserve order through the whole/parts form' (Verran 2010: 173). This can also be described as a move from multiplicity to homogeneity, that is, taking a series of specific instances and bringing them together in a multiplicity (one/many), or – starting the other way round – taking the whole and describing the individual elements as subordinate to it (whole/parts). For the *Capital Growth* project, for example, it is the shift from thinking of these projects as individual efforts by groups and communities that could be brought together under one umbrella to thinking of them as existing only as and of that project. This is important as it takes a grassroots, community-led and -initiated project and co-opts it into a centralised initiative. Value is bestowed through being affiliated to the *Capital Growth* project rather than through recognising the power of the specific grassroots initiatives and making policy that supports them. Conserving order through reference to an external metric, such as the arbitrary 2,012 gardens, is exactly the way

in which capitalist modes of exchange work, whether it is the water systems that Verran writes about or the agricultural systems of concern here.

An example of a recent project that engages numbers' capacity to materialise relations rather than acting as iconographic signs is the *R-Urban* project by Atelier d'Architecture Autogerée (AAA). Designed as a strategy for retrofitting cities to deal with the growing ecological crisis, it is based around what AAA have termed 'Recycle, Reuse, Repair, Re-think' (Petcou and Petrescu 2012: 64). The project is based in Colombes, a Parisian suburb, and is conceived, as the name of the project suggests, as a mediator between the rural and the urban. The project uses lots of numbers: to quantify carbon dioxide emissions, numbers of jobs created, percentage of waste recycled or water consumed. Each time numbers are used in the project, they not only perform the function of ordering, but they give an indication of value. In the cycles of waste, consumption, construction, food, etc., what is foregrounded is the way in which these practices of enumeration create certain social, ecological and political effects. Numbers are used with a full knowledge of their capacity to mediate in these relations; they are neither thought of as neutral nor passive. Numbers are mobilised to serve a purpose that is explicit.

Agency

Alongside questions of value are those of agency and the *R-Urban* project foregrounds the importance of participative strategies and the importance of thinking of urban agriculture as one aspect of a wider strategy of resilience that encompasses social and economic aspects. The term 'agency' also foregrounds the role of practitioners, such as AAA, who act as initiators or agents for alternative practices in the city. A recent book describes 'spatial agents' as 'neither impotent nor all powerful: they are negotiators of existing conditions in order to partially reform them' (Awan *et al.* 2011: 31). Whilst this comment is made primarily on the role of architects as spatial agents, it could equally be true of the other inhabitants of space who transform it in some way, or act in it in another way. To act with agency is to have a degree of power, to be able to articulate and legitimise certain ways of inhabiting space. 'Agency' also encompasses questions related to *who* is able to act otherwise in the city. Whilst this includes questions of cultural confidence, such as who has the privilege of visibility in a society where the other is excluded, it also includes practical questions of knowing *how* to claim a space. In order to set up a space for growing, do you squat in a vacant plot or do you apply for planning permission? Who is allowed temporary uses and who is not? Whilst the first concern relates to questions of subjectivity, the second is more technical. Architects often deal with the second, setting up spaces for communities to use, but, since the first question is left unaddressed, often projects remain underused or are even destroyed in more difficult contexts.[1]

There is a whole range of recent initiatives where people are claiming space for themselves, one such example from Germany is the *Perivoli* garden in Berlin-Neukölln (anstiftung *n.d.* c). Initiated in 2002 by a group of senior Greek women, *Perivoli* sits in the midst of a large area of *Kleingärten* [allotments]. The *Kleingärtenkolonie* is common across Germany, consisting of areas of equally sized, often largely identical rectangular plots that form a uniform patchwork of gardens with well-groomed lawns, fences and a large room or shed at the back. Whilst parallels can be made to the English allotment, the *Kleingärten* are more common, define a certain German lifestyle and are also usually more ornamental. The *Perivoli* garden feels very different from the traditional *Kleingärten*; in the simple spatial move of taking off the fences that demarcate the individual family plots, *Perivoli* announces a different way of thinking about the use of open space – as communal rather than individual. In contrast to the Kleingärten, which are usually not productive spaces but more related to ideas of relaxation and retreat, *Perivoli* is a space of collective production.

In comparison to initiatives led by architects, *Perivoli* works at a more informal level. It is self-managed, as the women who initiated it are still very much in charge of the space. They use their knowledge of small-scale growing practices and transmit it to younger members through spending time in the garden. This type of inter-generational exchange is often based around strong family and friendship ties and it is no different at *Perivoli*. Perhaps the most difficult aspect for places such as *Perivoli* is to keep them open and inviting for others, since groups based around a shared ethnicity or national background are inherently exclusive. Yet, they are also a necessary step towards agency, especially in a society where questions of multiculturalism and diversity are still problematic. *Perivoli* is now at a point of transition: the women who run the garden have an agency which could be used to invite others in by shifting the garden's emphasis from shared ethnicity to shared interests. In fact, this is already beginning to happen with a beekeeping initiative, which required the skills of others beyond the immediate group.

What emerges from the examples of *Perivoli* and *R-Urban* is that urban food-growing initiatives are well placed to contribute towards a wider goal of changing lifestyles in response to our planetary crisis, but in order to do this they must necessarily be about much more than the growing of food. Whilst it is an important factor, food growing can also be understood as a foil for wider questions of agency and responsibility in our relationships to the planet and to each other. How far we are able to think along the chain of interdependencies often depends on specific circumstances, but what is clear is that these circumstances are in flux. The women of *Perivoli* who started as members of a marginal community now have an agency that can include others within a space they have claimed, whilst AAA hope that the marginalised suburban residents of Colombes, through being involved in the setting up and management of the strategy for their area, will lead the way in retrofitting cities through a trans-local research centre (Atelier d'Architecture Autogerée 2012b).

Agential exchanges

Much of the discussion in this essay has been based around a series of false dichotomies, where one side is often given more value than the other. The distinctions between use value and exchange value create a situation where the production of commodities takes precedence over all other types of production. In the battle between nature and culture, what is obscured are the real opportunities for inventiveness and change that occur through an understanding of the hybridised nature of the interdependent world in which we live. This is nowhere more apparent than in the distinctions between approaches that couch themselves as qualitative or quantitative, meaning that numbers are able to perform as icons and obscure important questions of value, whilst the potential of the empirical as creating synergies between these two approaches is left unrealised.

Notions of agency must also be reconceptualised in this context as encompassing more than the human subject. Karen Barad's concept of 'agential realism' extends agency beyond the human subject through foregrounding the performative capabilities of objects, molecules, and entities of all kinds... (Barad 2007: 132–85). Just as Verran's understanding of numbers as materialised relations describes numbers as performative, agential realism defines agency first and foremost as a relation. It does not reside in the individual subject but emerges through relational exchanges. The New Alchemists understood this: for them, agency was located as much within the synergies between members of the group as it was between the fish and the plants, or as it emerged in the knowledge commons created through the distribution of their journal.

The approach outlined in this chapter acknowledges the entwined relations between science and culture and raises questions around the nature of measurement and value. In a world where targets must be met, or yields counted, questioning the very nature of measurement – of instruments as performative social and physical apparatus – allows for a more nuanced understanding of what could be considered a 'success'; how much production is productive enough?

Note

1   A practice that understands this dynamic well is muf architecture/art, whose Tilbury community garden and park project was set up in the context of vandalism of previous projects. muf's long-term participation strategy ensured that their project survived where the others had not (Long 2005).

Shrinking cities and productive urban landscapes

Philipp Oswalt in an interview with Bohn & Viljoen

The world is urbanising, albeit unevenly: across the globe, some cities expand whilst others contract. However, some cities are facing persistent negative growth – the phenomenon of Shrinking Cities – which demands not temporary solutions, but wide-reaching visions and encouraging opportunities. From the body of your research, we are especially interested in your work concerning shrinking cities and the question of how or whether their contemporary planning processes could be influenced by urban agriculture.

For the project *Shrinking Cities,* we conducted investigations at several locations.[1] In an intercultural comparison, it was interesting to see how differently the theme urban agriculture was addressed.

In the example of the Russian city of Ivanovo, urban agriculture was subsistence farming, i.e. contributing to the basic food supply. This was a result of the two economic recessions in Russia – one at the beginning and one in the middle of the 1990s. During this time, it was simply a question of sustenance: how and from what will one survive? The entire daily rhythm of life adapted to agricultural production cycles. And no matter how well one was educated and what labour structures one was part of, in order to make sure one had food to eat, one had to leave the city and go to the countryside during important seasonal events such as planting and harvest. This extended even further and was not limited to activities in the countryside, such as the mere growth of produce, but also included the preservation and pickling of vegetables and fruit for times after the actual harvest. Ever since the recessions, this has been a major urban influence in and around Ivanovo, and the rhythm of life has adapted to the agrarian rhythm. In Russian history, this is not without precedence. After the Russian revolution at the beginning of the 1920s, an exodus took people from the major cities of Moscow and Saint Petersburg to the countryside. During this time, half of the population of Saint Petersburg fled the city due to food shortages.

Detroit was very different from Ivanovo. The USA is not a country that offers a lot of social help services. For example, our German post-war understanding of social-democratic welfare does not exist in the same manner in the USA. Nevertheless, there is some sort of minimal provision. Different from Russia – and this is the bitter truth about post-socialist history – in the USA, the question of what one might eat tomorrow doesn't arise. Such hardships are buffered by society, even though there isn't an official form of social help.

In Detroit, just as in other American cities, urban agriculture presents itself as a social alternative, rather than a basic existential necessity. Urban agriculture in Ivanovo is largely defined by family structures, i.e. not individually organised, but still rather privately run. In Detroit, we mostly find communal activities with an abundance of utopian ideals and efforts to establish social work.

In Detroit, the *Urban Agriculture Network* exemplifies this social and communal approach.[2] It integrates people who are on welfare, those who have recently been released from prison or single teenage mothers into projects that convey strong ideals of community and society. Foucault would have named these projects 'heterotopias'.[3] They constitute a counter-example to dominating American models of society, and are consciously critical of the status quo, trying to shape a different sense of togetherness on a small scale.

This is very typical for the American situation, where scarcely any critique of urban planning and development can be heard and hardly any open debates take place, but – this at least was my experience in Detroit – a culture of counter-concepts does exist. The universities, for example, offer access to community design centres that volunteer in different parts of the city where they work on concrete projects. Neighbourhood and community groups understand their function in offering and leading hands-on approaches to specific situations, rather than criticising those in power.

These examples from Russia and the USA all imply claiming ownership of one's own public space.

Doubtless this springs from a certain socio-critical self-understanding. However, it manifests itself more significantly in the attempt to create something of one's own. The *Urban Agricultural Network* in Detroit, for example, encompasses many different organisations, such as a Christian one that is part of a monastery and works in various initiatives with homeless people. The *Ferguson Academy* is an educational centre for underage mothers, and its training programme includes working in adjacent gardens and fields.[4] Caring for something on a longer-term basis is part of the educational concept, because it communicates an understanding of sustainability and longevity. Whilst the aim of the project is to support women, the project draws on urban agriculture to achieve this. Here, agriculture is the means to a higher goal.

Most examples in the USA stem from New York's community gardens movement, which started in the early 1970s and is still active.[5] These too are not private, but communal ventures that were developed in the context of shrinking processes at the time. With the suburbanisation of the early 1960s, New York was suffering deficits in public financing and losing strength due to the economic crisis. This resulted in many vacant or brownfield sites, with the properties' ownership reverting to the city council, because their owners were no longer able to pay the high property taxes. Community gardens developed as a counter-culture to these shortcomings – not in a private context, but as a project *for* the neighbourhood *by* the neighbourhood.

So, the idea of productive urban landscape, in which urban agriculture takes place, can only be understood in the context of the shrinking cities phenomenon?

Not by any means, no. However, in Germany it is striking that many urban agriculture landscapes within

shrinking situations are subsidised landscapes. Two projects are exemplary: the *Jahrtausendfeld* in Leipzig[6] – a by-project of the Expo 2000 – and the *Landschaftszug* in Dessau.[7]

For the Expo in Leipzig, a vacant plot of industrial land was turned into a field by filling it with fertile soil from the construction site of Leipzig airport. For one year it was cultivated as a field, and a neighbouring theatre acted as the stakeholder. I do not want to criticise the project, but it was indeed embedded in a certain type of state organisation. For the Expo, there was certainly a flow of state subsidies and communal statutes to keep the project alive. The *Landschaftszug* in Dessau was developed in the context of the IBA, Germany's International Building Exhibition, with German federal and EU support.

Could one assign different chances of success to the different approaches discussed in your German and US-American examples?

In these two respective situations we are dealing with very different social contexts, so it's hard to draw a direct comparison between the different experiences. For example, even though Detroit is a metropolis, its budget for culture amounts to one million dollars per year, with the cultural council counting four employees. This cannot be compared to German circumstances, where every small town's cultural activities have more state support. The US-American planning policies are completely different as well, leading to a certain *laissez-faire* atmosphere. In the USA, the public spending ratio, i.e. the proportion of public spending to total spending, is about half of what it is in Germany; in Germany it lies at 50%, in the US at 25%. In this very different political and economic framework, things that work in the USA cannot work in Germany and vice versa. Comparisons like these really give one the chance to better reflect on the individualities of societies, and one's own position.

*I am interested in the main tools needed to make produc-
tive urban landscapes successful. What do processes, as you
describe them, mean for the self-determination of citizens,
be they individuals or collective initiatives, when wanting to
be involved in the appropriation of urban space?*

As part of the project *Urban Catalyst*, I have been
researching temporary uses of space, and one of our
focus points has been the tools and methods of implementation. For me, this is therefore a very important
question.

The first question is the availability of space: how is land
made available? For this, certain instruments have been
developed: licence agreements, for example, regulating
the use of private property outside of rental agreements.
In my opinion, control over space must be linked to use
of space, not simply to the question of proprietorship.
German constitutional law, for example, limits certain
claims by declaring *Eigentum verpflichtet* [property
entails obligations]. This means that the proprietor is
not the absolute sovereign over their property, but certain rules apply to his powers. In Dutch legislation, for
example, it is defined that in the Netherlands, after one
year, a vacant building may be squatted legally. In many
countries with an Anglo-Saxon jurisdictional culture,
or in Brazil, vacant land is ascribed to whoever utilises
it over a long term, thereby acquiring ownership-like
entitlement through utilisation. The owner, who does
not use their land, ultimately loses the title to their
property. Whether they are not able or do not want to
use it, ultimately the community is not afflicted by the
non-use of the space. This question is vital because it is a
precondition for how space can be made available.

In addition to the question of ownership, there is the
question of liability. In Germany, the problem often
becomes twofold: because proprietors will not be fully
relieved of their liabilities, they might not be willing
to make their space available. As a result, attempts
are being made to alter this with licence agreements
between the public authorities, private owners and
users. This way the state can function as guarantor,
taking on liability which allows third parties the use of
private property.

*Practically asked: the spaces we are speaking of, what
dimensions do they have? Is their size important?*

These spaces can be of various sizes, as they always
depend on the urban situation. It is not only the size
of the area that plays a role, but also it's setting. Three
square metres of Berlin's open space at Potsdamer Platz,
right in the city centre, possess very different possibilities from three square metres in Marzahn-Hellersdorf
at the city's North-Eastern periphery. However, size
is important for certain uses that require minimum
areas. In the context of urban agriculture, size becomes
relevant in forests or fields that have to be economically
viable, as in the model case of the industrial forest at
IBA *Emscher Park*.[8] Gardens, on the other hand, can be
quite small.

*Making a CPUL infrastructure will require major inter-
ventions within the structure of a city and a fundamental
rethinking of how cities, especially traditional European
cities, could be used. Would you understand such urban landscapes in terms of reuse, residual or temporary use? Or could
they be understood within a theory of demographic and
urban change as a planned longer-term solution?*

Yes, they may of course be seen as longer-term. Such
concepts could be very concrete and real, and there are
historical precedents for them.

During the *Gründerzeit* in 19th-century Germany,
industry boomed and construction took place at high
density. At the same time, large plots were reserved
for *Schrebergärten*, allotment gardens. In various ways,
these green areas complemented the building development of the Gründerzeit: on the one hand, light, air and
sun were needed, and on the other, the economic and
social situation of the city's inhabitants was precarious.
The allotment garden fulfilled a central urban function
offering citizens environmental qualities, the possibility
of a subsistence economy and potential extra income.

In the late 19th century, one could also find city-owned
farms, *Stadtgüter*, in Germany. Throughout the early
phase of modernity in Berlin, before transport became
as cheap and the distribution of labour as advanced as
today, it was a matter of course that a large proportion

of food supply was provided within the city and its immediate urban surroundings. Historically this was the norm.

The situation that has come about after World War II is actually the exception. Today, we have food shipped from all over the globe and use enormous amounts of energy to subsist. What we consume is seldom fresh, but relatively sterile and standardised. Consumers are not able to relate to the goods they buy. Nowadays one needs the qualifications of a university professor just to shop ethically; according to which criteria must we judge food? What is harmful to us? What is socially and what is ecologically sustainable? In this complete estrangement, one needs very detailed and constantly responsive insights to shop conscientiously. Quite obviously, this is a phase of modernity that is coming to an end. Already now, there are interesting counter-movements.

Recent debates about urban agriculture are often accompanied by the term 'behaviour change' touching on some of the aspects you mentioned. In our context, behaviour change refers especially to the change of individual eating patterns, in order that consumption becomes more beneficial for one's own health. One might think that small changes like this can have a greater impact on sustainable urban development than attempting to alter urban food production.

Such concepts go beyond concrete practice and can serve, by extension, as models. With the new forms of urban agriculture, we depart from the current model of consumer society and its associated separation of production and consumption. And if one leaves this classic model, one also leaves the emphasis on the monetary. As a consequence, social processes, such as exchange, donation and help become relevant.

The contemporary trend can better be described by the term 'prosumer', which arose at the end of the 1990s.[9] It stems from the digital world and entails the revocation of producer and consumer. Just as we have relinquished the idea of the functional city and come to understand that it was a mistake – the concept of zoning (separation) by use, which undeniably had its legitimisation in a phase of modernity – we are now

arriving at a point where we must leave the idea of the classic consumer society behind, i.e. a complete decoupling of consumer and producer. In our everyday lives we are almost nothing but consumers, and only within the narrow framework of our profession may we be producers.

The new theories stem from the world of media, from principles such as 'open source software' and 'commons', in which a user is also a producer. If we look at human history, this was in fact always the case. However, with the intense modernisation after World War II, the consumer society and its strict division of producer and consumer was enforced. In the course of this, all processes were assessed on monetary terms. The exchange of goods nowadays is only mediated by money; other criteria no longer play a role. It is the price that dominates what we buy, and a majority of people buy poor goods, often of dubious quality, because they are cheaper.

Through urban agriculture, people could develop a different relationship to their nutrition. Every apartment could, on a larger or smaller scale, be turned into a farm, starting with five pots of herbs on the windowsill. However, such changes are not solely based on food, but have to do with reshaping everyday life and, consequently, with rethinking urban space. Urban agriculture practice might then reach larger brownfield sites on which food would be produced in a quantitatively significant manner.

Even though people still experiment with how economically strong and commercially viable urban agriculture could be, do you think a new urban productivity could arise from its integration into everyday life?

It's a question of the economy of time, since food production is time consuming. Economic strength strongly depends on lifestyles. Tending a garden or a field requires one's presence at the location. This, however, often stands in conflict with today's urban lifestyles. If one is not at home during the week or sometimes away months at a time, it is even less possible to maintain food growing. Unless it is shared communally; then others tend the field during one's own absence.

Lifestyles, however, could still shift in other directions: in a digital work environment, many live somewhere out in the countryside, say in Brandenburg or the Alsace, and are able to work for distant employers or clients independently of a set work space. This allows for new forms of rural living.

The term 'productivity' is a construct, and one has to ask how to define it. Our classic definition of the Gross National Product does not recognise goods that are not on the market for trade. Goods that are swapped or personally consumed are not included. What is not on the market cannot be taxed and is therefore not quantified. This is where the problem of the term lies. One could state that the Gross National Product is higher when apples are imported from New Zealand or South Africa, compared to those from your own dacha, which are not accounted for. Here we can see the problem with using this term.

There is another problem too: the often considerable collateral damage, the large amounts of energy used in production, should be assessed in productivity calculations. Often, these all add up to a negative productivity.

So we have to clarify what concept of productivity we are actually talking about. There are shifts, because urban agriculture takes time, and it has to be planned how to make this time available. For all that, perhaps, an urban gardener or city farmer no longer fosters the desire to fly to the Maldives in springtime, simply because she or he now has a very different experience of nature.

Regarding the spatial effects of food growing on a shrinking city, do these cities necessitate different observations on productivity and economic viability? This is especially important, considering that – as you stated earlier – we are arriving at the end of a certain lifestyle and economic approach.

City-integrated agriculture is close to the individual. In the 19th century, city farms, such as the *Stadtgüter* in Berlin, lay at the outskirts of the metropolitan area. There, not far from the city, one could find market gardens and orchards. Within the city, one would find the farmers' market, selling products from the environs. When we speak of sustainable provisions of food,

we always have to think about relations between the city and its hinterland. This is not a problem though: it awakens new desires. Over the past decades, these desires have developed, and new stakeholder and space use models for urban agriculture have developed, such as self-harvesting projects: farmers plant strawberry fields and passing-by citizens are able to buy the fruit directly from the field. Many hybrid forms of involvement exist in this context; on one hand, the option to tend a field all year round, or on the other – the lean version – to merely participate in the harvest.

In the context of shrinking cities, the debate should focus on spatial cohesion, on unity within the city. Here in Europe, we debate this problem quite differently from the USA. In Detroit, I came to realise that the understanding of a city continuum does not actually exist and rather that landscape can be used and then abandoned. Generally in Europe, we want all parts of urban space to blend into a larger framework. Here, territory as a whole is integrated into society.

So, when demands on space usage cease to apply, it should be debated how such space can be reintegrated into the urban realm. New forms of extensive use have to be applied to these areas that no longer have any purposeful uses tied to them, and these may well pertain to agriculture and forestry. The phase of totally intensive space use, of perpetual compaction is over for many places: today we are looking at processes of de-compaction of urban space. The agricultural model of usage allows the planning, maintaining and cultivating of areas with a lesser density of investment and people.

At the other end of the spectrum, in a growing city such as London, we call our approach 'Ecological Intensification': densification that should not only be thought of in the sense of 'more people per square metre', but also of overlapping types of usage in the same open space. Open space will then not only be used as a park, but also as an office or a circulation route, as well as a place for food production.

I find it feasible to use larger inner-city areas for urban agriculture. But I can rather imagine them in places where there's not a high competition for usage. In densely populated situations, say Tokyo, urban agriculture will always only fill small niches. In a city such as London, it is currently not necessary to force large-scale agriculture within the city. Agriculture can take place on the outskirts. In Detroit, to the contrary, there are many spaces for which there is no demand and these could well be used productively on a larger scale.

However, it will always be important to reserve space for such functions as urban agriculture in order to improve the quality of urban life and not only organise it according to a fiscal point of view. For example, if city politics were merely motivated by capital, *Schrebergärten* would no longer exist in Berlin, because the state could sell the plots for tremendous prices on the market.

London is highly compacted and growing without signs of it shrinking in the near future. Nevertheless, according to calculations – partially conducted by us – one could allocate sufficient space to produce maybe 30% of the necessary fruit and vegetables consumed in Greater London instead of importing them. And all this without London losing any of its urban qualities.

At this point I would like to refer back to your earlier question: what view of the city is created or underlies these visions?

The discourse about the European city is conducted very conservatively. It is characterised by formal ideals on perimeter block development, corridor streets and the limitation of eaves' heights. For more conservative urban thinkers, like Hans Stimmann, former head of Berlin's planning department, urban agriculture is out of the question. Such protagonists would consider it 'un-urban' and find that it destroys public space.

This, however, is an utter misconception of public space and of the essence of European cities. One can also debate this fact in a different way: in Europe, an urban understanding exists – different to the US-American one, for example – that aims for cohesion and would like to see the urban structure or territory planned and designed as a whole. This includes considerations for social balance. As part of such an understanding of the European city, urban agriculture can play an important role in creating spatial and social cohesion.

Cities are much rather about embedding sites into the public realm and creating a structure of responsibilities that can be integrated into a larger cohesive framework. The actual practice and use of a city is about something very different than the narrative of the corridor street, for example. For urban space to work, clearly defined responsibilities are necessary. One problem of classic modernism, for example, is the *Abstandsgrün* – the green space separating buildings' entrances from the pavement.

But then, urban agriculture could be understood in similar terms: as a quasi-socialist model, in which no one owns the land on which isolated buildings stand. This, though, has never worked. In everyday life, it is rather about defining the public space of streets, squares and parks and creating adjacent, publicly accessible areas.

Such 'adjacent areas', however, can be subject to very different, even opposing currents. How would the spaces we are talking about remain public in a broader sense, i.e. by accessibility or by lines of sight?

The surrounding is visually important, but it is also significant for one's own local interaction. The same applies for the experience of open spaces. Picture, for example, a totally fenced-off plot, an accessible plot of barren and unsafe land, a publicly accessible and well-kept park, a plot of land used by residents for food production only open to certain people, or a plot open to everybody but only at certain times. Each of these urban situations creates completely different possibilities for interaction. Considering such spatial factors helps to create a pleasant inner-city situation.

For me, open, public spaces within the European city have to be defined from a pedestrian's perspective, or from the impression one gets riding a bike through the city; what possibilities of use are there for a certain space? What potential lies in it for activities and contact? It is significant which spaces border such a public open area and how porous these boundaries are. Public space is vital once it is supported and activated by its adjacent sites. Here, urban agriculture can be significant, especially when managed collectively and in an integrating rather than mono-functional way. Urban agriculture is not a simple transplantation of standard agricultural fields into the city, but is characterised by the integration of social and public functions.

Depending on whether urban agriculture can support and be integrated into urban space production – without endangering the formation called the 'European city' – it can become a key component of such a formation.

The creation of new forms of open space brings new types of usage. Today, young, often middle-class, city inhabitants have demands that cannot be compared to those of 50 years ago. How do you think this will develop in the near future?

I am reluctant to speculate about the future. Cities are highly complex entities and, sometimes, utterly different, even conflicting developments play a role. Questions of economic flows feed as much into these developments as cultural or technological currents do. At times, a general trend is hard to pinpoint. Thirty years ago, nobody was able to predict the city of today, and today we are in a similar situation. Developments of the past decades and the current status quo are important factors to analyse. Our ideals of cities are outdated. We would already have won a lot, if we perceived and understood the present without prejudices. Then certain trends can be extrapolated: what may come in the next few years, even though we cannot fathom how cities will look in 30 years.

Immanently – and today more than ever – the question of social well-being arises from these developments. Over the past two or three years, neoliberal ideology in Germany has been discredited, perhaps because we still do not have a clear societal concept of what might come next.

However, the recent changes to urban stakeholder structures appear crucial to me. I would like to relate this to the theme of temporary use.

In the last few years, using concepts about the temporary use of space, different places have been experiencing an increase in civil participation in urban space production. The temporary use of buildings or sites mobilises contrasting inhabitants and brings them

together. This has to do with culturalisation processes and partially – although perhaps not in the case of agriculture – with new media. By now, these strong social individualising forces have led many citizens to take the initiative and be part of creating urban space, often without much financial capital.

Various social milieus become part of these projects; from the upper-middle-class, educated and employed in the cultural sector, to those with migrant backgrounds and economies. Not everyone participates though; these are not 'embracing models' that are inclusive to society as a whole. Usually, urban design is coupled with large investments, hence, usually, the city is formed by those who control capital. In temporary use projects, it is interesting that beyond the city's focus on private investment, suddenly very different protagonists have appeared. They might not be eligible for large-scale credits, but they want to shape the city themselves. They are willing to invest energy and time and are capable of doing so. Often, a group of people comes together, investing their social capital, time and other resources. The city politicians are increasingly taking these new stakeholders seriously. Political decisions around the *Tempelhofer Feld* in Berlin[10] are a good example reflecting these new demands.

Values have shifted. Only ten years ago, temporary use was not discussed in urban development. Today, it is widely recognised, with new discussions taking place about a different type of stakeholders who are able to find long-term and sustainable new projects. Temporary use has turned into a sort of starter drug.

Cities cannot be understood as form. Urban formations are the result of social processes. It is important to understand the economic processes and the constellations of stakeholders that underpin these forces. Depending on these factors, one is able to realise how constellations can shift, sometimes for the better. If one succeeds in involving a larger number of individuals into the production of cities then, for me, this is social progress.

Notes

1. for project details see: Shrinking Cities Project (2008) *Shrinking Cities*, Online: <http://www.shrinkingcities.com> (accessed 16 May 2012).
2. for project details see: Detroit Agriculture Network (2006) *Keep Growing Detroit!*, Online: <http://detroitagriculture.net> (accessed 16 May 2012).
3. see: Foucault, Michel (1967) *Of Other Spaces*, Online: <http://foucault.info/documents/heteroTopia/foucault.heteroTopia.en.html> (accessed 16 May 2012).
4. for project details see: Catherine Ferguson Academy (2011) *Catherine Ferguson Academy*, Online: <http://www.catherinefergusonacademy.org> (accessed 16 May 2012).
5. see chapters by Cohen and Meyer-Renschhausen in this book.
6. for project details see: Reinhardt, R. (2003) *Das Jahrtausendfeld*, Online: <http://www.jahrtausendfeld.de/> (accessed 16 May 2012).
7. for project details see: Stadt Dessau-Roßlau and Station C23 (2008) *Leitfaden Landschaftszug Dessau-Roßlau*, Online via: <http://www.dessau.de/Deutsch/Bauen-und-Wohnen/Stadtentwicklung/Stadtumbau/Konzepte/Leitfaden-Landschaftszug/> (accessed 16 May 2012).
8. for project details see: Regionalverband Ruhr (no year) *Emscher Landschaftspark*, Online: <http://www.metropoleruhr.de/freizeit-sport/emscher-landschaftspark.html> (accessed 16 May 2012).
9. see: Toffler, A., *The Third Wave*, London: Bantam Press, 1984.
10. for project details see: Tempelhofer Freiheit (no date) *Open space for the city of the future*, Online available: <www.tempelhoferfreiheit.de/en> (accessed 16 May 2012).

Laboratories for Urban Agriculture: The USA – New York City

André Viljoen and Katrin Bohn

In 2011, the University of Columbia's Urban Design Lab published a report titled *The Potential for Urban Agriculture in New York City*. Its executive summary headlines as a key finding that, in New York City, 'Urban agriculture can play a critical role as productive green urban infrastructure' (Urban Design Lab 2011b: 2).

Although this productive green urban infrastructure remains to be fully realised, New York already has a varied, dynamic and radical history linked to urban agriculture. Proposals for 'vertical city farms' have been developed by Dickson Despommier (Despommier 2010), and a number of community-based initiatives address poverty, employment and hunger. The city has one of the most articulate, resilient and resourceful networks of community gardens, the benefits of which, in relation to health, well-being and community building, are

beginning to be recognised. After a long struggle and with some compromises, community gardens have been given a legal status in the city. Several in-depth publications provide a good overview of the city's community gardens, all of which, to varying degrees, cultivate edible crops (Campbell and Wiesen 2009; Mees and Stone 2010).

New York City's newest and most visible manifestation of urban agriculture, rooftop farms, provide the focus for this chapter, and those echo an earlier work created by Agnes Denes, who planted a two-acre wheat field in downtown Manhattan. This installation – *Wheatfield, a confrontation* – was made in response to world hunger (Greenmuseum 2010), and for many it has become an evocation for a new type of urban space and a seminal provocation in favour of urban agriculture.

Documentary images of *Wheatfield* show a horizontal sea of wheat before a vertical backdrop of sky scrapers. Almost twenty years later, these same characteristics are being displayed in the city's rooftop farms.

We will analyse two of these pioneering rooftop farms, *Eagle Street Rooftop Farm* and *Brooklyn Grange Rooftop Farm* (p. 188), using the four themes of the *CPUL City Actions*. Both practise intensive open-air soil-based organic cultivation, are accessible to the public, well managed and media-savvy. *Eagle Street* is focused on education and social engagement within its neighbourhood, and *Brooklyn Grange* on commercial viability.

CPUL City Action: Visualising Consequences

When developing the CPUL concept, we had assumed that due to the ease of cultivation and logistics, ground-based urban agriculture would develop more rapidly and extensively than rooftop farming. In practice, rooftop cultivation has also quickly expanded, and in NYC this is primarily found in the borough of Queens, across the East River from Manhattan. The relative scarcity and

high cost of urban land provide some straightforward reasons for the popularity of urban rooftop farms, yet, beyond these, it seems that the constrained, secure, defined and elevated territory of a roof may of itself be attractive.

Aerial organoponicos

Spatially, rooftop farms have many of the characteristics found in Cuban organoponicos as described in our project *Laboratories for Urban Agriculture: Cuba* (Viljoen and Howe 2005). Principal amongst these is the dominance of the horizontal field with wide views towards the horizon. The optical arrangement of viewer, field and surrounding buildings is, however, fundamentally different for rooftop farms: In Cuba, organoponicos are viewed from above or from their edge and looked across. Rooftop farms are rarely viewed from the edge; the predominant view is by an observer within the planted field. Their elevated nature and the need to seek out sites that are not overshaded by adjacent buildings all contribute to their island-like character. The experience of entering a rooftop farm – after a journey through the building from the pavement to the top – is captured by the architect for *Brooklyn Grange Rooftop Farm*, Jerry

Fig 1: *Eagle Street Rooftop Farm*. View towards Manhattan across the farm on this New York warehouse roof.

Caldari, who, when asked what surprised him most about the farm, said it was 'the universal child-like amazement of people who come to see it, whoever these people are' (personal communication Aug 2011).

This characteristic of a "world within a world" and of a "second nature" within the city contribute to the farm's ability to provide a place of refuge and relaxation, a private, visually expansive open room in the city. New York's rooftop farms also tend to have what Dutch architect Aldo van Eyck, when writing about the design of architectural spaces that encourage sympathetic occupation, calls 'right size' (Eyck 1962). Although there is no *one* "right size" – because of context, including the number of people using a space – the dimensions of New York's rooftop farms usually are comparable to those of organoponicos or mostly fit into a 19th- or early-20th-century city block. From observations within our project *Laboratories for Urban Agriculture: The USA* it appears that, if at least one linear dimension of a rooftop farm is in the order of 20 to 40 metres, and there is one or more gathering space for small groups of people, say 10 to 20 in number, this helps to attain an intimacy and openness that leads to "right size". *Eagle Street Rooftop Farm* presents a good example of "right size": it is an intensively cultivated but relatively small farm with a plan area of approximately 15 by 20 metres including a small seating area that can accommodate up to a dozen people and is reached by walking through the field. From the seating area, an expansive view opens across the East River towards Manhattan.

The much larger *Brooklyn Grange Farm* has two designated gathering spaces; one is a long banqueting table constructed from scaffolding components, and the other a "found space" under the building's elevated water tank offering a shaded place for workers to rest and relax.

The potential to use urban agriculture sites as "celebratory space" was identified in our 2005 *CPUL* book, and is demonstrated in NYC, where rooftops are often used as venues for celebrations, such as weddings, anniversaries and birthday parties. The rent from hiring out space for events provides an important additional revenue stream for urban farmers.

CPUL City Action:
The Inventory of Urban Capacity

The *CPUL City Actions* recognise that space and design on their own are not sufficient to initiate and sustain urban agriculture initiatives. Each individual project requires constant management and maintenance. New York, like many cities, benefits from a rich pool of motivated, enterprising and educated individuals, providing significant social and managerial capacity and entrepreneurial energy.

Eagle Street Rooftop Farm was established in 2009 as the result of a collaboration between the building's owners who run a stage design business and a green roofing contractor, both jointly funding the construction of the rooftop field. The farm itself operates at many levels: selling produce for profit, working with local charities and educational establishments as a resource, running a weekly market, operating an apprenticeship scheme for urban farmers and being a place to visit. Delivery of all these programmes is coordinated by an employed farm manager. During its first year of operation, two managers ran the farm, Annie Novak and Ben Flanner. At the end of 2009, Ben Flanner left *Eagle Street* to set up the *Brooklyn Grange Rooftop Farm* (Eagle Street n.d.).

A sequence of e-mail communications regarding Bohn&Viljoen's *Laboratories for Urban Agriculture* project, conversations with staff and volunteers, as well as site visits, allow us to formulate observations about *Brooklyn Grange Rooftop Farm*. A core group of five motivated, (media-)savvy young graduates initiated *Brooklyn Grange*, bringing to the project both determination and a recognition of the financial and legal realities of establishing a new enterprise. This is particularly interesting because of their aim to operate a commercially viable, independent farm using the principles of organic farming. Starting without access to significant capital, the additional cost of lawyers, accountants, engineers and architects had to be covered.

As a commercial enterprise, the farm utilises a full spectrum of finance including 'private equity, loans, grassroots fundraising events and crowd-funding platforms'. The farm 'broke even in our first year and showed 40% growth in our second year. Our expansion to an additional acre of cultivated rooftop (Building 3 at Brooklyn Naval Yard) in our third year promises even greater growth, and we plan to continue expanding in the coming years' (Brooklyn Grange 2012). Ten- and twenty-year leases on the Grange and Naval Yard buildings' roofs provide the security necessary for the farms to bed down and to make investment worthwhile.

In setting up *Brooklyn Grange Farm*, the initiators looked for investors who supported the project's goals and could offer financial input or direct input: "sweat equity". Some consultants, such as the architects Bromley Caldari, became partners/investors, and others required payment as consultants. At the moment, all profits are ploughed back into the business, but once the business becomes profitable and, for example, consultancy jobs materialise, the investors could do well.

Apart from the labour put in by the five founding partners, the *Brooklyn Grange Rooftop Farm* relies on interns and volunteers to operate and, one year into the project, some partners relied on external "rent jobs" to supplement their farm-derived income.

Maintaining an online and media presence is essential for recruiting interns, volunteers and customers, and both *Brooklyn Grange* and *Eagle Street* have relied on and maintained comprehensive websites since their inception, detailing events and providing considerable background material for interested parties.

CPUL City Action: Researching for Change

There are numerous transferable lessons from these two projects. Here, we will concentrate on initial design research related to the integration of rooftop farms into buildings and the characteristics of the physical infrastructure they require (another urban capacity). Our conclusions are based on personal observations of several rooftop farms and an interview held in August 2011 with *Brooklyn Grange*'s architect Jerry Caldari of Bromley Caldari Architects

The design challenges for rooftop farms include the choice of materials, topographical manipulation and spatial definition – subtle challenges for landscape architecture, but crucial when working at the scale of an

Fig 2: *Brooklyn Grange Rooftop Farm.* Currently the 'world's largest rooftop soil farm', this farm is located in the heart of Queens in New York City.

urban roof. The degree to which these are addressed will depend on the attitude adopted towards issues like the degree of public access or the number of ancillary commercial activities catered for in addition to food growing. Environmental, structural and practical criteria play a significant role in determining which rooftops are suitable for cultivation: exposure to sunlight, the availability of water and rainwater, the physical access to the roof, preferably also by a goods lift, the building's structural strength, the potential for getting soil onto the roof, access to the roof out of "office hours" and, ideally, a storage bay at ground level are all important. In the case of *Brooklyn Grange*, finding an appropriate site and then negotiating a contract took about nine months.

Once a suitable site has been identified, the designer's role is to establish the location of planting areas and paths, etc., to deal with waterproofing of the rooftop and to ensure that drainage is suitably detailed, so that the planting medium does not lead to blockages of downpipes or the like. The prevalence of ornamental and "non-productive" planted rooftops simplifies research and specification processes because proprietary waterproof root barrier and drainage systems are now readily available. Planted roofs are classified as "extensive" or "intensive". The former term is being used where a thin growing medium supports a largely maintenance-free and self-seeding ground cover, such as sedum. For

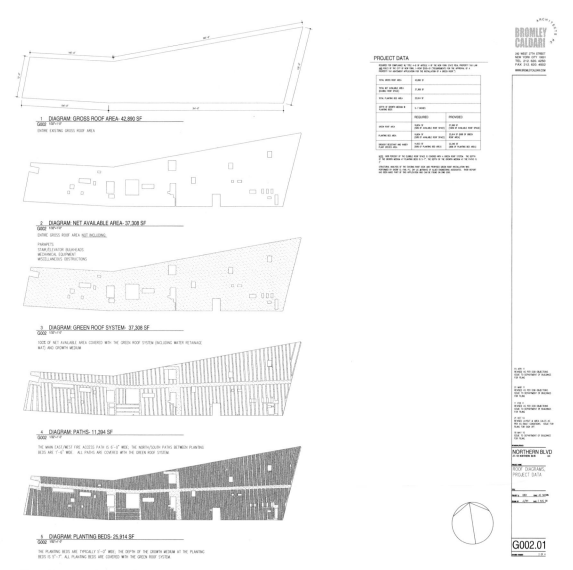

Fig 3: Designing for urban agriculture. Bromley Caldari Architects' plans for Brooklyn Grange prepared for NYC's Department of Buildings. Sixty percent of the roof's gross area is cultivated. (image: Bromley Caldari Architects PC, 2011)

non-hydroponic rooftop farms, a minimum depth of soil is required, and these thicker roofs are called "intensive green roofs". Structural conditions will determine what depth of soil is possible, but it is surprising how little soil is needed for non-root crops, such as beans or marrows. At *Brooklyn Grange*, the roof is made of 200 millimetres [8 inches] thick reinforced concrete, supported by a grid of so-called 'mushroom columns', capped by thickened drop panels at approximately 6.7 metre [22 foot] centres. This roof has the capacity to support an additional load of 19 newtons per square metre [39 pounds per square foot], which allowed for the addition of 180 mm [7 inches] deep soil for planting.

Installing the soil at *Brooklyn Grange* required the placing of a proprietary waterproofing substrate. After the waterproofing was in place, soil in large builder's bags was lifted by means of a mobile crane onto the roof of the six-storey building. Using wheelbarrows and spades, the soil was then manually shifted into its final position. This operation took six days and required temporary access to space at ground level for the crane and vehicles delivering soil.

Once the farm became operational, day-to-day access to the roof was essential for workers, for the supply of materials and goods, such as compost, and for the distribution of the harvest. Cultivation on a scale similar to Brooklyn Grange, with a growing area of about 2.3 hectares [25,000 square feet], requires permanent access to a large goods lift. At *Brooklyn Grange*, an existing goods lift stopped two flights of stairs below the roof, so, during the summer of 2011, as part of the lease agreement, it was being extended to exit at rooftop level. Prior to this, produce for sale and heavy boxes of compostable waste from restaurants were being carried up and down the final two flights of stairs in back-breaking human convoys.

CPUL City Action: Bottom-Up and Top-Down

When the two farms were conceived, NYC had just introduced a green roof tax credit for building owners as part of an overall environmental sustainability policy supporting heat island mitigation and the reduction of stormwater runoff following heavy rain. Surprisingly, rooftop farms were not classified as "green", but generic extensive sedum-type roofs were, despite the latter potentially absorbing much less water. To benefit from the tax credit, the city authorities require a three-year commitment to the maintenance of green roofs, which was well covered by the farms' substantially longer leases. Architects Bromley Caldari made a case for Brooklyn Grange to the relevant authorities that the roof's edible plants should be classified as "green". In the summer of 2011 their arguments prevailed and the tax credit was awarded based on the entire roof area of 3,809 square metres [41,000 square feet] including footpaths that were also covered with protective layers of earth. This tax credit is a significant incentive for building owners contemplating the installation of a productive rooftop.

Given the bottom-up challenges involved in getting rooftop farms rated as green roofs, it might be thought that they are not considered resilient in the face of the stormy weather predicted as a result of climate change. This concern seems to be unfounded because since their founding, *Eagle Street* and *Brooklyn Grange* have withstood a number of storms, including tropical cyclones.

Additionally, unlike some other cities in the United States, New York has not defined urban agriculture as a specifically recognised land use. According to Jerry Caldari, as part of the process of embedding urban agriculture within everyday planning, an application will now be made to redesignate the rooftop at *Brooklyn Grange* as an occupied manufacturing space (personal communication Aug 2011).

The processes to normalise rooftop farms within the planning and general regulatory frameworks associated with urban development are not overly complex, but it is important to establish a working relationship with the relevant authorities in order to demystify the concept of a rooftop farm and to establish local precedents and procedures. With respect to both planning frameworks and actual physical design parameters, it is far easier to plan for accommodating a rooftop farm at the design stage than to retrofit existing buildings. Being proactive and allowing for

Fig 4: Adapting the host building for agricultural use.
Brooklyn Grange volunteers expose the concrete roof slab prior to the building's goods lift being extended to exit at rooftop level.

Fig 5: Tailored space production. The space below Brooklyn Grange's water tower is used as an informal kitchen and area for relaxation.

rooftop cultivation at the design stage provides for future proofing at a marginal cost.

Beyond planning frameworks and business plans, a loose coalition of individuals and organisations are collectively recording the outputs and impacts of urban farms in New York. Universities, the city's Botanic Gardens, the Parks Department and the mayor's office communicate via channels that are often based on individual contacts established by common interests and objectives. These interests range from large politically and electorally significant issues, such as the future of community gardens, to wider diet-related public health issues. Many of the key players generating the evidence and metrics that will determine the future for particular types of urban agriculture are doing this in parallel with academic studies or other employment. One such bottom-up project is called *Farming Concrete* and records the quantities of fruit and vegetables actually produced per annum by participating community gardens. Another project, *Seeing Green,* records the rainwater retention capacity of rooftop farms (see chapter *Productive life in the city*, p. 40).

Rooftop farms' programmes and operational modes
At *Brooklyn Grange*, supporters, neighbours and the general public can engage with the operation of the farm via its online presence or physically through a number of activities. One of the challenges faced by *Brooklyn Grange* is that they are inundated with requests for guided tours, interviews and access to the farm, all of which help to build relationships and reputation, but also demand time from staff who need to deliver the farm's core business of fruit and vegetable production. To manage the conflicting aims of being a profitable enterprise while promoting an alternative environmental agenda, the farm operates two modes of access: one on a strictly commercial basis and the other by providing opportunities for volunteering.

To better understand this, André Viljoen attended a volunteering session in 2011, led by Anastasia Cole Plakias, one of the farm's directors. The session ran on a Saturday between 10am and 4pm. In a relaxed atmosphere, volunteers did as much work as they wanted to or could, and with no recriminations, could chose to spend some time photographing or walking about. Anastasia, on the other hand, was working non-stop, engendering an atmosphere of "do as I do". Apart from directing our team of about eight volunteers, she also hosted a tour of about ten elderly women, briefed a chef who was going to prepare a meal for "very wealthy" families on the farm roof and shovelled a lot of earth, despite wearing a splint to protect a broken foot.

For volunteers, the day started with weeding followed by some watering. We then went down two flights of stairs into the building to carry some boxes of compostable material from a local food market onto the roof. This was heavy work, and one of the farm's regular workers required assistance from two volunteers to simply get a box of compostable material onto his back, before carrying it up the staircase onto the roof. The rest of us needed two people to carry a box onto the roof. After that, bricks had to be carried up to the roof, used to hold down exposed waterproof roofing membranes where the roof would be cut open to allow the building's goods lift to be extended to the farm level. The need for the lift became obvious during our earlier exertions carrying items up to the roof.

A lunch break on the roof, sitting in the shade of the building's raised water tower provided time for talk. The volunteers came from many places: a Dutch graduate designer, a Bolivian planning to establish an urban farm, a recent US architectural graduate, two sisters and a young internet-based bookseller. During the afternoon, two Chinese visitors joined us. Most volunteers came for a day, but about a third were regulars. Informal discussions gave everyone a good sense of how the farm operated, while also providing networking opportunities. At the time of this visit, volunteers were predominantly young, either students or recent graduates.

Brooklyn Grange's expansion to include a second, larger rooftop farm at Brooklyn Naval Yard and other new initiatives in the city, often linked directly to restaurants, demonstrate the growing interest in developing commercially viable prototypes. The fact that these projects are thriving when everyday food prices in the Global North continue to be at historically low levels and, as is the case of NYC, the growing season for unprotected crops is very short due to long cold winters, demonstrates the underlying desire for productive spaces, a desire that goes beyond the pragmatic. The absolute contribution of food from these pioneering projects may be small within the city's overall food consumption, but, being produced in projects testing out future scenarios, it makes significant.

Conclusions

Contemporary New York is home to a vibrant and well-established network of food-producing community gardens, while also hosting a growing number of rooftop farms. The development of rooftop farms has been rapid and will help to advance theory and practice.

As well as realised projects, design research is underway and one of the most ambitious studies is being undertaken by architect Michael Sorkin (Sorkin 2012). At the time when *Eagle Street* and *Brooklyn Grange* were establishing themselves, Sorkin's studio presented their project *New York (Steady) State* at the 2010 Venice Biennale. This project rightly places urban agriculture within a wider political and economic context, although its conclusion – that the world may revert to a medieval model of autonomous and self-sufficient city states – is depressing, if not that far from the truth, unless we collectively grasp the future. However, Sorkin's formal design investigations need not be tied to one particular future economic and social scenario, and the realisable environmental and qualitative benefits arising from increasing the productivity of cities can be better envisaged as part of a wider national and international system of governance. Indeed, the concept of achieving 100% self-sufficiency within urban boundaries is not one that is envisaged in the *CPUL City* concept, which rather aims to enhance environmental benefits by establishing more effective exchanges with the hinterland. In relation to CPUL theory, *New York (Steady) State* undertakes yield investigations that closely align with the concept of site yield introduced in our 2005 *CPUL* book (Bohn and Viljoen 2005), where the aim is to maximise the yield of food and energy harvested from renewable resources within the curtilage of a given site. In Sorkin's case, the target is to ascertain energy and food self-sufficiency within the political boundary of NYC. Initial design studies that achieved 100% self-sufficiency in food production from within the curtilage of individual city blocks were soon rejected by the architect due to the overwhelming impact they would have on public space, access to daylight and urban qualities in general. Assessing various options for the "right size" urban agriculture, Sorkin concludes that the "sweet spot" lies somewhere in the region of 30% self-sufficiency in food production from urban agriculture. This figure is the same as proposed by Bohn&Viljoen ten years earlier for their 1999 *Urban Nature Towers* mixed-use development integrating horizontal and vertical food-growing landscapes within a scheme achieving densities of 440 persons per square metre (Bohn and Viljoen 2005: 258).

What New York confirms is that productive urban landscapes contribute more than food to a city; they aim for longevity, and more innovation is underway. Whilst theoretical studies indicate the potential in food yields, realised projects go beyond this, demonstrating benefits that are social, enhance quality of life and include pleasures less easy to articulate, but none-the-less tangible – as evidenced by urban spaces like the rooftop farms at *Eagle Street Farm* and *Brooklyn Grange*.

Laboratories for Urban Agriculture: The USA – Detroit

André Viljoen and Katrin Bohn

New York and Detroit – a brief comparison by Nevin Cohen:

Like New York City, Detroit has a rich and extensive urban agriculture network, with more than 1,000 community gardens, including several large non-profit farms, and many backyard gardens (Pothukuchi 2011: 59). These spaces of food production, community development, education and social justice organizing are supported by community-based urban agriculture initiatives, including the Detroit Black Community Food Security Network, the Greening of Detroit, and Earthworks Urban Farm, as well as Wayne State University's "SEED Wayne" programme and extension services from Michigan State University. Unlike New York, however, Detroit faces serious economic challenges as a result of decades of deindustrialization, job loss, and population decline from approximately 1.5 million in 1970 to 714,000 in 2010.[1] As a result of its economic and population losses, the city has an estimated 40 square miles of vacant land within city limits, and certain neighbourhoods in close proximity to the downtown are virtually depopulated, with many blocks containing just one or two remaining houses. The large quantity of unproductive land results in enormous per capita costs to provide city services, diminishing the capacity of Detroit's municipal government to meet the city's many long-term needs. At the time of writing, the State of Michigan was poised to appoint a manager to take over the city's finances, creating uncertainty and turmoil in government and drawing attention away from other municipal matters.

You would be hard pushed to find somewhere better than Detroit to illustrate the full spectrum of possibilities for how urban agriculture can be practised under conditions of stress. The demographic of practitioners and advocates cover wide variations in wealth, economic approach, social outlook, ethnicity, politics and age. The size of urban agriculture plots also varies from small-scale community gardens to heroic endeavours by individual urban farmers and corporate enterprises with ambitions to create 'the world's largest urban farms'.

The only common feature to all these endeavours is that, for the moment at least, they are all "ground based". Like in Cuba, Detroit's urban farmers grow in the earth. But even this might change in the future if planned new schemes come on stream.

No discussion about Detroit can take place without acknowledging that it is a shrinking city and there is some debate as to whether its population has stabilised. Whilst what is undeniable is the extreme degree to which it became depopulated is undeniable. The city has been bedevilled by a loss of industry and jobs, and this is compounded by ethnic tensions and inequalities. Within the 100 years of the 20th century it has witnessed an amazing transformation, driven by Henry Ford's vision of mass production that enabled the car to become an everyday consumer object. The industrial, social and physical transformation achieved was phenomenal. In the case of Detroit, the decline of the city has been as rapid as its original expansion at the start of the century.

Despite having an extensive and sprawling suburban fringe, Detroit has a relatively small and compact urban core with some magnificent early skyscrapers, and many empty office blocks and abandoned city lots. Its suburbs, predominantly consisting of modest, detached, timber-framed houses have vast tracts of empty and where houses have been abandoned and then demolished. For a visitor it is difficult to escape the observation that nature is taking over and reoccupying the city; suburbs look like a rural landscape with small houses dotted about. The problem for the city is that individuals remain living in these now isolated homes, without services and, in many cases, work; there are few easy answers for how to address these problems. John Gallagher's book, *Reimagining Detroit: Opportunities for redefining an American city* (Gallagher 2010) provides a comprehensive overview of the city's history and its complex contemporary challenges.

Dan Carmody, a planner by training, who runs Detroit's thriving Eastern (food) Market, describes the city's food situation as follows:

Detroit has the opportunity – because it's more broken than other American cities – to write some new rules and to try some things outside of the box that other places won't: to experiment, to see what works and what doesn't, to be open to experimentation. Many of the problems that Detroit has are the same problems that are affecting the rest of the country. We've just got a worse strain of it. To a certain extent, depending on how the overall economy goes, the rest of the country could look a lot like Detroit. Food is typically one of the central organizing elements. Food is where justice meets economic vitality and environmental sustainability. If you don't have those three things, you can't have a society that endures ... You can't have a food system where 20 percent of the people at the lower end of the economic totem pole eat only one-seventh of the amount of fresh fruits and vegetables that the people at the top eat. Society can't afford the health care costs of treating diabetes and hypertension and coronary disease because of their poor diet. We as a society have to figure out a way that people of all incomes can afford and access healthy eating. The Eastern Market is much loved in this region because it's where food and place come together. So the conviviality is every bit as important [...] as the good food is here; for changing that mix as it affects our diet, as it affects the health of the region, and as it affects the country in terms of what people eat.

(Broder 2011)

Despite the different political and economic contexts, there are parallels between the situation in Detroit and that found in Cuba during its "special period"; both can be understood as situations dealing with scarcity. They may not cases represent the most desirable models for all aspects of post "peak everything" societies, but with respect to design and planning, they offer many lessons about how new food systems can create better lives and places.

In Cuba urban agriculture was initiated spontaneously and out of necessity by citizens, and then introduced systematically. The government and municipalities quickly put in place schemes to train would-be farmers, identify suitable land and generally coordinate production. Detroit's urban agriculture is far less systematically practised (see chapter *Policies to support*

Urban Agriculture, p. 138), and a large number of different groups and individuals are exploring different approaches to growing. They tend to focus on individually supplying particular user groups, although there are mechanisms in place to facilitate the coordinated sale of produce from growers at fruit and vegetable markets. Based on observations in Cuba and Detroit there is a greater diversity of types of urban agriculture practised in Detroit, both in terms of production size and managerial aim.

Up to 2012 Detroit had not amended its planning regulations to directly support urban agriculture, none the less, it is evolving along several tracks. One, exemplified by the efforts of the Detroit Black Community Food Security Network (DBFSN), is oriented toward issues of social justice as well as food security. The network operates the multi-acre *D-Town Farm*, which offers educational and youth development programming and distributes its produce through several markets throughout the city. Similarly, one of the major policy issues among grassroots food organisations is linking food justice to social, economic and environmental justice. The Detroit Food Policy Council has been working to make connections between people and those resources which add value to food processing and enable the start-up of food-related businesses. In that vein, a community youth kitchen is under construction at *Eastern Market*, also comprising of a three-acre farm that is growing and selling produce via farm stands throughout the city.

Fig 1: 'Where food and place come together' (Dan Carmody).
On market days, Detroit's residents occupy the street in front of *Eastern Market*.

The other Detroit model for urban agriculture is much larger in scale, with both social and commercial goals. The non-profit organisation Self-Help Addiction Rehabilitation (SHAR) has a comprehensive proposal for food production, processing, and retail cluster of businesses, called *Recovery Park*, which would create jobs for SHAR's clients and provide revenue for the organisation. Another proposal has been advanced by *Hantz Farms*, a company that wishes to build a commercial farm in Detroit (described on the company's website as 'the world's largest urban farm'). The plan has evolved from a proposed fruit and vegetable farm to a Christmas tree farm, to *Hantz Farms*' current proposal to purchase 200 acres of vacant city property for the cultivation of oak and other hardwood trees that could be harvested for timber in the future (Berman 2012).

Spatially, the city has started to develop proposals for landscape corridors – 'greenways' – and the first greenway has been constructed along the Dequindre Cut, the route of an abandoned railway line. This has been strategically positioned to connect some of the city's most significant places, including public space along the city's river front, architectural heritage sites, alternative transportation networks, food markets and urban agriculture sites. If expanded as envisaged these greenways have the potential to become prototypical components for a *CPUL City*.

The purpose of this chapter is notr to present definitive case studies of each urban agriculture project in Detroit, but to register the different motivations and organisational methods found in the city based on an extended field research visit in the summer of 2011. Each of the projects referred to has vast resources of practical knowledge gained thorough experience, and most projects have websites that provide contacts and additional detailed project information. Each project's approach has resulted in persistent presence in the city, although not all have realised their aims. They are important references for the *CPUL City* concept, which by its nature will need to accommodate a variety of types of urban agriculture within its network of productive landscapes. We believe that different types of ground-based urban agriculture, are generic and likely to be encountered in many cities across the world. Our aim is to articulate these findings in such a way that planners, designers and practitioners can begin to see how different approaches work together may make a whole. Size of inytervention would have been a neat filter for

Fig 2: Eco-farming micro-enterprise. Caroline Leadley's approach to sales, transportation and cultivation.

categorisation, but it does not correlate well with the aims of different individuals and groups; for example, an ecological farmer can operate from a window box or several hectares. Our three key definitions are therefore loose, overlap and, to a degree, the parameters are subjective, with the essential approach and character of operation being determined by the grower's aims.

Detroit Types

Eco-farmers and micro-enterprises

MOTIVATION: Driven by environmental and ethical concerns. Entrepreneurial aim for economic viablility.

CHARACTERISTICS: Scaled to individual or family-sized production. A network of modestly sized fields, often abandoned housing plots, of about 200 square metres. Part of a social network, for example family and friends help out with getting to the market; facilitating a resilient community. Housing often close to the farm, integrating a cool store. Distance to markets and customers will determine the viability of the mode of sale, e.g. food markets or farm gate.

CHALLENGES: Access to cheap land and markets.

EXAMPLE: These micro (eco) enterprises are happening on relatively small areas of land and the practitioners benefit from access to land at minimal or no cost, sometimes squatting. Furthermore, adjacent housing is available at low cost, but requires major renovation. It is reported that abandoned housing can be purchased for the order of $5000 (Kalish 2011). Caroline Leadley, who runs the micro-enterprise *The Rising Pheasant Farm*, and her partner are "self-renovating" a house in a very poor state of repair, adjacent to her farm sited on an abandoned suburban lot. This approach is similar to that championed by the late German/British architect Walter Segal, whereby municipal authorities would make "awkward sites" available to self-builders at low cost. There is no reason for the land to be in the suburbs, nor that it could not be on a rooftop; the issue is that its cost must reflect the potential income an individual can generate.

Urban farmers operating at this scale should be valued for their contribution to the wider community by producing food, but also by offering a market for urban compost, improving biodiversity and providing sustainable drainage. The *Rising Pheasant* model is exemplary in its commitment to a wider low-impact approach, exemplified by the use of bicycles for transport; somewhat remarkable in a city that is so synonymous with the car. Bicycles are equally used by Cuba farmers to deliver goods to urban markets. *The Rising Pheasant Farm* utilises a convoy of three or so bikes, each pulling customised 2m-long lightweight trailers. The implications of this are immediate: whereas most farmers have a truck big enough to hold a day's goods, Leadley needs helpers to transport her produce to market. We can see how her mode of sale requires a networked approach where mutual dependence between individuals is made explicit.

The location of urban farms determines the ease of access to customers. In the simplest scenario: the urban farm is located in an area with sufficient population and through traffic to allow for sales from a farm gate stall. We can imagine how urban farms utilising space adjacent to or over railway stations and bus stops could provide ideal outlets for produce. Small urban farms also require cool storage space for crops once harvested; in Leadley's case produce includes fruit, vegetables and cut flowers. Finally Leadley lives next to her fields – not essential, but very convenient.

Corporate Urban Agriculture

MOTIVATION: Two commercially led approaches: one, to expand to the maximum; another driven by corporate responsibility aiming to benefit employees and the public realm. Motivations do not necessarily stem from a desire to improve food systems, but may be based primarily on a business opportunity that happens to be food related.

CHARACTERISTICS: Cover the full spectrum of scale and employment (paid work or volunteering); either working to achieve a profit or funded by the corporation for social/employers' and employees' benefit. Projects engage formally with the city, and its various authorities and regeneration schemes. Capacity to use professional advisors and project managers.

Fig 3: Corporate urban agriculture. Compuware's *Lafayette Greens* in the heart of Detroit's business district.

CHALLENGES: Access to areas of land identified within business plans for commercial schemes. Building community support and respect.

EXAMPLES: John Hants, who runs a large financial services business, is trying to initiate an ambitious large-scale commercial urban agriculture venture called *Hantz Farms*™ *Detroit* (E. Smith 2010). *Hantz Farms* apply the most traditional top-down business approach to urban agriculture. They have found it difficult to negotiate access to land within the city, possibly because it is neither intimately connected to, nor working with

Detroit's farming community, planning department or a wider demographic.

Another Detroit corporation, Compuware, has taken a different approach by setting up a highly visible public garden, *Lafayette Greens*, on an empty site in the heart of the city's business district. Its motivation is less ambitious with respect to the scale and represents the desire for a mutually beneficial solution between the corporation and the city. Metrics of production are less important than cultural and behaviour change impacts. Food growing becomes the means by which urban regeneration and corporate need are served. The site of about 2,000 square metres is cultivated on a voluntary basis by Compuware employees with the support of an employed and experienced urban farmer, Gwen Meyer, who had previously worked on *The Rising Pheasant Farm*. Produce from the garden is either used by Compuware volunteers or passed on to a community food bank. *Lafayette Greens* is one of a few urban agriculture sites in Detroit designed by a professional landscape architect and built to a high material specification.

Urban Agriculture as a social enterprise

MOTIVATION: Driven by social, ethical and environmental concerns.

CHARACTERISTICS: Serving communities of circumstance. Wide range of practice; typically operate at a neighbourhood or city scale; food production is significant and linked to social benefit. Often working with interest groups and individuals; utilizing digital technology for communication and networking; schedule of regular, consistent and engaging events and workshops. Affiliated to larger formal or informal regional, national and international networks; activist agendas. Core funding for activities and staff.

CHALLENGES: Reliance on external funding by foundations or similar; risk of programmes being driven by funders' objectives. Building community confidenceand managerial capacity. Maintaining ability to liaise across agencies, organisations, disciplines and demographics.

EXAMPLES: *Earthworks Urban Farm* is one of the most comprehensive and yet localised operations. It forms part of a much wider social support network linked to, or working with, the *Capuchin Soup Kitchen*, established by the Capuchin Brothers, whose monastery is situated close by. The *Earthworks* farm consists of several plots along Meldrum Street where the soup kitchen is located. Although called an 'urban farm', like many of the city's urban agriculture sites, it would more accurately be described as 'suburban'. The farm, which includes community orchards, a youth garden and highly productive fields, is sited on former suburban housing plots, with remaining houses and some commercial activity dotted between.

Fig 4: Earthworks Urban Farm. This early afternoon exhibits the characteristics of a productive landscape: protected cropping in the background, a bicycle repair workshop in the farm's forecourt, adjacent to a kitchen and store.

The spatial opportunities in Detroit that enable *Earthworks* to occupy and animate three blocks are likely to be unique to shrinking cities unless they would be identified when development plans are drawn up. However, what is immediately transferable to any situation is the mechanism by which *Earthworks* fits into a catalogue of community development initiatives. When compared to other urban agricultural initiatives in the city, *Earthworks* diverse food activities – soup kitchen and farm – are intimately connected to their wider social support systems assisting individuals who have fallen on hard times. The individuals who are helped do form a community that is less geographically or philosophically self-defined and more of a community of circumstance, operating at a scale where personal relationships are likely to bind participants together.

Another organisation with a very particular focus on individual rehabilitation is the already mentioned SHAR (Self Help Addiction Rehabilitation) (Recovery Park *n.d.*). It operates residential rehabilitation programmes in the city and was established in 1969. Since 2008, SHAR Incorporated have started to extend its concept of rehabilitation to include work training and job creation. Drawing on Detroit's opportunities for establishing urban agriculture and ancillary food processing

Fig 5: Planning aquaponics. An abandoned old people's home is being considered as a possible site for an aquaponics centre by Gary Wosniak, president of the Recovery Park Organisation.

initiatives within its extensive and depopulated suburbs. SHAR is proposing to facilitate an extensive development called *Recovery Park*. Whereas *Earthworks* was geographically rooted from the outset, due to the location of the Capuchin Monastery, *Recovery Park* have taken a community-design-led approach to identifying potential sites and to creating a vision and proposal for the park.

As a result, a 30-acre (12 ha) farm, consisting of clusters of 2- to 3-acre sites, is planned as the starting point for development. In seeking to define its role and ambitions, *Recovery Park* does offer a new model, for large-size urban agricultural operations with potential efficiencies of scale, while retaining a focus on neighbourhood and individual farm workers. The challenges of setting up such a large project, and learning about its operation, can only be judged in the future.

Unlike the newer *Hantz Farms* and *Recovery Park* proposals, the not-for-profit organisation *The Greening of Detroit* has an established track record dating back to 1989, for using urban agriculture as a tool for revitalising neighbourhoods that have suffered population loss. Ashley Atkinson, who is responsible for urban agriculture within the organisation, has built up a highly valuable transferable knowledge base and programme of practice. At the heart of it is a co-design process whereby *The Greening of Detroit* help to facilitate community

development by working with local residents. This process rejects the traditional top-down approach that some consider inseparable from schemes run by external architects and planners. Although communities are central to their method of working, *The Greening of Detroit* bring an agenda to the table, broadly promoting community building and ecologically sustainable development. This agenda necessitates a very clear programme for running community development and for selecting communities with whom the organisation can work effectively.

The Greening of Detroit brings an evolving process to projects, but not a proposal. It is this process that designers can learn from and may want to engage with. It is robust enough to accommodate external design input, but it is very noticeable that the role of designers is viewed sceptically, no doubt due to the recognition of the extensive, prolonged and committed engagement that is required to work with neighbourhoods that are severely stressed.

For urban agriculture projects, Ashley Atkinson has developed initial selection criteria to identify neighbourhoods with which to work: first, a diverse and solid community is sought, second, a minimum density of remaining dwellings is required, so that vacancy does not exceed about 50%, and finally the areas should lack access to retail outlets and be so-called 'food deserts'. This latter condition is nearly universal in Detroit, where dollar stores selling alcohol and junk food from behind bullet-proof glass predominate.

The Greening of Detroit, rather than bringing things in from outside, aim to create community-based and personal food distribution systems, named "bring-your-own-box" schemes that, as a spin-off, mean people engage in exchange and get to know each other. This is like a 'grounded Slow Food movement', far from Tuscany, and working within its own context. Perhaps even more important than defining selection criteria are the lessons learnt from the high proportion of participants in workshops and outreach activities who eventually become urban farmers cultivating sizable plots.

Regular food-realted workshops and classes have proved to be important if people are to participate in neighbourhood development schemes for the long term. The subjects and content for these classes are driven by a

community feedback loop, which determines what type
of classes are run and what is grown in community
gardens. People grow a diversity of crops – about 70
varieties of plants have been identified in their community gardens – and much of the teaching comes from
within the community. In short as a considerable body
of expert local knowledge does exist, any workshop's
content tends to be "cutting edge".

The Greening of Detroit runs many citywide events
annually; hundreds of people participate and the classes
continue to grow. Food is brought and consumed at
workshops; the policy is one of 'open house', mixing fast
food and traditional fare. Experience has shown that
children will eat what they grow, so events become big
communal gatherings combining teaching, harvesting
and cooking. In 2011, Ashley Atkinson estimated that
there were about 1,350 community gardeners in Detroit,
with 80% involved for the education and 60% also
participating in associated neighbourhood social events.
In a typical neighbourhood group attending urban
agriculture workshops, about 30% of the original cohort
go on to participate in leadership training programmes,
and at this point, Atkinson thinks, participants feel
that they are truly "part of a movement". It is also these
neighbourhood groups who seek further opportunities
to engage locally, not only as farmers but also setting
up things like bike shops, arts and education projects.
About 10% of community gardeners grow produce for
sale, and finally about 2.5% of the original cohort that
attended initial workshops set up market gardens, typically earning about $10,000 per acre. Ashley estimates
that 3 acres [1.2 hectares] are manageable by a family.

In Detroit, urban agriculture initiatives combine with
other green infrastructure projects aimed not only
at improving the environment, but also at stabilising
neighbourhoods, rebuilding esteem, connecting communities to resources and developing employment. A
veritable toolbox of differently-sized projects has been
developed for reference in various situations. One of
the simplest of these tools is called 'creative mowing',
whereby demolished housing plots are mown and
tended to make them appear intentional, rather than
abandoned. This act reminds of one of the drivers for
the *CPUL City* concept: namely to give a sense of coherence to urban landscapes by creating a physical productive continuity between individual plots of land.

Note
1.   <http://quickfacts.census.gov/qfd/states/26/2622000.html>
     accessed 3/21/12

Policies to support Urban Agriculture: Lessons from New York and Detroit

Nevin Cohen

Urban agriculture policy-making in the USA has generally consisted of rezoning as a first step towards recognizing, legalizing and regulating the gardens, farms and related food production, processing, and distribution infrastructure that are part of the urban agriculture system. The rezoning efforts underway in cities across the USA (e.g. Portland, Oakland, Minneapolis) have typically addressed issues of farm scale, operational or performance standards, the sale of farm products, and ancillary uses like greenhouses (Hodgson *et al.* 2011). In some cities, zoning decisions have been informed by land surveys to identify new sites for food production (Mendes 2008: 436).

Cities are also attempting to address *emerging* forms of urban agriculture, including gardening and farming at an increased scale, new types of rooftop and commercial farms and other forms of building-integrated agriculture, temporary and flexible farming projects, animal husbandry and beekeeping, and the use of diverse growing technologies such as aquaponics.

Advocates and policy makers in US cities continue to debate whether and to what extent urban agriculture is an appropriate use of city land, and its potential impact on social, economic and environmental needs. This chapter presents case profiles for New York and Detroit, and suggests lessons learned from each that can be applied by other cities interested in supporting emerging forms of urban agriculture.

New York City

New York has a rich and robust agricultural network; one of the largest of any US city. As of 2011, there were more than 700 farms and gardens citywide that grow food (Cohen *et al.* 2012). By comparison, Seattle's famous *P-Patch* community gardening program has approximately 85 (Seattle *n.d.*), and San Francisco has approximately 65 gardens on city property (SPUR 2012: 10). The New York City Department of Education supports nearly 350 school gardens, including a garden-to-school café program in 63 schools that incorporates student-grown produce in school lunches (grow to learn *n.d.*). Dozens of non-profit and commercial farms, including several rooftop farms, operate throughout the city. New York City farmers and gardeners use a wide range of growing techniques at various scales to produce food throughout the five boroughs.

Policy and planning context

Two important factors enable New York to support such a large and diverse agricultural system. For one thing, it has very permissive public policies. Unlike many other US cities, New York City's zoning ordinance allows agriculture (gardening and farming) virtually everywhere (NYC 2009). The Health Department permits raising chickens and bees (NYC 2010). In 2010, the city adopted rules that offer community gardening groups annual licenses to operate gardens on city property, with provisions for automatic renewal provided that gardens comply with the license terms and conditions, and a complex public review process required if the city wishes to evict gardeners and develop a site (Blachman 2010: 2549).[1]

New York City also has an extensive network of technical assistance providers, advocacy organizations, philanthropies and private businesses that support gardeners and farmers (Cohen *et al.* 2012). This network of intermediary organizations runs farmers' markets that sell city-grown and -raised food, organizes neighborhood-scale composting projects, designs and builds gardens and chicken coops, provides training and technical assistance, lends gardening tools and advocates for supportive public policy. A small but expanding number of restaurant owners back urban agriculture by buying produce from city farms and supplying organic waste for composting, as well as by growing their own food. Groups have launched an urban farm school to train prospective farmers, helped immigrants with farming skills gain access to farmland, and have begun planning an urban farm incubator.

Recent strategic plans and policy papers also emphasize the value of urban agriculture to the city's sustainability. The mayor's 2011 update to the citywide sustainability strategy, *PlaNYC*, endorses the growth of urban agriculture, as do two additional food policy reports prepared by New York City elected officials (NYC *n.d.*).

City sustainability strategy: *PlaNYC 2030*
PlaNYC 2030 states that the city is 'committed to promoting community gardens and other forms of urban agriculture' and gives several specific guarantees to expand urban gardens and farms:

- The New York City Housing Authority (NYCHA) will create at least one urban farm and 129 new community gardens on Housing Authority land.
- The Department of Parks and Recreation will identify farm or garden sites on city-owned properties,

increase the number of gardeners registered with the city's *Green Thumb* gardening program by 25%, and establish five new farmers' markets at community garden sites.
- The city's *Brownfield Cleanup* program will pilot a community garden on a remediated brownfield site.
- The Department of Education will register 25 new school gardens per year.
- The Department of Sanitation will reinstate leaf and yard waste composting and evaluate the feasibility of residential organic waste composting.
- The Departments of City Planning, Buildings, and Parks and Recreation will review laws and regulations to reduce impediments to agriculture.

While *PlaNYC* articulates broad goals and commits agencies to specific actions, it is a strategy document of the current Mayor's administration, not an adopted and enforceable plan to which city actions must conform.

Policy plans
Two documents prepared by city elected officials – written with input from citizens, stakeholders and policy advocates – offer recommendations to support and grow the city's gardens and farms: *FoodNYC: A Blueprint for*

Fig 1: Arbor House. This municipal housing project by a team around Blue Sea housing developers contains a commercial rooftop greenhouse expected to yield 80,000 to 100,000 pounds of fresh produce a year. (image: Bernstein Associates, 2012)

Fig 2: Arbor House. The produce of the commercial rooftop greenhouse will be sold to the building's residents as well as to local markets in the Bronx, New York. (image: Bernstein Associates, 2012)

a *Sustainable Food System*, a white paper issued by the President of the Borough of Manhattan in February 2010; and *FoodWorks*, a report issued by City Council Speaker Christine Quinn in November 2010. Although neither is an official city plan, they have had the effect of increasing the salience of certain issues and building support for programs and the adoption of new local laws.

FoodNYC calls on the city to 'establish urban food production as a priority in New York City for personal, community, or commercial use by the year 2030' (Stringer 2010). It advocates a large-scale urban agriculture program and policies to facilitate the construction of rooftop agricultural greenhouses. *FoodWorks* urges identifying city-owned buildings with rooftops suitable for agriculture and providing financial incentives for rooftop farms, as well as support for the development of new urban agriculture technologies (Weiss 2011). *FoodWorks* has led to the adoption of several local laws that require the city to track and make publicly available information about the food system, to maintain an online list of vacant land suitable for urban agriculture and to purchase New York State-produced food for its many feeding programs when feasible.

Policy innovation in New York City has also come from various NGOs. The New York City Community Gardening Coalition lobbied for stronger protections for gardens located on city property (NYCCGC 2010); *Just Food* rallied members to lobby successfully to legalize beekeeping (Just Food 2010); the Design Trust for Public Space published recommendations for policy innovations that address issues raised by practitioners, advocates, funders and government officials (Cohen *et al.* 2012); *Farming Concrete* helps urban gardeners track how much produce they have grown (Farming Concrete *n.d.*); and the *596 Acres* project identifies and helps residents to gain access to farm vacant parcels in Brooklyn (596 Acres *n.d.*).

Emerging forms of Urban Agriculture

ROOFTOP AGRICULTURE: New York has numerous rooftop farms and greenhouses: non-profits (such as *Georgia's Place*, an assisted living facility for formerly homeless adults in Brooklyn) use roof spaces for

therapeutic gardens (Seeds To Feed *n.d.*); housing developers (e.g. Blue Sea Development) are building rooftop greenhouses into their residential projects;[2] entrepreneurs have started commercial rooftop farms (e.g. *Eagle Street Rooftop Farm* (Eagle Street *n.d.*); *Brooklyn Grange Farm* (Brooklyn Grange 2012)); and grocers (e.g. *Eli Zabar's* (Eli Zabar *n.d.*)) and restaurants (e.g. *Bell, Book and Candle* (BBC 2012)) are growing food on their roofs. The potential for expanding the number of rooftop agriculture projects is substantial. New York City has an estimated 3,000 acres [1,200 hectares] of flat rooftops on buildings likely to be able to support the weight of rooftop farms without major structural improvements (Ackerman 2011: 40).

Two policies make it easier for buildings to accommodate rooftop greenhouses. *Local Law 49* of 2011 amends the building code by adding greenhouses to the list of rooftop structures (such as water tanks and ventilation equipment) that do not count towards building height limits, provided that the greenhouses occupy less than a third of a roof's area.[3] Another policy is designed to address the approximately 1,200 acres of rooftop space on buildings that are at or over the maximum amount of floor area allowed on the building's lot. To make it possible for the owners of these buildings to install rooftop greenhouses, the New York City Department of City Planning (DCP) amended the city's zoning to exclude rooftop greenhouses atop commercial buildings from the lot's floor area and height limits. To qualify for the exclusion, a greenhouse must: not be on buildings with residential units; only be used to grow plants; not exceed the building height limit by more than 25 feet; have mostly transparent roofs and walls; be set back from the perimeter by at least 6 feet if it exceeds height limits; and incorporate a rainwater collection and reuse system (NYCDCP 2012).

BUILDING-INTEGRATED AGRICULTURE: New York City has issued innovative requests for proposals and offered financial support to encourage developers of affordable housing to design agriculture into their projects on the roof and elsewhere within the building's footprint. For example, the City's Department of Housing Preservation and Development (NYCHPD 2006) issued a request for proposals that required respondents to consider incorporating access to nutritious food, a fitness theme, and places for social gathering into the development.

The winning project, a building called *Via Verde* that has 151 rental and 71 co-op apartments, includes rooftop gardens (including a small apple orchard) to provide opportunities for residents to engage in fruit and vegetable cultivation and to have space for passive recreation and social gathering, while also providing stormwater control and building insulation (Via Verde *n.d.*). Working with the non-profit *GrowNYC*, the development company designed raised garden beds and provides on-site horticultural workshops and food preparation and tasting demonstrations for building occupants (GrowNYC *n.d.*).

The New York City Housing Authority (which is the largest public housing authority in North America, with approximately 179,000 apartments and more than 400,000 residents) sold a parcel of land at a Bronx public housing project to a developer for the construction of 124 units of affordable housing.[4] The development, which opened on February 21, 2013, features an 8,000 square foot hydroponic rooftop greenhouse operated by a private firm, *Sky Vegetables* (Sky *n.d.*), which will grow produce on a commercial basis for the surrounding low-income community (GreenHome *n.d.*). The financial support of the Bronx Borough President and the City Council covered the costs of the purchase and installation of the greenhouse.[5]

AGRICULTURE AS GREEN INFRASTRUCTURE: Like other US cities, New York is under federal and state mandates to reduce combined sewer overflow (CSO) – the mixture of stormwater and sewage that is discharged to waterways untreated when it rains to avoid inundating the sewage treatment facilities. In 2010, New York City's Department of Environmental Protection (DEP), the agency in charge of water and sewer infrastructure, negotiated a consent order with state and federal officials allowing it to use low-tech, landscape design techniques – 'green infrastructure' – to reduce the quantity of stormwater that reaches the sewer system by slowing its flow and allowing it to absorb into the ground through pervious surfaces (NYCDEP *n.d.*). To implement this plan, DEP committed to investing $187 million in such green infrastructure over the next four years, and over $2.4 billion by 2030. As part of this program, DEP funded several new urban agriculture projects: a non-profit rooftop garden that provides social services; a vegetable garden near the Gowanus Canal,

which has been declared a toxic site under the federal *Superfund* program and suffers from CSO pollution; and a commercial rooftop farm atop an industrial building in Brooklyn. By including urban farm and garden sites in this program, the city is simultaneously tackling the CSO problem and providing other multidimensional benefits associated with urban agriculture (Cohen and Ackerman 2012).

Detroit

Policy and planning context

Detroit completed a multi-year comprehensive planning process called *Detroit Future City* in January 2013 that begins to address the role of urban agriculture in the city (Detroit Works *n.d.*). *Detroit Future City* is a long-range plan to articulate a vision for the future of the urban realm, with policy recommendations and implementation strategies. As part of the planning process, *Detroit Future City* published a series of 'policy audits' that outlined observations, information, and tentative ideas on issues considered important to the city's future. One policy audit addressed urban agriculture, describing broadly the state of urban agriculture in Detroit, related its food policies, the leading proposals for expanding urban farming, and urban agriculture policy and planning precedents from other similarly sized cities (AECOM 2010).

The final plan recommends the integration of urban agriculture into the city, including an entire land use category designated 'innovation productive' (DFC 2013). In the innovation productive zones, land that is currently vacant is envisioned being used for growing food and as cultivated urban forests, as well as for fields landscaped to clean contaminated soils, research plots to test new horticultural ideas, and aquaculture facilities. The plan also calls for green residential neighborhoods that include single- and multi-family dwellings, as well as productive landscapes, such as gardens and farms. Green mixed-rise neighborhoods would integrate productive uses like community gardens and forests, as well as green infrastructure and urban habitats, into medium- and high-density multi-family housing. *Detroit Future City* also envisions the links between small-scale urban gardens, farms and local farmers' markets to larger urban farms connected to employment districts, the food industry, and the existing food distribution network, including *Eastern Market*, the city's historic public food market.

To accommodate urban agriculture, Detroit had to revise its zoning ordinance. Unlike New York's agriculture-friendly zoning, Detroit's zoning had no definition of urban farming or food production until it was amended in April 2013. The amended code defines different types

of urban agriculture and related infrastructure: from farms and gardens to aquaculture, aquaponics and hydroponics facilities to greenhouses and farmers' markets. The code now permits agriculture as of right in all residential zoning districts, and with some limitations in all other districts. It requires farms to go through site plan review and conform to standards for agricultural use. It also grandfathers pre-existing farms as non-conforming uses. While permissive with respect to the

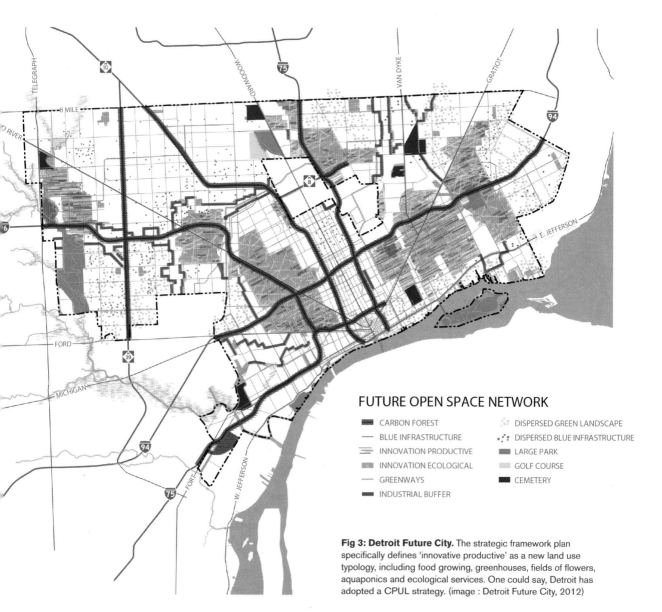

FUTURE OPEN SPACE NETWORK

- CARBON FOREST
- BLUE INFRASTRUCTURE
- INNOVATION PRODUCTIVE
- INNOVATION ECOLOGICAL
- GREENWAYS
- INDUSTRIAL BUFFER

- DISPERSED GREEN LANDSCAPE
- DISPERSED BLUE INFRASTRUCTURE
- LARGE PARK
- GOLF COURSE
- CEMETERY

Fig 3: Detroit Future City. The strategic framework plan specifically defines 'innovative productive' as a new land use typology, including food growing, greenhouses, fields of flowers, aquaponics and ecological services. One could say, Detroit has adopted a CPUL strategy. (image : Detroit Future City, 2012)

type of infrastructure allowed on farms and gardens, the code prohibits farm animals, invasive species of trees and certain crops deemed likely to attract rodents, like oats, wheat and rye.

The major difference in how the urban agriculture issue is framed in Detroit compared to New York City relates to Detroit's economic woes, the large quantity of vacant and derelict properties, and its long-range planned shrinkage of the city. Some urban agriculture advocates in Detroit have been able to conceive gardening and farming as a low-cost and relatively near-term strategy to put vacant land back into productive use as a means to achieve food sovereignty and local economic development. One of the leading organizations advocating local control of land for urban agriculture is the Detroit Black Community Food Security Network, a coalition of organizations and individuals working to build food security in Detroit's African-American community. The network has focused on the importance of building self-reliance, food sovereignty and food justice, and operates *D-Town Farm*, a seven-acre farm on Detroit's west side that has organic vegetable plots, mushroom beds, four beehives, four hoop houses for year-round food production and a composting scheme.

Emerging policy questions

The preceding chapter indicates the extent to which urban agriculture in Detroit is evolving along different tracks, one community-based and the other large-scale. Yet, there remain two unresolved policy questions at the heart of both community-based and large-scale commercial urban agriculture, especially given the current economic crisis Detroit faces. One relates to social justice and disparities in access to city resources, like low-cost land and preferential treatment by city officials. The other is long-term control of city land. Individuals in Detroit's food policy world, particularly members of the Detroit Black Community Food Security Network, are concerned that the appointment of an emergency financial manager for the city in March 2013, who has control over operations and budgeting, may increase efforts to sell vacant land throughout the city to outside investors as a way to quickly raise revenue and reduce the city's inventory of vacant parcels. Advocates argue that such land sales disadvantage the Detroit residents who wish to expand grassroots urban agriculture ventures

and make it difficult to plan the growth of the city's community-based urban agriculture system.

Lessons for planners (cross-referenced to the *CPUL City Actions*)

Engage in Urban Agriculture planning (*CPUL City Action*: IUC)

While New York has language in its sustainability strategy about urban agriculture, there is no overarching plan grounded in commitments to land use for urban agriculture and budgetary support for the infrastructure needed for a vibrant urban agriculture sector. In Detroit, questions about how agriculture fits into the cityscape may be addressed in the *Detroit Future City* plan, but these issues have not been resolved and may be complicated by the financial crisis that the city now faces. The two cases suggest the need to move beyond rezoning efforts and specific policy and program development to comprehensive urban agriculture planning, as the city of Minneapolis did in 2011 (Minneapolis 2011).

An urban agriculture plan would improve governance structures, practices, and programs to broaden participation in urban agriculture policy-making and provide more equitable access to material and financial resources. Specifically, it would be a process by which a city determines its goals and objectives for expanding urban agriculture, recognizing the potential capacity for food production, the costs of increasing production, opportunity costs for using farmable land and the potential for urban food growing to meet the needs of different communities. A plan is a vehicle for assessing the land and rooftop space needs for a variety of urban agriculture scenarios over the next decade, including identifying opportunities for emerging forms of urban food growing, such as rooftop spaces. It is also a process for determining the long-term capital and annual operating budgets required to adequately support the city's urban agriculture program. *Detroit Future City* identifies the land uses that can support urban agriculture, but a plan for disposing of vacant parcels and financing their conversion to productive open spaces remains to be developed.

Integrate urban agriculture into the regional food system (*CPUL City Action*: R)

One of the lessons of the emerging commercial urban agriculture efforts in both New York City and Detroit is that urban gardeners and farmers are not only networked horizontally within the city, but they are connected to and appreciate their integral relationship with the regional food system and the farmers in the wider foodshed. To support commercial and institutional urban farmers, cities can facilitate relationships with commercial farmers outside of the city. This would help urban farmers to expand their production capacities through partnerships with larger landholders, and share business and farming advice with farmers who focus on production and sales rather than the social goals of community gardening and non-profit farming. Even community gardeners have formed working relationships with rural farms, in many cases through the farmers' markets located at the gardens that serve as distribution channels for regional produce. To make it less expensive for rural farmers to participate in these markets, cities can invest in 'food hubs' that make aggregation, processing, and distribution more cost-effective. Detroit's *Eastern Market* is one example, but different models and scales may be appropriate in other cities.

Address race and class disparities in Urban Agriculture (*CPUL City Action*: U+D)

Significant race and class disparities exist in both New York and Detroit's urban agriculture systems, with resulting negative impacts on urban agriculture programs, not to mention to the individuals and communities most directly affected by these disparities (Cohen and Reynolds 2012). Philanthropic dollars, city grants and in-kind assistance often are not equally accessible to all practitioners because information about opportunities often flows to organizations already connected to funding networks. In New York City, urban farmers and gardeners feel that dollars often flow to emerging forms of urban agriculture, like rooftop farms, because they are novel and are run by young, primarily white individuals who have easier access to media and funders. In Detroit, as noted above, grassroots activists are concerned about preferential treatment of large-scale commercial farming proposals.

One step to address these concerns is to ensure that all practitioners in the city have full access to information about funding opportunities and agency programs that support their missions. Leveling the playing field means that agencies and philanthropic organizations need to affirmatively seek out and assist organizations that have historically not been successful at winning grants and contracts, and by funding institutional capacity building in these organizations so that they are better able to compete for funding opportunities. Addressing disparities also means looking at ways for agencies to create links among the urban agriculture community that foster increased sharing of knowledge and resources.

Data gathering is essential for practitioners and policy makers (*CPUL City Action*: R)

Because food systems have not, until very recently, been part of the planning process, cities have little information on basic parameters of the food system, such as the provenance of food purchased by city agencies, the land (and rooftops) for urban food production, the accessibility of healthy food, and the management of food residuals. A fundamental project of many cities is to collect, organize and analyse this data for the purposes of planning, program management, policy-making and establishing a baseline for progress evaluation. Given the fiscal constraints cities are currently facing, often this information gathering requires external funding or is done by NGOs instead of city agencies.

Elsewhere in this book, reference is made to organizations measuring the outputs from urban food growing, and a recent study in Detroit estimates that urban agriculture has the potential to meet a substantial part of the city's demand for vegetables (Colasanti and Hamm 2010: 41). Studies like these can serve as a benchmark for evaluating the productive capacity of urban agriculture programs, yet food production is only one of many important indicators. Activities such as educational programs, effects on the diets of gardeners and farmers, ecological data, and other benefits must be tracked to make the policy case for support of urban agriculture.

Financial support to enable gardeners and farmers to track these metrics would begin to produce the data needed for program improvements, for funders to target their investments, and for government officials to design more effective programs and policies. Lending support, so that intermediary organizations can better track and evaluate the impacts of their programs, would also provide valuable information for the organizations themselves to improve their programming and for the philanthropic community to understand the impacts of their funding.

Integrate agriculture into multiple-agency missions (*CPUL City Action*: U+D)

Many aspects of city government are affected by food and affect the food system, from food procurement to public health programs designed to reduce obesity, to zoning, planning and city property management, to waste disposal. Yet city charters do not designate food as an explicit responsibility of any single city agency. A challenge for food systems planning is to ensure that agencies are both empowered and encouraged to address food system sustainability, and that innovative food system policies are designed to support the missions of specific agencies. Cities like Detroit that are undergoing comprehensive planning, or those with sustainability plans like New York, have to some degree been able to integrate food into these efforts.

There is an enormous opportunity to incorporate food production into various aspects of the city's operations or physical development by encouraging agencies to consider how urban agriculture can help them to address diverse programmatic issues, from affordable housing production to waste management. Urban agriculture should be treated as a cross-cutting issue that warrants consideration throughout the planning processes that happen at the agency level. This means that city agencies, from Sanitation to City Planning, to the Office of Management and Budget, should integrate thinking about urban agriculture into their programs, plans and long-range strategies. The example from New York City's green infrastructure program illustrates that urban agriculture can fulfill not only the goals of increased food production, but also the pragmatic needs of agencies not connected to the food system, such as the water utility's need for low-cost stormwater management techniques. Other multidimensional benefits of considering urban agriculture can accrue to agencies that might otherwise consider food as part of their purview.

Conclusions

The lessons from New York City and Detroit suggest that urban agriculture planning and policy-making should evolve from a focus on zoning to support the existing networks of gardens and farms in cities to a more comprehensive assessment of emerging forms, scales and configurations of urban agriculture as well as forward-looking planning to support these new typologies; and innovative ways to weave these new gardens and farms into city agency activities. A planning process that engages urban farmers, gardeners and grassroots advocates in a meaningful way is essential to ensure support for new forms of urban agriculture from various constituencies in and outside of government, and to address disparities that may emerge in the urban agriculture system due to underlying race and class disparities that exist in cities. The result is likely to be the development of continuous productive urban landscapes that include both large-scale urban farms and gardens, as well as interconnected networks of small-scale gardens, building-integrated farms, and other forms of edible green infrastructure.

Notes

1   note the addition of a New Chapter 6 to Title 56 of the Official Compilation of Rules of the City of New York.

2   for press release see: <http://www.prlog.org/11833817-old-castle-precast-helps-construct-green-affordable-housing-for-families-in-need.html>.

3   for a download of the document see <http://www.nyc.gov/html/dob/downloads/pdf/ll49of2011.pdf>.

4   for details see: U.S. Department of Housing and Urban Development Office of Public and Indian Housing – New York City Housing Authority: *Final PHA Plan: Annual Plan for Fiscal Year 2012*, pg. 7. Accessed at <www.nyc.gov/html/nycha/downloads/pdf/FY2012-AnnualPlan.pdf> on 20 Jan, 2012.

5   for a planning and housing focused report see: <http://www.nyc.gov/html/nycha/html/news/new-york-city-and-state-officials-join-blue-sea-development-to-celebrate-the-opening-of-a-new-healthy-and-energy-efficient-affordable-housing-development-in-the-bronx.shtml>.

Community gardening in Berlin and New York: A new eco-social movement

Elisabeth Meyer-Renschhausen

Local politicians and city planners of the Global North are faced with a new phenomenon: a fresh enthusiasm for community gardening can be seen across many major cities in many parts of the world. Community gardeners, guerilla gardeners and intercultural gardeners are reclaiming common land for their social and gardening activities. The media follow. No community gardening activity can take place in Berlin without photographers or researchers watching. Intentionally or not, the urban cultivation of vegetables has become fashionable.

This kind of new 'urban agriculture' – as I would call it, following Jac Smit (Smit *et al.* 1996) – has become a symbol and a form of positive protest; a protest against land grabbing in all its variants and against developer-driven communal policies. Collective vegetable growing has become *the* sign of the fight against a food dictatorship which has brought devastation, destruction and genetic engineering to the world without consulting with the people.

Independently founded community gardens and agricultural projects recall the kitchen gardens and allotments of the past, which were originally tended by women in the context of their housework. Remember the so-called "rubble women" in Berlin, who were the driving force behind the reconstruction of many bombed-out cities after World War II? They also grew their own potatoes in public parks (Warneke *et al.* 2001; Meyer-Renschhausen *et al.* 2002, Meyer-Renschhausen 2011a). In times of crisis and need, informal, casual work and self-help have always reappeared in cities, for example after the Thirty Years' War (Meyer-Renschhausen and Holl 2000). In such times, we – especially the younger generation – rediscover the value and pleasures of working for one's own subsistence and living sustainably; a development welcome for both individuals and society as a whole, especially in times of rising unemployment.

Community gardening has become a kind of invisible university in the postmodern age. People who cultivate vegetables among the weeds of the urban wasteland begin to reflect on their own eating habits and on a climate-friendly 'diet for a small planet' (Moore Lappé 1971). Long-forgotten and unappreciated varieties of vegetables resurface, such as French spinach, heritage potatoes or Swiss chard. The new freelancers, independent artists and career surfers teach each other and the rest of us how to live a good life with little or no money. They teach the socially excluded and the unemployed how to reclaim the commons, i.e. the land that is publicly or collectively owned (Hynes 1996; Ferguson 1999; Linn 1999 and 2007; Campbell and Wiesen 2009).

Over the last 30 years, the globalisation of poverty resulting from the "global brutal" politics of privatisation (Chossudovsky 1997; Krugman 2003; Davis 2006) have generated a new class of urban poor and, as an answer, new social movements to 'Reclaim the Commons' (Linn 1999 and 2007). Guerilla gardening has become a popular means of taking action against the politics of land speculation – these politics that even the leftist and the far-left political parties tolerate and sometimes support. By constantly having to fight for the land they have reclaimed, and to maintain existing community gardens, people who had previously been marginalised become citizens again. The new gardeners see themselves as active members of a world society working to preserve the One World. It is a movement fighting for democracy and for a food independence threatened by commercial interests, especially by those of big multinational seed producers (Lamborn Wilson and Weinberg 1999; Shiva 2006).

The roots: international social movements and their achievements – the example of Berlin

Cities shrink in times of rising unemployment. This will become an increasingly common phenomenon in Northern and Western societies if their economies continue to shrink.

Within this, Berlin is a strange city, where at the moment somehow nothing is growing except its gardening movement. Berlin, a stronghold of what I like to call "survival artists", has just very recently become a capital of community gardening. But, as I shall explain, it has always had a strong affinity for forests, gardens and social movements.

The first garden settlement in the greater Berlin area was founded in 1893, to the North of Berlin, in order to give the unemployed the opportunity to feed themselves. This first intentional garden community, later called *Obstbaukolonie Eden* [Orchard Colony Eden], was located near the Berlin suburb of Oranienburg at the end of the municipal railway line. It began as a vegetarian cooperative (its foundation was planned in a vegetarian restaurant in Charlottenburg) and, in the course of the roaring twenties, evolved into a type of "Northern Ascona", with all kinds of lifestyle and social reformers as well as artists living there together. In 1932, it hosted the World Congress of the Vegetarian Movement.

In 1899, the book *Garden cities of to-morrow* was published by the English social and land reformer Ebenezer Howard (Howard 1902), after reading Edward Bellamy's *Looking backwards,* and after having visited Long Island in 1880, which was then largely a summer refuge for New York City residents. Howard's idea was to restore a healthier way of life to a working-class and lower-middle-class community. In 1899, the first Garden City Association was founded in England and in 1902 *Letchworth Garden City* was built near London, followed by *Welwyn Garden City* in 1920 (Miller 2010).

The first German garden cities of this generation included the *Gartenstadt Rüppurr*, founded in 1907 by the well-known author Paul Kampffmeyer in the village of Rüppurr south of Karlsruhe (today a part of Karlsruhe) (Kampffmeyer 1913), as well as the *Gartenstadt Hellerau*, established by the furniture

manufacturer Karl Schmidt in 1909 in Hellerau, east of the city of Dresden, today a part of Dresden (Hartmann 1998). Around 1910, a large number of new garden cities were created on the Berlin periphery. The *Gartenstadt Staaken*, for example, was set up in 1913 by the sociologist and land reformer Franz Oppenheimer in Staaken near Spandau, a town to the Northwest of Berlin (Oppenheimer 1964). Today, both Staaken and Spandau are part of the municipality of Berlin. Astonishingly many garden cities were founded in 1913, i.e. just one year before the outbreak of the First World War, and then completed in the 1920s, for example to give war invalids, the unemployed and people with small salaries the possibility to get or build their own homes and to feed themselves from their home gardens. Several of these garden cities were designed by well-known architects, such as Bruno Taut's *Hufeisensiedlung* [Horse-shoe Colony] in Berlin-Britz, realised between 1925 and 1933.

Some of the garden enthusiasts of this era left town and became small-scale farmers. Among them was Henny Rosenthal (1885–1944), the mother of well-known US-American community gardener Karl Linn (1923–2005). After graduating from the first college for young women in Berlin, Rosenthal became the first woman to work at the Berlin Stock Exchange. Later she quit that job and bought a piece of land, a *Rentengut*, a type of smallholding, from a land-reform society which had purchased land with the intention of selling it on to subsistence farmers, unemployed people and idealistic garden enthusiasts. Helped only by her mother, she founded her small farmstead near Dessow, a village with a train station about one hour north of Berlin. Her farm consisted primarily of an orchard that she planted during the First World War with apple, cherry and pear trees. She also kept chickens, pigs and cows. In addition, she used the farm to teach Jewish girls the skills of horticulture and lived with them in a Kibbutz-style community (Linn 2007; Meyer-Renschhausen 2008).

In 1920, Berlin incorporated nearly all of the surrounding municipalities. In the midst of the revolutionary post-war era with its many social reforms, this new Greater Berlin became a green city, with 18% of its area covered with forests. In 1930, Berlin had about 4 million inhabitants, and since many were long-term unemployed without any kind of social security, about

6% of Berlin's surface was covered with allotment gardens (Warnecke *et al.* 2001).[1] Allotment gardens were strongly supported by a new law of 1919, the *Reichsklein-garten-und Siedlungsverordnung*, which became possible as result of the November Revolution in Germany (War-necke *et al.* 2001). Under this law, everyone in need had a right to a so-called *Schrebergarten* on land provided by the municipality (Gröning and Wolschke-Bulmahn 1995; Meyer-Renschhausen 2004a). During the inter-war period, internationally people were as enthusiastic about gardening as they had been before World War I. The 1920s and 1930s witnessed the second garden-ing wave of the 20th century. In Berlin, many rooftop gardens were created during the 1920s, in an abundance that was never reached thereafter. At least one of my grandmothers grew vegetables in her urban backyard, as your grandmother may also have done.

In the United States, garden cities for the unemployed were founded during the Great Depression. In 1937, for example, unemployed textile workers from New York were given the opportunity to move to the Jersey Homestead, renamed Roosevelt in 1945, near Trenton, New Jersey. During both world wars, especially World War II, so-called Victory Gardens were founded in many English and US-American cities.

After World War II, in East and West Germany, new settlements for refugees from the former German prov-inces of Silesia, Pomerania and East Prussia were estab-lished, both in the countryside and on the outskirts of big cities. We can see these settlements as a second or third generation – as well as a variation – of garden cities, since they offered to the settlers small detached, semi-detached or terraced houses with large gardens for a functioning subsistence economy. In cities like Berlin, Leipzig, Hannover, Hamburg, Bremen and Cologne, thousands of allotment garden colonies fed the hungry during the hard times after the war. While in the post-war United States, the wartime Victory Gardens were soon sacrificed to developers in the housing industry, in Germany, Poland and Austria most of the inner-city allotment gardens survived at least into the 1990s.

The second wave: community gardening – the example of New York City

During the world financial crisis due to the Vietnam War in the early 1970s, a wave of community gardeners in the United States took over empty lots in many parts of major cities. The *Liz Christy Garden* was the "first" community garden founded in Manhattan's Lower East Side in 1973.[2]

In Europe, a similar "squatters' movement" arose as a reaction against rising speculative housing and land vacancy. The squatters took over empty lots and created the so-called children's farms – in London, Amsterdam and Copenhagen as well as in Berlin. Later, they formed the European Federation of City Farms (EFCF *n.d.*). In Berlin, the first founders of these children's farms were often young women with small children or students. They planted trees, flowers and vegetables and kept goats, sheep, horses, pigs, rabbits and chickens for their youngsters. Mostly without any help from the authori-ties, they created beautiful green places where German mothers could meet Turkish mothers and families from other countries in an informal setting (Rosol 2006).

As a result of the world financial crisis of the 1970s, the North American tax system passed the burden of the economic downturn on to the municipalities. Growing industrial unemployment resulted in urban decay. In 1975, the global city of New York was facing bankruptcy. The Republican-led national government, dominated by the suburban upper-middle-class and mid-sized cities of the Midwest, refused to help. The harsh "structural programmes" that were then imposed on the unloved metropolis were in fact no different to those being imposed on South America by the World Bank and IMF since the early 1970s, as well as on indebted developing countries worldwide since the early 1980s. Many parts of the city of New York became neglected regions with broken windows, vacant buildings, and poorly main-tained streets and public transportation. These included the Lower East Side of Manhattan, large parts of the Bronx, Harlem, and parts of Brooklyn, such as East New York, Red Hook and Williamsburg. These quarters were perceived as being too dangerous for white people to live in or even to travel through. Many of them, including East New York, became ghettos (Häußermann and Siebel 1993; Marcuse 1998; Thabit 2003; Sites 2003). On the

Fig 1: *Allmende-Kontor*'s **community garden** a former Tempelhof Feld airport in Berlin.

Fig 2: **Community-supported agriculture meeting** in the Garden of Union, Brooklyn, New York City.

brink of bankruptcy, the city of New York was compelled to collaborate with private investors in order to increase tax revenues. New York became a pioneer in the sad business of excluding the poor while publicly subsidising real estate speculators. Since that time, municipal policies have been dictated by an advisory board dominated by bankers. This board was forced onto the Democratic Mayor Ed Koch in 1975 in order to rescue the city's finances. The advisory board recommended that the city cancel a long list of social programmes and disengage from entire districts, which were then deliberately left to decay. In East New York, for example, the administration stopped fixing the roads and planting trees. Public property was not maintained and the garbage was left uncollected on the streets. This created areas of "no man's land" open to large-scale speculation – as the New York City planner Walter Thabit showed in his study on East New York (Thabit 2003). Soon after 2000, the construction of overpriced new housing got their owner-contractors into trouble (Smith 1993; Sites 2003; Thabit 2003).

That is one side of the story, but such heavy crises also bring new opportunities. A municipality that can no longer afford to sustain itself must honour and support the efforts of citizens to help themselves. If it can do nothing against the shrinking process of the city, it is in its own interest to acknowledge the growing willingness of citizens to create, for example, gardens on empty lots. Thus, even a municipality as large as New York City pragmatically adopted a sort of subsistence perspective of its own. It was a question of daily survival. The self-subsistence perspective found favour within the administration, because this new kind of self-help was seen as preventing urban decay and the growth of criminality connected with it. The mayors of the boroughs realised the ability of community gardens to promote social peace. Since they provide an excellent protection against attacks and violence and create a new feeling of safety for people, such gardens offer a healing process for both body and soul (Hynes 1996; Grünsteidel and Schneider-Sliwa 1999; Grünsteidel 2000; Gröning 1997 and 2002; Stone 2002; Meyer-Renschhausen 2004b and 2008).

The policy of the administration regarding community gardens remains unfortunately ambivalent. Several other interest groups, including short-term, medium-term and long-term interests, compete with each other. This becomes apparent when community gardens are supported in one case, while being threatened elsewhere. Self-initiative and self-help remain welcome in those parts of the city that no one is economically interested in. But as soon as people have succeeded substantially in improving their neighbourhood, the speculators appear on the scene again and we can watch

149

Fig 3: The *Prinzessinnengärten* in Berlin-Kreuzberg understands itself as a nomadic urban agriculture project.

of new community gardens and with communication between gardeners and the city. In 1995, *Green Thumb* became part of the Parks and Recreation Administration (Meyer-Renschhausen 2004b; Stone 2000, 2002 and 2009; Gittleman *et al.* 2010). By adopting *Green Thumb* into City Hall, federal and local governments have acknowledged that community gardeners enhance the urban environment not just for themselves, but for everyone. It is a proven fact that gardeners and their supporters contribute to healthier living conditions (Meyer-Renschhausen and Holl 2000; Svendsen 2009; Stone 2009). Small green spaces are enough to reduce pollution from car exhaust, offer pleasure, healthy work and rest for all. Urban green reduces stress. Trees and bushes reduce noise and are refreshing in the hot summer. Community gardens are an important part of the environmental movement worldwide, probably one of its most effective components. They are a landmark on the way to a sustainable environmental policy in the sense of the Rio de Janeiro 1992 *Agenda 21* agreement, when municipalities committed themselves to contribute to the reduction of greenhouse gases (Svendsen 2009).

The most recent developments in this string of open space production are commercial rooftop gardens, for example in the New York Borough of Brooklyn.

the process of gentrification. However, the need to find meaningful uses for vacant lots – and for people – and shrinking incomes while costs exploded, especially rent in the housing sector, led to authorities committing to an expansion of urban farming in Philadelphia, Boston, Detroit, Chicago and many other urban areas. The aim was and still is to turn vacant lots into open green spaces full of fresh air, sunlight, shade and the twitter of birds.

Starting in 1975, New York City created the *Open Space Greening* and the *Plant a Lot* programmes; two self-greening programmes by the Council on the Environment to support community gardens. Today, the Council is still financed by sponsorship, but is under the direct authority of the mayor. Liz Christy, the founder of the city's first community garden, was chosen as the first head of the Council's new advisory board (Meyer-Renschhausen 2004b; Stone 2000, 2002 and 2009). The Council on the Environment still supports the greening of new vacant lots, in addition to fighting waste proliferation and promoting environmental education and new farmers' markets.

Shortly afterwards, in 1978, New York City's key organisation, *Green Thumb,* was founded as *Operation Green Thumb*. Its main task was to help with the creation

The third wave: growing vegetables – the example of Berlin

In the last 20 years, a third wave of community gardening took over more and more open spaces in North American cities, reaching London in the early 1990s and European continental cities in the late 1990s. Contrary to earlier intentions of community gardening, in this new wave the focus is on vegetable growing. In the US, these vegetable-growing community gardens are founded and run in poor neighbourhoods, so-called "ghettos". The majority of North American gardeners now are people of colour. The gardeners often are long-time unemployed or earn too little to be able to act as citizens participating in the public sphere of their society (Stone 2009; Svendsen 2009).

In Berlin, the *AG Kleinslandwirtschaft und Gärten* [Working Group for Small-Scale Agriculture and

Gardens] was founded as a research team in 1997 at the Humboldt University (AG Kleinstlandwirtschaft *n.d.*) and since then plays an important role in promoting community gardening in the German capital.

Today the German city state of Berlin has an official unemployment rate of about 15%. Every fifth inhabitant is poor and receives some form of state benefit. Every second person is self-employed, the majority in low-wage professions, such as freelance artists, sausage vendors and bicycle rickshaw drivers who take tourists around the city. The average Berliner earns half of what people in other German cities earn. That means about €18,600 (about $26,364) a year. In poor neighbourhoods with a high population density and often over-crowded apartments, such as Berlin-Neukölln, east of the former Tempelhof Airport, 60% of boys from families with an immigrant background neither finish school nor receive a vocational training, meaning that they never enter the formal labour market (Meyer-Renschhausen 2011b; Amt für Statistik 2012).

Berlin has 3.5 million inhabitants. Half of the tax-paying residents who lived in East and West Berlin at the time of the city's reunification in 1990 no longer live there, having moved to Western Germany in search of work or to the outskirts of Berlin in search of greener surroundings. They have been replaced by newcomers from all over the world, especially from Poland and Eastern Europe, many of them fleeing the effects of "disaster capitalism" (Klein 2008), such as high unemployment and poverty, authoritarian and oligarchical governments, and growing racism against racial and ethnic minorities. However, the city of Berlin cannot provide enough jobs and these newcomers do not automatically become high-earning taxpayers. Some of them bring their elderly parents with them, although they often do not even earn enough money to support themselves. Therefore, the newcomers need gardens. In particular the newly founded community gardens give the older family members something meaningful to do: providing families with vegetables to eat and perhaps also to sell. Even in the comparatively wealthy western part of Berlin, low-income people, including students, artists and immigrants from Turkey, have started to grow potatoes and other vegetables and fruits for their own subsistence.

Fig 4: The neighbourhood garden *Rosa Rose* had to move from its squatter site to a new location in Berlin.

In Germany the first of these mainly vegetable-growing community gardens were founded in 1996 in the city of Göttingen, 100 km south of Hannover. These community gardens were set up by refugees from the Bosnian war; women from Bosnia Herzegovina, together with their (female) social workers. Originally called 'Internationale Gärten Göttingen' [International Gardens Göttingen], they changed their name a few years later into the now more commonly used term, *intercultural gardens*. The *International Gardens Göttingen* received their land from the local Protestant church for growing vegetables. In 2000, the *Perivoli Garten* in Berlin was established on the southern fringes of the borough of Neukölln as part of a German-Greek women's project, later opened up to the whole community of immigrants. Another such garden, set up in Leipzig in 2001, was explicitly modelled after the example of the North American community gardens. This garden, called *Bunte Gärten Leipzig* [Colourful Gardens of Leipzig], was especially created for refugees and asylum seekers from Afghanistan, Iraq, Sudan and elsewhere. The gardeners sell a part of their harvest to a local farmers' market and pay language teachers with the revenue.

Since 2003, Berlin has become a rapidly growing capital of community gardening in Germany. The first official Interkulturelle Garten was founded in the same year in

Berlin-Köpenick near the River Wuhle. During a workshop in Köpenick at the turn of 2002–2003, *Stiftung Interkultur* was created as a new part of the anstiftung & ertornis foundation with the main aim of promoting intercultural gardens nationwide. The anstiftung & ertornis foundation's office in Munich supports the creation of new gardens and coordinates today, after just a decade, more than 120 gardens (anstiftung *n.d.*a). The foundation's coordinating work is an important factor in the rapid development of German community gardens. Each year, *Stiftung Interkultur* organises a nationwide network meeting. But, of course, the community gardens' success depends crucially on those many activists doing voluntary work and organising round tables all over the country, now and for over 20 years.

Today, Berlin has more than 80 community gardens (Madlener 2009). Beside this, Berlin has various other ongoing urban agriculture projects. Often, these projects feed their initiators and many others – in both meanings of the word. The best-known projects are the *Prinzessinnengärten* in Berlin-Kreuzberg and the *Allmende-Kontor* on the former airport of Tempelhof.

Since the founding of the World Trade Organization in January 1995, a so-called "austerity policy" of the European Union and of the European national governments has brought municipal communities, countries and states into serious difficulties. In 1995, Berlin was drastically deprived of its earlier subsidies as the "best-supported city" during the Cold War. As a result,

the city and state of Berlin has run into debt, initially without any fault of its own. To exacerbate this, ruling politicians of this period fell to corruption. They gave too much as investor guarantees from the Berlin-owned Landesbank to large housing projects, ending in a financial disaster and additional debt increase. By 2012, Berlin had used up all of its financial resources. The national policy of privatisation has deprived it of its freedom to act. Berlin politicians are still unclear about what to do with a major new vacant area, the former airfield in Tempelhof (still famous for the airlift action by US "raisin bombers" to feed Berlin during the Soviet blockade at the beginning of the Cold War). It took a wild and carnivalesque summer day in June 2009, when a couple of thousand squatters faced nearly as many policemen and policewomen in riot gear to convince the administration to open the area for Berlin citizens. Today people are allowed to use the Tempelhof field on a temporary basis, and there are about ten different gardening projects accepted as official "pioneer projects". The biggest of these community gardening projects is the previously mentioned *Allmende-Kontor* [Bureau for Commons], run by a small group of 13 activists and supporting more than 800 gardeners on over 300 raised beds on an allocated area of 5000 square metres, lost in the huge airfield. The *AG Kleinstlandwirtschaft* (see above) is one of the project's founding groups. Many more *Allmende-Kontor* gardens could be created on the field: the interest is immense and growing, as shown by a long waiting list. Will the administration understand this reality fast enough and help the core group finance

Fig 5: Allmende Kontor. Urban gardeners grow crops in individually made planters. Spaces in between are used communally. (image: Bohn & Viljoen, 2011)

and manage the organisation of this huge community garden in a difficult neighbourhood?

An unpleasant tug-of-war over another large urban wasteland had developed a few years back between the Federal Government, in this case its privatised railway company, and the state of Berlin and its boroughs over the Gleisdreieck area, a former freight station near Potsdamer Platz in the city centre. The local citizen's initiative *AG Gleisdreieck* promoted the creation of international community gardens on the large vacant area of the Gleisdreieck (Kotanyi 2007; Bauer 2009; Bauer *n.d.*) as well as safeguarding existing allotment gardens on the site. After many years of negotiation, this large area was designed to accommodate both community-oriented gardens and a prestigious urban park initiated by the council.

Conclusion

Community gardens are no longer utopia. They contribute urgent solutions to problems resulting from a capitalist market economy and the growing gaps in our societies. Community gardens belong to the future of cities as a self-help activity for marginalised people and dispossessed municipalities. Today – in the Global South, as well as in the inner-city ghettos of the North – the term *urban agriculture* means growing food (Bakker *et al.* 2000). In Europe, this is the result of a policy of

austerity we have been facing since 1989. In Berlin, the conversion of urban (waste)land into green spaces open to the public and to community gardening is still hopelessly slow, calling for much patience from the city's garden activists, but during the last ten years a lot has changed. The most important effect of community gardening in both North America and Germany has been the discovery of a new form of cooperation among different cultural, ethnic and social groups as a result of their common fight to save their land from "developers". In many cases, the community gardens of New York have spurred new forms of community involvement and civic participation in a country where half of the population tends not to vote. Furthermore, community gardening creates a different understanding of the global needs, beyond the industrialised North. In doing so, formerly disenfranchised community gardeners become active citizens not just in their own countries, but also for the whole world.

For sure, 'cities that feed themselves' – as Jac Smit once wrote (Smit 1996) – are now on the political agenda, and not only the agenda of the UN's Food and Agriculture Organization.

Notes
1   Today, 2.9% of Berlin is covered by allotment gardens.
2   This garden has recently been included into the *Common Ground* catalogue of the Architecture Biennale in Venice 2012 (Krasny 2012).

CPUL
CITY
ACTIONS

An introduction

Katrin Bohn and André Viljoen

Productive landscapes comprise more than urban agriculture, but agriculture is central; reintroducing it to cities, planning and design remains a radical act. It is not surprising that the numerous municipal initiatives being developed in and by cities such as San Francisco, Vancouver, Rotterdam, Berlin or London, to name but a few, are somewhat piecemeal and patchy given the conceptual change required in thinking and acting if productive urban landscapes are to become truly sustainable and extensive.

With this in mind, the *CPUL City* concept has been extended by developing a toolkit of *CPUL City Actions*, to provide a comprehensive, multi-scaled, interdisciplinary strategic framework of actions for the practical and planned implementation of localised, long-term urban food systems. Four distinct "actions" categorise the various tools most relevant to the architectural, urban design and planning professions. They acknowledge the complex interdependencies within food systems planning, but also help to define particular tasks within the competency of an individual. We visualise them as the "*CPUL City* Clover", a unity of four actions that must happen jointly. Each action can take on different size and shape depending on their particular context (Bohn and Viljoen 2010b).

The current uneven mix of policy, planning and design guidance on urban agriculture has not prevented the establishment of successful initiatives worldwide, initiatives that now stand out as case studies for a vast array of aspects of urban food growing. These range from building-integrated agriculture to rainwater harvesting, to the design of boundaries and planting, to the art of seed collection, to setting up urban farmers' co-ops, food policy councils and more.

The reasons for this uneven development within the architectural and planning professions are complex and intertwined and include:

- the complex nature of urban food systems,

- different local contexts for countries, cities, regions and individual sites, including their different food cultures, physical and logistical site conditions and trading patterns,
- diverse agricultural practices and organisational structures for urban agriculture operations even within one city,
- a lack of long-term experience with urban agriculture projects, other than allotments and community gardens,
- little evaluation of comparable projects as well as the inconsistent dissemination of transferable knowledge,
- competition with commercial developers for valuable urban land within expanding cities and a lack of resources for infrastructure projects within shrinking cities,
- scepticism regarding urban agriculture's legitimacy as an urban land use.

In many respects, practice is outstripping policy and other strategic urban development tools, and the advancement of both individual projects and urban achemes can be very contingent and often lack coherence. In some cases, with Detroit being a well-documented example, different development strategies and approaches can result in a highly contested environment, where issues of food sovereignty, political approach and economic rationale can polarise opinion (Gallagher 2010).

There are by now various good guides available that focus on the transfer and dissemination of useful knowledge from one project to another, as well as to other future urban farmers. However there is very little direction on how to set up, design, run and reflect on urban agriculture projects in more strategic ways that enable and advance their long-term presence in the Global North.

Some of the *CPUL City Actions* overlap with tools and guidance covered elsewhere, for example in the Transition Towns' *Local Food* book dealing with practical and transferable information aimed above all at communities with engaged activists (Pinkerton and Hopkins 2009). Moreover, in the past few years a series of "specialised" guidance books have been published that either belong to a special location or a particular school

of thought. In the UK, amongst these are the *Manual for Growing Food in Front Gardens* by a group of authors from Leeds Metropolitan University, the Back to Front Community Group and Leeds City Council (Oldroyd *et al.* 2011) or the Transition Town Brixton's *Grower's Pack* (Noy *et al.* 2010). The former describes ways to transform a neighbourhood productively, the latter focuses on practical advice on how to start a community garden in Brixton, South London. In the USA, the guidebooks can be ten years older, and concentrate on specific projects/sites, as exemplified by The Food Project's *Urban Grower's Manual* for its community gardeners (Cather 2003), or on operational aspects, as in Urban Partners' *Feasibility Analysis and Next Steps* advising Pennsylvania council on farming in Philadelphia (Hartling 2007). With its shorter history of urban agriculture, Germany takes a scholarly approach to the instruction book, analysing practical examples and drawing applicable conclusions, as the *ZFarm* project in Berlin aims to do with its research on productive roofs (ZALF 2011).

Additionally, case study collections stamped with the proof of "having done it" exist today in all three countries. Here, the achievement can lie in making information comparable and thereby implicitly giving guidance for different types of urban agriculture; essential if practitioners and policy makers are to understand, and therefore plan, how and in which direction a project might develop. *Die Produktive Stadt*, an exhibition about existing food-growing projects in Berlin and Munich, is representative of such collections and was held in a number of German cities in 2011 (TUB 2011). The online database about *Capital Growth's* 2012 food growing spaces in London provides a similar resource (Capital Growth n.d. a). Bridging the gap between strategic and hands-on case study collections is the North-America-based *Carrot City Project*, which boasts more than 100 international examples, many of which offer practical information, as well as visionary ideas on designing for urban agriculture. Its database, divided into five categories from urban design to detailed components, is available online (Ryerson University 2009) with selected examples being published in the book *Carrot City: Creating places for urban agriculture* (Gorgolewski *et al.* 2011).

CPUL City Actions aim to provide clarity by focusing on the key strategic, yet practical steps necessary to implement urban agriculture as part of a designed and

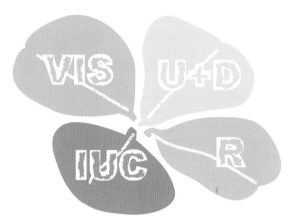

Fig 1: The *CPUL City* Clover. Four joint actions enable the successful implementation of productive urban landscapes:
Action VIS = Visualising Consequences: The visualisation of urban agriculture's contributions to urban life,
Action IUC = Inventory of Urban Capacity: The careful study of each site's capacities and opportunities,
Action U+D = Bottom Up + Top Down: Cooperation between food growers, local councils and neighbourhoods,
Action R = Researching for Change: Constant research for best practice and the adaptation to changing contexts.

planned productive urban landscape. The Actions work within a larger framework by referencing existing best practice, derived from international case studies and contexts, but their message is condensed down to four points relevant to every individual project whatever its scale, location and purpose: *visualise, inventorise, negotiate, keep up to speed.*

The Actions can be thought of in terms of "localisation agendas", but they also explicitly recognise the need for coherent municipal and regiuonal planning frameworks to manage their infrastructural implementation. Food systems by their very nature have to look beyond the local, and the aim here is to maximise the positive contribution that urban agriculture can make to a city's food system. As evidenced in our three case study countries by way of example, there is demand for systematic, practical, graphically descriptive and transferable guidance for those involved in the planning and establishment of productive urban landscapes. We suggest to work with simultaneously these four Actions whatever the urban agriculture task may be. The Actions address activists and urban farmers, as well as the design, planning and governance professionals who can jointly

provide a managed and strategic overview at the level required for implementing productive urban landscapes as elements of urban infrastructure.

In this part of the book, we discuss these four actions with a number of experts involved in the development and/or realisation of implementing urban agriculture projects. To practically mirror the requirements of the *CPUL City Actions*, we present case studies, most of which have been generated within our own work or describe projects that we have been involved in. A summary of the Actions is provided at the end of this section of the book.

Action U+D = *Bottom-Up + Top-Down*

Infrastructural, as well as individual food-productive projects need parallel top-down and bottom-up initiatives, and integrative design and planning.

An urban agriculture project will have the best chance of long-term success, when it can rely on a strong base of local supporters, active and passive, and when these are steadily engaged in negotiation processes with those entities that govern their lives, for example local councils or food distribution systems. The larger, i.e. more infrastructural, a project is, such as a CPUL, the more interdependencies it needs and creates.

Cuba's organoponicos were – and still are – good examples from the 1990s (Viljoen 2005); New York's 1970s *Green Thumb* initiative (Green Thumb 2010); London's *Capital Growth* project (Capital Growth *n.d.* b) represent pioneering efforts now. A spectrum of bottom-up motivations can be identified ranging from community-led to entrepreneurial initiatives. Within each of these motivations, further differentiation can be noted, for example community-led programmes that are driven by imperatives of empowerment and ex-/ inclusion, e.g. *Growing Power, Inc.* in Milwaukee (Growing Power 2011), Germany's intercultural gardens (IKG 2011), or those initiatives, often in more affluent areas, that aim for broader educational and lifestyle choices, such as *Fortis Green Allotments* in London (FGCAT 2010) or *Domäne Dahlem* in Berlin (Lummel 2009). Entrepreneurial-led projects similarly range from those advocating small-scale, but individually viable market gardens, e.g. the social enterprise *Growing Communities* in London (Growing Communities 2008) or the commercially viable "self-harvest" project *Bauerngarten* in Berlin (Grafenstein 2010), to larger-scale "corporate" approaches, e.g. *Hantz Farms* in Detroit (Hantz Farms 2011).

James Godsil unravels in his chapter *And every city deserves a Sweet Water and a Growing Power!* the many facets of co-founding and running one of the USA's recently much-discussed urban agriculture projects, the 'hybrid enterprise experiment' *Sweet Water Organics*. Much in the sense of this action, he describes *Sweet Water* as a 'social business and innovation centre' advancing at the same time the commercialisation and democratisation of aquaponics as 'an ecological method of food production' and a major response to the challenge of food security.

In the work of social design collective *Urbaniahoeve*, similar relationships are being explored: Debra Solomon and Mariska van den Berg take stock in their chapter *Urbaniahoeve: Event-based practice and Urban Agriculture*. The authors understand their work – as exemplified by their project *Foodscape Schilderswijk* in The Hague – as 'a classic case of *event practice*', as 'collectively installed public space edible landscapes that, in time, form an *ecological framework* within the city'. Negotiating productive landscapes between residents, funders and the local council changes the attitude of all of them to their environments, because, so *Urbaniahoeve* believes, 'food appears to encourage generous behaviour'.

When looking at top-down and bottom-up approaches to urban agriculture, it is of great interest to study these interdependencies in communities that have not (yet) found the energy or means to actively engage via the food growing agenda with their local environment. Here, it might be "outsiders" who feel that the joint building of a productive urban landscape would benefit those particular neighbourhoods. In this case, the ignition for action – then coupled with funding – can successfully come from local governments or institutions such as in the 2,012-food-growing-spaces *Capital Growth* project in London or in the one-off neighbourhood renewal *Spiel/ Feld Marzahn* project in Berlin. For the *Urban Farming Project* in Middlesbrough, stakeholders, residents and

council representatives jointly engaged in a celebration of food, food growing sites and food consumption.

What is required now is the evolution of policy to support diverse bottom-up initiatives and accommodate these within a mutually beneficial framework of top-down decisions that add to urban experience, urban resilience and the quality of urban space. For this to happen, the consequences of integrating productive urban landscapes into contemporary cities need to be visualised.

Action VIS = *Visualising Consequences*

The qualities and aims of urban agriculture and productive urban landscapes, such as CPULs, need visualising to inform decision makers and raise public awareness.

Visualising ideas and concepts is one of the primary skills of architects, planners and designers. Usually, this is done through the design and/or prototyping of the idea in question, thereby predicting and discussing its potential outcomes; spatial, user, environmental or financial. In the case of productive urban landscapes, this action widens to include a range of urban agriculture experts and practitioners in the process. It encompasses the public and visually descriptive dissemination of ideas, data and best-practice examples, mostly in the form of exhibitions, installations, prototypes and online/paper/live presentations. Here, the design professional becomes the "agent of change", carrying on a long, and at times problematic, tradition of the architectural manifesto as a herald of future change and challenges. One can broadly identify two main, sometimes overlapping ways of visualising the consequences of productive urban landscapes: the creation of new mental images and the creation of 1:1 working prototypes.

The international exhibition *Vertical Gardens*, first shown in 2009 at Exit Art in New York (Exit Art 2009), for example, brought together a range of mostly unbuilt projects by international architects inviting visitors to think again when considering urban food growing. The temporary *Salatfeld* by the artists' installation collective myvillages.org enabled visitors for the duration of one week to taste the produce of a salad field floating on one of Berlin's man-made ponds (myvillages 2011). Since 2011 The *Farm:Shop* in London, a shop-front terrace converted into a food-producing workspace has acted as a prototype for studies on building-integrated urban agriculture and closed-loop systems (Something & Son *n.d.* a).

Sabine Voggenreiter describes in her chapter *Initials CPUL* how arts practice can enable the adaptation of food concerns, by various local stakeholders in an area of Cologne, Germany. One of the starting points for her project *Design Quartier Ehrenfeld* is the conviction that 'to share a "vision" means first to work on common images'. To develop these images, Voggenreiter curates a combination of participatory and artist-/architect-led workshops and installations which, in the case of a community garden, led to the actual production of space. For Voggenreiter, an art historian, there is a 'close relation between creativity and green productivity in the city', as 'both processes are highly productive and both are community processes'.

Such approaches can be instigated relatively quickly and on a short-time basis, as exemplified by the temporary public installation and event *The Continuous Picnic*, or it can be built up and nurtured over several years, as in the participatory project *Urbane Agrikultur in Köln-Ehrenfeld*. In either case, the aim of such urban transformations is to generate an awareness of open urban space to create a basis for integrative planning discussions and to, ultimately, implement change of use, based on a changed desire. Here the visualisation of productive urban landscapes can be experienced at a 1:1 scale and with all senses. Contrary to that, the ideas project *Urban Nature Shoreditch* explains how architectural visualisation can bridge the communication gap between urban agriculture protagonists and design professionals.

Whilst the visualisation of qualitative characteristics is important in winning support for the urban agriculture case, quantitative assessments of the actual spaces will lay the ground for their environmentally, socially and economically successful integration. It is preferable that prior to any productive activity the chosen site or sites are inventorised.

Action IUC = *Inventory of Urban Capacity*

An inventory is necessary for each location, especially of spatial, resource, stakeholder and managerial capacities in order to best respond to local opportunities.

At the beginning of the relatively short history of the urban agriculture movement in the Global North, (planning) emphasis was given to identifying (i.e. location, state of use, availability/ownership) and mapping (i.e. sun direction, soil quality, pollution, water, exposure to wind, adjacency to markets and compost) open urban space as shown, for example, in the city of Portland's *Diggable City* report (Balmer *et al.* 2005) or the *Elephant & Castle Study* for London (Tomkins 2009). In recent years, it has become clear that stakeholder and managerial/maintenance capacity is as important. Moreover, available resources need to be recorded and systematically integrated into the planning and execution of productive urban landscape projects.

Evidence for different approaches is appearing, e.g. the increase of local growing capacity through active community inclusion work by the Bankside Open Space Trust in London (BOST 2011) or the increase of maintenance capacity when it is shared between council and urban farmer as practised by Lichtenberg council and the *Agrarbörse* in Berlin (Agrarbörse 2011). While available space is often finite (although sometimes underestimated), stakeholder and managerial capacity can be increased. One of the top-down approaches that has proven successful is the funding of extension programmes focused on developing agricultural and managerial skills (business and social enterprise), most notably in Cuba (Viljoen 2005).

In her chapter *Recording the unrecorded* Marit Rosol presents the roots, processes and insights of a stakeholder-focused inventory of Berlin's community gardens. To understand how urban space can be appropriated, Rosol looks primarily at 'the motivation and the individual contexts in which the gardens had developed'. She makes a clear distinction between strategies of 'how to find lots', i.e. spatial inventories, and those – equally important – concentrating on other ingredients of space production, such as stakeholder and managerial capacities. In the Berlin case, she highlights that 'even if the city council offered the perfect lot of land and funding, the future users may not feel addressed'.

The three case studies discussed as examples of this *CPUL City Action* aim to show the diversity of approaches when creating *Inventories of Urban Capacity*. Milwaukee as a whole is one of the US-American cities that can be studied nowadays as a *Laboratory of Urban Agriculture* showcasing a whole range of successful, mostly activist-led initiatives usually developed alongside very detailed inventories of sites, stakeholders or commercial/managerial potential. In the *London Thames Gateway* feasibility study, the task was to identify sites allowing both connectivity and substantial food growing with a clear focus on spatial planning. The *Urban Agriculture Curtain* worked on a very different scale: here it was important to respond to the mostly quantifiable requirements of a small food system ranging from production to consumption to recycling.

Establishing an *Inventory of Urban Capacity* and considering its different components – as appropriate for a given site or a number of sites – is again a transdisciplinary action crossing traditional boundaries that existed (and frequently still exist) between planners and activists, urban farmers and designers, council members and social researchers, and so on. The case for such inventories can be made stronger when it is supported by subject-relevant, up-to-date and state-of-the-art research.

Action R = *Researching for Change*

Constant research, development and consolidation of productive urban landscape projects and concepts is needed to respond to changing circumstances.

Social and environmental conditions can change rapidly – locally, regionally, nationally and globally. To keep pace with such developments, but also to scrutinise the achievements of concepts such as *CPUL City*, urban agriculture projects have to undergo repeated evaluation and evolution. Theory and practice need to be able to accommodate change, to anticipate the future by having understood the past. Shorter- and longer-term research is needed to improve on different procedural, spatial,

user and business models for various scales of production. Three main directions of research are currently identifiable: design/applied research dealing with the physical consequences of productive landscapes, such as the *Greenhouse Project* by New York Sun Works (Sun Works 2010); quantifiable research, especially providing ecological, economic and plant-based arguments for urban agriculture, such as the writing by James Petts about London for UK-charity *Sustain* as well as for the *WHO* (Petts 2001a and 2001b); and educational and social research close to human and user needs as for example the professional training and networking project *Urban Gardening* in Berlin (Aenis 2012). The main partners for this action are the multidisciplinary experts and researchers in universities or other research institutions on the one side and the practising urban farmers on the other.

Howard Lee, Stefan Jordan and Victor Coleman in *The devil is in the detail* describe how the necessity of addressing issues of food security has impacted on the work of staff at Hadlow College in the UK. It is this type and amount of detail that will turn the ideas and concepts of productive landscapes and urban agriculture into reality. After noting that 'knowledge of likely yields from urban and peri-urban food production sites is limited due to the lack of documented assessments', the authors then move on to theoretically investigate protected options for urban and peri-urban sites. Their literature, components and prototypes research concludes by highlighting that 'most importantly though is the demonstration to local groups' as 'there will be a need for confidence building for people who know little about growing vegetables or rearing fish but are concerned about and want to improve their food security.'

Gianluca Brunori and Francesco Di Iacovo have the final word and present their research in *Alternative food networks as drivers of a food transition*, arguing that it will be alternative food networks which can provide the 'concrete outcome to innovative visions and values'. According to these authors, both of whom are agricultural economists, alternative food networks with their 'double identity as social movements and economic activities' could drive the repositioning of the urban food system towards a more sustainable future. Much in the sense of this action, alternative food networks are considered as "niches" meaning that they act 'as laboratories to test innovative socio-technical subsystems that may be integrated at higher level' into society at a later stage.

The *CPUL City* concept has aimed from the outset to underpin its "vision" with a concrete body of research. For example, prototyping and in-situ testing of growing arrangements are two of the most efficient ways of evaluating design options. We have found that exhibitions and installations provide a good initial setting for what seem fairly straightforward design propositions, as exemplified by the temporary hydroponic *Growing Balconies* developed and tested with specialists from Hadlow Agricultural College. McGill University's seminal *Edible Campus* project has inspired the ongoing and expanding student-led *Edible Campus* at the University of Brighton, enabling students to empirically design and research a small productive rooftop and social space. At an urban scale, research is being extended into the community in Brighton by projects such as the event-based *Unlocking Spaces* installation and community gathering.

Present actions lead to future infrastructure

The examples of actions presented in this part of the book are from the start of a process, and they will remain relevant for cities exploring future strategies. It is also likely that these case studies will soon be overtaken by more extensive and permanent examples of urban agriculture, especially if urban agriculture continues to develop at the same rate as it has over the last decade. If the economic and social infrastructure can be put in place to support it, we could build something far more abundant and significant than what is often envisaged by a romantic notion of "growing your own". Urban agriculture will then be well on the way to providing *more experience with less consumption*.

Laboratory for Urban Agriculture

Milwaukee, USA, 2011– ongoing

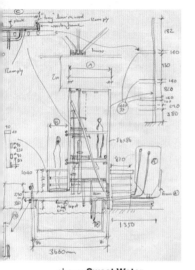

Field-based research, identifying the human and spatial capacities supporting urban agriculture in Milwaukee.

- **SPACE AND ORGANISATION:** Prearranged site visits. Documentation (drawings and photographs) of active urban agriculture sites with community and commercial goals. Interviews with practitioners and city officials.

- **FUNDING:** University of Brighton and Bohn&Viljoen Architects.

- **PROJECT TEAM:** Bohn&Viljoen Architects.

- **FOOD PRODUCTION TYPE:** Diverse typese depending on project, including open-field, vertical, indoor, hydroponics, aquaponics.

- **USE OF HARVEST:** Communal or commercial or bath, depending on project.

- **CLIENT:** University of Brighton and Bohn & Viljoen Architects.

above: **Sweet Water Organics' aquaponic mainframe.** Survey drawings provide a record of construction, a resource for future design development and a reference for teaching. Here, the multiple layering of crop trays resulted in the need for significant levels of artificial lighting.

right: **Sweet Water Organics, September 2011.** Milwaukee's large experimental aquaponic system (combined fish farm and hydroponic vegetable production) is located within a disused railway repair shed. This view shows about half of the entire installation, which was developed in an attempt to rapidly up-scale aquaponic systems. IBM and Harvard Business School had independently reported favourably on the system's potential, and the city provided an advantageous loan, conditional on job creation. The building housing Sweet Water is not ideal, with relatively low levels of daylight requiring artificial lighting for plants and with poor thermal insulation resulting in fish tanks requiring significant heating, problematic given Milwaukee's long cold winters. The scale of the project and the degree to which it was experimental, made its viability as a business extremely challenging. It ceased trading in 2013.

left: **Constructing for growing.** In September 2011, *Sweet Water Organics* constructed new daylit hoop houses / poly tunnels to improve the aquaponic system's energy balance by using daylighting and solar gain for heating. Maximising the use of renewable resources (i.e. daylight, solar heating and finding natural/unprocessed fish feed) is essential for establishing closed-loop systems.

above: **Growing Power.** Will Allen's pioneering urban agriculture project *Growing Power, Inc.* is generating capacity, both within its own organisation and, increasingly, through consultancy and outreach elsewhere in the USA and beyond. The original urban farm and market includes multiple intensive cultivation systems, favouring a low-technology approach. Active solar systems and rainwater harvesting are being introduced to upgrade traditional glasshouses.

above: **Fondy Market.** Managed by the Fondy Food Centre, this fresh food market provides an infrastructural capacity that enables small-scale farmers to make a living by selling their produce locally.

below left: **Alice's Community Garden.** This community garden was designed by the not-for-profit organisation The Centre for Resilient Cities with neighbourhood activists. It provides food growing plots for residents and cultural activities. We can identify three capacities: the garden (space, soil), activists and gardeners and a social enterprise.

below right: **Managerial capacity.** Milwaukee's urban agriculture serves multiple demographics, for example this suburban site is managed by *Growing Power*.

COMMENTARY

Milwaukee is a medium-sized city (population approximately 0.5M) with a rich mix of the capacities considered necessary for supporting urban agriculture.

Not always ideal, but space is available due, in part, to the city's industrial past.

Stakeholder capacity includes established and experimental food-producing social entrepreneurs typified by Will Allen's organisation *Growing Power*. The city itself is a major supportive stakeholder, as represented by Mayor Tom Barratt's evidence-based support for established and more "risky" urban agriculture projects.

Practitioners typically build management skills slowly. Here, not-for-profit civic organisations like The Centre for Resilient Cities or the Fondy Food Centre increasingly foster management capacity within start-up projects.

In terms of resource capacity, significant quantities of organic waste are available in the city for composting. Confidence can also be considered a resource, and is here evidenced by the positive impact that a 2011 IBM smarter cities award had when it concluded that developing aquaponics would be "smart". As the *Sweet Water* experiment has shown, risk cannot be eliminated if innovation is sought.

Fieldwork confirmed that bottom-up and top-down linkages are essential for facilitating urban agriculture. In Milwaukee's case, this happens mainly by the city not putting unnecessary barriers in place to preclude its implementation. Constant research and development by practitioners is very evident, technical (i.e. aquaponics), social (i.e. not-for-profit capacity building for small-scale producers) and political (Growing Food and Justice for All Initiative). Not evident was systematic spatial visioning and visualisation of what the city would be/look like, if productive landscapes were fully integrated into its fabric.

We found significant challenges for aquaponics in relation to closing the cradle-to-cradle loop (i.e. in fish feed and artificial lighting) and, more generally, maintaining the multiple income strands necessary to achieve financial viability.

above: **Growing Food and Justice for All.** Mural created by participants attending the 2011 annual initiative in Milwaukee. These anti-racist and empowerment gatherings were established in 2008 by *Growing Power* and represent one of the most powerful and unique capacity-building exercises to be found anywhere in the world.

left: **Aquaponics.** *Growing Power*'s low-tech aquaponic system predates the *Sweet Water* system and is combined with several different approaches to organic cultivation.

below: **Investing in composting.** Utilizing organic waste harvested from the city is central to *Growing Power*'s cradle-to-cradle ambition.

The Urban Agriculture Curtain

London, UK, 2009

above and below: **Working with what is there.** An installation using industry-standard hydroponic planter trays to produce a range of salads, herbs and vegetables.

A fully functioning prototype for small-scale/small-space building-integrated urban agriculture – installed as part of an urban agriculture exhibition.

- **SPACE AND ORGANISATION:** Vertical farm, closed-loop indoor food system.

- **FOOD PRODUCTION TYPE:** Hydroponic production for salads, herbs and vegetables.

- **USE OF HARVEST:** Crops for in-house café.

- **CLIENT:** Jackson Hunt (curator), The Building Centre, London.

- **FUNDING:** The Building Centre London, Hadlow Agricultural College (in kind).

- **PROJECT TEAM:** Bohn&Viljoen (supported by Marcel Croxson, Jack Wates) with Hadlow Agricultural College (Stefan Jordan and students).

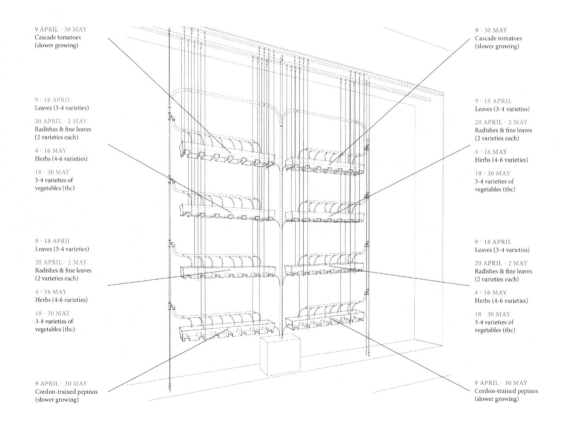

9 APRIL - 30 MAY
Cascade tomatoes
(slower growing)

9 - 18 APRIL
Leaves (3-4 varieties)

20 APRIL - 2 MAY
Radishes & fine leaves
(2 varieties each)

4 - 16 MAY
Herbs (4-6 varieties)

18 - 30 MAY
3-4 varieties of
vegetables (tbc)

9 - 18 APRIL
Leaves (3-4 varieties)

20 APRIL - 2 MAY
Radishes & fine leaves
(2 varieties each)

4 - 16 MAY
Herbs (4-6 varieties)

18 - 30 MAY
3-4 varieties of
vegetables (tbc)

9 APRIL - 30 MAY
Cordon-trained pepinos
(slower growing)

9 - 30 MAY
Cascade tomatoes
(slower growing)

9 - 18 APRIL
Leaves (3-4 varieties)

20 APRIL - 2 MAY
Radishes & fine leaves
(2 varieties each)

4 - 16 MAY
Herbs (4-6 varieties)

18 - 30 MAY
3-4 varieties of
vegetables (tbc)

9 - 18 APRIL
Leaves (3-4 varieties)

20 APRIL - 2 MAY
Radishes & fine leaves
(2 varieties each)

4 - 16 MAY
Herbs (4-6 varieties)

18 - 30 MAY
3-4 varieties of
vegetables (tbc)

9 APRIL - 30 MAY
Cordon-trained pepinos
(slower growing)

left: **Prototyping indoor growing.** The *Urban Agriculture Curtain* provides an interface between a public café and the street. Its utilisation of sunlight and daylight for plant growth was balanced against the requirements for natural light in the café's interior. This site had adequate daylight access, but much less would have been problematic.

above: **Working inside and out.** The installation advertised the exhibition, tested vertical system, produced crops and helped to publicy disseminate the qualities of building-integrated urban agriculture. It increased the site's capacity for urban food growing.

above: **Detailing the support structure.** The prototype adapted a proprietary suspension system that usually supports display panels. Using industry-standard trays and pipework, the only customised parts are aluminium supports for each tray. Design and setting-up time went into a careful arrangement of the junctions between all these parts.

Seeds germinated
in a greenhouse

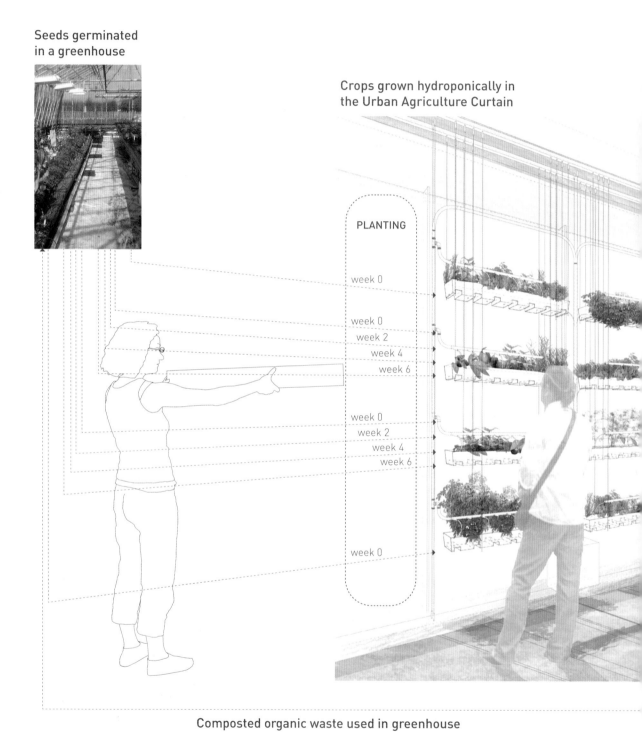

Crops grown hydroponically in
the Urban Agriculture Curtain

PLANTING

week 0

week 0
week 2
week 4
week 6

week 0
week 2
week 4
week 6

week 0

Composted organic waste used in greenhouse

COMMENTARY

'What is the potential for building-integrated urban agriculture and what capacities are required to support it?' Working with the Building Centre in London and Hadlow College, we tested hydroponics as an efficient way of cultivating fresh crops for use in the centre's restaurant. The site's managerial capacities led to practical design and process decisions such as that crops were germinated in a greenhouse off site and varieties were selected for harvesting on a two-week cycle.

Maintaining the hydroponic system was relatively straightforward, as was convincing the restaurant staff to use the produce. Composting the harvests' non-usable parts was difficult. With respect to urban capacity, the greatest challenge will be identifying sites with sufficient daylight for crops to thrive, without the need for artificial lighting. Another practical design issue is the ease of access to crops, here addressed by means of a mobile ladder and mobile planters.

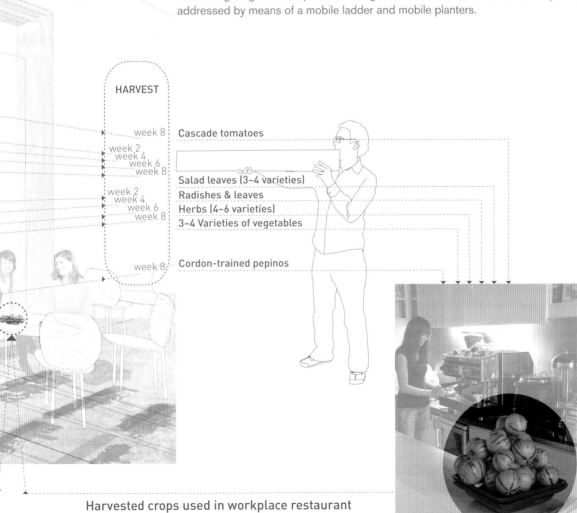

HARVEST

week 8   Cascade tomatoes

week 2
week 4
week 6
week 8

Salad leaves (3–4 varieties)

week 2
week 4
week 6
week 8

Radishes & leaves
Herbs (4–6 varieties)
3–4 Varieties of vegetables

week 8   Cordon-trained pepinos

Harvested crops used in workplace restaurant

left: **Changing the café's spatial quality.** The Urban Agriculture Curtain in use as part of the exhibition *London Yields*. The system developed with Hadlow Agricultural College produces fortnightly crops for use in the Building Centre's restaurant.

above: **Detailed indoor view.** View of the interplay between support system, irrigation pipes and planters. Each planter consists of two trays, the upper-one holding the crops and growing medium, while the lower-one acts as a reservoir for water and nutrients. This arrangement also simplifies the fortnightly exchange of plants.

London Thames Gateway

London, UK, 2004

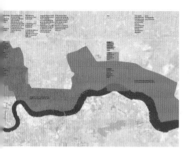

above: **Spatial needs.** A first study worked out the areas needed to meet all the fruit and vegetable requirements for the projected new residents in the two Thames Gateway zones examined. These footprint areas have been calculated for different types of urban agriculture, ranging from high-yield professional market gardens to low-yield leisure allotments.

A feasibility study, exploring the potential for the integration of urban agriculture into London's Green Grid and planned eastward expansion.

- **SPACE AND ORGANISATION:** CPUL.

- **FOOD PRODUCTION TYPE:** Open-field and infrastructure-integrated production.

- **USE OF HARVEST:** Supply for local residents.

- **CLIENT:** Architecture and Urbanism Unit, The Greater London Authority.

- **FUNDING:** The University of Brighton, The Greater London Authority (in kind), Bohn&Viljoen Architects (in kind).

- **PROJECT TEAM:** Bohn&Viljoen (supported by Michael Aling, Alice Constantine, Kabage Karanja, Katja Schäfer) with CUJAE Havana (Jorge Peña Diaz).

right: **CPUL strategies.**
Two different strategies were proposed for the two zones examined, Lower Lea Valley (Stratford zone) and London Riverside (Barking and Dagenham zone). Whereas London Riverside (right-hand side) lends itself to the creation of one or more CPULs, the Lower Lea Valley (left-hand side) allows for the development of individual productive "secret fields" or biodiversity stepping stones.

Open space types and their capacities:
- River Thames and its tributaries and lakes
- existing open space, partly belonging to the regional "Green Grid"
- existing open space, important for connecting this study's proposal to a wider, even rural landscape strategy
- parks/ open space
- vacant/ derilict sites (industrial)
- allotments

First proposal for implementing a CPUL including:
- CPUL walking landscape using existing underused open space (reclaimed landscape)
- CPUL 'organoponicos' (high-yield fields)
- CPUL edges containing primarily leisure, trading, educational activities
- CPUL urban (market) squares
- CPUL new or extended pedestrian bridge

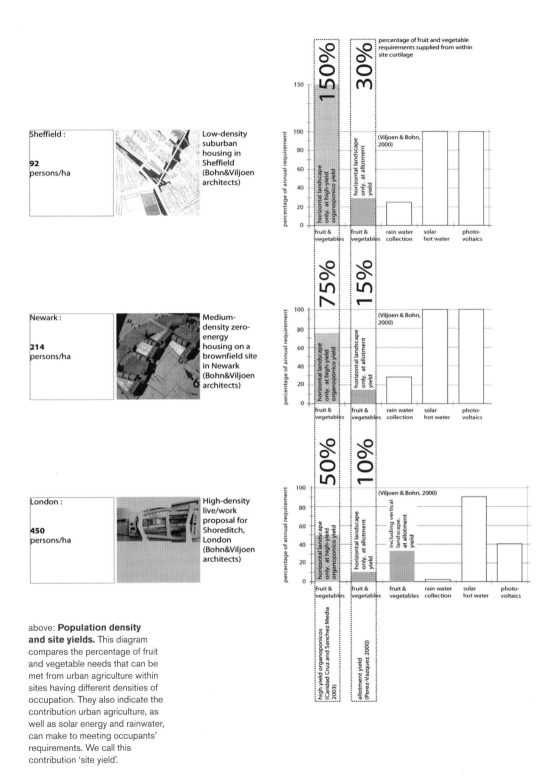

Sheffield : **92** persons/ha		Low-density suburban housing in Sheffield (Bohn&Viljoen architects)

150% horizontal landscape only, at high-yield organoponico yield
30% horizontal landscape only, at allotment yield

percentage of fruit and vegetable requirements supplied from within site curtilage

(Viljoen & Bohn, 2000)

fruit & vegetables | fruit & vegetables | rain water collection | solar hot water | photo-voltaics

Newark : **214** persons/ha		Medium-density zero-energy housing on a brownfield site in Newark (Bohn&Viljoen architects)

75% horizontal landscape only, at high-yield organoponico yield
15% horizontal landscape only, at allotment yield

(Viljoen & Bohn, 2000)

fruit & vegetables | fruit & vegetables | rain water collection | solar hot water | photo-voltaics

London : **450** persons/ha		High-density live/work proposal for Shoreditch, London (Bohn&Viljoen architects)

50% horizontal landscape only, at high-yield organoponico yield
10% horizontal landscape only, at allotment yield
including vertical landscape, at allotment yield

(Viljoen & Bohn, 2000)

fruit & vegetables | fruit & vegetables | fruit & vegetables | rain water collection | solar hot water | photo-voltaics

high yield organoponicos (Caridad Cruz and Sanchez Media 2003)
allotment yield (Perez-Vazquez 2000)

above: **Population density and site yields.** This diagram compares the percentage of fruit and vegetable needs that can be met from urban agriculture within sites having different densities of occupation. They also indicate the contribution urban agriculture, as well as solar energy and rainwater, can make to meeting occupants' requirements. We call this contribution 'site yield'.

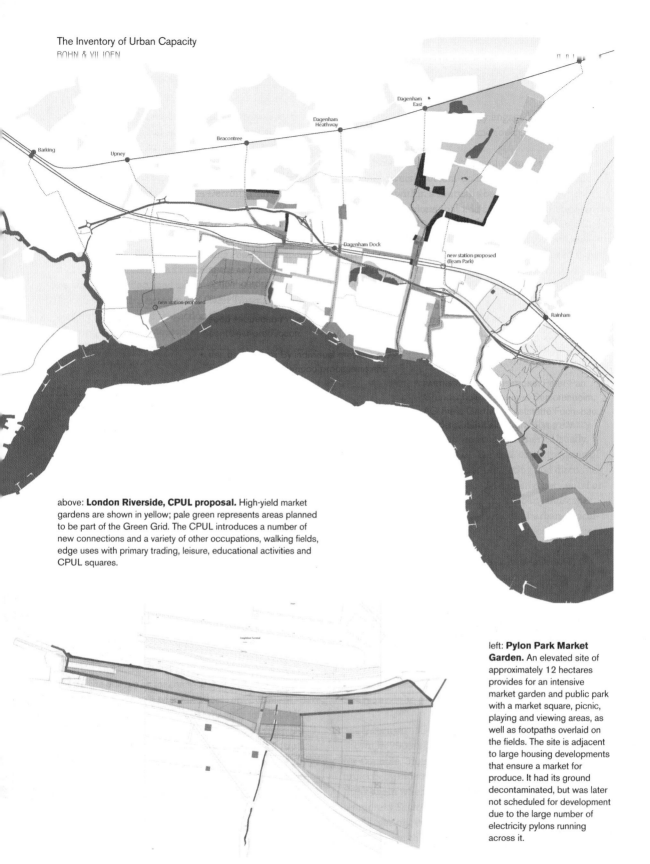

above: **London Riverside, CPUL proposal.** High-yield market gardens are shown in yellow; pale green represents areas planned to be part of the Green Grid. The CPUL introduces a number of new connections and a variety of other occupations, walking fields, edge uses with primary trading, leisure, educational activities and CPUL squares.

left: **Pylon Park Market Garden.** An elevated site of approximately 12 hectares provides for an intensive market garden and public park with a market square, picnic, playing and viewing areas, as well as footpaths overlaid on the fields. The site is adjacent to large housing developments that ensure a market for produce. It had its ground decontaminated, but was later not scheduled for development due to the large number of electricity pylons running across it.

COMMENTARY

This study represents a comprehensive Inventory of Urban Capacity focusing on the space available for urban agriculture; a complex exercise due to multiple landowners and developers with interests in the area. The study was undertaken with the Architecture and Urbanism Unit (AUU), who were promoting proposals for an All London Green Grid as a multifunctional network of connected open urban spaces, with many CPUL characteristics, although urban agriculture was not explicitly named as one. Subsequent to this study the Green Grid strategy was amended to 'promote sustainable food growing'. Our study reinforced the need for a coordinated top-down and bottom-up approach for such large projects. However, at the time of writing, the ambitions of London Riverside remain largely unfulfilled. A major obstacle to developing a CPUL was the lack of a single statutory authority capable of implementing, a coherent spatial plan. The AUU, for example, was limited to "promoting" strategies. In 2005, a London Thames Gateway Development Corporation was established to deal with planning issues, only to be abolished in early 2013 with planning returned to local boroughs.

above: **Productive infrastructure.** Existing infrastructure is connected into the CPUL's walking and cycling network. Railway stations and bus stops help to define nodes within the network. The A13 motorway is one of the only pieces of land that is owned by "London". A proposed walk and cycle way suspended below the A13 reads as an artificial landscape, providing continuity and coherence by connecting otherwise isolated and inaccessible pockets of landscape.

above: **The Suspended A13.** A proposed walk and cycle way utilises space below the elevated A13 and bridges between market garden sites. It touches the ground at its western edge adjacent to Dagenham Station and a proposed new rapid transit system. The southern edge provides the opportunity for vertical landscapes and the space below can shelter storage, market and meeting spaces.

right: **Inventorising land.**
A major part of this feasibility study involved detailed research into the availability of open space, while taking account of its many other uses and use restrictions. Consequently, the project's initial spatial layout had to be adapted repeatedly to suit both the CPUL strategy and the site's overall possibilities. Extended site visits, meetings with planners and photographic analysis enabled us to identify constraints and opportunities for individual sites, resulting in a viable CPUL with If the CPUL was developed to incorporate high yield market gardens we estimated that the fruit and vegetable needs of about 39,000 people could be met. To put this into context, 21,754 new housing units were planned by 2016, for the area in the study.

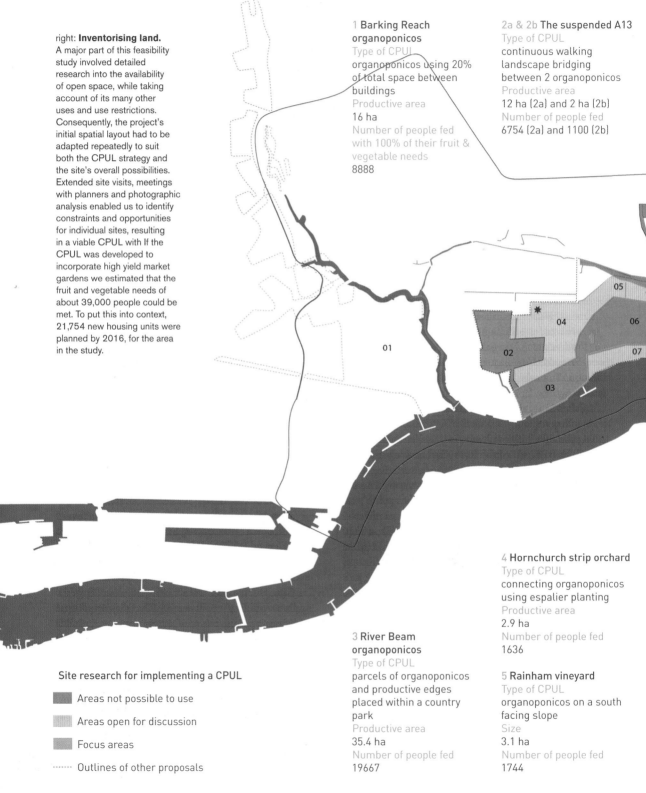

1 **Barking Reach organoponicos**
Type of CPUL
organoponicos using 20% of total space between buildings
Productive area
16 ha
Number of people fed with 100% of their fruit & vegetable needs
8888

2a & 2b **The suspended A13**
Type of CPUL
continuous walking landscape bridging between 2 organoponicos
Productive area
12 ha (2a) and 2 ha (2b)
Number of people fed
6754 (2a) and 1100 (2b)

4 **Hornchurch strip orchard**
Type of CPUL
connecting organoponicos using espalier planting
Productive area
2.9 ha
Number of people fed
1636

3 **River Beam organoponicos**
Type of CPUL
parcels of organoponicos and productive edges placed within a country park
Productive area
35.4 ha
Number of people fed
19667

5 **Rainham vineyard**
Type of CPUL
organoponicos on a south facing slope
Size
3.1 ha
Number of people fed
1744

Site research for implementing a CPUL

Areas not possible to use

Areas open for discussion

Focus areas

.... Outlines of other proposals

01 Possibility for continuation of CPUL strategy into Creek Mouth and Barking

02 Possibility (to discuss within Maxwan proposal)
03 Possibility (to discuss within Maxwan proposal)

04 Not available (build on, info B&V)
05 Not possible (highly toxic, info LBB&D)
06 Possibility (to discuss within Maxwan proposal)
07 Not available (scientific interest, info LBB&D)
08 Possibility (to discuss with LBB&D)
09 Possibility (to discuss within Maxwan proposal)
10 Not available (Innogy, info GLA)
11 Possibility (to discuss with GLA)

12 Not available (Innogy, info GLA)
13 Possibility (to discuss with GLA)
14 Not useful any longer (as route impossible, info GLA)
15 Not available (Ravenbourne, info GLA)
16 Possibility (to discuss within Mac Creanor Lavington proposal)

17 Not available (SETS, info B&V)
18 Possibility (to discuss with GLA)
19 Not available (Ford, info GLA)
20 Not useful any longer (as route impossible)
21 Possibility (to discuss within West 8 proposal)
22 Not available (info GLA)
23 Possibility (to discuss with LDA)
24 Possibility (to discuss with GLA)
25 Not available (info GLA)

26 Not available (flood defense / reedbed, info LBD&B)
27 Slight possibility (to discuss with Havering Council)
28 Slight possibility (to discuss with Havering Council)
29 Not available (flood defense / local nature reserve, info LBD&B)
30 Possibility (to discuss with Havering Council)

31 Slight possibility (to discuss with Havering Council)

32 Not available (part of Beam Valley Park, info LBD&B)
33 Possibility (to discuss with Havering Council)

34 Rainham Arc (possibility of CPUL strategy)

35 Possibility (to discuss within Latz+Partner proposal)
36 Not advisable (north slope)

Recording the unrecorded: A community garden inventory for Berlin

Marit Rosol in an interview with Bohn & Viljoen

You translated the term 'community gardens' into German and thereby defined a new urban space typology for German cities.

For my PhD thesis, I studied community gardens in Berlin, coining the term 'Gemeinschaftsgärten' in the process. I never thoroughly checked whether I was the first to do this, but I did publish the first PhD thesis and book on this type of urban garden.[1] My active research took place from 2002 to 2005. I tracked down various projects for which, back then, there was no name. These gardens did not refer to themselves as 'Gemeinschaftsgärten'. There was not any definition. It was quite a lot of legwork finding all these projects in Berlin. None of the initiators were networked and, for example, the *Stiftung Interkultur* did not yet exist.[2] Therefore, instead of applying what I saw to an established concept, I had to extrapolate new trends. What I found were people who had suddenly started planting on public spaces, mostly on a voluntary basis, sometimes with support from or as part of an initiative of the city.

The particular plants being cultivated was not my focus. Very few of my case studies implemented urban agriculture with food production as their primary goal. Fruit and vegetables were grown, but mostly for education purposes: to show to children or to demonstrate that this was actually possible in the city. The projects I found showed various forms of active creation, appropriation and usage of open public spaces. I realised that, even though the individual initiatives were very different from each other, they were in fact similar to, maybe inspired by, the community gardens in New York.

What role did quantitative research play in your work?

Quantitative evaluations are very good for the creation of models and predictions. Whether these then become

a reality is dependent on economic and political decisions. It is, for example, not possible to concentrate only on what a suitable property can theoretically be used for and in what way. The distribution of power, political majorities and possibilities of implementation have to be taken into consideration.

I only used quantitative data for the exploration of various contexts. First, I examined the changed role for civic involvement in planning and creating free space. A further point of reference was whether planning or urban construction deficits could be detected in the areas in which the gardens were being developed. In this context, I then questioned whether the garden initiatives corresponded with local planning or urban design deficits. With particular focus on the last question, I analysed and interpreted in what way the provision of green spaces is strictly quantitative. This concerned (a) which green spaces are there, their distribution, location and their size, and (b) in what context these locations relate to each other, and what is the official opinion about the landscape planning of these areas.

Interestingly, the gardens did not only emerge within city limits, where there is an absolute absence of open space, but also on the outskirts, where there is enough green space and where one can also find private gardens. When studying these garden projects more carefully, it becomes clear that there are different motivations and different reasons for initiating the gardens. So it is actually really important where the gardens are located.

However, I neither collected any quantitative data, nor did I interpret any statistics. My primary explanations were the motivation and the individual contexts in which the gardens had developed. These two factors were described in qualitative case studies.

The interaction between quantitative and qualitative research is very important to us. It corresponds to these goals of our work that are qualitative: creating productive urban landscapes networked into the city tissue. However, our experience has been that quantitative research is needed to reach qualitative goals. To give an example: in order to develop such urban landscapes, we advocate first recording an Inventory of Urban Capacity that gathers data about particular urban sites. This can then be used to convince a city council to give the site to urban farmers, because their working of these plots of land would improve soil quality and biodiversity, produce food and social inclusion or reduce greenhouse gas emissions in a wider sense.

Principally, I was interested in the phenomenon itself: what was it that was developing. I wrote my PhD in a graduate school for urban ecology dealing with green spaces and urban ecology. Mostly, however, the focus was on natural scientific questions, on flora and fauna in the city or climate. My general topic was *the usage* of green spaces. I had indeed intended to develop my thesis based on statistical evidence, but during the course of my work I found the various individual forms of usage to be much more interesting. I was curious what other forms of usage there might be for spaces that were being created by the users themselves without becoming private but still being open to the general public. Consequently, I studied the opportunities and risks these projects bring with them. The results were classified and presented according to different criteria: on the one hand, the potential in respect to land-use planning, as well as to ecology, politics, social and economic questions. On the other hand, the problems and risks of the same. My aim was to give an overall picture of the various projects: what motivates people to start the projects; why do they participate; which concepts work and which don't; what opportunities and problems might arise. My very last step was to develop recommendations as guidance for similar projects. These, however, I published in the appendix, because strictly speaking they weren't my main focus. My goal wasn't to compile a toolkit or contrive a persuasive pamphlet.

I did not take commercial agriculture into account; my topic was strictly unpaid work – voluntary, civic participation [Bürgerschaftliches Engagement]. Both your and my work approaches overlap on the forms of urban gardening. Your focus, however, highlights strategies, such as "how do I find lots" and, "how do I convince city councils". I didn't work on that.

However, I did touch upon the advantages of using these strategies: my research showed that top-down strategies are not very useful in voluntary projects. Even if the city council offered the perfect lot of land and funding, the appropriate future users may not feel addressed. Ideally, a ready-formed group of people who are in search of a site approaches the city administration or a landowner. If one of these two factors doesn't apply, one has to put a bit more effort into the process: either, in absence of the land, the group has to continue searching for a plot or, in absence of the group, a very dedicated city council has to find motivated users.

Such a situation occurred in the district of Friedrichshain in Berlin: the redevelopment commissioners invested a lot of energy to find people for the fallow land around Dolziger Straße.[3] They had designated three garden sites in the neighbourhood *Samariterviertel* and not only provided the land, but also invited people to take walks around it. They were very creative in handling funding guidelines to secure the project and attract gardeners. At least one side has to take on the active part in order for something to happen.

In your opinion, was there a moment in time when such insights in relation to urban space production suddenly became apparent or were they always known or applied?

That is where nowadays the difference lies to my first book and the research I conducted between 2002 and 2005.[1] Back then the phenomenon was still unknown; hardly anyone had studied urban agriculture and community gardens. Berlin's councils' parks and gardens departments were still very sceptical, especially because of the many problems that may arise if people work voluntarily on public land ranging from insurance issues to securing continuity and standards. So, the city council partially raised viable objections and apprehensions. Additionally, the interested groups did also not exactly know how to go about it or who to turn to. Everything was still very uncoordinated. Now, only ten years later, it has become much less difficult to go to the city council and say that you intend to cultivate a garden. Over the past years, projects have been proven to work and the city council has become more approachable and receptive.

During my research, it was very helpful to visit sites in person. I flew to Toronto and Seattle, examined the North American projects and conducted interviews. The people involved in these projects encouraged me, for example explaining how insurance difficulties could be overcome. They also suggested it might not be so bad if projects died after five or ten years – thereafter, lawns could be grown on the plots. After all, there is no loss from the temporal usage as gardens, even if they might deviate from the regulations of a parks and gardens department.

Do these American examples advocate temporary use as means of evading failure?

Addressing temporary use is ambivalent. On one hand, it is important to explain to the city council that there is nothing wrong with temporary use. Concurrently, people who would like to cultivate a garden need a long-term prospect, because a garden takes time to grow and develop. Especially when setting out to plant an all-purpose garden and to raise more than seasonal vegetables it takes time until everything has grown in.

Temporary use of outdoor space has been an ever-increasing topic in Berlin since the end of the 1990s. It was promoted by certain groups, and the city council has warmed to it. By now, it is much more accepted. Temporary use is not a bad thing. However, fundamentally, a long-term perspective should be secured. Otherwise frustrations might arise; if the gardeners are offered a short-term contract of only a year, with a four-week notice period, they won't really be motivated to become involved. Temporary use can be problematic and often gardeners reject this option. This is where I laid the focus of my research. If it's about planting vegetables, people might be satisfied with merely one season. However, it's a different story when trying to establish a garden that exceeds the desire for vegetable production.

Often, it is not a great master plan or toolkit that is needed, but realistic judgement of the political circumstances: how much money is available; what interests does the city have; is it a priority for them to secure the site?

For example, in the already mentioned *Samariterviertel* neighbourhood in Berlin, users agreed to short-term notice periods in their contracts. They weren't very happy with the clause, and always hoped the city might acquire the private property the gardens were on. Logic supported creating and sustaining a green space in this densely populated area. From an urban point of view and considering the enthusiasm of the participants, it would have been great if the city could have acquired the lot and secured it as green space for further use. However, the city did not. Even though the *Samariterviertel* project was very successful, it was discontinued. The property owner had the development rights and started building on the site. If the city had wanted to ascertain the use by gardeners, it would have had to purchase the property and pay a high level of compensation to the owner. The city couldn't – or didn't want to – afford that kind of money. This is an example of an unpredictable political decision despite all quantitative evaluations. Only with qualitative research are we able to detect such factors. Quantitative models, however, are a good way of showing general advantages and possibilities. Statistical surveys are very good for the detection of the demands of people in the neighbourhood due to their analysis of the land utilisation, the population and its needs.

On the face of it, it seems that Berlin's community gardens are a very characteristic element of urban agriculture in this city. Looking at North America, urban agriculture also seems to be distinguished by yield.

I approached Berlin with the question of how "other" open spaces can be generated, how – from a user's perspective – independent open spaces can be created by and with people. After all, this is the main topic many people here are concerned with – so, of course, it became my focus. Furthermore, educational aspects and pedagogic approaches fed into this, as well as ecological and political ideals, for example ideas about the food system and genetic modification.

I did an internship in Toronto, held interviews and visited many urban agricultural sites. The theme there was strongly tied to issues such as nutrition, food security and fairness in the distribution of healthy food. Producing food within gardens is an important topic, but only in combination with an unjust and unequal access to healthy food. In Toronto, 'food deserts' and 'food banks' have strong connections with community gardens. Great solidarity exists in this network; with donations to the food bank, the community gardens produce good, nutritious food for those in need. In Berlin, for a long time, such issues were not a topic, although now they are being debated more frequently.

It is now nearly a decade since you conducted your research in Berlin. Can you already detect such a trend?

From what I've gathered more recently in Berlin, food production has always played an important role in the intercultural gardens.[4] They have always helped to financially relieve the gardeners and been used to grow unusual plants that are not widely found. So, these gardens have to do with heritage, with cultural roots.

In Germany, radical changes followed the introduction of the new social welfare system Hartz IV in 2005. By now, *Tafelgärten* have been established: garden projects that specifically provide produce for food banks and people who are reliant on food donations.[5] Such changes brought food production back to the attention of people, just as it has always been an important matter during times of crisis.

However, today the well-known *Prinzessinnengärten* in Berlin is centred around economically viable fruit, vegetable and herb production.[6] At the same time, they are comparable to community gardens with all the social activities they offer. Here, urban agriculture is accomplished because it can be economically viable.

Moreover, *Prinzessinnengärten* has addressed temporary use in a new and productive way. They have lent it a new flexibility with their nomadic strategy; the possibility of moving to another site at any time. This is something other garden projects do not (yet) pursue. *Prinzessinnengärten* took temporary use, which has become a trendy political subject, and made it accessible for everyone involved.

Earlier on you mentioned that you are interested in 'the creation, appropriation and utilisation of public open spaces'. At first glance, it seems the three terms describe similar activities. Where do the fine differences lie?

There are very central differences. Typically, public use of urban space is provided in a legal context, but only to a certain extent: inhabitants are allowed to ride their bike through the city, lie in parks, play football, perhaps even barbecue in the urban environment. However, the usage is restricted and limited. Creating one's own space, getting involved, changing things, sowing grass, planting a fruit tree or building a fence are usually not allowed. With gardening activities, space is created and changed – or left unchanged. These alternative forms of utilisation are of course a way of appropriating space: space is used and taken into possession in a different way than with ordinary open urban space. This stands in contrast to private gardens, which are perhaps laid out according to one's own ideals, but don't have the same possibilities community gardens do.

I recently reviewed a book on community gardens on the Lower East Side in New York. The author speaks about these gardens in the context of gentrification, the up-valuation of city districts and change of the resident structure. She made an interesting point: in the late 1990s, these gardens were in danger of being sold off. A lot of them could be saved, a few could not. There were different organisational models for the gardens, and the great majority of them were planned out to provide nutritious food and guarantee self-sufficiency.

Many of the gardens were run by certain ethnic groups. The Latinos from Puerto Rico, for example, played an important role. For them, gardens were also a public living room, a comfort space. The gardens that were run by the white middle class usually possessed an idea of landscape architecture. They were planned out as "picturesque" gardens; appealing to the eye, which one enjoyed meditating over and stepping into – even as an outsider. Throughout the rescue mission, the latter had a much greater chance of being saved, because they were more accessible and were therefore able to win over a much larger lobby. Gardens that were being used only by specific groups were not designed to delight, but were optimised to very particular needs and uses of a small face-to-face group. These gardens had a much harder time

sustaining themselves, establishing a lobby and convey-
ing broadly acceptable reasons to continue to exist. They
had to put up hard fights, which they often lost.

It seems that in New York too, the more common concep-
tions and prevalent perception habits of what a garden
should look like are more widely accepted. This clashes
with the idea we have of agriculture when speaking of
urban agriculture as practised in community gardens.

It is also always interesting to look at who is manag-
ing the gardens, who (institutionally) supports them
and who they have as their lobby. Being careful when
legitimising gardens to city councils is important
because there are very different needs and demands.
Marginalised groups tend to fall through if their needs
are different or perhaps not as familiar. The interesting
thing about urban gardens is that they can satisfy such
differing needs: the need to grow (crops/produce), the
need for social life, to improve climatic conditions, the
need for flora and fauna, for ecological priorities. These,
however, are all always combined with social interaction.

To fulfil the social component, it is not that important
what the garden looks like. To fulfil other aspects, however, it is important. It is important to judge carefully
who the garden is for, who is involved in it and for what
reasons certain needs should be satisfied.

*How can these needs best be recorded? What would be the
appropriate tool in your opinion?*

Talking to people, interviewing them or conducting ethnographic research. "Ethnographic" entails staying in the
field longer, participating, integrating, observing – using
the same methods as in cultural anthropology or partially
in sociology. By observation, modes of utilising and creating space can be detected, as can the questions of who uses
the space, why and how often. By enquiry, the motivation
of the participators becomes clear; what significance the
garden has, what is so important about it. Both the active
user and those not using the garden can be asked in order
to find out what in general might be missing.

During my fieldwork in Berlin, it became apparent that
community gardens, temporary use, use of fallow land

or neighbourhood gardens often created difficult spatial
categories. This interrelation of space and society is
most important. The gardens created a spatial category
people could not decipher. They were caught off guard as
to whether they were allowed into the garden, whether
they may participate, whether it was private or public,
what they were allowed to do in it and whether it
belonged to the city or an individual. This was not clear.
Sometimes, problems resulted in utilising the gardens.
However, this unpredictability is not bad. The important
thing is to find an appropriate response to it. Composition and information are certainly two ways of tackling
this unpredictability and can help to explain in what way
a garden is intended to be used.

*On the one hand, community gardens create new spaces
for residents; however, on the other hand, there is a certain
danger of the state shifting particular responsibilities.
Why do you think this might be a problem and not an
opportunity?*

My book depicts clearly that community gardens arise
from social changes. With these changes come a new
understanding of the state's role and accordingly a new
understanding of what a citizen is able to do in a city.
The opportunity entails citizens actively changing and
creating spaces, literally *winning* free space. Simultaneously, there is an apprehension that public parks
currently tended and managed by parks and gardens
departments might, in parts, be handed over to citizens'
initiatives, simply because these community gardens are
such a great model.

This, however, would be extremely problematic. There
are, for example, some activities that people like doing,
because it involves the ability to implement their own
ideas and visions. Contrary, tasks such as weeding
flower beds or raking – in general, all repetitive and tire-
some chores – are not a primary interest and motivation
in the context of community gardening. Be that as it
may, the main fear is that community gardeners could
be understood as a cheap replacement. It is dangerous substituting paid labour with unpaid labour. This
means saving at the expense of others. In the course of a
neoliberal social development, public authorities try, for
example, to cut jobs. Related skilled crafts and trades are

jeopardised. Community gardeners, however, often do not have the same skills as trained landscape gardeners. The goal should be to bring professional knowledge and the interests of the users closer together. This can even be implemented in existing gardens.

Cities know that the handing over of parks is double-edged. On the one hand, they do want to give people open space. On the other, though, city councils act in accordance with the need for money. Municipalities, especially Berlin, are subject to a strict austerity programme. Since they do not have much money to spend, they are forced to find it. However, outsourcing responsibilities to non-profit or voluntarily working hands is not the way to do it. It would overburden people. They lead their own lives, have their own work and, despite the positive aspects of involvement and self-determination, they cannot additionally run public kindergartens, public swimming pools, public transport and public parks. The idea that voluntary work and civic commitment could fill all the gaps that financial cuts have torn in the public budget is an illusion and a politically unreasonable one at that.[7]

Unequal supply would become apparent, with some groups being better able to articulate their needs than others. The middle class for example has a distinct language and is better capable of asserting their interests. People who are juggling three jobs to make ends meet do not have much time for voluntary work; it is a luxury they cannot afford. If, however, the green spaces within the city in close proximity to a home are tied to voluntary work by the resident, spaces in indigent neighbourhoods might not be viable. Community gardens are a wonderful development and should be supported – but as an additional option.

Community gardens are a variation of urban agriculture. With urban agriculture, we mainly envision urban sites that are to be operated by urban farmers who trade their produce.

My theories don't really grasp commercial urban agriculture, because it is not about voluntary work. However, as an urban geographer, I know that in a city, whatever form of utilisation earns the highest profit and yield is the one that comes out on top. It is most likely the case that agriculture does not fulfil this maxim – or if it does, then only with the type of agriculture that is most intensive. In such a case, it is also a decision of whether one wants the farmer who can pay the highest rent or someone else who for example fulfils ecological or organic demands. Consequently, there should be priorities. It's dangerous to act solely on economic interests. We have to define how we want to live in our cities; how we envision a quality of living.

My assumption is that urban agriculture – at least in certain locations – has to be subsidised. Any form of development is more likely to pay off than agricultural usage. That precisely is the reason why there is less agriculture within the city. Food production is more favourable everywhere else, outside of the city. However, inner-city production starts making sense when other advantages are taken into consideration, for example transport routes and distances.

So, we should continue researching?

Absolutely.

Notes

1   Rosol, M. (2006) *Gemeinschaftsgärten in Berlin: Eine qualitative Untersuchung zu Potenzialen und Risikenbürgerschaftlichen Engagements im Grünflächenbereich vor dem Hintergrund des Wandels von Staat und Planung*, Berlin: Mensch & Buch Verlag.

2   for project details see: <http://www.anstiftung-ertomis.de/die-stiftung/stiftung-interkultur>.

3   for project details see: <http://www.stadtentwicklung.berlin.de/staedtebau/foerderprogramme/stadterneuerung/de/samariterviertel>.

4   for details on intercultural gardens, see chapter *Green theory in practice and urban design: Germany* (p.92).

5   for project details see: <http://www.kleingarten-bund.de/projekte/tafelgaerten>.

6   for project details see: <http://prinzessinnengarten.net>.

7   for a detailed argument see: Rosol, M. (2012) *Community volunteering as a neo-liberal strategy? The case of green space production in Berlin*, in: Antipode, no. 44 (1), pp. 239–257.

The Urban Farming Project

Middlesbrough, UK, 2006–2007

above: **Farms around the city.** Extract from Bohn&Viljoen's Opportunities Map that, at the request of the Dott team, 'a child must be able to understand'.

A top-down initiated, city wide participatory event, envisioning, encouraging and establishing urban food growing by individuals, groups and organisations.

- **SPACE AND ORGANISATION:** CPUL + community garden, school garden, house garden, windowsill.

- **FOOD PRODUCTION TYPE:** Open-field, container and domestic production.

- **USE OF HARVEST:** Food celebration (The Town Meal) + joint processing/cooking and consumption events.

- **CLIENT:** John Thakara, director of DOTT 07, the citizens of Middlesbrough and Middlesbrough Council.

- **FUNDING:** Design Council, One North East, Middlesbrough Council; in kind: Middlesbrough Primary Care Trust, Middlesbrough Sure Start, Groundwork South Tees, Middlesbrough Environment City and the Soil Association.

- **PROJECT TEAM:** John Thakara, David Barrie, David Barrie & Associates (producer); Nina Belk, Zest Innovation (producer); Debra Solomon, Culiblog (producer); Robert+Roberta Smith (consultants); Bohn&Viljoen (consultants); citizens of Middlesbrough.

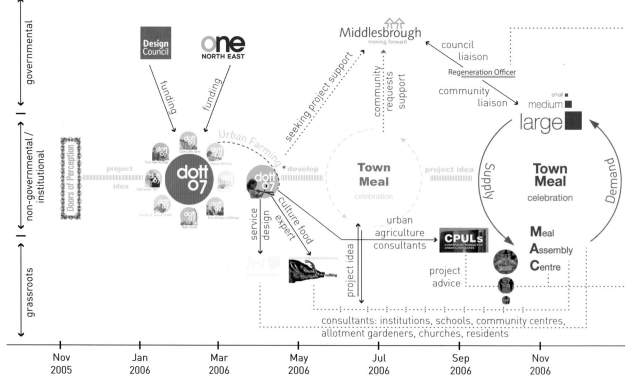

* David Barrie, Producer

above and right: **S – M – L.** During the two growing years, people all over the city planted edibles into more than 200 purpose-designed (S) mall, (M)edium and (L)arge growing containers'. (images: David Barrie, 2007)

above: **Discussing productive urban landscapes.** The project provided localised, individual food-growing opportunities, but also a strategy for the planning and development of productive urban landscapes.

below: **Working across the lines.** The *Urban Farming Project* has been nationally commended for its far-reaching impact on Middlesbrough's population. Its success has been the result of intense capacity research from the start, an excellent relationship between local residents and local government and extended community consultation.

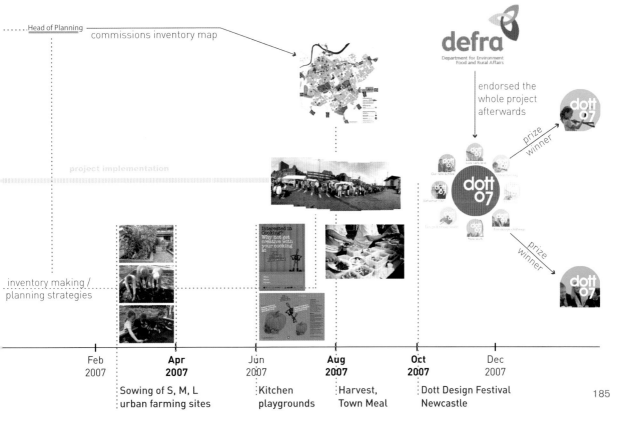

above: **Food growing for a public event.** Many growing sites were run by schools or community organisations. Produce was harvested and used in neighbourhood meals, culminating in the huge celebratory outdoor 'Town Meal'. The Town Meal has since become an annual event in Middlesbrough. Food growing in public spaces managed by the city's Parks Department was well received by residents and came the closest to showing what commercial market gardens would add to the city. (image: David Barrie, 2007)

right: **Food growing and personal health.** A series of local gatherings enabled reflection on the project, recruiting participants and the learning of growing and cooking skills. Harvesting, cooking and eating the produce grown provided the opportunity for local communities and individuals to reconnect with the seasonality of homegrown food and with their fellow growers. The positive health impacts of the project, due to healthy eating and obesity reduction, have been recognised and incorporated into a Healthy Town Initiative, established in 2008 after winning a 4 million pound National Health Service award. (image: David Barrie, 2007)

COMMENTARY

The Middlesbrough *Urban Farming Project* formed part of the UK Design Council's two-year initiative Designs of the Time 2007 (DOTT07), which asked the question, 'Wouldn't it be great if… we could live sustainably by design?' The project was managed and produced by David Barrie, who developed initial concepts with a team including Debra Solomon (see chapter *Urbaniahoeve: Event-based practice and Urban Agriculture*) and Bohn&Viljoen.

During 2006 contacts were established – with community groups, individuals, enterprises and institutions – all were invited to participate and indicate if they wished to take on a growing site. In 2007, the main food growing activities took place culminating in a celebratory Town Meal. By this time, many local residents had taken up urban food growing initiatives. The city's Director of Regeneration, Tim White, and his team supported the project and were critical to its success.

Bohn&Viljoen worked with the project team to devise a participatory strategy, which included a concept for developing small, medium and large food growing sites. This enabled a wide variety of partners to join, from individual residents to the city's Parks Department who took the radical step of planting large areas in the city centre with fruit and vegetables rather than ornamental plants. Feedback from the Parks Department was of particular interest; first vandalism was not a significant problem, and second, urban agriculture was no more expensive to maintain than ornamental plants.

From the start the intention was to use crops for local consumption, and ensure that the project was experienced as a part of everyday life. A number of citywide initiatives introduced people to urban food growing; from horticultural workshops to cooking and eating events. The sustainability organisation Groundworks South Tyneside and Newcastle was employed to provide planters and plants. Debra Solomon initiated the very effective "Kitchen Playground" programme, whereby cooking classes were run at a number of community centres throughout the city. Workshops and gatherings were notable for the cross-generational participation they encouraged and for how "memories of grandparents' food growing" were recalled. The most ambitious event curated as part of the project was the "Town Meal" for which the city's approximately 2,000 new urban farmers produced fruit and vegetables for a shared community feast held at Middlesborough's main city square in August 2007. It ran concurrently with The *Really Super Market* curated by artist Bob and Roberta Smith, combining art and food, and attracting about 8,000 participants.

above: **The Kitchen Playground**. Regular cooking events were held to jointly process and consume the produce grown.
(image: Nina Belk, 2007)

left: **Showcasing The Urban Farming Project.** The two-year Middlesbrough project concluded with the Dott07 Design Festival in Newcastle. Here, all five Dott themes were presented and debated in a series of public meetings.

right: **An Opportunities Map for Middlesbrough.** Commissioned by the city's regeneration team, this map combines a strategic vision and the project's actual food-growing sites. Public open space, urban agriculture sites and a biodiversity network gain coherence in the CPUL strategy.

Reflecting in 2013 on the DOTT07 project, in a personal communication, the city's regeneration team noted:

More than 2,000 residents, including children, schools and eight community centres participated, culminating in a Town Meal feeding over 2,500 residents with locally grown food. The project captured the imagination of the people of Middlesbrough and resulted in a number of spin-offs, continuation activities and new opportunities. In particular, the Opportunity Map helped us identify further green spaces we could utilise for growing, building on the success of the initial project. In 2008, even more people got involved – particularly schools who saw it as an opportunity to teach their children about healthy eating and sustainability. It also allowed schools to supply their own kitchens with school-grown food, thus minimizing the carbon footprint. Further allotment development took place at Gresham Neighbourhood Management Centre, and funding was secured for the reintroduction of allotment capacity at the former "Cabbage Club" allotments in Whinney Banks. The legacy of the DOTT07 project and the DOTT team's work is apparent – the project is still running six years later, and the Town Meal is an annual event. The project is now managed by Middlesbrough Environment City, an environmental charity which promotes healthy and sustainable living.

The UK's Commission for Architecture and The Built Environment (CABE) observed that Middlesbrough followed a 'project-led approach' rather than a 'strategy-led approach'; spatial and social design interventions led the way. This is akin to another *CPUL City* Action, Visualising, which provides stakeholders with a critically important qualitative experience of the strategy

Dott 07 Opportunities for a green and edible Middlesbrough

01 An urban design concept
* plant continuous open space corridors (CPUL) thereby connecting the city with the rural, the wild
** benefit from this new landscape productively in a variety of ways :

02 movement
* improve non-vehicular movement and access by foot or bike throughout the entire town
** reroute traffic

03 energy (economics)
* use the ground more effectively in economic terms, esp. through new types of urban farming sites
** provide employment and invigorate districts through productive elements of the new landscape

04 school
* offset the building density with extra large open space to provide children with healthy and self-sufficient activity options
** improve safety for children with play space weaving through their town

05 health
* offset industrial/noise pollution with contrasting calming and oxygenising open space
** improve air flow in and out of the city through open corridors

06 food
* plant urban agriculture sites in the heart of the town producing organic and local food
** improve the sense of place, the food and eating culture by providing space for food production and processing

07 An urban lifestyle
* preserve the greenbelt by offering the rural on the urban doorstep (within a CPUL)
** enhance people's relationship with and enjoyment of nature, the year's seasons and weather

The DOTT 07 Urban Farming Project in Middlesbrough

represents the first practical testing of a concept for continuous productive urban landscape (CPUL). Individuals and organisations participated by growing fruit and vegetables in small, medium and large containers. Over 200 containers were distributed across the city. There was and is a positive acceptance and enthusiasm for urban farming, evidenced by the number of participants who wish to continue growing fruit and vegetables next year and several who wish to expand the area under cultivation. People enjoy being close to edible landscapes.

When imagining how Middlesbrough may develop the CPUL concept in the future, it is important to realize that it does not require everyone to grow their own food. It rather proposes that commercially viable market gardens would form part of the city's network of open urban spaces. In this way, the city would significantly reduce its ecological footprint while at the same time enhancing its urban environment. CPUL provides more experience with less consumption.

Bohn & Viljoen Architects 2007

An edible Middlesbrough

Middlesbrough CPUL

What if more land in our towns and cities were given over to edible landscapes? The raised green panels show how a network of spaces for growing food, circulation and leisure could be introduced in to the town in the future. These spaces would incorporate market gardens for growing fruit and vegetables and could form part of the town's network of open urban spaces. We call this a network of spaces a "continuous productive urban landscape" or CPUL. CPULs are a way to enhance the urban environment and reduce its ecological footprint.

Middlesbrough today

Allotments

There are already many allotments in Middlesbrough. They show that the town already has an infrastructure of urban agriculture. In the future, allotments could become an essential part of an extended network of edible landscapes that run through the town.

The DOTT07 urban farming project

Small containers

142 Window boxes and barrels were distributed as containers for food to be grown in by individuals and organizations.

Medium containers

66 medium containers, one metre square in area, were used for growing fruit and vegetables. These were looked after by schools, community organizations, hospitals and amenity groups.

Large containers

48 large containers, two metres square, were cultivated by schools, neighbourhood centres and other local organizations.

Food was also grown in the town's parks and open spaces by the horticulture department of the local authority and the town's principal art gallery - the Middlesbrough Institute of Modern Art (MIMA).

Across the growing season, Middlesbrough's new 'urban farmers' harvested and ate food they had grown and the final harvest yielded a bumper crop that was shared by over 2500 people in a celebratory town meal.

Spiel/Feld Marzahn

Berlin, Germany, 2011– ongoing

above: **'Kräuter' is the German word for 'herbs'.** Signs form an important part of the project, initially to inform residents about its intentions and later to publicise food growing events. (image: Kristian Ritzmann (FG Stadt & Ernährung TU Berlin), 2011)

A fully functioning prototype – encouraging and establishing urban food growing on suitable, longer-term sites.

- **SPACE AND ORGANISATION:** A community and school garden incorporating a composting system.

- **FOOD PRODUCTION TYPE:** Open-field and container production.

- **USE OF HARVEST:** By individual growers plus crops for neighbourhood processing and consumption.

- **CLIENT:** Head of Planning, Borough of Marzahn-Hellersdorf, Berlin.

- **FUNDING:** Senate of Berlin, Technical University (TU) of Berlin.

- **PROJECT TEAM:** Fachgebiet Stadt & Ernährung at the TU Berlin (Katrin Bohn, Kristian Ritzmann), landscape architecture students core team (Griephan, Hasenstab, Keil, Knoll, Otters), local residents.

- **PARTNERING ORGANISATIONS:** Peter-Pan Grundschule, Alpenland Seniorenheim, AG Freie Gärtner, Gaststätte Fuchsbau, Kindergarten Felix, Agrarbörse e.V.

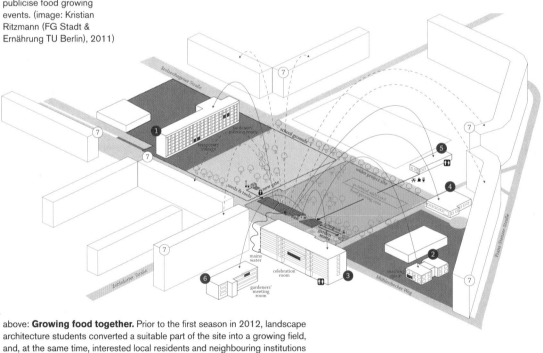

above: **Growing food together.** Prior to the first season in 2012, landscape architecture students converted a suitable part of the site into a growing field, and, at the same time, interested local residents and neighbouring institutions began to network. (image: Nishat Awan, Kristian Ritzmann and Susanne Hausstein (FG Stadt & Ernährung TU Berlin), 2012)

left: **Marking up qualities.** During the project's pilot phase, temporary installations highlighted spatial qualities unique to the larger brownfield site.

below: **Preparing the site for spring planting.** The perimeter of the growing field follows the outline of a former school from the 1970s site. It provides a memory of past use and proposes a vision for future use.

bottom: **Working in context.** The site remains open to the public throughout the year. Paths that had been created by residents before are retained and cross the new field.

above: **Public consultation.**
Before any construction
started, alternative proposals
for the urban agriculture field
were exhibited next to the site
alongside a public footpath.
They were later discussed
during public events on the
brownfield site.

below: **Autumn, winter,
spring and summer.** The
growing field is visible from an
adjacent old people's home
and, as seasons pass, provides
an ever-changing view. It
becomes imaginable that this
parcel of open land will be
the start of a food productive
landscape in Berlin.
(images: Kristian Ritzmann,
2011 (left), Any Paz, 2012
(centre left) (FG Stadt &
Ernährung TU Berlin))

COMMENTARY

Spiel/Feld Marzahn is an urban agriculture project aiming to instigate the spatially effective, food productive use of a brownfield site while also strengthening local engagement and offering lifestyle choices. At the time of writing, the project consists of a 600 m² food growing field, a purpose-built store and greenhouse, a composting system and an emerging group of local food gardeners.

Development pressure in the Berlin borough of Marzahn-Hellersdorf is low and maintenance of redundant sites is a burden for the local council. The council's Nature and Environment Department has initiated a borough-wide urban agriculture strategy aiming to match interested urban farmers with good value land. The *Spiel/Feld* project sets a spatial precedence for a certain type of agricultural use in the area. Moreover, it can help to firmly root urban food growing as a valid and desirable space use option in the borough.

The part of the borough where the *Spiel/Feld* project is located is considered to be deprived. Unemployment is high and household earnings are low. Despite the fact that the area houses many people, there are comparatively few choices for leisure activities. The participation of the neighbourhood in development initiatives is low, although people identify positively with their homes.

Spiel/Feld is therefore run as a participatory top-down project with the university team as mediator where decisions are made with the community and hopefully later by the community. The aim is not only to benefit the development of this specific piece of land, but to start a constructive public discourse about local planning issues. The project has a focus on ecological education, for example by working closely with local school children from the neighbouring primary school and by offering meeting opportunities and workshops for gardeners.

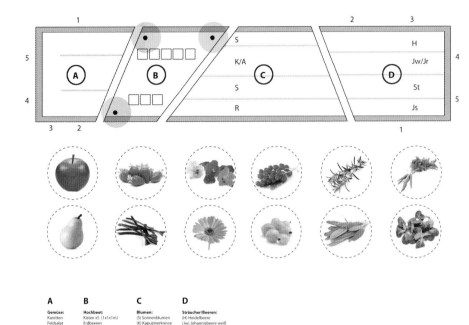

left: **Planning to plant.** The 'Big Field' planting plan and a selection of crops planted during the first year. The field is naturally subdivided into four zones by existing footpaths, providing the framework for a dynamic landscape. During the first year of cultivation, plots were used as follows: Zone A was cultivated by a children's centre and an after-school club, Zone B was a public gathering space and included fruit trees and raised beds cultivated by residents from the adjacent old people's home, Zone C was subdivided into a number of plots cultivated by individual residents living on the estate and Zone D was used by pupils from an adjacent school and students from the Technical University of Berlin. As more was learnt about how residents used the site or which crops thrived and which need to be rotated, changes due to evolving patterns of use and occupation overlaid the first plan.
(image: Michael Keil (FG Stadt & Ernährung TU Berlin), 2011)

right: **Means of communication.** As part of the design process, different neighbourhood groups were engaged in discussions about the project. Young school children made their own drawings of how they imagined the site. (image: Sunny (a local school child), 2011)

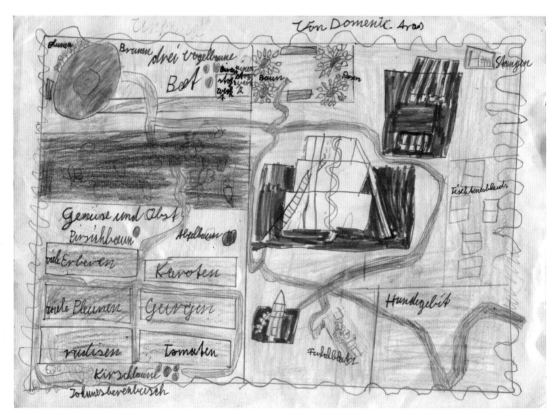

above: **Linking food and schools.** This drawing by a school child makes clear their understanding of the connection between the school and the field. (image: Domenic (a local school child), 2011)

Spiel/Feld Marzahn aims to visualize how design quality and participatory processes can enhance the spatial layout of urban agriculture sites and lead to solutions that are positively received by residents and council officials alike.

After two years it is noticeable that although there are more and more residents who use the site, they are not yet ready to take on its day-to-day management. Whilst the project's Inventory of Urban Capacity has informed most decisions, it is the strengthening of that capacity which is one of the project's main actions.

right: **Prototyping.** The tool shed and greenhouse designed by the students and staff at the TU Berlin's Department for City and Nutrition, led by Katrin Bohn, is significant as a base for residents using the urban agriculture field. Overlooking the field, it is located within the adjacent school's grounds for security. Apart from providing storage and a place for germinating seeds, a terrace with a façade that unfolds to form a table makes a space for gardeners.

below: **Teaching ecological literacy.** Particular school classes, and individual school children with an interest in food growing helped (and help) to grow crops and maintain the beds.

And every city deserves a *Sweet Water* and a *Growing Power*!

James Godsil

Sweet Water is an emergent, hybrid enterprise experiment, a social business and innovation centre, advancing the commercialisation, democratisation and globalisation of aquaponics, an ecosystem method of food production. But *Sweet Water* offers more than food produce and protein production. *Sweet Water* is a science lab, a school, an eco-tourist destination, an artist and tinkerers' workshop, a community and new enterprise centre. *Sweet Water* aspires to grow urban farmers, green tech start-up businesses, communities and... organic cities!

The stars aligning for great aquaponics experiments

A sequence of events inspired me to team up with a web of partners to launch the *Sweet Water* experiment. The first happened in 2005, when young citizens at a public meeting in Riverwest Milwaukee, the most successful "integrating neighbourhood" in Wisconsin, challenged the community to constructively respond to an incident

Fig 1: *Growing Power*. Will Allen at *Growing Power*'s headquarters in Milwaukee talking to delegates from the *Grow Food, Growing Justice* gathering in summer 2011. (image: Bohn&Viljoen, 2011)

of "black on white, straight on gay" violence rather than pound drums of race rage. This motivated me to check out Will Allen's *Growing Power*, which, I had heard, involved an African-American ex-pro basketball player harvesting urban waste streams to grow rich soil for use by teams of urban youth, transforming vacant lots into community gardens. I was "seized as if by a madness" by the *Growing Power* "magic" and decided to intensely promote Will's teams through the MilwaukeeRenaissance. com wiki platform. My work led to a front-page story about Will in the local alternative weekly *The Shepherd Express* and a position on the *Growing Power* Board.

I focused on the *Growing Power* model, both its food production systems, especially vermiculture and aquaponics, and its methods for 'growing farmers and communities' with a hybrid model, aimed at both multiple income streams through standard market sales as well as funds from workshops, tours, foundations, donors and public–private partnerships.

A number of other developments were critical in setting the stage for the *Sweet Water* aquaponics experiment. In the spring of 2006, Michael Macy, a State Department cultural attaché, lent great lustre to Milwaukee's urban agriculture movement when he orchestrated a London visit by Will Allen to address the Royal Society for the Encouragement of Arts, Manufactures and Commerce as well as a visit by an eminent group of London "agrarians" to Milwaukee in the fall of 2007. The "London Farmers" then published the now classic report *Edible Cities* including *Growing Power* projects in Milwaukee, Chicago and New York. The Milwaukee Urban Agriculture Network (MUAN) became both an inspirational/ educational coalition as well as a grassroots political force. In March 2008, MUAN organized a highly successful international urban agriculture conference at which the head of Milwaukee's Department of City Development, Rocky Marcoux, proudly proclaimed Milwaukee as the centre of American urban agriculture. A month later, urban agriculture made front-page news in Milwaukee, for the first time, with a report on a partnership between Fred Binkowski of the Great Lakes Water Institute and *Growing Power* to raise 10,000 perch in Will's aquaponic system. Jon Bales' Urban Aquaculture Centre connected Will to Binkowski, as well as drumming up community awareness of urban fish farming's possibilities. In September 2008, Will won the coveted MacArthur genius award. My daughter Rachel Godsil, a law professor and convener of the Obama Urban Policy Team, introduced me to some of that group's leadership, increasingly intrigued by the flaws of oil-based, unhealthy and polluting industrial agriculture systems. My business partner Josh Fraundorf led our roof system restoration company to a $40,000 profit for *Sweet Water* investing. His friend and business associate offered very low rent – $15,000 in capital – and the promise of another $20,000 in sweat equity as a partner in *Sweet Water*. Emmanuel Pratt, a doctoral candidate in Columbia University's Planning and Architecture Department, filmmaker, and close associate of Will Allen, signed on to help out with the social business, democratising and globalising vision. Josh and Steve focused on the commercial upscaling.

A "grand alliance" was manifesting! The stage was surely set for an impressive commencement on 31 December 2008, when the Mayor's City Development chief, Rocky Marcoux, along with Will Allen, pledged to provide support for what has become an audacious experiment called *Sweet Water*.

Fig 2: *Sweet Water.* *Sweet Water*'s vision shared at *Wild Flower Bakery*. Will Allen in the centre with James Godsil to his right and Rocky Marcoux to his left.

Milwaukee: a fertile field for earth-friendly, science/engineering-enhanced food production

Milwaukee is a city with a history that made *Sweet Water* possible. While the people who imagined the business, the farm and the "academy" came forth with money, time, work and a noteworthy emotional/spiritual investment, the core founders are embedded in a community within a region whose active leaders very brilliantly prepared the way across many sectors. Milwaukee is the leading industrial and commercial city of Wisconsin, home of naturalist environmentalist icons John Muir, Aldo Leopold and Earth Day founder Gaylord Nelson. Milwaukee is renowned for its food and beverage industry (i.e. cheese and beer), its machine tool, engineering and medical technologies enterprise, and its embrace of education, culture and commonwealth support, like its renowned Olmsted parks or the heralded public health initiatives of the "Sewer Socialist" city government of 40 years standing up through the 1950s. Will Allen's breakthrough, so critical for *Sweet Water*'s emergence, was only possible because a vanguard of diverse supporters helped create the political climate that inspired the City Government at all levels to help adjust city law and zoning rules to minimise archaic, industrial city obstacles to this new "bio-technology", which integrated biological engineering systems into urban agriculture architecture – that is, food production using vermiculture and aquaponics.

Internet resources for a Milwaukee spring

While Milwaukee's abundance in human capital and social formations was a necessary condition for *Sweet Water*'s emergence, the early harnessing of the power of the internet was fundamental for its progress. E-mail exchanges and wiki platform resources played a vital role in pulling together the "Grand Alliance". The internet's ability to connect people across social sectors and identity groups and institutional boundaries was key for the original web of *Sweet Water* supporters from government, business, educational and new agrarian circles. Information and images were narrowly and widely diffused providing inspiration for and documentation of new possibilities. The digital exchange was augmented by meetings at cafés or the *Sweet Water* site, all of which provided good times and inspired commitments. The internet exchanges via e-mails and collaboration platforms eventually found their way to local hard-copy media outlets and, eventually, with enormous significance, to the metropolitan dailies, *Wall Street Journal*, *New York Times*, NPR and *NBC Nightly News*. National collaborative platforms like Tufts University's Comfoods – the "Comfoodies" – played an important part. Some early *Sweet Water* challenges around issues of proper lighting and plant:fish ratios would have been avoided had the founders been wired into some now international sharing sites like *Aquaponics Gardening* and *Backyard Aquaponics*. Fundraising events and governmental, banking and investor connectivity were all substantially enhanced, with much more "bang for the buck" by virtue of the miracle of the world wide web. Recent development in data design and graphic presentations have made the conveyance of complex concepts, hypotheses and modelling much more intelligible in real-time meetings as well as cross-national exchange.

An IBM 2011 film included the statement that *Sweet Water*'s experiment could be the mainframe for the 'organic city revolution'. Its accompanying report stated that 'Milwaukee could become more economically viable and help the world feed itself through urban agriculture and aquaponics – water-efficient systems that can transform abandoned factories and vacant lots into urban farms that raise fish and vegetables'.

Fig 3: Sweet Water. James Godsil introducing the *Sweet Water* project to visitors at a regular Sunday tour. (image: Bohn&Viljoen, 2011)

Multiple bottom lines and income streams

The *Sweet Water* "proof of concept" for the sustainability of the world's first fish and vegetable farm in a repurposed factory building reconciles different points of view.

Some of the expanding circle of partners believed that there would be sufficient revenues from the sale of tilapia, perch and the produce they nourished to validate the system and inspire replications large and small.

Others viewed *Sweet Water Organics* as a necessary research and development project with too many unknowns to expect a quick financial return. *Sweet Water* was seen as a science lab, a multifaceted 21st-century school "without walls", an eco-business incubator, an emerging community centre, and, possibly, a model for urban infill development with a "Sweet Water Village" potential. This group proposed a focus on multiple bottom lines, e.g. ecology and equity, as well as multiple income streams, e.g. fish and produce sales, but also compost, worms, worm castings, small-plot intensive garden structures, workshops, tours, urban agriculture and aquaponics installations.

Some also advocated a hybrid business model for *Sweet Water Organics* that would involve the establishment of a non-profit, i.e. the *Sweet Water Foundation*, to harvest the hard-won information derived from research and development and incorporate it into education and inspiration for schools and community. *Sweet Water Organics* would profit from the goodwill and expanding web of competent and committed partners in the urban agriculture/aquaponics evolution!

Sweet Water for all

Since digging the first of six 8,000-gallon tanks housing over 25,000 fish in 2009, *Sweet Water*'s transformation of a century-old, 25,000 sq. ft. derelict factory complex has mainstreamed aquaponics and inspired scores of replications, large and small. Responding to a laudatory *Harvard Business Review* note on *Sweet Water*, the *Economist* opined *Sweet Water* as 'what's right about America'. The *Wall Street Journal*, *New York Times*, NBC

Nightly News and *NPR* have echoed this notion. IBM has urged Milwaukee to invest millions in an Aquaponics Innovation Centre to harness the business-relevant R&D of Milwaukee's new School of Fresh Water Sciences showcasing the learning, demonstration, labour and market capacity building of urban agriculture platforms like *Sweet Water* and Will Allen's *Growing Power*.

Sweet Water currently consists of *Sweet Water Organics, Inc.*, i.e. "The Farm", the *Sweet Water Foundation*, i.e. "The Academy", and a globalising enterprise ecosystem, i.e. "The Grand Alliance". The *Sweet Water* Farm focuses on providing fresh, safe and sustainable food for local communities. The Academy harvests knowledge for lifelong learning and resilient community creation through tours, workshops and digital training modules in sustainable urban agriculture practices. The emerging global *Sweet Water* Grand Alliance is networking partners large – e.g. IBM, UN Global Compact Cities, major universities, city governments and business associations – and small – e.g. 40 Chicago and Milwaukee primary and secondary schools, veterans and community gardening groups, start-up co-ops and family businesses, interested in local, national and international collaboration. Many of the *Sweet Water* partners share a vision that 10% of the world's homes and schools will be harvesting knowledge and food from miniature aquaponics farms within a generation or two, facilitated by global open-source knowledge sharing among networks of "aquapons" as well as a major aquaponics innovation centre in every city. Milwaukee School of Engineering professor Shajan John, who has orchestrated an aquaponics start-up collaboration connecting 12 University of Wisconson-Madison students, *Sweet Water* and partners from Kerelea in India, has his eyes on the prize of 100,000,000 aquaponics miniatures across the world by 2025. *Sweet Water Foundation* educators Emmanuel Pratt, Jesse Blom and Jill Frey see their US Department of Agriculture grant to equip teachers with aquaponics systems and curricula as a first step toward the introduction of a pedagogical method of transformative possibility, not only for science, technology, engineering and mathematics, i.e. STEM competencies, but also for the acquisition of a higher sensibility and ecological and global citizen mindfulness. The Academy recently won a $175,000 MacArthur competition for digital media and knowledge through life learning.

Asset-based sequential economic and community development

The *Sweet Water* founders believed that harnessing the resources available to them in pursuit of a vision that was "in the grain" of the needs of the time, they would set in motion a self-organising process that would bring new partners with new resource sets, who would bring yet more partners with yet more resources, in a virtuous cycle of evolution and growth.

Some of the initial resources brought to the project were:

- a mammoth 10,000 sq. ft. building with three built-in, concrete-lined, below-ground fish tanks waiting for transformation from their original use as a rail road car repair pit,
- an acre of secluded land outside amenable to large-scale composting without bothering any neighbours (there are rail road tracks and lightly used factories nearby),
- a start-up capitalisation of about $50,000 that the Community Roofing partners were able to bring forth during the first six months,
- a wide and deep network of artisans, mechanics, horticulturalists and fish scientists already showing up in various edge-of-history Milwaukee urban agriculture projects, e.g. *Growing Power*, Great Lakes Water Institute, Milwaukee Urban Agriculture Network, Urban Ecology Center, UW-Extension, the Victory Garden Initiative, *Walnut Way*, *Alice's Garden*, *Future Green* and more,
- a track record of collaboration with complex and dangerous projects marked by the Lindner/community projects during the previous five or more years,
- communications connectivity with the mainstream media and the increasingly dense internet platforms available to attract local, national and international help.

STOP PRESS
In 2013, the highly ambitious and experimental Sweet Water Organics Aquaponic Farm *ceased trading due to financial difficulties. The* Sweet Water Foundation *continues with its educational work.*

Urbaniahoeve: Event-based practice and Urban Agriculture

Debra Solomon and Mariska van den Berg, Urbaniahoeve

Urbaniahoeve Social Design Lab for Urban Agriculture was established in the Netherlands in 2010. In Dutch, 'Urbaniahoeve' means, 'the city (as a) farmyard'. We initiate and coordinate structural forms of urban agriculture in public spaces by creating a contiguous, resplendent, fertile and, of course, edible ecological framework in the existing greens of the city. Collaborating with the local population in all its diversity and roles, *Urbaniahoeve* transforms (visually) green spaces into social spaces, and as well produces a source of *free,* organically grown fruit, herbs, flowers and vegetables. Our contextual framework lies in spatial planning and public space, and we see ourselves as producers of (food system) infrastructure, creating park-like, food-bearing ecosystems.

Urbaniahoeve comprises artist Debra Solomon (artist/art director), art historians Mariska van den Berg (writer/researcher of bottom-up public space infrastructure) and Annet van Otterloo (producer and project coordinator of artist-initiated urban regeneration). Between us, we have considerable experience utilizing event-based practice, supported by municipal policy, to realize artists' interventions in public space and urban regeneration propositions.

Our work asks how a collectively set up *foodscape* can function for a neighbourhood, and whether the local community can maintain it. Can artists and designers coordinate with local food entrepreneurs to infuse new life into a tired urban outdoor market? Can an elementary school maintain its own edible landscaping as a learning platform?

Our project *Foodscape Schilderswijk* in The Hague is an example of infrastructural, experiential, agrarian, material, social and ecological event practice. In the context of art, we refer to our work as a 'critical spatial practice'. It demonstrates the empirical application of a holistic approach to the human–city–nature complex, a qualitative reconsideration of the *real and actual* city's public space, rather than the objective application of a statistical and quantitative enquiry on its usage.

The project can trace its roots back to 2005, when reading *Continuous Productive Urban Landscapes: Designing urban agriculture for sustainable cities*. Debra was inspired by the notion the book put forth: that the city could seed its green spaces with productive greens and grow these spaces like ink spots into corridors to feed the city. She remembers reading:

CPULs do not yet exist.
In type, they will be new,
in type they will be productive.

and thinking, "CPULs must soon exist". In 2007, Debra was fortunate to be the food domain expert and part of the design team *DOTT 07 Urban Farming* that cooperated with *Bohn&Viljoen Architects* to initiate a temporary CPUL sketched with planters filled with soft fruit and vegetables for an urban farming project in Middlesbrough, England.[1]

Fig 1: *Foodscape Schilderswijk.* Section of densely layered planting including espaliered semi-dwarf fruit trees (e.g. plum), raspberry bushes, nectar plants (e.g. phacelia), and perennial herbs (e.g. lavender).

Later in 2007, Debra was commissioned by the *Free-house Collective,* an artist-initiated urban regeneration collective, to map the existing food-system infrastructure and food surplus generated by the Netherlands' largest outdoor market, the Afrikaandermarkt in Rotterdam Zuid. The resulting *Lucky Mi Fortune Cooking Free Kitchen*[2] tapped food flows and under-programmed facilities to transform the (perishable) food surplus (e.g. uncountable boxes of blueberries or crates of overripe pears from Argentina) into more versatile, longer-lasting food products (jams, syrups, pickles, drinks, soups and savoury snacks). The notion of connecting existing (food) facilities with social infrastructure was inspired by the merging ink spot dynamic of green spaces in the city described in the *CPUL* book.

The term 'foodscape' indicates an urban landscape that not only includes (under-programmed) green space, but (under-used) professional kitchens and open-air markets, as well as an under-accessed urban *socialscape,* e.g. neighbours, high-school biology students and their devoted, flexible teachers, or an elder-living group with

Fig 2: Continuous Productive Urban Foodscape. Hand-drawn chalkboard map of the Hague borough the Schilderswijk as a Continuous Productive Urban Foodscape. (image: Debra Solomon and Jacques Abelman for Urbaniahoeve, 2010)

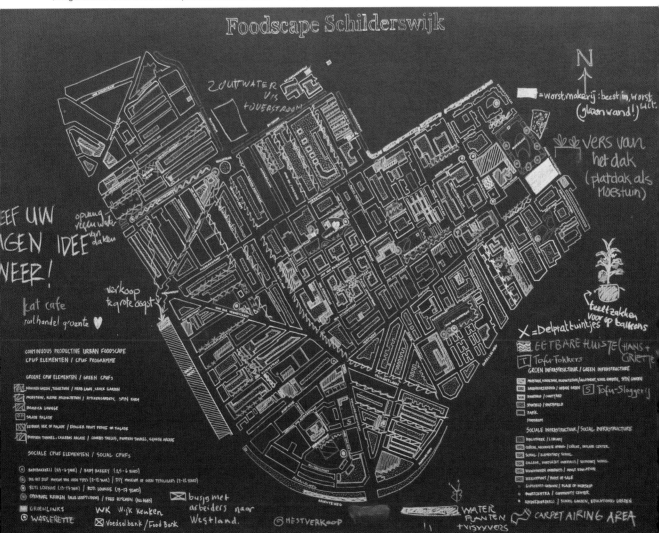

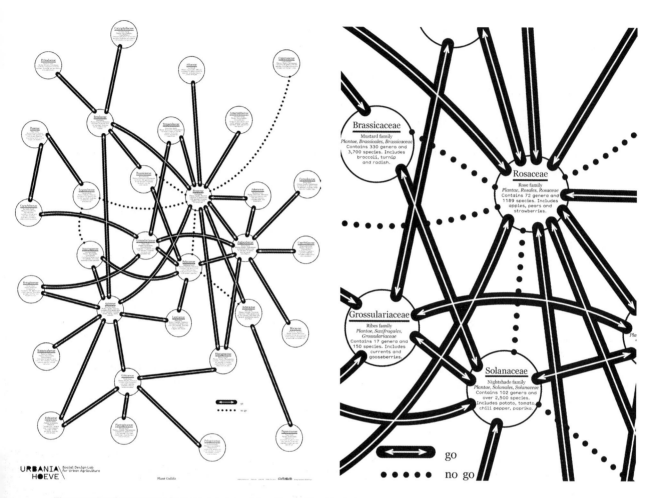

Figs 3 and 4: Plant guilds. Diagram showing collaborative relationships between
various food and nectar producing plant families.
(image: Debra Solomon and Jaromil Roio for Urbaniahoeve and DYNE.org, 2012)

a garden club. Expanding the CPULs' *land*scape into a
*food*scape could also accommodate an intricate layer of
existing urban programming comprising diverse forms
of social work at the neighbourhood level. In the meantime, CPULs do in fact exist, because *Urbaniahoeve* and
The Hague borough Schilderswijk have been building
one in the public space since 2010.

From 2010 onwards, and in close collaboration with
the art and architecture centre *Stroom Den Haag*,[3] the
Urbaniahoeve team have worked on *Foodscape Schilderswijk*, a continuous productive landscape in the
existing green infrastructure, built with the borough's

neighbours and organizations. *Foodscape Schilderswijk*
is a series of public space orchards, installed and
maintained by numerous and varied local groups
within the municipality. It is a classic case of *event
practice* for the sort of urban agriculture that *Urbaniahoeve* promotes, namely collectively installed public
space edible landscapes that, in time, form an *ecological framework* within the city. The harvest from these
locations (fruit, berries/soft fruit, artichokes, rhubarb,
perennial herbs and flowers) is public and free for the
picking. The more "abstract" harvest of this project, i.e.
public space programming, increased social cohesion
and community solidarity, and a radical and steady

increase in biodiversity and conviviality, is also free for the community to enjoy.

'Realistic utopianism without irony' is one of the slogans emblazoned on the *Urbaniahoeve Foodscape Schilderswijk* project posters. This tongue-in-cheek expression underscores our intention to cooperatively implement edible landscapes that form a working example of the sort of urban agriculture that we actually desire, namely: in public space, park-like and an important foundation in a city's ecological framework.

Urbaniahoeve Social Design Lab for Urban Agriculture

The Hague's Schilderswijk was designed in a 1980s wave of Dutch urban renewal and is populated with a demographic that supports and would utilize a well-programmed public space. The design of the existing public greens is primarily "defensive", e.g. fencing, monocultures of landscaped barriers. For an urban agriculture event to be successful in the Schilderswijk, it must positively impact resilience at ecological, social and nutritional levels. Our team's practice and experience in neighbourhoods in Schilderswijk and Amsterdam[4] has taught us that growing nutritive food crops and the social landscape that can support them is far more valuable to a neighbourhood than the production and sale of consumer-grade food products. The *Foodscape Schilderswijk* community (read also Amsterdam Nieuw West, Amsterdam Noord, Rotterdam Afrikaanderwijk)[5] possesses neither the means nor the ambition to benefit from buying organic produce. In these neighbourhoods, the awareness of the value of locally grown fruit and vegetables, of a healthy biotope, of a healthy relationship with one's neighbours, will come readily when that "product" is free for the picking, both in terms of consumption and participation.

The project participants of *Foodscape Schilderswijk*'s planting, harvesting and cooking activities are diverse. Participants include children (aged 8–12), together with their mothers directly after school, high-school students, a fathers' group, and even once or twice per year an expert group of municipal greens gardeners interested in *espalier* pruning. Aside from the *Urbaniahoeve*

project coordinator (local, highly experienced in artist-initiated urban regeneration), we work with a social worker (local, specialized in social permaculture, and a beekeeper) and a local project permaculture expert.

Although it would be a stretch to say that Schilderswijkers are motivated to participate in *the foodscapes* due to their interest in or knowledge of urban agriculture, deep ecology, imminent resource depletion or even a desire to access locally produced organic fruit, the child-participants do seem to be aware of these issues through their elementary school curricula. Early in the project, we chose fruit above vegetables as the primary planting, because (the eventuality of) a neglected orchard is, at worst, poetic; a neglected kitchen garden, on the other hand, is a mucky disaster. Yet, it is the fact that these fruit crops require so little maintenance that the core team can steadily initiate new, adjacent locations to secure and establish community engagement. Two years into *Foodscape Schilderswijk*, the orchards thrive with and without care, and should anyone decide to make a go at a cottage perfume or essential oils business this year, the locations yielded enough lavender to consider this a viable endeavour. The rhubarb harvest was so large that we conducted cooking classes to teach the new Dutch teenagers from the participating high school how

Fig 5: *Foodscape Schilderswijk*. Child participant prepares signs alerting neighbours and passers-by to 'Let the plants be, they have been planted by the neighbourhood children. Greetings from Safia, Youssef, Oumaima and Sara'.

to prepare it, and *Foodscape Schilderswijk* distributed recipes to encourage its consumption. By the third year we expect to not only have a copious crop of berries, but enough berry bush cuttings that we won't need to buy plant stock for the newest locations. That's nice about rhubarb, berries and artichokes: once you get the plants into the neighbourhood you can propagate cuttings for next year's locations!

An important element that contributes to the success of *Foodscape Schilderswijk* is our healthy working relationship with the parks and greens department *Groen Beheer*.[6] In the coming season, we will further strengthen this relationship by producing administrative templates for work/planting packages, encouraging further cooperation between our organizations. Not only can we support each other with plant material, labour and technical knowledge, Groen Beheer has proved a valuable ally in convincing sceptical bureaucratic parties during the early phases of *Foodscape Schilderswijk*. Groen Beheer provides us with local, strategic advocacy.

Part of the protocol maintained with Groen Beheer is that *Foodscape Schilderswijk* may begin work at any public space location as long as we can show that we have sufficient constituency to finish and maintain the planting. After researching a potential project location and developing contact with neighbours and in-situ institutions, we simply discuss (yes, verbally) the project with Groen Beheer and then proceed to get on with our work. Our contact is generous with suggestions regarding plant engineering and is facilitating with regard to works requiring machinery. By now, we are well acquainted with the municipality's ambitions and timetables for the Schilderswijk, just as Groen Beheer is acquainted with *Foodscape Schilderswijk's* ambitions and landscape *language*.

Public reaction

Not all *Schilderswijk* neighbours react positively to *the foodscapes*. A non-participating, vocal minority greets each new location with a negative attitude towards the possibility that a participatory landscape in the public space could affect civic behaviour. Along the southwest

facing wall of the *Hanneman Hoek*,[7] adjacent to a sanctioned dog-poop zone, mothers and children from the elementary school planted a collection of pear trees flanked with currants, abundant and over-productive rhubarb and artichokes. The local high-school biology class planted aromatic tread-plants to overpower the nearby poop along the dividing fence. In one year's time, the *Hanneman Hoek* has flourished with a significant, albeit rhubarb-rich, harvest for the neighbourhood and increasing numbers of ad hoc visits. Neighbours who once vocally eschewed the edible landscape now openly agree that the location is a success and focus their abundant negativity towards our rhubarb recipes.

In the spring of 2012 we planted a new location with large fruit trees (apple, pear and plum – donated by Groen Beheer) on the way to the dog-poop zone with a group of 36 local enthusiastic child-volunteers. Although four months later some of the plants have been stolen and some dog owners still allow their dogs to poop on the strawberries, we are certain that, within a year, this behaviour will change for the better as it did at every other location. And in the event that the bad civic behaviour doesn't change (enough)? We'll simply replace the strawberries with bee forage or a soft fruit that crops a little higher up. Although a minority of vocal sceptics may think otherwise, in our experience, the presence of food appears to encourage generous behaviour. We want to emphasize that *Urbaniahoeve* produces both examples and vocabulary (that is, event practice) of community-installed edible landscaping as a sorely needed tool for community agency. Although each new location is met with scepticism, to date, and within one year of completion, each *Foodscape Schilderswijk* location has been adopted, accepted and appreciated.

The structural problem with small-scale, event practice Urban Agriculture infrastructure

After two years of financing *Foodscape Schilderswijk* largely through the cultural sector, the time came for the municipality to invest in the continuity of its *foodscape*. As of this writing, *Urbaniahoeve* has spent more than four months to secure funding for 2013 and in so doing has hosted more than 60 MPs and local politicians on site during working hours. In a particularly grim funding search episode, three different parties (a local political party, a social work funding platform for the Schilderswijk and the local housing corporation) proceeded as if to cover our budget equally among them. After months of discussion, honing the proposal and the budget, we discovered that two of these parties were planning on tapping the same, rather inadequate fund that represented a mere one tenth of our total budget. This process squandered our time (not to mention our spirits); a pity considering that urban agriculture infrastructure production activities are season-bound. Now, six months later, *Foodscape Schilderswijk's* project continuity is uncertain.

The contextual and financial bubble of artist autonomy that was a strong agent for culture-driven urban agriculture and urban regeneration in the Netherlands burst when, in 2011, the Dutch minority cabinet announced draconian funding cuts to culture. Like other contemporary 'bottom-up infrastructure producers' in the era of the partially dismantled government, *Urbaniahoeve* now operates in precarity. We have since prioritized forming strategic alliances at the nexus of the ministries of culture, agriculture, infrastructure and the environment in the hope that searching higher, rather than lower, will yield the continuity that our vision of urban agriculture requires.

Urbaniahoeve's vision of the urban public space as a *foodscape* posits a productive, socio-natural city. However, aside from network actors such as the aforementioned Groen Beheer, who maintain the city's green spaces, and the local educational framework (environmental education (DSB/NME), and the public school system), the institutional framework with which *Urbaniahoeve* currently works is inadequate in its understanding of our vision, let alone its ability to sustain the inherently long-term aims that we adopt. In times of austerity, when true socio-environmental costs remain hidden, an urban agriculture event practice can provide a platform to develop new forms of long-term support frameworks, promoting a deepened dialectical foundation for urban agriculture; not exclusively a producer of urban food infrastructure, but a generator of new notions of socio-environmental relationships, horizontally produced urban infrastructure, and 'innovation under austerity'.

Notes

1. for project details see: Social Design Site (2007) *DOTT07 Urban Farming Project*, Online: <http://www.socialdesignsite.com/content/view/150> (accessed 10 Apr 2013).
2. for project details see: Culiblog.org (2008) *Lucky Mi Fortune Cooking*, Online: <http://culiblog.org/category/lucky-mi-fortune-cooking/> (accessed 10 Apr 2013).
3. for details see: Stroom Foodprint Programme (2009) *Stroom Den Haag Foodprint Weblog*, Online: <http://stroom.typepad.com> (accessed 10 Apr 2013).
4. for project details see: URBANIAHOEVE projects (2010) *Urbaniahoeve Social Design Lab for Urban Agriculture*, Online: <http://www.urbaniahoeve.nl/project-locations/?lang=en> (accessed 10 Apr 2013).
5. Amsterdam Nieuw West, Amsterdam Noord, Rotterdam Afrikaanderwijk are low-income, culturally diverse boroughs by Dutch standards. These boroughs represent different demographics and urban typologies.
6. *Groen Beheer* is a Dutch term describing a (municipal) parks and greens department.
7. *Hanneman Hoek* is a multi-level polyculture orchard planted by schoolchildren with their mothers, and it is part of *Foodscape Schilderswijk*.

Fig 6: Hügelbed. DemoGarden volunteers fabricate a 'Hügelbed' from in-situ wood litter and local cardboard waste. The advantages of growing urban food on Hügelbeds include contact mitigation with potentially contaminated (or poor) urban soils, radical increase in growing surface, carbon and water sequestration, and a wonderful use for abundant urban waste streams.
(image: DYNE.org for Urbaniahoeve, 2012)

Urban Nature Shoreditch

London, UK, 1998

Architectural design proposal (1999) extended for international exhibition (2009) – exploring the integration of food production within a high-density urban setting.

- **SPACE AND ORGANISATION:** High-density, high-rise, mixed-use incorporating vertical and horizontal fields/market gardens for a site in central London.

- **FOOD PRODUCTION TYPE:** Commercial and self-grown using open-field and building-integrated production.

- **USE OF HARVEST:** Neighbourhood supply.

- **CLIENT:** 1999 competition coordinated by the Architecture Foundation, 2009 exhibition curated by Exit Arts NYC.

- **FUNDING:** None.

- **PROJECT TEAM:** Bohn&Viljoen, supported by Eva Beniio Benito and Lucy Taussig in 1998 and by Jonathan Gales, John Hibbett and Áine Moriarty in 2009.

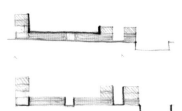

above: **Topographical study** into the use of slopes and level changes to control visual continuity and physical separation between public and private space, including market gardens.

SOUTH NORTH SECTION 1:500 90M HIGH TOWER

above: **Section through one of the towers.** By means of vertical layering, the towers accommodate a mixed-use programme, including public and private spaces, such as apartments, offices, shops, a nursery and a swimming pool. Such mixed-use briefs, although rarely achieved, are central to the concept of sustainable, high-density urban development. A primary goal was to achieve a naturally daylit and ventilated high-rise building, and this has determined the building's narrow section. The cranked profile in plan is to aid structural stiffness.

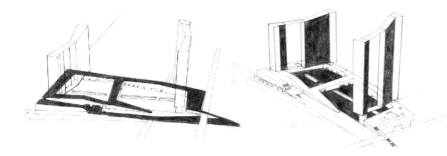

far left: **The landscape is layered** so that at the upper level a linear public park connects to a larger network of pedestrian and cycle routes.

left: **Vertical and horizontal productive fields** are visible to all, but, by means of level changes, are also secure for commercial or private growing.

above: **An aerial view** showing how the public park frames the urban agriculture fields.

right: **Personalised urban agriculture.** Vertical planting on the façade, using espaliered fruit trees, providing a seasonal crop as well as an important connection with nature. Protected hydroponic planting is placed internally to supply salad crops and herbs. A continuous floor finish creates continuity between inside and outside.

below: **The original prototypical proposal by Bohn&Viljoen from 1999.** It demonstrates principles of Ecological Intensification, such as integrating food growing, rainwater harvesting, active solar hot water, PV and passive solar design for the building's daylight and ventilation to collectively minimise the project's ecological footprint. The design was revisited in 2009 for the Vertical Gardens exhibition hosted and curated by Exit Arts in New York and later exhibited by the American Institute of Architects in San Francisco.

COMMENTARY

Urban Nature tested the provision of tall, thin buildings with natural lighting and ventilation, incorporating vertical "fields" on major facades and allowing ground and roof space for the cultivation of crops.

The design was a response and a challenge to the publication in 1999 of the *Urban Task Force Report*, commissioned by the UK government in an attempt to define sustainable strategies for urban regeneration. Urban food systems did not feature. Our own research was indicating that remote food production had a significant negative environmental impact on cities. In this project, we wanted to visualise how urban agriculture could be combined with a development accommodating 450 persons per hectare.

With hindsight, the *Urban Nature* towers can be seen as one of the first proposals for vertical city farming, governed by the need to provide plants with daylight to avoid energy-intensive artificial lighting.

Visualisation occurs at the urban, architectural and personal scale, providing a sense of what a *CPUL City* would be like to inhabit. Aspects requiring further research include adjustable wind protection systems for the vertical fields and optimising these for internal daylighting and natural ventilation.

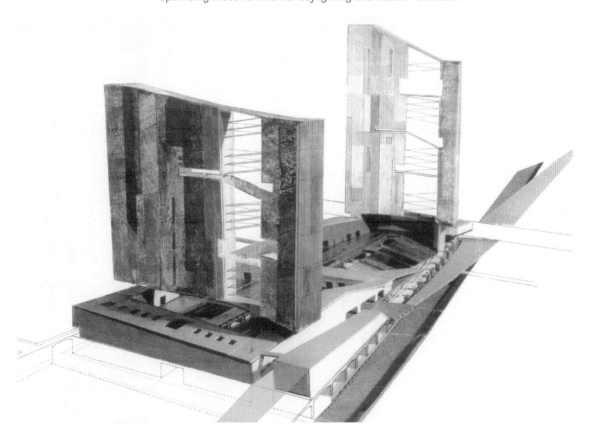

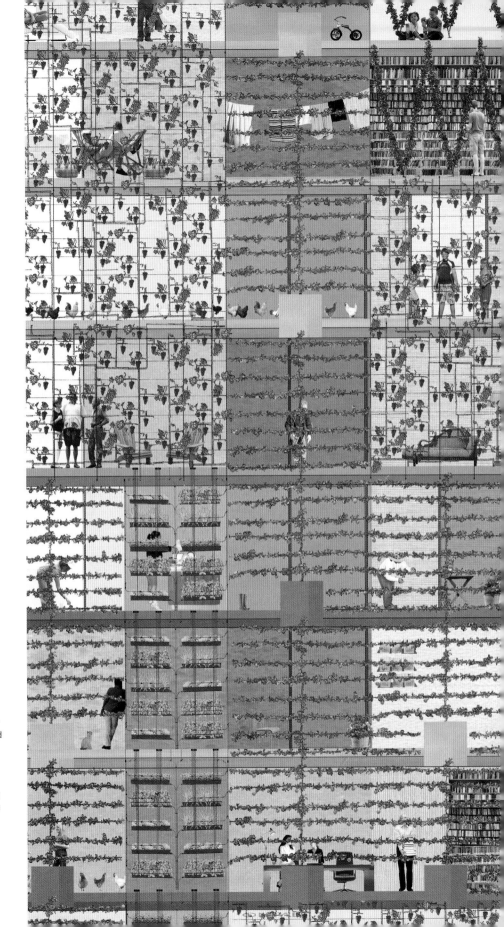

right: **Vertical Gardens.**
Part elevation showing how
the vertical fields are formed
and vary according to crop
type. Complex mechanisms
are avoided, and access
is provided by means of
balconies that enable direct
access to crops. Cultivation
can either be managed
centrally or directly by the
building's occupants.

The Continuous Picnic

London, UK, 2008

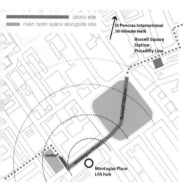

above: **A continuous landscape.** The picnic site made a physical connection between existing open spaces.

A day-long public event run as part of the London Festival of Architecture, asking, 'How does London feed itself?' and demonstrating how major public spaces could be transformed if productive urban landscapes were adopted.

- **SPACE AND ORGANISATION:** CPUL.

- **FOOD PRODUCTION TYPE:** Individual and community cultivation.

- **USE OF HARVEST:** In a public picnic.

- **CLIENT AND FUNDING:** London Festival of Architecture with additional financial support from The Arts Council, The London Development Agency and the London Borough of Camden.

- **PROJECT TEAM:** Bohn&Viljoen with input from, Studio Columba, Charlick+Nicholson Architects, David Barrie, Andrew Stuck, Abby Taubin, Jo Foster, Jonathan Gales, Mikey Tomkins and second-year University of Brighton Architecture students.

- **PARTNER:** The SEED Foundation, Global Generation, The Calthorp Project, as well as many helpers on the day.

right: **Seed Packets.** Artefacts were used to publicise the picnic and promote a discussion about London's food system. Working with the organic seed supplier Tamar Organics, we designed new labels for seed packets that were distributed as fliers in shops around the picnic site and also given as prizes for some of the growing competitions.

above: **Challenging the perception of open space.** Picnickers using the space in front of the event's *Inverted Market*. Normally, this space holds no market and is used as a road. (image: Clare Brass SEED Foundation, 2008)

below: **The picnic underway.** Montague Place, directly behind the British Museum, was transformed from a bus parking road, into a short CPUL during the London Festival of Architecture.

below: **The Project Process Diagram.** The diagram visualises the web of interactions typical for delivering collaborative actions, such as the *Continuous Picnic*.

COMMENTARY

The *Continuous Picnic* was designed as a day-long event celebrating local food and the city. It took place on Saturday the 5th July 2008 in Bloomsbury, central London, occupying Montague Place (behind the British Museum) and Russell Square. Working with a team of architects, community gardeners, designers and food enthusiasts the project aimed to engage Londoners and visitors in a dialogue about urban food production and an alternative use of open space, showing how both could be combined advantageously in the future.

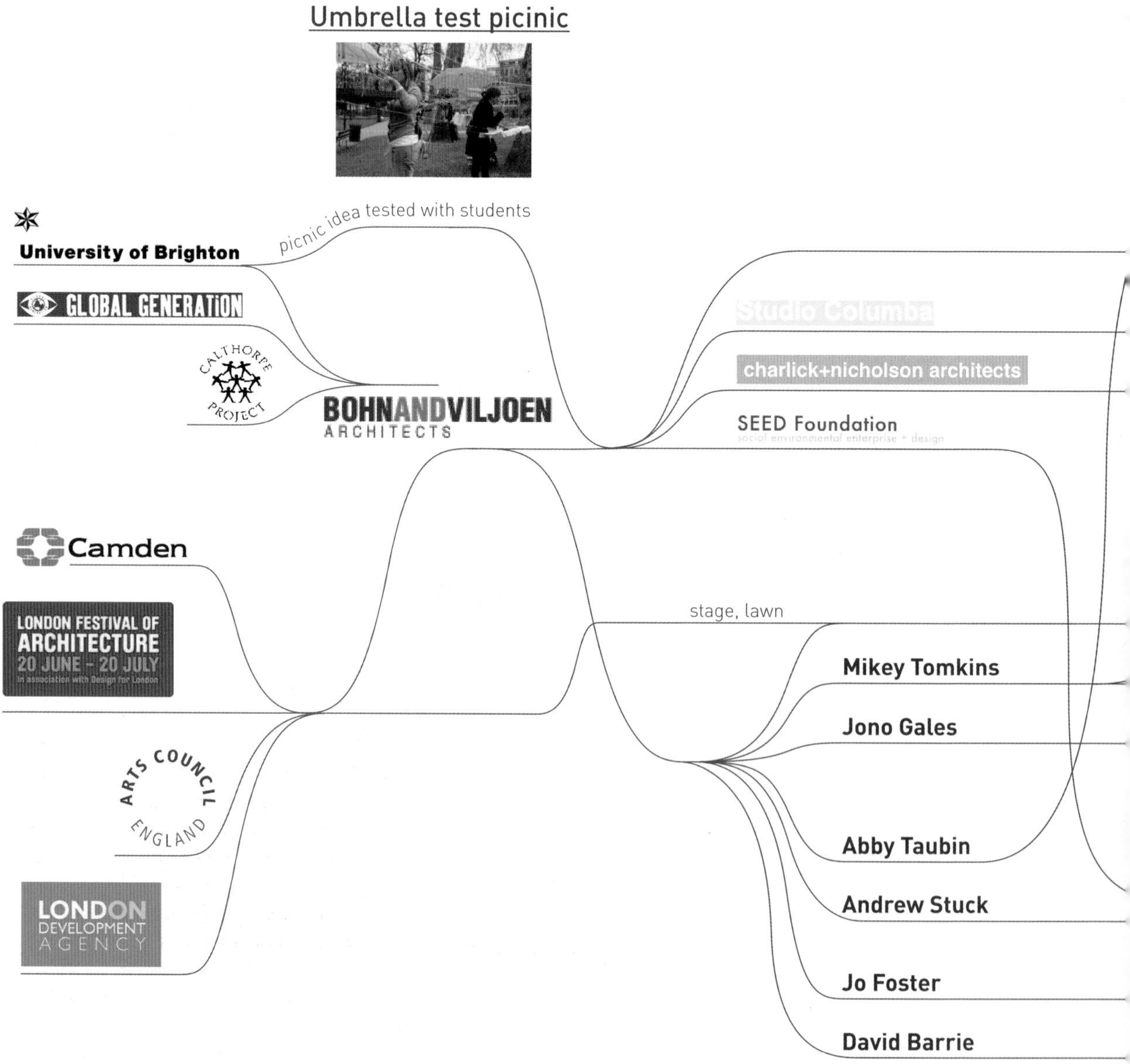

Umbrella test picinic

picnic idea tested with students

University of Brighton

GLOBAL GENERATION

CALTHORPE PROJECT

BOHNANDVILJOEN
ARCHITECTS

Studio Columba

charlick+nicholson architects

SEED Foundation
social environmental enterprise + design

Camden

LONDON FESTIVAL OF
ARCHITECTURE
20 JUNE – 20 JULY
In association with Design for London

ARTS COUNCIL
ENGLAND

LONDON
DEVELOPMENT
AGENCY

stage, lawn

Mikey Tomkins

Jono Gales

Abby Taubin

Andrew Stuck

Jo Foster

David Barrie

It was advertised as 'The picnic with a difference: A fresh food market installation followed by a giant public picnic in one of the most beautiful parts of central London... a continuous picnic of infinite personal encounters and fresh food events... a free outdoor event for everybody to celebrate good food and company'.

The day started early in the morning with the *Inverted Market*, a 150-metre long fresh food market installation. 'Inverted' referred to the market's call to the public

below: **The Project Process Diagram.** Although planned and designed (top-down), the successful realisation of the event depended on the active participation by community groups, social enterprises and, ultimately, the public (bottom-up).

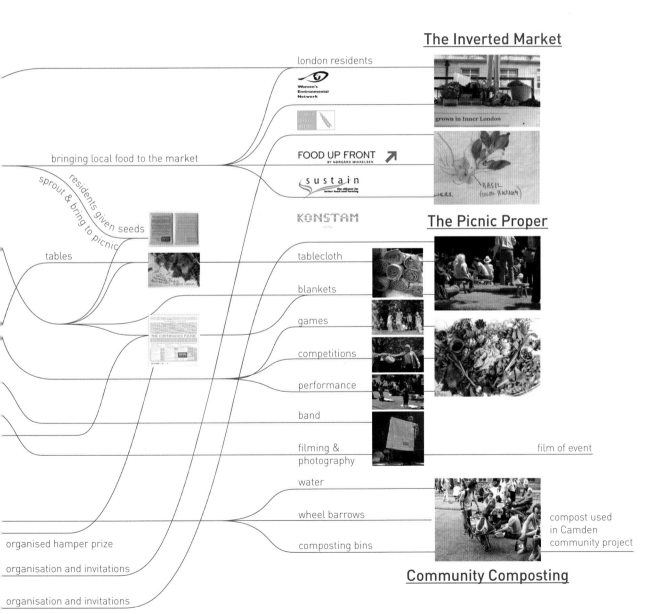

The Inverted Market

london residents

Women's Environmental Network

bringing local food to the market

FOOD UP FRONT
BY NORGÅRD MIKKELSEN

sustain
the alliance for
better food and farming

grown in Inner London

BASIL
(COLN. HACKNEY)

KONSTAM

sprout & bring to picnic

residents given seeds

The Picnic Proper

tables

tablecloth

blankets

games

competitions

performance

band

filming & photography

film of event

water

wheel barrows

organised hamper prize

composting bins

compost used in Camden community project

organisation and invitations

Community Composting

organisation and invitations

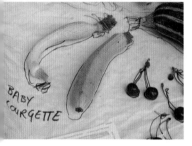

to bring food, either self-grown or grown and bought within central London, to the market. Market tables were set up to provide a visual record of the distance between Montague Place and where the food had been grown.

At mid-morning, in the tradition of summer fair produce competitions, a number of fresh fruit and vegetable competitions took place, all judged by leading practitioners in the field of London's local and sustainable food movement. Competition categories included, The Allotment Award, judged by Richard Wiltshire, allotments advocate and campaigner, The Edible Flower Award, judged by Louise Gates, *The Calthorpe Project*, The Food Miles Award, judged by Ben Reynolds, *Sustain*, The Grown-on-concrete Award, judged by Seb Mayfield, *Food up Front*, The London Eco Chef Award, judged by Oliver Rowe, Konstam Restaurant, The Schools' Urban Agriculture Award, judged by Jane Riddiford, *Camden Environmental Education Network*, The You'd Never Believe You Could Grow This In London Award, judged by Christine Haigh, *The Women's Environmental Network*, and The Jelly-It Award, judged by Bompas & Parr, *The Jellymongers*. The awards ceremony effectively became an impromptu and informal masterclass on London's food system, both in a top-down and bottom-up

above: **The Inverted Market.** Produce grown in London was brought to the market, laid out according to the distance it travelled and later consumed by the picnickers. Outlining on paper table cloths where each contribution had been grown and its type, recorded and visualised. Food miles, local produce and biodiversity.

below: **The Inverted Market.** The market's tables were rearranged during the day to accommodate different stages of the event, for example display, preparation and, in some cases, eating.

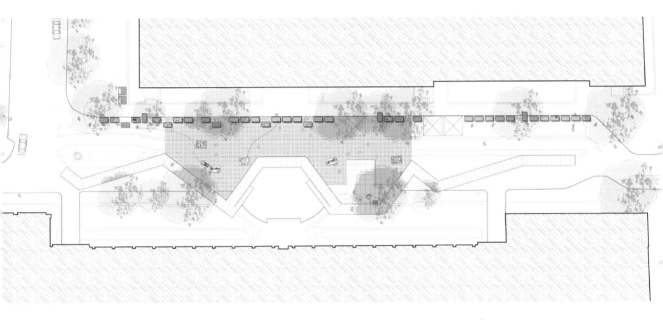

above: **The Continuous Picnic site.** Plan of Montague Place as reconfigured for the event. The 150-m long *Inverted Market* lies to the north and a temporary elevated walkway by architects' Carmody Groarke to the south side of the road. (image: Bohn&Viljoen using a plan supplied by Carmody Groake, 2008)

sense. London's former deputy mayor and sustainability campaigner, Jenny Jones, introduced this public dialogue.

The picnic began at midday, allowing for the prepartion of produce from the *Inverted Market*. It was supplemented with fresh bread supplied by one of London's re-emergent organic and ethical bakers, Flour Power City Bakery, as well as a selection of other picnic ingredients.

A *Community Composting* event concluded the day, when all compostable remains were collected and returned to local communities for reuse.

Alongside the picnic, a number of workshops, performances and children's food games animated the day. Despite having to contend with a very wet morning, the picnic continued well into the evening, long after the *Community Composting* had ended.

The *Continuous Picnic* confirmed the desirability of CPUL space within a city, amply demonstrated by the number of people stopping in the space during the day. The event was less successful at building an Inventory of Urban Capacity, i.e. recording and documenting the quantity and variety of crops already grown in London. For such a big task, the project was much too small. The differences between visualising the consequences of urban agriculture and researching or inventorying them, became very evident.

Urbane Agrikultur in Köln-Ehrenfeld

Köln, Germany, 2010–2011

above: ***Ehrenfeld, was isst du?*** The first paper-based mapping made with residents showing where food was grown or processed.

Arts-based practice leading urban regeneration.

- **SPACE AND ORGANISATION:** CPUL strategy applied to a post-industrial landscape.

- **FOOD PRODUCTION TYPE:** Open-field and container production.

- **USE OF HARVEST:** Communal cultivation for neighbourhood processing and consumption.

- **CLIENT:** Plan 10, DQE, City of Cologne [Köln].

- **FUNDING:** European Fund for Regional Development, Department of Trade and Industry North Rhine-Westphalia, City of Cologne, GAG Immobilien AG.

- **PROJECT TEAM:** Bohn&Viljoen Architects, Dirk Melzer Landscape Architect and Environmental Engineer.

above: **Baskets represent a map of streets in Ehrenfeld,** with actual neighbourhood produce placed in the baskets according to the production's location. (images: Dirk Melzer, 2010)

COMMENTARY

The city of Cologne runs an established architecture biennale; whose 2010 edition, entitled "plan 10" included the project *Ehrenfeld, was isst du?* ['*Ehrenfelt, what do you eat?*']. Exploring how urban agriculture might contribute to the regeneration of the Ehrenfeld neighbourhood, this project acted as the catalyst for larger European-Union-funded project called *Urbane Agrikultur in Köln-Ehrenfeld*. Utilising a number of different visualisation techniques and participatory processes, *Ehrenfeld, was isst du?* generated an overall CPUL strategy for the neighbourhood, including three specific urban agriculture proposals: an orchard, the Low Line Linear Park and an urban vineyard. At the time of writing, all three of these projects have developed from visualisations into trial projects in cooperation with residents, city officials and developers.

The success of *Ehrenfeld, was isst du?* as a catalyst is due to the combination of initial visualising work, with top-down and bottom-up strategies, developed to build upon existing desires and skills within the neighbourhood – or, in other words, upon existing urban capacities.

below: **Plan10 and Design Quarter Ehrenfeld (DQE).** DQE occupies a vacant industrial unit, and this unique space became the central focus during Cologne's Plan10 Architecture Biennale for the multiple activities visualising Ehrenfeld's existing food networks and emerging urban food and productive landscape strategies. The space accommodated meeting, making, cooking and exhibition areas, collectively facilitating a multi-stakeholder design process. (image: Bohn&Viljoen and Nishat Awan (FG Stadt & Ernährung TU Berlin), 2012)

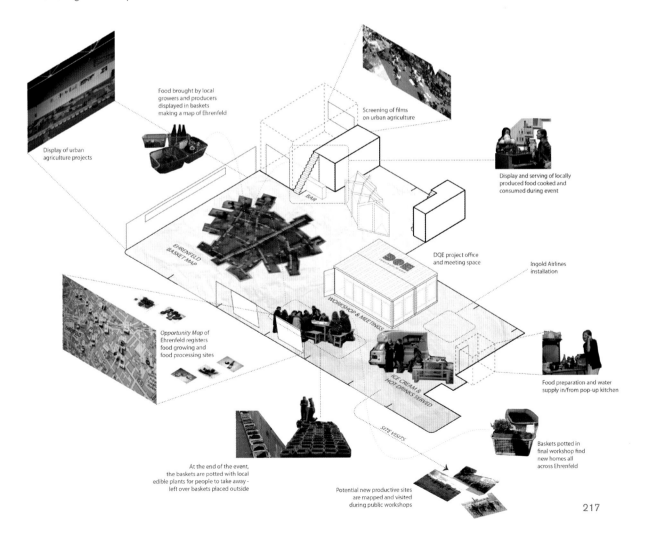

Display of urban agriculture projects

Food brought by local growers and producers displayed in baskets making a map of Ehrenfeld

Screening of films on urban agriculture

Display and serving of locally produced food cooked and consumed during event

EHRENFELD BASKET MAP

BAR

DQE project office and meeting space

Ingold Airlines installation

Opportunity Map of Ehrenfeld registers food growing and food processing sites

WORKSHOP & MEETINGS

ICE CREAM & HOT DRINKS SERVED

Food preparation and water supply in/from pop-up kitchen

SITE VISITS

Baskets potted in final workshop find new homes all across Ehrenfeld

At the end of the event, the baskets are potted with local edible plants for people to take away - left over baskets placed outside

Potential new productive sites are mapped and visited during public workshops

217

right: **Developing visions.**
Site visits, followed up by
design strategy meetings and
food growing workshops at the
DQE headquarters resulted
in a strategy for continuous
productive urban landscapes
as shown below.
(images: Dirk Melzer, 2010)

A possible walking / cycling
connection between a large open
space to the North (Takufeld) and the
city forest (Stadtwald) to the South
was identified as a major necessity

The connectivity between the city
centre (to the East) and the edge of the
city (to the West) could be improved

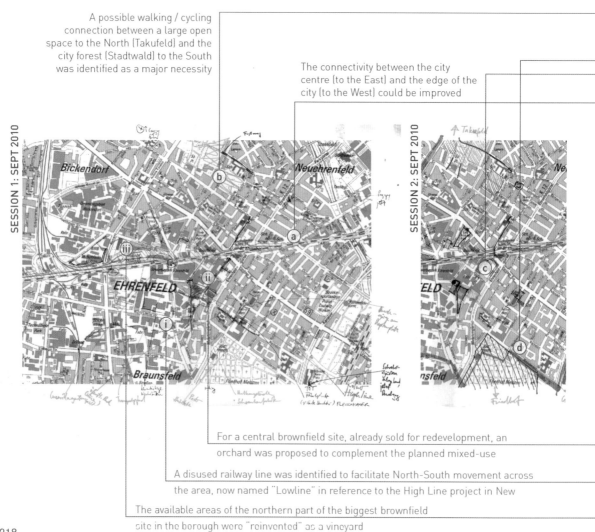

For a central brownfield site, already sold for redevelopment, an
orchard was proposed to complement the planned mixed-use

A disused railway line was identified to facilitate North-South movement across
the area, now named "Lowline" in reference to the High Line project in New

The available areas of the northern part of the biggest brownfield
site in the borough were "reinvented" as a vineyard

below: **An Opportunities Map for Köln-Ehrenfeld.** Chronological sequence of maps developed over three workshops, showing certain strategic decisions and how they evolved. (image: Bohn&Viljoen, local residents and Nishat Awan (FG Stadt & Ernährung TU Berlin), 2012)

The four most desired urban strategies engaged with during workshops

a East to West productive green connector

b North to South productive green connector

c Redevelopment of the Heliosquarter

d North-West to South-East green connector

The need for a productive connection to the South-East towards the inner-city emerged during the workshop

The Heliosquarter was identified as a potential hub for food growing activities in the area

SESSION 3: MAY 2011

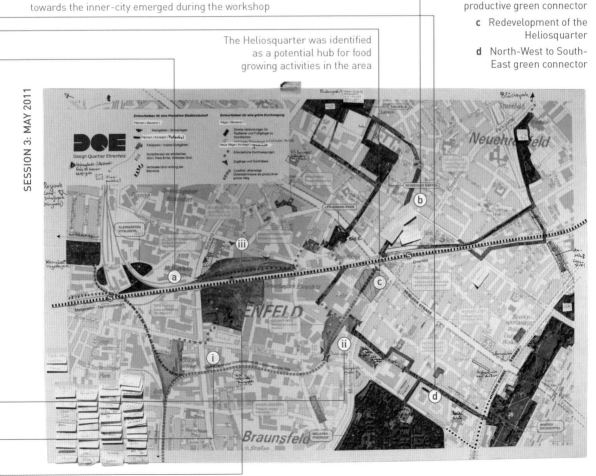

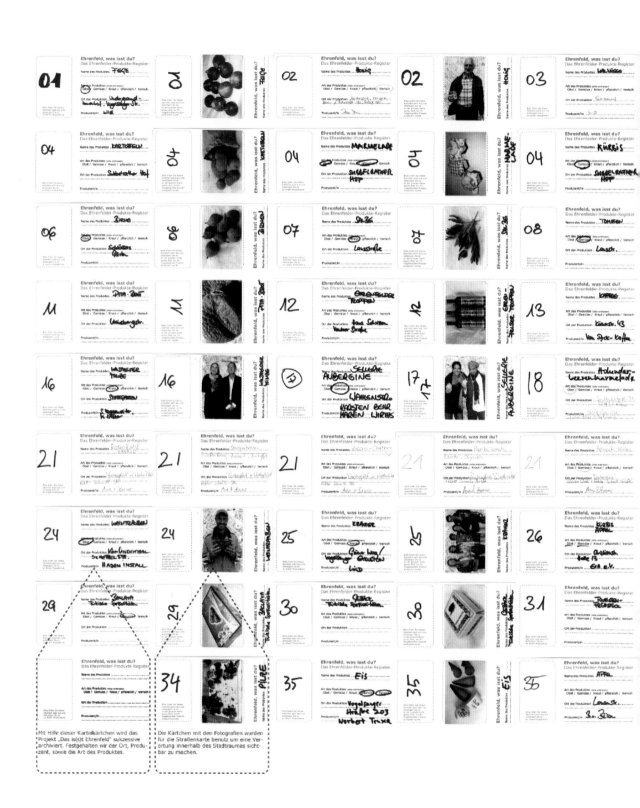

left: **Ehrenfeld, was isst du?** A sample of register cards from the first project looking at food in Ehrenfeld. After recording what food was grown or processed in the neighbourhood, the actual produce was subsequently included in an installation set up at the DQE headquarters. The register cards where then located on a neighbourhood food map. As an action in the visualisation process, a chef prepared a neighbourhood meal using local produce. Overall, this exercise was part of the Inventory of Urban Capacity informing the later CPUL strategy, and it was equally significant in establishing the community of residents who wished to advocate urban agriculture within the wider network of neighbourhood stakeholders.

Initials CPUL:
Regenerating the urban

Sabine Voggenreiter in an interview with Bohn & Viljoen

When planning the DQE work in Köln-Ehrenfeld, why did you choose urban agriculture as strategic starting point?

When we started planning the *DQE* work in Köln-Ehrenfeld, we decided to not just set individual "creative" topics but take a wider approach, looking at different ways of being involved in the organisation of everyday life in neighbourhoods and in community-driven processes.

DQE – Design Quartier Ehrenfeld – aims to develop a creative urban district in Cologne. The project was the winner of a competition, *Create.NRW*, run by the North Rhine-Westphalia Department of Trade and Industry on behalf of the European Union. Our project explores strategic concepts for structuring the Ehrenfeld district spatially and conceptually – and will successively transform this former "working-class neighbourhood" into a creative urban space and a centre for creative industries. The awareness that cities and economies (can) grow like biological organisms, for example in a garden, forms the central motivation for our project which brings new/alternative categories into play, such as: urban design, sustainability, spatial qualities, links to the location's history, regional economies, new living and working environments, neighbourhood, ethics of economies (and politics) and the "nature" of growth.

We assume that small-scale and sensitive urban and socially interactive planning of the "city" will help it survive on a long-term basis and (re)generate it, and that creative micro-economies are the development engines for a European city to flourish on a sustainable basis. It is unique that a cultural scientist like me (joined by an urban practitioner) was enabled to do research by practice in realising such a project. I think this is related to the fact of urban planning being confronted with new topics that the conventional method of the master plan could no longer address. There is a new spatial interest and new spatial need, and new questions and challenges

are set, like creating identity, urbanity and public urban space and altogether building a community. Our work also reflects and evaluates the production of knowledge and creative practice.

So, on the one side, we created cultural events and programs in collaboration with the urban creatives. There is a pool of approximately 600 creatives who want to be part of the process. Thus we started *Design Parcours Ehrenfeld* with about 79 venues all over Ehrenfeld and with about 60,000 visitors during one week, *Pop Design Festival (pdf)*, an event format about the topics of pop and design culture, and a decentralised fashion festival with do-it-yourself happenings and catwalks.

On the other hand, we started a movement we called "Urbane Agrikultur Ehrenfeld" with a workshop and several happenings in the context of *plan10* which allowed us to multiply energies and create synergies by interlocking different art events.

plan is a decentralised biennial exhibition in Cologne, which addresses the interplay of architecture, city and the arts. During the past 15 years, and not only in Germany, the analysis – as well as the interpretation and evaluation – of architecture and city, of urban and suburban spaces, has undergone an enormous change. The near-artistic approaches taken by city planners and architects on the one hand, and the great interest artists and cultural theorists have in these topics on the other, have brought about numerous (primarily temporary) projects with a playful, symbolic and metaphoric – but also very precise, pragmatic or even socio-political – orientation. As diverse as the respective positions and intentions may be, all share a common interest in bringing about a change in perception: in seeing situations and places, spaces and areas within the architectonic/urban structural context in a different way and in drawing productive conclusions. And the "best way" to generate sensibility and awareness in this regard is still the artistic approach – with the corresponding strategies and methods.

For *Urbane Agrikultur Ehrenfeld* this meant that the *plan10* events were followed by a workshop programme *Ehrenfelder Frühling* in 2011 when we opened our first "urban garden" in Ehrenfeld in the very neighbour-hood of the *DQE* headquarters and on a post-industrial brownfield site: the *Obsthain Grüner Weg*.

The DQE project aims to establish a 'creative' quarter in Ehrenfeld. How do you think urban agriculture helps to this aim?

The centre for urban agriculture initiative in Ehrenfeld is the *Obsthain Grüner Weg*, a fruit orchard realised as a co-operation project between *DQE* and the local housing company GAG Immobilien AG.[1] This mobile community garden with its 30 apple and pear trees, consisting of old varieties for the most part, opened in May 2011. Since then, it has developed into a location for leisure activities, learning and production in which gardening

enthusiasts from Ehrenfeld raise a very broad variety of edibles, cultivate varieties of fruit and vegetables that have grown rare and receive instruction in herbal medicine and even beekeeping. The project is now home to some 130 different useful plants. The plot of ground on which the garden is located belongs to GAG and is the site for the *Grüner Weg Wohngebiet*, a residential estate now under construction, where in future the open spaces will be planted with these very trees. As building progresses, the fruit orchard that is currently growing in mobile plant containers will migrate, little by little, to its final location. So it will ultimately become a com-munity garden for the new residents living here: overall, an extraordinary project in new housing construction

Fig 1: **Seed project.** Planting event at *DQE* headquarters as part of the plan10 project *Ehrenfeld, was isst du?* (image: Bozica Babic, 2010)

Fig 2: **Kölner Palme.** Mobile plantation of a native type of field salad – Palm of Cologne – on the roofs of *DQE* headquarters as part of the plan10 project *Ehrenfeld, was isst du?* (image: Bozica Babic, 2010)

in which the first thing to develop, before all else, is a garden.

In projects of this nature, an important factor, in addition to the actual sources of agricultural experience and knowledge, are the social networks that develop within the respective neighbourhoods and beyond – the food growing garden becomes a space to relax in, an educational entity and a meeting place for groups of all ages. Cooperation and contacts with other community gardens are also important in this regard. For us, this meant, amongst other actions, a workshop held in March 2012 with the initiators of the *Prinzessinnengärten* in Berlin;[2] working with the successful concepts they use, scenarios were drawn up for the planning and development of similar community gardens based on a location analysis. This provided models or checklists for the three projects in Cologne: *NeuLand*, *Pflanzstelle* and *Obsthain Grüner Weg*.[3]

After two years, our project was presented in detail to all interested individuals during *plan12*: using a video documentation *Urbane Agrikultur und Produktive Stadtlandschaften in Köln-Ehrenfeld* [Urban Agriculture and Productive Urban Landscapes in Köln-Ehrenfeld] by Sybille Petrausch, a digital slide show, a presentation in the *Obsthain Grüner Weg* publication series, a garden meeting held on 22 and 24 September 2012, an exhibition with design studies on productive urban landscapes

in Köln-Ehrenfeld by your [Katrin Bohn's] students from the Technical University Berlin and your lecture on this topic during the major autumn festival day on 23 September 2012, where guests could also taste the first honey from the fruit orchard on Grüner Weg. The urban agriculture movement is alive and growing in Köln-Ehrenfeld too...

I have just seen a short film on the DQE website about the project Urbane Agrikultur in Köln-Ehrenfeld. In the film it is stated that 'participation necessitates reception'. This seems very close to one of our CPUL City Actions, the one we call 'Visualising Consequences'. Could you please expand on such strategies from the DQE point of view?

If we wish to be able to change and further develop our cities with the requisite imagination and creativity, new forms of observation must arise from time to time. In this sense you, (Bohn&Viljoen Architects) have been working with the notion of the 'productive urban landscape' for years. Your work attempts to elevate urban gardening and the practice of agriculture to an urban-structural dimension, and to establish these as an

Fig 3: *Obsthain Grüner Weg*. Summer party at the community garden which developed out of an urban agriculture planning workshop with local residents. (image: Pauline Rühl, 2012)

Fig 4: Local knowledge. Consultation and workshop in plant propagation at the community garden *Obsthain Grüner Weg*. (image: Pauline Rühl, 2012)

overall design approach with sweeping positive effects for urban life. Such changes necessitate participation, and participation necessitates being able to share into a common vision. A practical manifestation of theoretical reflections such as these is the communal fruit orchard *Obsthain Grüner Weg*, described above. The idea for this project was the result of the workshop entitled *Ehrenfeld, was isst du?* [Ehrenfeld, what are you eating?], which you and landscape architect Dirk Melzer organised and ran during *plan10*. In your follow-up workshop in 2011, a concept was developed with committed residents from the neighbourhood, and this provides for a green layout of Ehrenfeld, accompanied by smaller and larger areas for agricultural use. An initial building block in the direction of planning and implementation is the *Karte der guten Gelegenheiten* [Good Opportunities Map] in which, along with fallow areas, "green paths" are also featured linking Ehrenfeld with adjoining districts of the city. The discontinued rail freight routes of the former industrial location thereby offer the potential for creating a 'Low Line Linear Park' for pedestrians and cyclists. This can be supplemented with environmental and education programmes, such as a community food centre. So far, we have reached more than 700 people who have taken part in the actions and happenings like *Ehrenfeld, was isst du?* or in the gardening workshops and open garden events.

As mentioned earlier, everything that had been designed and implemented for *Obsthain Grüner Weg* could be seen on display during *plan12*, but, most importantly, the additional workshop you hosted enabled the joint planning and launch for three new orchard "offshoots" in Ehrenfeld, and hence the decentralised extension of areas of self-sufficiency. Part of this work will consist of an analysis of the specific features of each individual area and the preparation of a 'mini-transferability study'. The method used – 'spatial, geographical and organisational mapping' – will be further developed as the conceptual and planning work for the 'Low Line Linear Park' continues. The first results of this workshop were shown as "work in progress" throughout the entire *plan12* week and publicly presented and discussed during an event with residents and expert critics.

'Participation necessitates reception'.

I guess successful reception also shows in the way ideas are being taken forward, expand and grow beyond our project. Now that *DQE* is drawing to a close, what will stay or continue? The idea of the "offshoots" is being taken forward; amongst its sites is a triangle of open space studied in the last workshop and a seemingly rural

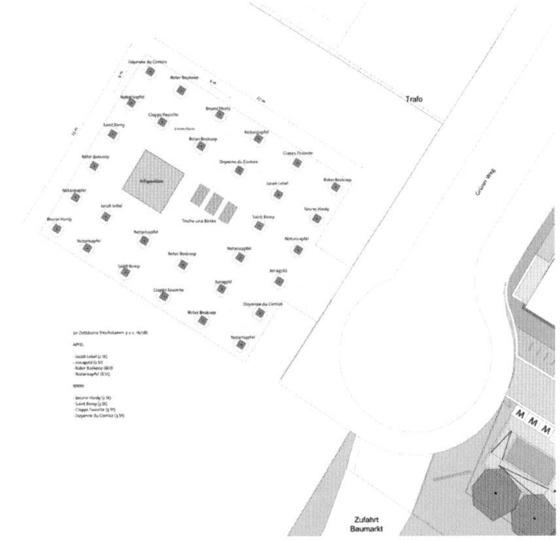

Fig 5: *Obsthain Grüner Weg.* Site planning of the *DQE* project by scape Landschaftsarchitekten as part of the GAG housing association development.
(image: GAG Immobilien AG, 2011)

Fig 6: Local resource. The community garden's apiary is used to produce honey as well as knowledge about bees and beekeeping.
(image: Pauline Rühl, 2012)

brownfield site identified and mapped during an earlier workshop. The beekeepers' group at the *Obsthain* community garden has been contracted to run environmental education projects over the next months, especially with local children. The gardening group at the community garden is being portrayed in a small local TV series. The fruit trees will be planted into their final locations in the housing development during next year. Together with the housing company GAG, we are now planning their 'Mietergärten', housing-related residents' gardens, starting with the setting up of a gardeners' association. Along the road Grüner Weg, the first section of the 'Low Line Park' will go into its two-year trial phase starting in 2013 with support from the City of Cologne, the local council of Ehrenfeld, the housing company GAG and the environmental charity *Klimakreis Köln...*

processes. Creative work awakens an approach to the productive work of food growing, as it means contemplation, togetherness, sharing knowledge and experiences, all of which are open-source processes in creative communities and gardening communities. It also stimulates the impetus of directly designing one's own sphere of life and planning processes in the city. Both envisage a responsible and democratic bottom-up development within a community or the different communities of a quarter at the (small) scale of a city neighbourhood; the interaction of different communities – creatives, immigrants, older residents – considering the endogenous urban progression of an entire neighbourhood in relation to the importance of a "good life" for everyone.

Your work mostly involves the artistic professions and art practice in a purposefully wide sense. How or where do you see the role of artists in the creation, perception and dissemination of urban agriculture ideas?

There is a close relation between creativity and green productivity in a city or in a neighbourhood: both processes are highly productive and both are community

Fig 7: Low Line Linear Park. Planning work for a continuous landscape at the workshop Scaling 1:3 during plan12. (image: Pauline Rühl, 2012)

Fig 8: Working with the need to move. Mobile potato plantation at *Obsthain Grüner Weg*. (image: Pauline Rühl, 2012)

Within the urban agriculture strand of the *DQE* project, common actions are driven by common experiences. Its do-it-yourself productions are led by the ideas of a new economy, alternative working structures, models of a new work and life ethic developed by informal learning in an informal community set-up.

'Die Wahrheit ist immer konkret' [The truth is always precise].[4]

Although we are also part of the theoretical or abstract discussion about creative cities on the one hand and of social and political implementations of urban agriculture on the other, *DQE* is very much focused on the special, real situation where we can work on experience and the development of images and models on the spot, simultaneously or dialectally. Envisioning is a necessity when deciding whether to start acting in reality and to be part of an active community. To share a "vision" means first to work on common images. So, our experience is that common images are more convincing than logical talking. It is not only that we reach the creative communities in this way, but also, and even more so, the broad public and the municipality – and we meet the 'Alltagskreativität', the 'everyday creativity' of the neighbourhood's people.

Is there a future for urban agriculture? How do you imagine such a future for Köln-Ehrenfeld?

The aim of the first *DQE* workshop *Ehrenfeld, was isst du?* is now a reality: the open space of social housing project *Grüner Weg* by housing company GAG will be an urban garden with apple trees, herbs and vegetables for the people living there, but also for the neighbourhood. The latest workshop *A scale of 1:3* has shown ways of spreading food producing community gardens within the neighbourhood of Ehrenfeld. There is now a strong movement of urban gardeners in the quarter. Last but not least, we developed the community-driven project 'Low Line Linear Park' with a productive green along the former industrial railway line.

And the future? The site *Grüner Weg Wohngebiet* is now seen as the starting point of an old railway line, which we would like to convert into a linear productive park

contributing to the community's subsistence and well-being, into a demonstration project for the whole neighbourhood, and into part of the programme to transform Ehrenfeld into a productive urban landscape. Both sites could share a community food centre aiding networking and outreach and providing room for stakeholder capacity-building workshops. The development of foot and cycle paths on the *Low Line* would offer the inhabitants of Ehrenfeld a green and safe way, without much car contact, to the Cologne green belt (500 m distance) and the *Stadtwald*, a 200 ha park in the adjacent quarter of Braunsfeld. Biomass, produced through the care of the landscape, and organic kitchen waste, could be used to produce energy or compost for the housing development at Grüner Weg. A planting and climate action plan will be created for Ehrenfeld, taking into consideration the experiences of other pilot projects and reflection from the implementation processes. This plan will be established with community involvement and developed from the *DQE* workshop results that have already been achieved...

I hope that we have initiated an urban agriculture future in the heads of the inhabitants...

Notes

1. GAG Immobilien AG is a Cologne-based housing association aiming to provide good and affordable accommodation especially to citizens on a lower budget. Germany has many similar housing companies.
2. for project details see: Nomadisch Grün gGmbH (2009) *Prinzessinnengärten*, available online: <http://prinzessinnengarten. net> (accessed 14 July 2012).
3. for project details see: Kölner NeuLand e.V. (2011) *Ein mobiler Gemeinschaftsgarten für Köln*, available online: <http://www. neuland-koeln.de> (accessed 30 Sep 2012) and Pflanzstelle: grenzenlos gärten e.V. (2011) *Soziokulturelle und urbane Landwirtschaft in Köln-Kalk*, available online: <http://pflanzstelle. blogsport.eu> (accessed 30 Sep 2012).
4. see: Lenin, W. I. (1905) in: *Zwei Taktiken der Sozialdemokratie in der demokratischen Revolution*, Berlin: Dietz Verlag 1961.

Unlocking Spaces

Brighton, UK, 2010

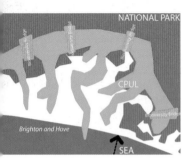

above: **CPUL strategy** for Brighton, incorporating biodiversity bridges between the city and the Sussex Downs to the north.

A university/community-based project exploring how a neighbourhood could develop and implement a productive urban landscape.

- **SPACE AND ORGANISATION:** CPUL fragment temporarily installed on Shaftesbury Place in Brighton, an underused public road/ square. Cooperation between a planning and design team and local residents enabled a tangible legacy.

- **FOOD PRODUCTION TYPE:** Individual and community cultivation.

- **USE OF HARVEST:** By residents.

- **CLIENT:** The Creative Campus Initiative.

- **FUNDING:** Higher Education Funding Council of England.

- **PROJECT TEAM:** Bohn&Viljoen, Vaida Morkunaite, Kirsty Sutherland, Ditchling Rise Residents Association, Studio Columba, Jonathan Gales, Mikey Tomkins, Master of Architecture students from University of Brighton.

right: **Continuous landscapes.** A scale map showing potential "green links" between the city centre and open space surrounding it. Much of the surrounding land belongs to Brighton and is farmland, most of which now given over to leisure uses such as riding schools. The soil conditions are not especially fertile for horticulture, but could be made so, if the city's organic waste was composted and used to establish market gardens. This land represents a major underutilised spatial capacity.

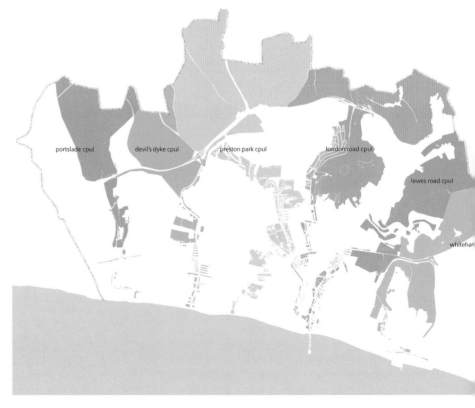

above: **Shaftesbury Place** in regular use as a car parking area. This site in front of London Road railway station was selected with residents for installing a temporary productive urban landscape.

above: **Shaftesbury Place** transformed into a temporary productive urban landscape. Residents are collecting plants for their own use at the end of the daylong installation. The plants – vegetables, lettuces and herbs – were all supplied by a local nursery.

below: **The timeline and process** for implementing *Unlocking Spaces*. The project researched the potential for small-scale neighbourhood urban agriculture sites. Findings fed into the larger city-wide initiative *Harvest Brighton & Hove*, which led to the adoption of a planning advisory note on urban agriculture by the city council.
(image: Bohn&Viljoen and Nishat Awan (FG Stadt & Ernährung TU Berlin), 2012)

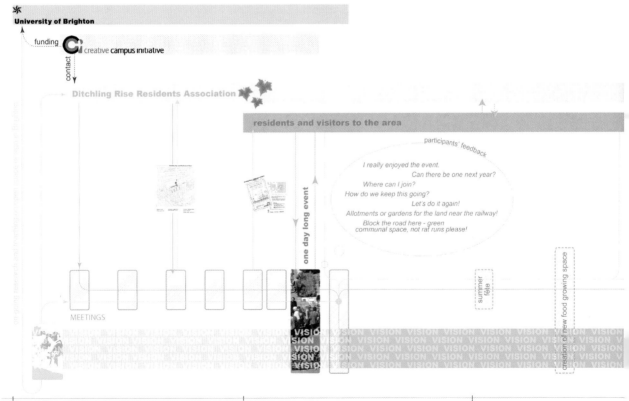

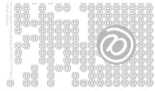

UNLOCKING SPACES @ Shaftesbury Place

above: **Communication.**
Purpose-made fliers were
distributed to advertise the
event in the neigbhourhood.
The symbol @ was also used
on the day to graphically
symbolize planted fields.

below: **The installation as
tool for visualising change.**
Apart from the physical and
visual experience of a food-
productive landscape, a small
exhibition provided a focus
for discussion, as did a public
meal.

COMMENTARY

Prior to London hosting the Olympic Games in 2012, a number of public engagement events were set up in the UK. The Creative Campus Initiative was one of
these with the aim of inviting the cultural and academic communities to, 'help stimu-
late new forms of creative exploration, research and learning […] in the Olympic
spirit'. This provided an opportunity to work with a neighbourhood in Brighton
looking at ways of reimagining open space as productive with respect to potential
use for urban agriculture and for exercise – a so-called 'health-enabling approach to
the city'.

Architectural students had been researching Brighton's potential for developing
a CPUL strategy, in parallel with a city-wide food-growing initiative called *Harvest
Brighton & Hove.* The Harvest project was run by run by the Brighton and Hove
Food Partnership, with the University of Brighton being one of several research
partners. *Unlocking Spaces* aimed to enable a local residents' association to envisage very specific proposals for their surroundings.

A forecourt area adjacent to a railway station was chosen to model possible urban
transformation. Through a series of joint meetings, a design was generated and
then made visible on site using over 700 germinated vegetable plant seedlings, and
by marking further planting beds on roads using chalk and stencils. The installation coincided with the annual "Big Lunch" day that occurs each summer in the
UK. Plants were distributed to residents who went on to grow them at home, and
a small, underused space adjacent to the site has now been established as a communal food-growing site.

above: **Recording the transformation.** Architectural drawings complemented
the more visually accessible temporary installation. As with many schemes aimed at
reoccupying streets, a balance needed to be struck between reasonable provision for
car parking and proposed new uses. The increasing prevalence of car-sharing schemes
makes this more viable in the future. (image: Bohn&Viljoen and Nishat Awan (FG Stadt
& Ernährung TU Berlin), 2012)

The Edible Campus

Brighton, UK, 2008

A university-based cross-disciplinary elective module for students, using an action research approach with the aim of introducing sustainable urban food growing and its wider environmental, cultural and social impact.

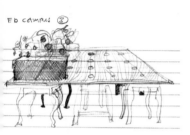

above: **Cradle to cradle.** An early sketch for raised planters constructed using recycled furniture. Researching cradle-to-cradle options runs as a thread through all learning in this module.

- **SPACE AND ORGANISATION:** A rooftop terrace, above the university's Faculty of Art and Design campus restaurant. Students elect to complete the *Edible Campus* module, which runs during the whole of an academic year, allowing for a full cycle of growing, from germination of seeds to harvest. Community partners are encouraged, as are events using the produce.

- **FOOD PRODUCTION TYPE:** Organic cultivation of vegetables and herbs (for seasoning and tea).

- **USE OF HARVEST:** By students and in the faculty restaurant.

- **CLIENT:** University of Brighton.

- **FUNDING:** Initial start-up funding from the University of Brighton for materials and specialist workshops.

- **PROJECT TEAM:** André Viljoen and university colleagues.

right: **Productive space makes place.** Abundant planting, interspersed with areas for sitting, invites occupation during public events like the faculty summer exhibition. Restaurant staff have direct access to fresh produce and in turn compost their organic waste for the *Edible Campus*. The project contributes to the university's catering department's fair trade and local sourcing policies.

above: **Setting up the *Edible Campus*.** The south-facing roof terrace above
the faculty restaurant has good access to sunlight and is visible from adjacent
teaching spaces. Students mapped solar access throughout a year to determine
the best location for crops based on microclimates.

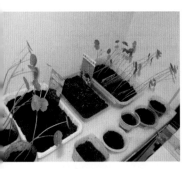

above: **Students grow crops** from seeds, practically experiencing the challenges of food growing, not least how long it takes. This includes participation in Brighton's annual Seedy Sunday, a seed-swapping event in February, and experimenting to find suitable indoor spaces for germinating seeds. (image: Alice Freeman (Edible Campus), 2012)

COMMENTARY

The Edible Campus, set up by Professor Vikram Bhatt at McGill University in Montreal, provided the inspiration for this project. The need for constant research and evaluation of the way we produce food is taught using the city as a laboratory, working with its many food and sustainability organisations, and referring to international case studies. Students are guided to "discover" issues linked to achieving sustainable urban food systems.

The *CPUL City* Action Visualisation is achieved through direct participation in growing, harvesting and cooking, as well as in debates about lifestyles less dependent on passive consumption. Existing and potential urban capacities are explored within Brighton's food supply chains, such as those of the city's hospitality industry and the university. Furthermore the project builds new capacity directly, as a number of students take up food growing outside of the university, or begin to introduce food-related themes into their chosen disciplines. Top-down and bottom-up relationships are explored through engagement with Brighton & Hove's several food- and sustainability-related organisations such as the Permaculture Trust, Brighton & Hove Organic Gardeners Group, Brighton & Hove Food Partnership, or the city council's sustainability office. Projects like this need programmes with regular and reliable events for students and community partners. They do not "run themselves". A particular challenge has been maintaining the project's momentum during the summer holidays when students are no longer on site.

below left and right: **The concept of harvesting** is extended to include the sourcing of construction materials. Planters use durable Douglas fir timber, from trees planted 60 years earlier within 100 kilometres of Brighton. The "hungry season", when few crops are available, occurs during the academic year and reinforces the need for protected cropping to extend the growing season, food preservation techniques and sustainable urban food systems.

left: **Researching for Change.** Within undergraduate teaching, research takes on various forms, many of which relate to daily routines related to food. Cooking and baking using produce from the *Edible Campus* provides a powerful but simple action bridging productivity and sociability. In this case, students are selling cakes and savoury dishes they have prepared to raise funds for *Edible Campus* materials and advertise a student-run food co-op, supplying locally sourced fruit and vegetables to staff and students. This entrepreneurial approach is encouraged and often leads students to working with partners outside of the university.

below: **The Edible Campus in May.** Early crops begin to appear. Warmer weather and a large table encourage people to use the site as an outdoor classroom.

Growing Balconies

London, UK, 2009

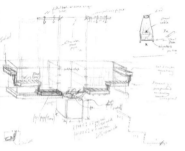

above: **Drawn communication.** Early sketch by our agronomist partner incorporating ideas for gravity-fed water supply and support for tall plants. (image: Stefan Jordan, 2009)

Can a small, everyday domestic space become intensively productive and remain attractive?

- **SPACE AND ORGANISATION:** 2 m² prefabricated balconies with growing and sitting spaces. Designed as a "plug-in" system for new build or retrofit. Exhibited at the Royal Horticultural Society's Hampton Court Garden Show, London.

- **FOOD PRODUCTION TYPE:** Outdoor hydroponic fruit and vegetable production.

- **USE OF HARVEST:** By residents.

- **CLIENT:** *Capital Growth* project/Sustain.

- **FUNDING:** The Mayor of London.

- **PROJECT TEAM:** Bohn&Viljoen with Hadlow Agricultural College (Stefan Jordan and students).

right: **Making an action happen.** Research partners can benefit from different, but mutually supportive agendas, creating a virtuous circle. Here, the desire of the Mayor of London's *Capital Growth* project to publicly demonstrate food growing in unconventional domestic spaces enabled us to further test and disseminate (via BBC television coverage) ideas first explored in the *Urban Agriculture Curtain*. (image: Bohn&Viljoen and Nishat Awan (FG Stadt & Ernährung TU Berlin), 2012)

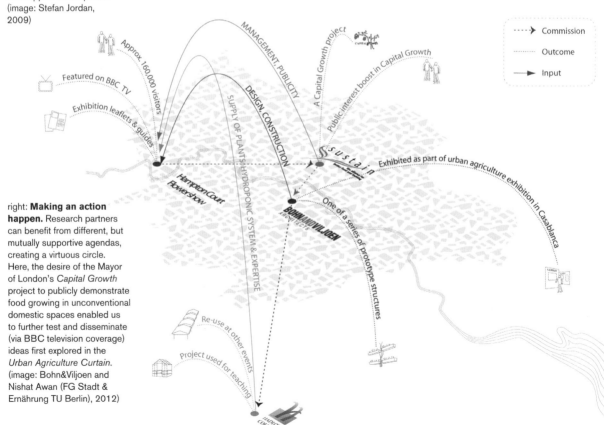

left: **Modular systems.**
The intention is to develop a
system that is no more difficult
to install than a washing
machine. The balcony's
simple framework allows
for adaptation and physical
extension. To prolong the
growing season, or if the
climate makes this necessary,
the frames can be glazed to
become a small greenhouse.

above: **Enjoying one's
balcony.** These multipurpose
balconies develop ideas for
intensive food growing in small
urban spaces without access
to soil. The design uses a
hydroponic growing system
and is suitable for situations
where high yields are required
and minimum gardening time
is available. Using hydroponics
externally is unusual as is
its application in a domestic
situation.

1 **existing balcony**
The food growing spaces do not
interfere with the balcony's diverse
occupations.

2 **structure**
The installation uses industry
standard components fitted to a
customised balcony and could
be adapted to a glazed balcony,
if climate makes this necessary.

3 **hydroponic growing system**
Suitable for situations where high yields
are required and minimum gardening
time is available. Designed to minimise
the need to pump plant feed by
allowing the feeder liquid to drain from
high to low level troughs.

4 **plants**
The balcony can supply day to day
salad and certain vegetables.

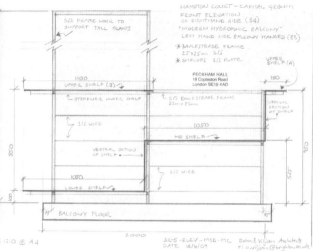

above and right: **Working with what is there.** The installation uses industry-standard components fitted to a customised balcony railing framework. The use of stainless steel reflects the low maintenance brief set for this project.

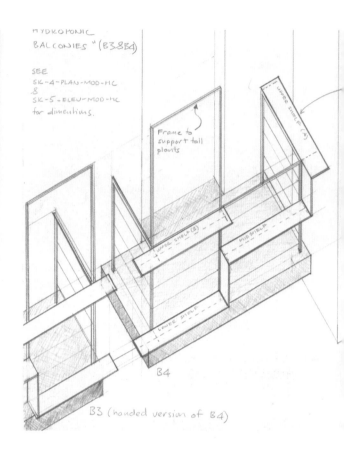

right: **Integrating desire, use and behaviour.** Good balconies should accommodate people's desires for fresh air, light, views and, at times, privacy. Food growing spaces do not need to interfere with balcony use and, as seen here, plants can be used to control degrees of transparency and shading.

left: **Designing for diversity of use:** Should an occupant not wish to grow food, the planters' support shelves may be used for pots, cups, books and the like while the balcony is in use or, more conventionally, for ornamental plants. The vertical frame for tall plants can also support sun awnings or privacy screens. This image of the prototype structure displayed at Hampton Court Garden Show does not include the minimal barriers that would be added to prevent objects accidentally falling from the planter shelves.

COMMENTARY

Researching for change can happen at many scales. During the growing season this small space will supply day-to-day salad needs and some vegetable require-ments. The balcony is designed to minimise the need for pumping plant feed by placing supports for planters so that they allow drainage from high to low level troughs. It could in the future be connected to a rainwater harvesting system, become "organic" by avoiding the use of processed nutrients, or be developed to operate as an aquaponic system, by integrating a fish tank.

With respect to other *CPUL City Actions*, the balconies address Visualising and represent one of the smallest urban capacities. Bottom-up and top-down are less directly addressed, but in reality the inclusion within apartment buildings or similar would require support from developers and residents.

The devil is in the detail: Food security and self-sustaining cropping systems

Howard Lee, Stefan Jordan and Victor Coleman

Some recent studies have highlighted the vulnerability of many cities to reduced food security, especially in Europe (Lee 2012). The majority of European citizens, including nearly 80% in Britain, now live in urban areas and their food security is of increasing concern. Thus, the potential of cities to produce at least some of their own food requirements is being investigated (Brown 2010) and three zones have been identified: the Urban (Zone 1), the Peri-Urban (Zone 2) and the Rural Hinterland (Zone 3). Zone 1 is generally described as higher-density residential/commercial and seen as presenting limited space for food production apart from residential gardens, rooftops and some municipal amenity areas. However, Zone 2 appears to have more potential, with a mosaic of residential sites, industrial estates and parcels of unused land (Lee 2012).

This chapter introduces different methods of production and cropping that are scalable and could be applied in urban (Zone 1) or peri-urban (Zone 2) areas. We consider the potential of combined hydroponic horticulture, aquaculture and protected cropping designs, which are suited to optimal yields from limited spaces either within or between existing built infrastructures. The principles of aquaculture and protected cropping may be applied at a number of scales ranging from the construction of integrated systems, such as small-scale building-integrated hydroponics (see the *Urban Agriculture Curtain* case study, p. 166), to commercial peri-urban enterprises.

Protected cropping to maximise yield baselines

Knowledge of likely yields from urban and peri-urban food production sites is limited due to the lack of documented assessments. One of the authors reviewed published data with most salad/vegetable crops achieving variable yields from approximately 20 to 40 t per ha per year (Lee 2012: 458). Evidence has been reported that

'yields from [glass]house crops are generally ten times more than comparable field-produced crops' (Cantliffe *et al.* 2001: 195). Similar results are also available beneath polythene, e.g. for tomatoes (Briar *et al.* 2011: 87). Even so, variations in local climate, soil conditions and management are likely, and such yield increases cannot always be guaranteed. However, there is a clear imperative to investigate protected options across urban and peri-urban sites. For many years, the humble 'poly tunnel' has been used for much protected horticultural salad/vegetable cropping, but new and updated designs of protected systems are commercially available and need consideration.

Design options for protected urban cropping

There is a need for protected cropping designs best suited to urban locations which are:

- relatively cost effective to manufacture,
- quick and easy to erect and dismantle (as land needs change),
- managed to optimise the growing environment inside: a major advantage of protected cropping is to allow an extension of the growing season for crops (Briar *et al.* 2011: 87),
- We are also interested in 'poly tunnel' cover systems that improve ventilation and thus reduce the risks of diseases and pests. (It is envisaged that production systems reviewed will be lower input, especially for pesticides.)

Glasshouses are not considered here, because of their relatively higher costs of construction, though their long-term cost effectiveness has been favourably reviewed elsewhere (Torrellas *et al.* 2012). Adapted poly tunnel designs are reviewed in this chapter, the details of which are discussed below. These new poly tunnel designs will need to be sited in quite small areas of land between industrial structures, with the disadvantages of reduced space and shading, but the benefit of water supplies from roof-rain-harvesting.

Aquaculture in urban and peri-urban food systems

Aquaculture has clear potential for development in tanks of harvested rainwater (Woods *n.d.*). According to Nick Pierpoint from Hadlow College, for the UK, carp (*Cyprinus carpio*) are especially promising due to their general resilience and ability to feed on various food wastes (personal communication 2012). Carp are tolerant of a relatively wide range of water conditions: temperatures 23 to 30°C and pH 6.5 to 9.0 (FAD 2012). In temperate zones, carp can reach 1 to 2 kg body weight after two to four rearing seasons (Karakatsouli *et al.* 2010) and can tolerate relatively high stocking rates without loss of previous weight gain: e.g. carp of a body weight of approximately 100 g at stocking rates up to 2.6 kg per litre min., equivalent to 85 kg per m^3 (Ruane and Komen 2003), as reported in Karakatsouli *et al.* (2010: 125). Yields are variable – indeed, this is true for all aquaculture species – and are affected by changes in water quality, which will need special attention for rainwater draining from roofs (Pierpoint,

personal communication 2012). Optimistic yields have been reported for aquaculture projects elsewhere, e.g. farm models for production per hectare of open water of 55 tons of seabream (*Spondyliosoma cantharus)* or 92 tons of salmon (family *Salmonidae)* per year (Neori *et al.* 2004). The contention here is that it is possible to achieve equally promising yields in urban sites: for temperate carp in hypothetical rainwater tanks of 10 x 5 x 2m (100 m^3) and based upon the above sources (85 kg per m^3 stocking rate and a harvest after up to four seasons), annual yields of approximately 1,000 to 2,000 kg per tank would seem reasonable. If we consider the known *per capita* consumption of fish in the UK (cited as 217 g per week (COT 2004), which equates to about 11 kg *per capita per annum*) and allow for losses from our projected yield due to preparation (20%?), then actual fish meat production could be 800–1,600 kg per tank. Thus, one tank seems likely to contribute annually to the diet of about 70–140 people.

Hydroponics for protected urban and peri-urban horticulture

Virtually no review is needed for demonstrating the importance of hydroponic systems for horticultural crop management, since there is now a substantial record of

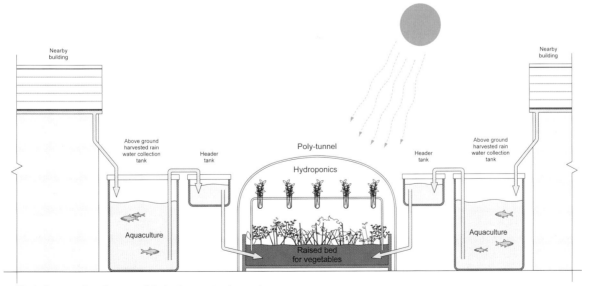

Fig 1: Aquaponics. Conceptual design for a system in an urban or peri-urban setting. (image: Howard Lee (redrawn by Ian Bailey Bohn&Viljoen Architects), 2012)

success and ongoing research, especially for tomatoes (*Lycopersicon esculentum*), modelling mineral relations (Massa *et al.* 2011) and quality issues (Toor *et al.* 2006), but also other crops, such as squash (*Cucurbita pepo*) (Rouphael and Colla 2005). The use of hydroponics is seen as especially beneficial for urban and peri-urban sites where water might be in limited supply and hydroponics have already been shown to have potential for such areas (Stefanelli *et al.* 2010). Yields of fruit and vegetables that might be obtained from protected hydroponics are very difficult to estimate, being affected by species choice, management strategies and environmental conditions.

Combining aquaculture and hydroponic horticulture in urban and peri-urban sites

An obvious development of the harvesting of rainwater and use of it for rearing fish is to then use that water in horticultural production. Such systems – termed 'aquaponics' – have already been investigated, and there are some very successful commercial examples, e.g. *Growing Power* (Growing Power 2011) and *Sweet Water Organics* (Sweet Water *n.d.* a) in Milwaukee, which are referred to elsewhere in this book. It is suggested here that aquaponic production can be viable across a range of urban and peri-urban scales, from micro-scale domestic units to commercially viable installations.

Fig 1 shows a sketch of a small-scale aquaponic design, sited mid-way between buildings to avoid shade, and with above-ground harvested rainwater fish tanks situated in the less useful spaces close to buildings. Below-ground water storage is not considered due to the relatively higher costs (Abdulla and Al-Shareef 2009: 201).

The poly tunnel would be managed to grow vegetables (and also some fruit) by (i) growth directly into the ground; or (ii) on raised beds, or (iii) hydroponically. In all cases, the irrigation water is provided from the rainwater fish tanks, after filtration. One key point to consider for such water is the microorganism load and implications for the human safety of horticultural crops eaten raw, such as salads. The importance of microorganisms in hydroponics has been reviewed generally (Koohakan *et al.* 2004) and specifically noted as a

potential issue for aquaponics (Graber and Junge 2009). There is a body of work devoted to the phytoremediation of water in horticulture (Adler *et al.* 2003; Malato *et al.* 2009) and specifically to that of water circulating from aquaculture to hydroponic horticulture (Tokuyama *et al.* 2004) where reed (*Phragmites communis*) was used, though isolates of *Nitrosomonas communis* were shown to persist. However, water can easily be cleaned of such organisms by ultra-violet light treatment and ozonation (Summerfelt 2003).

If space permits, some of the aquaculture tanks could be situated *inside* the poly tunnel. The enhanced environmental conditions would then allow a wider range of fish to be cultured, such as catfish (*Ictalurus punctatus*) or tilapia (*Oreochromis niloticus*), the latter being especially useful as herbivores for consumption of waste vegetable biomass (Pierpoint, personal communication 2012).

The ideal poly tunnel design for urban and peri-urban use

The most commonly used existing poly tunnel design has polythene sheets stretched over semi-circular metal hoops (Lovelidgge 2011). The growing environment inside such tunnels is adversely affected by temperature fluctuations, lack of ventilation and associated condensation risks, high relative humidity and a consequential increased risk of pathogens, especially fungal infections (*anon.* 2009: 92 *et seq*). New designs of coverings are needed that can be used on existing hoops, but allow better ventilation and improved growing conditions. Two developments are reviewed here:

Voen

Manufactured in Germany (Voen 2012), film strips are arranged in an overlapping system, similar to a tile roof, and stitched onto a base fabric (hail net). The film strips react flexibly to the wind, offering minimal resistance and providing good air circulation within the tunnel.

In this way, automatic ventilation is created, with pests such as birds excluded. The internal hail net mesh can also be fine enough to exclude insect pests such as the fruit fly (*Drosophila melanogaster*).

Haygrove

The *Haygrove* system seeks to overcome the problems of heat stress, internal condensation, high humidity and poor ventilation by the integration of permanent ridge level vents and side walls that can be raised by electrical motors (Haygrove 2012). The system requires a power supply and computer-aided environmental controls. It also requires the provision and maintenance of electrical and environmental services. The *Haygrove* system has the advantages that birds can be entirely excluded and the spectral filtering of the plastic covering can be selected at the time of construction to suit the crop.

These two poly tunnel designs are objectively presented: we are not stating a preference, but simply emphasising that new and better cover technologies are now available that can and should be considered for urban and peri-urban poly tunnel production projects. Yields from such systems are not yet established. Both coverings were originally developed for protected fruit tree production, such as cherries, and their application to protected tunnels is at an early stage. The lifespan of the new coverings is favourable: for example, the *Voen* covering is estimated to last six to eight years, depending upon level of care. This compares with three years for most polythene covers, which also allow less light to penetrate, as they age and become increasingly vulnerable to wear and tear (Foster, personal communication 2012).

Installing new poly tunnel designs in urban and peri-urban sites

The key production factors are thought likely to be:

1. Size of tunnel: whilst poly tunnel hoops can be supplied for widths of approximately 6–9 metres (Lovelidgge 2011), tunnel length can be adjusted to fit within fragmentary peri-urban sites and between existing structures.
2. Speed of development: such tunnels can be erected easily and quickly.
3. Irrigation water storage: harvested rainwater from nearby buildings can be stored in above-ground tanks, which is an established technology (Abdulla and Al-Shareef 2009), managed for fish production

(Woods *n.d.*), and then solar-pumped into header tanks for irrigation in the poly tunnel as required.
4. Soil contamination: if the site soil is not contaminated, then ground cultivation or raised beds can be used. If soil contamination is an issue, then badly affected soil can be excavated or left in place and sealed with geotextiles to allow raised bed production (Turner 2009) or hydroponic management.
5. Cropping management: once tunnels have been installed, a year-long production regime can be established (Salt 1999; Neville 2004), which is much more diverse and sophisticated than for unprotected cropping, hence the higher yields referred to above.

Conclusions

New poly tunnel designs combined with aquaculture for urban and peri-urban sites have profound implications for food security, achieving:

1. higher yields from less space – a vital consideration,
2. reduced risk from extreme weather events (Wagner 1999) – to be increasingly expected as part of climate change – and,
3. better working conditions for those growing the crops.

Most important though is the demonstration to local groups that impressive yields of food can rapidly and efficiently be grown. There will be a need for confidence building for people who know little about growing vegetables or rearing fish, but are concerned about and want to improve their food security (McCullum *et al.* 2005). Such groups will require advice and guidance from experienced and skilled horticulturalists and aquaculturists to help establish urban and peri-urban protected food production systems – from design and management through to maturity and harvest.

Protected cropping and aquaculture will be a key aspect of the move towards better urban and peri-urban food security. New protected tunnel designs combined with aquaponic systems need to be assessed to establish base yield potential and management priorities.

Alternative food networks as drivers of a food transition: The role of cities

Gianluca Brunori and Francesco Di Iacovo

Alternative food networks (Goodman *et al.* 2011) oppose local food to globalised food, direct links between producers and consumers to the opacity of products' origins, craftsmanship to industrial processes, agroecology to genetic engineering, and sustainable consumption styles to mass consumption. The growing attention of researchers and scholars to alternative food networks is related to the capacity of such networks to give a concrete outcome to innovative visions and values, creating spaces for alternative economies. Their specificity is their double identity: as social movements and as economic activities. This specificity has helped them to develop a strong capacity to adapt operating principles and practices to changing contexts.

At the beginning of the 1980s, alternative food networks centred their development on a narrative based on "resistance to modernisation". Facing an overwhelming trend to commodification, specialisation and scale enlargement, a relatively small group of farmers, most of them with urban origins, looked for alternative business models focused upon the local identity of the farm and its products. They put these models into practice by diversifying the range of products and services, re-internalising parts of the production processes – feed production, processing, selling – and taking an active role in the regeneration of rural communities (Ploeg *et al.* 2000). This process has been conceptualised as the re-embeddedness of farming in the local community and in the local environment (Sonnino 2007; Chiffoleau 2009), contrasting a movement in the opposite direction driven by modernisation. The most important allies of these farmers were a diversified group of consumers looking for alternatives to conventional food. These consumers ranged from people wanting to pursue consumption styles coherent with their political ideas to wealthy people looking for healthy and natural lifestyles, to people looking for gastronomic specialities. This business model developed mainly in remote rural areas. In fact, these areas had not been fully transformed by

modernisation, as they did not fit into dominant technical and organisational patterns, and by virtue of their "naturalness" they now became the object of renewed social demand in respect to the countryside's multiple functions. Policies at the end of the 1980s identified these business models as a key to rural development, because they could open markets based on resources specific to rural areas – nature, traditional culture, social capital – which could be mobilised to consolidate local economies (Ray 1999).

Organic food and protected "denominations of origin" labelling regulations paved the way to the expansion of these markets. They created an institutional space thanks to which new actors, not necessarily motivated by the same values as the initiators, could see such business models as a source of economic opportunities. The growing demand for organic and protected products has created pressure on the business component of alternative food networks. A large amount of research between the end of the 1990s and the beginning of the 2000s was dedicated to identifying the sources of competitiveness for alternative business (Brunori and Rossi 2000). The conceptual basis for this field of enquiry was found in the concept of 'niche', which identifies economic spaces that take advantage of "structural holes" emerging in the market (Ploeg *et al.* 2012). According to this approach, niches based on alternative models would find a suitable market in well-defined segments of consumers willing to pay for the higher perceived quality that their desired products offer.

A new phase began when the success of alternative food networks started to attract the attention of conventional business. Organic and quality foods have since increasingly invaded supermarket shelves. Specialised outlets based on "alternative" values are blossoming. The need to satisfy supermarket demand has shifted the attention of some of the farmers from values to business. Evolutionary patterns of concentration, scale enlargement and specialisation have also consolidated in this sector. Integration within the conventional supply chains, according to a growing critique, has made alternative food chains lose their capacity to 'transmit value-laden information' (Ilbery and Maye 2005) because of the former chains' control of communication with consumers. Although conventional chains make use of alternative values and symbols associated with the product, they insert them into different systems of meanings, so those values are not able to express their transformative potential.

The reaction to this process of 'conventionalisation' (Goodman *et al.* 2011) has taken multiple paths. Some farmers have deepened the niche approach by developing "excellence products" with high prices associated with radical values for selected consumers, as in the case of *Slow Food* products. This solution restores communication effectiveness, but limits the transformative potential. In fact, it is mainly consumer elites who demand this kind of product.

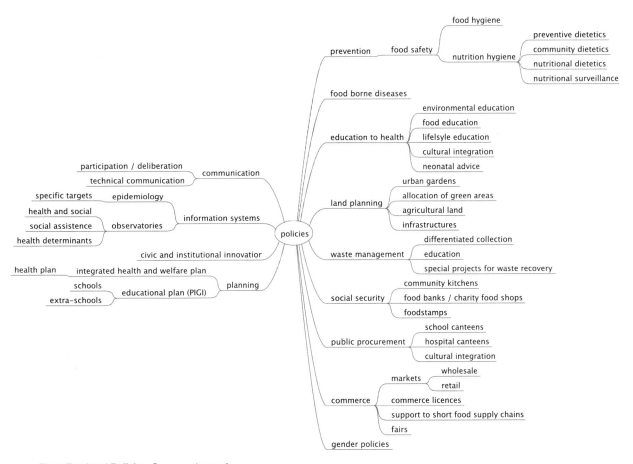

Fig 1: Food and Policies. Conceptual map of administrative competences related to food.

Another response has gone the opposite way. Focusing on the issue of affordability and working out the "everyday food" concept, a new generation of alternative food networks has emerged which strengthens the "movement" component. Their approach advocates a radical redefinition of consumption within a broader worldview (for example purchasing and food preparation habits), a rethinking of the meaning of food quality, a reordering of priorities and values associated with food and the food chain (Brunori *et al.* 2012). It also implies an active consumer involvement, opening the way to mobilising material and immaterial resources in the construction of alternative systems of provision that provide quality food while keeping prices affordable.

Will the alternative turn hegemonic?

The double identity of alternative food networks as movements and as economic activities has contributed to place its study within the field of transition studies (Brunori *et al.* 2012; Goodman *et al.* 2011; Seyfang and Smith 2007). This field analyses the evolution of socio-technical systems to identify avenues and drivers for change. Socio-technical systems have three levels of organisation: a micro level ('niche'), a meso level ('regime') and a macro level ('landscape') (Geels 2002). The key to understanding opportunities and barriers to change can be found at the interfaces between these levels. Transition approaches, in particular, consider niches as laboratories to test innovative socio-technical subsystems that may be integrated at a higher level when, also because of effects of changes in the landscape, a regime would not be able to solve the problems emerging within society. In this view, alternative food networks are considered (and, hopefully, addressed by innovation policies) as niches that foster transitions towards sustainability. In fact, they address economics, ecologies and health concerns with a clear orientation towards practice.

When considering the importance of alternative food networks as drivers of transition, the role of cities and local governments emerges as a key aspect. In their seminal paper, Pothukuchi and Kaufman state that 'the food system is implicated in the health of the local economy; to local land use and transportation; preservation of

agricultural land; to solid waste problems of cities; and to the quality of local water, air, and soil' (Pothukuchi and Kaufman 1999). Cities are the places where consumption and social movements are concentrated. Changes in consumption patterns can considerably change the way cities are organised. Cities can thus test technological, organisational or social innovation before they are extended at national level. Cities can also act as policy interfaces with national policy levels to remove barriers to a system's innovation.

Alongside modernisation, food has lost its centrality to urban policies. Technological developments, making food consumption independent from its place of production, have resulted in food provision being 'taken for granted' (Pothukuchi and Kaufman 1999). Supermarkets have appropriated the role of municipalities in organising food distribution, and competences related to food's diverse dimensions (health, environment, planning, commerce) have been distributed between different administrative bodies and kept separate. Only recently has the role of food as a key to innovative urban strategies for sustainability been rediscovered, and the number of cities developing their food strategies is growing fast. In general, urban food strategies are based on:

1. creating awareness of food issues,
2. promoting studies that collect evidence on issues related to food,
3. identifying priorities,
4. drawing plans for action.

These strategies have been particularly fruitful in the field of urban planning as, for example, the cases of Milwaukee's urban agriculture, the *Urban Farming Project* in Middlesbrough or Berlin's *Spiel/Feld Marzahn* show.

We will argue that alternative food networks can contribute to successful urban food strategies by addressing three aspects:

1. *Frames*: that is the way consumers, citizens and administrators perceive and conceive their environment as well as the way they justify their behaviour.
2. *Normative and regulative rules*: which are directly and indirectly related to food. Normative rules imply social sanctions and rewards, regulative rules imply

legal sanctions and rewards. Nutritional rules, for example, are normative rules as they don't touch people's freedom, but may become regulative rules once embodied into school menus.

3. *Material and immaterial infrastructures*: as in the case of (micro) logistics, communication networks or legal frameworks.

In this regard, the manner in which urban food strategies are implemented is crucial. In the following paragraphs we will test the *CPUL City Actions* methodology as a tool for assessing to what extent the process of implementation of urban food strategies contributes to developing new frames, rules and infrastructures.

Alternative food networks and urban strategies: two case studies

In order to reflect on some evidence about the role of local planning in food transition, two case studies are presented: the *Food Plan* for Pisa (*Piano del Cibo*) and the *Torino City to Grow* project. Both have been promoted in regions with an old food culture shaken by modernisation processes. In these cities, alternative food networks had already grown at the end of the 1980s, giving emphasis to small multifunctional farms, local biodiversity and organic production. This "food quality turn" was a first attempt in the redefinition of common concepts around food. In both areas it opened opportunities for innovative projects and for the organisation of new relationships between producers and consumers. After a while, radical initiatives evolved into "conventionalised" ones. The perceived conventionalisation stimulated local food movements

Fig 2: *Torino City to Grow.*
An interpretative summary.

	Action U+D – Bottom-Up and Top-Down	Action VIS – Visualising Consequences	Action IUC – Inventory of Urban Capacity	Action R – Researching for Change
frames	redefine the urban agriculture and agricultural land use in and around the city	public maps about actual potential use of public lands project initiatives from associations	inventory of public and private lands inside the municipality map of main actors involved and their internal resources	linking urban planning with food policy the city's sustainability in a wider perspective
rules	plans and procedures in order to mobilise urban and peri-urban public lands plan for common vegetable garden	municipality is redefining relevance of land use in urban planning	identification of the competences of municipalities and civic actors in relation to food and land use	how to introduce urban land use in municipal policies
infrastructures	organisational framework among associations and public institutions civic–public agreement on a city strategy for a better use of green productive areas local initiatives for short food supply chains	a net of gardening and productive areas is going to be designed	web tool to connect actors of local administrations, civil society, business and knowledge workers, and to share ideas and information	written memorandum of understanding between Turin City, Pisa University and local associations

and innovative project holders to activate new waves of innovation, introducing practices of civic agriculture, such as community-supported agriculture groups (CSAs), solidarity purchasing groups (GAS) [Gruppi di Acquisto Solidale] and social farming projects. The two case studies illustrate how urban strategies have connected a variety of initiatives – farmers' markets, social gardening, educational activities, public debates, and campaigns on specific food issues – which, until this time, had been carried out independently from each other. The growing number of initiatives was used to determine the rationale for a broader reflection on food and its implications. At the same time, these initiatives exercised pressure to reform institutional agendas, opening the way for the redesigning of new frames, rules and infrastructures.

Torino City to Grow

Torino, where the headquarters of the FIAT Company are located, is one of the most important Italian industrial cities. It is also one of the places where an interest around food has grown fastest in the last years. The *Slow Food* movement holds its bi-annual *Salone del Gusto* in Torino in an exhibition centre built in an old FIAT factory. *Salone del Gusto* has given international reputation to the city as a centre of quality food and of experimentation with innovative food production and distribution patterns. The Porta Palazzo Market, one of the biggest food markets in Europe, used to be a traditional municipal market where one could find a huge diversity of typical products from everywhere. Now, it is an important tourist destination. Torino is also the city where the headquarters and the first shop of *Eataly*, the biggest Italian retail outlet for traditional food, was established. The most important newspaper of Torino, *la Stampa*, regularly hosts the initiatives and disseminates the thoughts of *Slow Food*, dedicating a weekly page to it.

The vitality of the food discourse in Torino has motivated important actors in the 'regime' to change their strategies. *Campagna Amica*, an association that clusters educational and economic activities and promotes the dialogue between town and countryside, was born here by an initiative of the local *Coldiretti*, the biggest farmers' organisation. The provincial administration started to support local collective purchasing groups in 2000,

together with several innovative projects related to multifunctional agriculture and food production in peri-urban areas. All these initiatives have contributed to define a turn in the food discourse, generating political interest in public institutions, as well as in the economy. Between 1998 and 2008, the food industry was the only one to increase its employees, while the key industry of the city, the car industry, lost 20% of its staff.

It is in this new environment that the *Torino City to Grow* project was initiated in the framework of the EU's *Smart Cities and Communities* initiative. This initiative supports cities and regions in taking ambitious measures to progress by 2020 towards a 40% reduction of greenhouse gas emissions through the sustainable use and production of energy. The goal of the Torino project is to (re)vitalise urban agriculture, promote a better use of peri-urban land and to increase urban sustainability. Within the project, Torino Municipality organised a first meeting with local civic society organisations (CSOs) and *Coldiretti* with the aim of exploring the use of public land around and inside the city boundary. During the meeting, the technical staff of the city presented maps and ideas to illustrate the project. A first attempt by the municipality was to quantify and classify the total amount of municipal – public and private – agricultural areas and resources. Under the input of local stakeholders, a wider inventory of local initiatives was started, including traditional agricultural processes and products, social farming, urban collective agriculture, agro-tourism or urban forests to capture urban CO_2. Participating CSOs initiated a visioning exercise with innovative tools to identify solutions for the utilisation of some areas. *Coldiretti* mobilised their members to support the initiative and to make them aware of urban needs and demands, not only with regard to food provisioning, but also to relational/cultural initiatives and strategic planning. The project has already produced some important outcomes. The alignment of economically sustainable and professional projects has provided job opportunities for middle-aged unemployed. Torino Municipality has approved a plan for the organisation of public gardens. A research agreement between Torino City, *Coldiretti* and Pisa University is under development in order to accompany the process of change. More detailed urban planning is under discussion to promote specific initiatives and to link the sustainability of urban areas to the neighbouring rural ones.

The Pisa *Food Plan*

The agriculture of the Pisa Province had already lived its "rural renaissance" at the beginning of the 1990s, driven by the wine sector and agro-tourism and backed by new rural development policies and a strong orientation of the regional administration to multifunctional agriculture. As an effect of this renaissance, direct selling of organic and typical products grew fast in the last 20 years, and a business model based on diversification and intense communication with customers developed. New farm business models providing an increasing range of services – such as care, teaching, biodiversity conservation and environmental stewardship – have been encouraged. The City of Pisa is a university town with a strong concentration of students and academics. It also hosts a big hospital that serves the surrounding municipalities and, for many specialist services, attracts customers at a regional and national level. Pisa is also a tourist town, as the tower attracts hundreds of thousands of visitors every year. It was therefore a natural outlet for niche products, sold directly from farms or to specialist shops.

In recent years, another trend has emerged: *Solidarity Purchasing Groups* (GAS), consumer-initiated alternative food networks based on a strong voluntary work component and intense communication about general themes related to food, health and environment. These have involved a growing number of families and farmers. In 2012, more than 20 purchasing groups with about 50 families each were counted in the province. GAS have contributed substantially to create a food culture in the town. Farmers involved in GAS have progressively built their profile as "civic farmers", that is farmers who, thanks to their communication capacity and ethical profile, act as interfaces for improved city–countryside links. Likewise, consumers have progressively adopted a consumer-citizen profile, being

Fig 3: The Pisa *Food Plan*.
An interpretative summary.

	Action U+D – Bottom-Up and Top-Down	Action VIS – Visualising Consequences	Action IUC – Inventory of Urban Capacity	Action R – Researching for Change
frames	linking food to health and environment in an active environment devoted to innovation	conservation of agricultural land, especially in peri-urban areas conceptual mapping	exchanging information between food, health and environment administrative bodies	linking urban planning with food policy the sustainable diets concept
rules	*Food Plan* charter signed by municipalities	the province administration has mentioned the *Food Plan* initiative within the structural plan of the province	identification of the competences of municipalities in relation to food school food procurement standards	how to introduce local food into public procurement educational health infos on dietary rules
infrastructures	revitalisation of the school food commissions signature of the food strategy local initiatives for short food supply chains	google map with short food supply chains	web2.0 tool to connect actors of local administration, civil society, business and knowledge workers, and to share ideas and information	written memorandum of understanding between the Province, Pisa University and a spin-off

involved in the organisation of GAS systems of provision and in related events and communication flows. Local administrations have started to consider the multidimensionality of food, linking together agriculture, land planning, health and environment. One of the arenas where this multidimensional approach has consolidated is school food. Meeting the growing demand of parents, local administrations have activated initiatives to introduce organic products and local food into school meals. In this context, the Pisa Province has launched the *Piano del Cibo* project [Food Plan project] with the aim of coordinating private and public initiatives on food issues and promoting new institutional arrangements. Since 2008, several events on food issues have been organised jointly by civil society and public institutions under the *Piano del Cibo* umbrella. During these events, food, land use and environment emerged as three sensitive issues for diverse social groups of citizens. The *Piano del Cibo initiative* was made official in 2011 with an agreement between Pisa University and Pisa Province in order to implement, monitor and evaluate social and institutional processes of change around food via a multi-stakeholder dialogue. Meetings with specific groups (researchers, institutions, producers, civil society) were organised to reflect on food issues and their social and political implication, and to map ideas and related topics. The mapping exercise offered shared entry points and elements for planning activities.

Some initiatives were organised around more sensitive topics like urban strategies, short food supply chains and school public canteens. A website was launched in order to mobilise and empower local actors on food issues, providing information and support for local initiatives and facilitating active discussion and networks. Information accumulated from diverse activities has been organised in two political documents: a food *charter,* containing common goals and intentions (a city model, key points regarding food security, sustainable diet, food democracy and the definition of plan objectives and tools) and a food *strategy* where specific objectives are defined (health, food knowledge, sustainability, social justice, innovation and organisation) and political instruments were identified. The charter and the strategy were published online for discussion, presented in public meetings, and finally, 16 municipalities of the Pisa Province signed it.

The political initiative has generated local-level initiatives. With the support of a network of experts consolidated around the project, school food committees – consulting bodies of municipalities related to the organisation of school meals – have focused their activity around issues such as healthy and sustainable dietary rules, education, local provisioning and organic/sustainable food. Some of the principles elaborated during the process have been turned into tendering requirements for caterers. A borough of the Pisa municipality has officially endorsed the strategy and decided to promote the establishment of a food council with a consulting role on commerce and cultural activities.

Urban strategies: emerging lessons from the cases

Food is becoming a hot issue in urban areas. Urban food strategies, such as the examples above, open innovative spaces for consolidation of new discourses around food.

Having reviewed the two projects in terms of *CPUL City Actions*, we can see how new frames have been created through the activation of intense communication between local public and civic/private actors. These communication flows have generated new concepts, and collaboration has then translated them into visions and narratives that can be communicated to a wider public. The *Food Plan*, for example, evokes in people's perception a link between fields once kept separate: food, health, environment and land planning. The capacity to mobilise unexpected local material and immaterial resources into new perspectives, and the re-alignment of diverse policies and administrative tools in a new and more interlinked perspective around food issues are all part of strategies comparable to the *CPUL City Actions*.

The effort to build a new consensus on sustainable food at an urban scale opens ways to design new rules, from schools to commercial regulation to planning. Starting as a chaotic mosaic, urban strategies can progressively align the actors around pathways that can give order and a common frame to independent projects. Within an increasingly coherent frame, any new initiative has the potential to connect new people and to activate a change in conceived, perceived and lived food spaces. These initiatives have also created or contributed to establish new infrastructures. The food charter and the food strategy have set the priorities to fund infrastructures under a rural development plan. Online platforms have allowed communication among actors. New relationships between local movements, private businesses and institutions have turned into logistic arrangements and commercial flows. All of them can now better address their own action in a growing supportive environment.

New frames, rules and infrastructures are the components of new socio-technical systems. Focusing on food, cities can become open laboratories to test new solutions to the challenges of sustainability.

The moment before action:
A *CPUL City* summary

Katrin Bohn and André Viljoen

Designing for urban agriculture is a young discipline, and younger still is the international exploration of productive urban landscapes and how they may be implemented. Equally, as presented elsewhere in this book, measures to assess projects, especially when a focus on qualitative aspects (i.e. socio-political, cultural, well-being) rather than on quantitative aspects (i.e. yields, soil/air/plant/harvest types) have only just start to be developed.

As in many practice-driven processes, one can notice a simultaneity of "big and small" actions, of the strategic and the detailed, ranging from setting up a beehive to designing a greenway infrastructure, from negotiating a food policy document to installing a balcony growing system, or from building up a community garden to founding a rooftop farm. The *CPUL City Actions* address this by suggesting flexibility and appropriateness of scale and means. Within this simultaneity, two types of activities engage the designer and researcher as well as the practitioner and farmer: the enabling of urban agriculture and its assessment.

In order to create more sustainable, resilient and liveable cities, it is important to understand urban agriculture, both as part of an urban food system (or systems) and as part of a wider open urban space strategy. The *CPUL City Actions* take account of that by, for example, suggesting various forms of dialogue between stakeholders or the detailed inventorying of a project's capacities and requirements.

The four *CPUL City Actions* presented in this book categorise the multiple steps and tools most relevant to the architectural, urban design and planning professions. As said before, they can be condensed down to four points applicable to every individual project whatever its scale, location and specific purpose:

visualise, inventorise, negotiate, keep up to speed.

Enabling

The *CPUL City Actions* are intended as a toolbox when establishing urban agriculture projects. They work best when three interdependent prerequisites are ascertained:

- *Space*: a selection of suitable food-growing spaces is available,
- *Stakeholders*: there are local users with a desire to improve their access to healthy food,
- *Food*: "enough" food can be grown in the space with the involvement of the users.

If one or two of these prerequisites are missing, applying the Actions might help to generate them. However, the main use of the Actions begins when one or more stakeholders has expressed a desire to change the way in which an urban area is fed, by altering the way space in that urban area is used. The Actions will help these stakeholders – be they local residents, decision makers, property owners or other interested parties – to approach and navigate through their urban agriculture project, i.e. through the process of making urban space food-productive.

It is understood that urban agriculture activities are only one way of producing urban space. As such, they follow certain patterns of social and physical adaptation, with the specificity (and aim) of impacting on the local food system. These processes are dynamic and iterative. They might take place several times, consecutively or simultaneously. Not every attempt will be successful and/or satisfy all the desires that led to it. Depending on every project's individual context, many different parameters need to be considered, and the Actions can assist in finding the right methodology to filter options and agree on priorities. This will happen most intensely during the time in a project that we call "the moment before action".

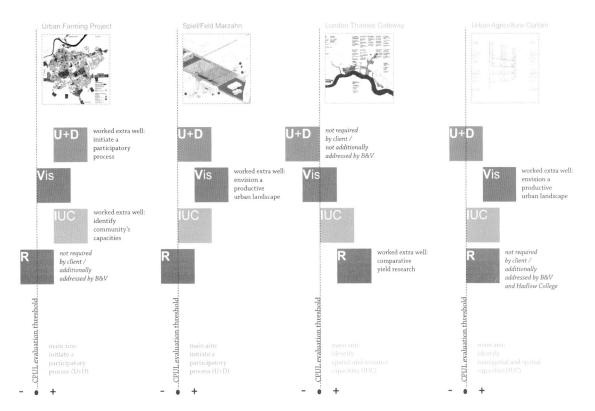

Fig 1: Assessing urban agriculture. Observing a food growing project with reference to the *CPUL City Actions* allows for the evaluation of a project's achievements against its aims and to decide on future priorities. The assessments of four of our projects are compared in this overview drawing.

Assessing

The *CPUL City Actions* can also be used as a tool for assessing food growing projects that are already underway. This, as a design research task, will become more important as more emerging projects engage in business planning, fundraising or negotiations with municipal authorities and other decision makers.

At the time of writing, we have used the Actions for assessment in two ways: we started to look at our own projects to understand how the interplay between and intensity of the four different actions shaped them, and we used the four actions to evaluate external projects. For example, in the case of *R-Urban*, a live project led by

French architects' collaboration AAA and exploring resilient, participatory and localised urban space production, applying the *CPUL City Actions* helped to sharpen the urban agriculture focus of one of the project parts, *Agrocité*. Here, applying the actions 'Inventory of Urban Capacity' and 'Bottom-up + Top-down' proved especially useful when discussing the various components needed to run a food growing project on this site in Colombes near Paris.

We would like to conclude with a summary of the *CPUL City Actions*:

Action U+D = Bottom-Up + Top-Down

Infrastructural, as well as individual food-productive projects need parallel top-down and bottom-up initiatives and integrative design and planning.

An urban agriculture project will have the best chance of long-term success when it can rely on a strong base of local supporters, active and passive, and when these are steadily engaged in negotiation processes with those entities that govern their lives, for example local councils or food distribution systems. The larger, i.e. more infrastructural a project is, such as a CPUL, the more interdependencies it needs and creates.

Within this action, it is important to address the following strategies, steps or tools necessary for a successful implementation of any urban agriculture project:

1. Develop multiple relationships between project protagonists, local communities and municipal decision makers in order to build a robust support network for the project.
2. Foster continuing negotiations with local food groups in the widest sense (i.e. organic seed suppliers, supermarket chains) in order to create closed-loop urban food systems that can fully integrate the specific food-growing project.
3. Stage events, create meeting occasions on the specific urban agriculture site(s) in order to increase the physical site's public visibility and its desire-in-use.
4. Jointly develop and advocate, discuss and refine, agree and contract aims, rules, design ambitions and process stages for the project in order to ascertain its commonly supported long-term future.

Action VIS = Visualising Consequences

The qualities and aims of urban agriculture and productive urban landscapes, such as CPULs, need visualising to convince decision makers and raise public awareness.

Visualising ideas and concepts is one of the primary skills of architects, planners and designers. Usually this is done through the design and/or prototyping of the idea in question, thereby predicting and discussing its potential outcomes – i.e. spatial, user, environmental or financial. In the case of productive urban landscapes, this action widens to include a range of urban agriculture experts and practitioners in the process. It encompasses the public and visually descriptive dissemination of ideas, data and best-practice examples, mostly in the form of exhibitions, installations, prototypes and online/paper/live presentations.

Within this action, it is important to:

1. Create images and visions – drawn, built and/or verbalised – that can convey the spatial, use and environmental values of urban agriculture projects to any members of the public in order to gain active and long-lasting support.
2. Advocate the potential for urban agriculture and productive urban landscapes as organic ornament in the city in order to broaden the public perception of what constitutes beautiful landscape and desirable lifestyles.
3. Think in three dimensions as well as temporally in order to maximise the potential impact of alternative urban food systems: raised beds, walls, roofs, fences, streets, etc. can become food-productive spaces and act as seasonal registers.
4. Provide visually descriptive guidance on the design-based realisation of productive landscapes in order to enhance their variety, usability, durability and aesthetic quality.

Action IUC = Inventory of Urban Capacity

An inventory is necessary for each location, especially of spatial, resource, stakeholder and managerial capacities in order to best respond to local opportunities.

At the beginning of the relatively short history of the urban agriculture movement in the Global North, (planning) emphasis was given to identifying (i.e. location, state of use, availability/ownership) and mapping (i.e. area, sun direction, soil quality, pollution, water, exposure to wind, adjacency to markets and compost) open urban space. In recent years, it has become clear that stakeholder and managerial/maintenance capacity around a site and in a food growing project are as important. Moreover, available resources need to be recorded and systematically integrated into the planning and execution of productive urban landscape projects.

Within this action, it is important to:

1. Map physical sites and resources taking into account that suitability for urban agriculture; includes issues such as land, orientation (sun), soil, air, boundaries, access, supply (water) and ownership in order to build a catalogue of spatial opportunities.
2. Identify potential goals and stakeholders for the project's different development stages from start-up to establishment to longer-term prominence, in order to ascertain and/or grow sufficient local capacity to maintain the project.
3. Aim for no-waste systems – grow, eat, compost, grow... – as one aspect of maximising the Ecological Intensification on open urban space.
4. Identify local resource and managerial capacities as a basis for new economic models, environmentally friendly production and fair trade for urban farmers.

Action R = Researching for Change

Constant research, development and consolidation of productive urban landscape projects and concepts is needed to respond to changing circumstances.

Social and environmental conditions can change rapidly – locally, regionally, nationally and globally. To keep pace with such developments, but also to scrutinise the achievements of concepts such as *CPUL City*, urban agriculture projects have to undergo repeated evaluation and evolution. Theory and practice need to be able to accommodate change, to anticipate the future by having understood the past. The main partners for this action are the multidisciplinary experts and researchers in universities or other research institutions on the one side and the practising urban farmers on the other.

Within this action, it is important to:

1. Stay flexible and open so as to be able to respond quickly and/or radically to changing circumstances – economic, climatic or socio-political – and defend the urban agriculture project.
2. Consolidate the project, be it built or conceptual, by constant search for and adaptation to both new agricultural research (plants, yields, soil, air) and emerging methods of urban space production and usage.
3. Understand productive urban landscapes as part of an urban food system or systems in order to develop economically viable structures for both a specific urban agriculture project and the resilience of its hosting community.
4. Think strategically – productive urban landscapes can become urban infrastructure – in order to respond to different urban conditions, such as lower and higher housing densities, socially deprived and well-off areas, inner cities and city edges or greener and less open neighbourhoods.

CPUL

REPOSI-
TORY

An introduction

Katrin Bohn and André Viljoen

In 2011, Joe Nasr inaugurated the *Jac Smit Memorial Library of Urban Agriculture*. The library is housed within *Food Share Toronto* (FoodShare *n.d.*) and holds about 4,000 paper-based items collected during Jac Smit's time leading *The Urban Agriculture Network (TUAN)* (TUAN 2009). It includes the texts, field notes and documentation that informed *TUAN*'s work and will continue to inform the work of researchers and practitioners.

In a subject area that is advancing and expanding as rapidly as urban agriculture is, it can be difficult to grasp where knowledge lies at any point in time, and so we can see the benefits of "freeze-framing" the knowledge base at particular moments, as is the case with Jac Smit's archive. With this in mind, we decided to apply a "freeze-frame" to the external resources currently underpinning the *CPUL City* concept and, by doing so, move a step beyond the conventional academic format for references. We have therefore collected all references used in this book into a single repository giving an overview of the sources informing it, archiving them according to their subject area and age and, in particular, providing a CPUL-relevant database. Because the *CPUL Repository* only lists resources specifically referred to in this book, they are predominantly from Germany, the UK and the USA – our three case study countries.

Urban agriculture projects are largely practice-based. Whilst books and papers are written *about* these projects, the information flow *between* them is mostly paperless. It is also fast, individual and open source. Despite urban agriculture's earlier reputation as a fringe, alternative, hands-on, and sometimes "luddite" activity with close local networks, its communication has for all of this century been far-reaching and nearly entirely web-based. By way of example, the sources and contacts in the 2005 *CPUL* book (Viljoen 2005: 271) listed nine organisations disseminating findings about urban agriculture. Almost all of these already had long-standing websites and almost all remain relevant and active today. Since 2005, online resources have expanded tremendously, and the urban agriculture communities in the USA, Great Britain and Germany are almost all online. The *CPUL Repository* therefore also aims to capture, as well as complement, the extensive online urban agriculture resources available today.

This last part of the book begins with short chapters from five authors who contributed to the 2005 *CPUL* book and who are still actively engaged with the topic. David Crouch, Ken Elkes, Jorge Peña Diaz, Graeme Sherriff and Richard Wiltshire reflect on particular developments since 2005 in community food growing, a concrete urban case study, allotment gardening and Cuba's urban agriculture, and conclude by recommending key resources that have appeared in the meantime – repository material.

The *CPUL Repository* closes this part of the book with its alphabetical listing of over 500 resources. To order the different types of reference, we have developed four non-hierarchical categories by which items are classified.

The four categories are:

PLANNING = Planning it
The planning, design and policy development for productive cities.

SPACE = Doing it
Spaces, projects and people involving/involved with urban agriculture.

ECOSYSTEM = Cooperating with nature
The significance of plants, animals and ecosystems for urban agriculture.

KNOWLEDGE = Setting the context
Knowledge contributing to a wider understanding of productive urban landscapes.

Fig 1: The CPUL Repository Timeline. This chart visualizes the data contained in the repository according to four areas of urban agriculture development. It also shows how the subject has expanded during the last twenty years.

ECOSYSTEM

KNOWLEDGE

PLANNING

SPACE

Neighbour

Lefebvre
Alward et al.
Moore Lappé
Georgescu-Roegen
Schumpeter: History Schumacher
of Economic Analysis   Slobodkin et al.
Schumpeter: Capitalism,   Steinhart et al.
Kampffmeyer Socialism and Democracy   Oppenheimer Leach Stanhill

Howard   Eyck

1978 Cityfarmer network
& later website

Brand: Whole Earth Catalog

1866   1902   1913   1943   1954   1964   1976   1982

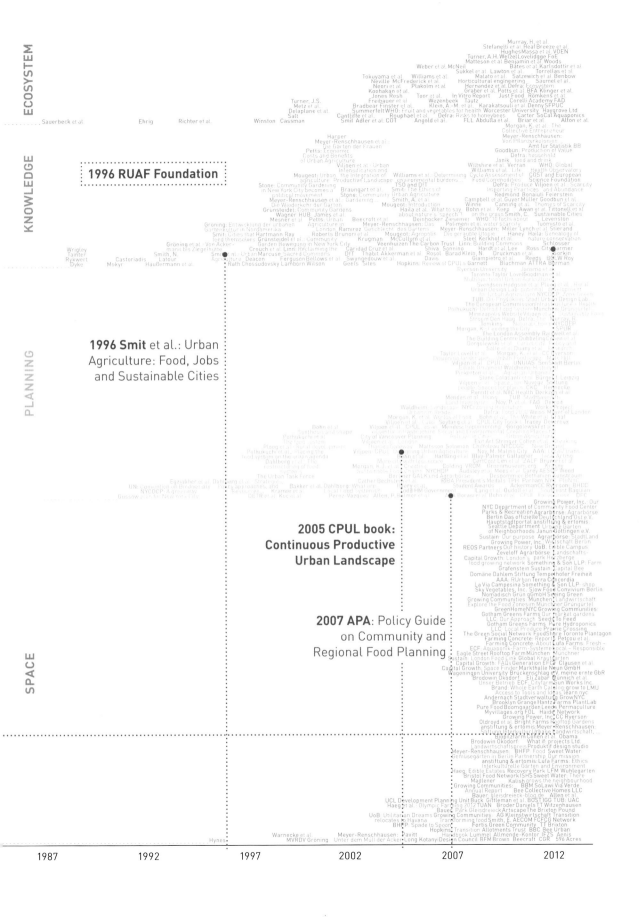

ECOSYSTEM

KNOWLEDGE

PLANNING

SPACE

1996 RUAF Foundation

1996 Smit et al.: Urban Agriculture: Food, Jobs and Sustainable Cities

2005 CPUL book: Continuous Productive Urban Landscape

2007 APA: Policy Guide on Community and Regional Food Planning

1987   1992   1997   2002   2007   2012

What has happened since *CPUL* 2005? The rise of community growing

Ken Elkes

Back in 2005, we highlighted the importance of the UK's thriving network of city farms, community gardens, school farms and allotment projects, which provided wide-ranging benefits to their communities.

In that sense, little has changed. Local groups still provide great opportunities and services from work training to after-school care. They continue to act as social hubs, bring together diverse ethnic communities and help create a sense of pride in often deprived areas. They also increase capacity for improving individual health and the general environment.

What has changed significantly, however, is the explosive rise in popularity of community-based urban food growing, fuelled by the "grow your own" message and an increased awareness of health, education outside the classroom and climate change. Statutory provision of land has been unable to keep pace with demand, so organisations at both national and local level have created a plethora of initiatives, from ad hoc guerrilla gardening and "Local Food Coalitions" to schemes like *Designs of the Time 2007* (*Dott 07*) – a ten-year programme of community projects in North East England that explored what life in a sustainable region could be like. Demand has also led to an upsurge in the need for support, information and guidance. Membership of the Federation of City Farms and Community Gardens (FCFCG) has risen greatly since 2005, with many newly established groups looking for advice not just on setting up, but also on being able to survive and develop.

FCFCG set up a project in England to increase its support to food growing groups – with funding from the Big Lottery's *Local Food Programme*. In Scotland, we have worked closely with the government to provide specific services tailored to its differing laws and needs, while a major programme called *Tyfu Pobl* [Growing People] was started by FCFCG in Wales in 2011. Over the last 18 months, there has been an expansion of activity in

Northern Ireland. FCFCG has also been instrumental in setting up the *Community Land Advisory Service*, an impartial partnership project designed to increase community access to land across the UK.

There has also been much activity around school farming and gardening, particularly from schools in urban areas. In 2006, there were just 66 school farms in the UK – now that figure tops 100 and is growing. Our work with the *School Farms Network* has helped increase the recognition of the educational and social benefits of school farms. Meanwhile, we are also running a successful pilot project to promote and support school gardening in the West Midlands. Since 2005, community-led activity has made the urban environment ever more productive, and the genuine, positive benefits created have been increasingly recognised by key decision makers at a regional and national level in the UK.

However, there are no guarantees about the future. Austerity measures have bitten deeply and many groups can no longer rely on grants from their local authority. A larger number of groups are competing for a shrinking pot of funding. As a result, we are committed to helping them become sustainable through diversifying their income into areas such as social enterprise and more innovative forms of fundraising, such as crowd funding and community shares. It's not easy, but the resilience that community farming and gardening has shown through its history will surely stand the movement in good stead in the coming years.

Urbanising food in Greater Manchester

Graeme Sherriff

There has certainly been a flourishing of urban food activity in Greater Manchester in recent years. A community orchard, a market garden trading directly with an organic supermarket, a fruit and veg van bringing produce to some of the most deprived communities and plans for a vertical farm in a disused building being some examples. The *Manchester Food Futures Strategy* promotes a model that aims to bring agriculture, processing and distribution into the city region. The aims of the strategy, which make reference to health, the local and global environment, the local economy, sustainable communities, and cultural diversity, reflect recognition of urban food as a key component of healthy, sustainable cities.

Since my research on permaculture, which informed my chapter in *CPUL 1*, I carried out participative research on a Manchester-based project informed by its principles: the *Bentley Bulk*. Like many similar projects, it depended on volunteer energy and arguably fell short of its full potential, but the fascinating thing about the project was that it brought many aspects of urban food together and, in doing so, aimed to create a 'healthy local food system'. Participants attended a weekly training seminar on food issues, including permaculture, followed by an afternoon of on-the-job training at a market garden. This work was remunerated with LETS currency (Local Exchange Trading Scheme) with which the participants could purchase produce grown on site. The project highlighted the importance of skills, culture and economy in a productive urban landscape, and of creating connections between these and the physical spaces of production.

Up the train line to Yorkshire is *Incredible Edible Todmorden*, a town-wide initiative to 'grow and campaign for local food'. Including innovative ideas, such as the station herb garden, weeded by local volunteers and giving busy commuters free access to fresh herbs to cook their evening meal, the initiative is working with community organisations such as schools, the police station and a health centre to both raise awareness and create a landscape of food production including fruit, vegetables, eggs and honey. Such projects have impact beyond food supply: they raise awareness about the impacts of food choices.

Whilst gaining momentum, these projects are still far from the mainstream, with the major supermarkets dominating food retail. Urban agriculture tends to be thought of as something separate from these businesses, so it is notable that one of them is currently running a scheme to promote food growing in schools. In considering the future of urban food, there are many pertinent questions. What is the future of urban agriculture, and how does it fit in the context of our food culture as a whole? How can we engage with people widely so that urban food becomes part of our cultural, as well as physical, landscape? What will be the role of supermarkets in a sustainable future? What other features of a sustainable city are competing for space: transport infrastructure, renewable energy, housing?

Fundamentally, to what extent are we trying to *urbanise* food such that cities (or regions) can feed themselves, or will urban food sit alongside the dominant food businesses, brightening up our cities and equipping us to engage with food culture more widely in a healthier and more sustainable way?

New designs on the plot

Richard Wiltshire

The role of allotments in emerging *CPUL*s has been transformed since *Designs on the Plot* (Crouch and Wiltshire 2005) as a successful route to expanding popular engagement with urban agriculture, but also as sites of new contestations.

The good practice guide *Growing in the Community* (Crouch, Sempik and Wiltshire 2001) was commissioned against a background of declining provision and widespread indifference. The *Allotments Regeneration Initiative (ARI)*, launched in 2002 to transform guidance into action, captured in its name a pressing need: to rescue allotments from obscurity and promote their relevance to multiple public policy objectives. A decade later, the majority of councils have allotment strategies (APSE 2012), a second edition of *Growing in the Community* celebrates the new popularity of allotments (Wiltshire and Burn 2008) – with an update to address consequent growth pains (Wiltshire 2010), and *ARI* is to be folded into the *National Allotment Society* (www.nsalg.org.uk), its mission of regeneration delivered. Waiting lists approaching six figures (Campbell and Campbell 2011) demonstrate the public's appetite for yet more provision, giving substance to the *CPUL City* vision.

Where land is plentiful, demands from aspiring growers have pushed councils to honour the 'duty to provide' embedded in the *Allotments Acts*, a duty fiercely defended against cutters of red tape. Plot size reductions have helped to ease waiting lists – and aided inclusion within the allotments model of today's busy lifestyles. Competition for urban land for new allotments has thrown up new conflicts, however, not only from existing users of the same space, for which designs need to embody political compromises (Wiltshire 2010), but also from alternative models of urban agriculture, with designs on the same space and narratives in the ascendancy.

The recognition of food growing as a tactic by movements addressing climate change, energy transitioning and food justice, has injected powerful ideologies into competition for urban space. Such movements bear benign intentions but, in stressing orchestrated collective action, place little value on neither the private idiosyncrasies that underpin the vernacular allotment landscape, nor the democratic and transparent principle of access that "allotment" entails. The conception of allotments as 'semi-closed, semi-privatised public open spaces' (Crouch and Wiltshire 2005) plays into the hands of those who advocate "community" food growing, without specifying who the community is and why collective labour is a necessary precondition of community life. Unequal competition is ensured by funding criteria which large organisations are adept at manipulating to their advantage. The erosion of traditional individual plotholding in New York's community gardens documented by Miranda Martinez is a cautionary tale of where such pressures can lead (Martinez 2010).

While not short of takers, therefore, the allotment requires a new narrative of 'vernacular foodscapes' and 'autotopographies' (Mares and Pena 2011), of decommodification and gifting, capturing the alternative values that it represents: self-confidence and self-actualisation, the autonomous formation and expression of individual identities – alongside community identities forged through the negotiation of difference, meeting the productive aims of the *CPUL* through a committed supply of labour imbued with a spirit of stewardship (Wiltshire and Geoghegan 2012).

The allotment and community garden

David Crouch

The arguments, issues and evidence in support of allotments and allotment sites, that Richard Wiltshire and I presented in our 2005 chapter, remain pertinent today and are likely to do for some time to come, as several key steps of change have developed, at least from the UK point of view, in the succeeding years.

Yet perhaps the most alarming example of a failure of design lurks in the "landscape" surrounding the *London Olympics* sites in North East London. The case, known as *The Manor Farm Allotments*, attracted a great deal of attention amongst celebrities, the wider London public and, most importantly, the affected allotment holders and other community gardeners across East London. The "landscape designers" of the *Lea Valley* area in London, also in the Olympics zone, produced a broad, sweeping kind of space and decided there was nothing to interrupt or punctuate their sweep. It happened that the *Manor Farm* site was somewhere in the middle of this design. Thus, it was deemed necessary to remove the whole site. A new site was eventually designated. Numerically, the plots and size remain much the same. The disruption to plotholders and the work to be invested in new plots was, and will continue to be, a burden for the individuals concerned. The designers failed to grasp the creative potential that the existing site and all of its well-used and cared-for plots – meaningful in the plotters' lives – had to offer.

Style in "living design" has crept further into the edges of allotment and community garden cultivation. In the UK, the National Trust has engaged in a significant scheme of providing plots on a number of their properties. Linking plots with designed spaces, renders a welcome engagement between the looser, living character of allotments and those designed spaces, thereby creating sustainable land. That is something that the design of *London Olympics* could certainly have attempted, but did not.

Somewhat different and as yet small, but spreading, interest in keeping animals on allotments has emerged, or re-emerged, in the UK after many decades of relatively quiet continuity at a very small scale (Crouch 2012). Keeping animals on plots places different design opportunities and pressures on allotments. Historically, significant areas of the UK had animals too, often held – very sustainably – amongst individual households with possibilities to share and to provide, typical of the reciprocity tradition of allotment holding.

Finally, the debacle over the UK government's effort to grasp open community-cultivated land in urban areas offers another means to critically examine the turns and shifts of sustainable and non-sustainable land use. The UK government sought to remove the generations-old requirement of local councils across the country to provide allotments – sites and plots – even though this was backed up since the 1998 *Government Enquiry on Allotments* by a renewed requirement for councils to promote the availability of plots on existing sites (Crouch 1998). This threat to sustainable land was wrested back through parliamentary debate that turned after a reading of key sections of the recent report on the demand and use of allotments (Crouch 2006). The 2011 success offers some optimism for the enabling of creative sustainable landscapes and land uses.

I complete this review with a brief reference to notions of sustainable design: Design can be a creative process, and comes through a responsive attitude and feeling towards land, growing, landscape. Landscape is a flexible, fluid process that can happen anywhere in everyday life, and through our activities we relate to spaces, sites, in a manner of flirting: of landscape not being merely "pre-arranged" by designers, as in film and in books, but constantly available, changing with our own actions, relations and feelings (Crouch 2010). Working allotments, the land, things growing, provides an intimate opportunity for this relationship.

UPA in Cuba:
On recent developments

Jorge Peña Díaz

The first decades of the 21st century witnessed the start of the partial recovery of Cuba's main economic indicators. Despite the strengthening of the USA financial and economic blockade against the country-island, its position within the international context has changed. New economic and political ties link Cuba to Latin America as exemplified by its insertion into South–South and regional cooperation schemes such as ALBA[1] and CELAC.[2] The overwhelming crisis responsible for Urban and Peri-urban Agriculture's (UPA) development as a response in the early 1990s situation has practically disappeared (Peña Díaz 2012). Nevertheless, global trends, such as the increase of food prices in the global market, as well as local ones, such as prevailing inefficiencies in the internal agricultural sector and the urgency of reducing food importation costs, have framed UPA's role within the local urban food system.

Political support for Urban and Peri-urban Agriculture has actually increased. The further consolidation of its regulatory framework could be interpreted as a result of the understanding of UPA as a key component of the national food system. For example, Urban and Peri-urban Agriculture proved its value in contingency situations when, after three major hurricanes hit Cuba one after another in 2008, UPA productive units were the only ones able to provide food immediately. These kinds of events seem to have contributed to the rise of its profile within food security policies and as part of the national security agenda.

This evolution is clearly reflected by the position Urban and Peri-urban Agriculture occupies within an important milestone of Cuban societal development: the *Guidelines for the economic and social policy of the Revolution and the Party* (PCC 2011). These guidelines establish a roadmap for the updating of the Cuban socio-economic model by including innovative features such as the fostering of self-employment, cooperatives and other non-state-based production forms, among other elements. Approximately 10% of the around 300 guidelines are dedicated to agriculture, and Urban and Peri-urban Agriculture finds a prominent position within them. Particularly suburban agriculture has been receiving more specific attention and is additionally backed by an innovative *Land Granting Scheme* easing access to land for many new farmers and the recovery of millions of hectares of idle land. Moreover, scientific knowledge transference related to this practice has successfully continued and production figures retain a positive trend.

Urban and Peri-urban Agriculture has gained additional recognition within planning tools. Notwithstanding this, despite having found resonance in local academic and artistic milieus, it continues to be paradoxical that the cities that have managed to set such a comprehensive implementation of UPA have developed almost no projects promoting urban and landscape design strategies using it as a key component. Accordingly – even though all the above-mentioned elements seem to ensure that UPA will remain strong in the immediate future – the integration of food-related policies into environmental agendas and urban design and landscape strategies at the local level seems to be one of the most interesting future challenges for evolving urban scenarios.

Notes
1 Acronym for Alianza Bolivariana de los pueblos de Nuestra América (Bolivarian Alliance).
2 Acronym for Comunidad de Estados Latinoamericanos y del Caribe (Community of Latin American and the Caribbean States).

5 x key references and resources

Jorge Peña Díaz recommends:

PCC Partido Comunista de Cuba (2011) *Lineamientos de La Política Económica y Social de La Revolución y El Partido*, PCC: Cuban Communist Party.

Peña Díaz, J. (2012) *Infraestructuras Urbanas Locales Sustentables: Agricultura Urbana de Cara a La Ciudad*, in: *Memorias 16 Convención Científica de Ingeniería y Arquitectura,* Palacio de las Convenciones, La Habana: Ministerio de Educación Superior (Cuban Higher Education Ministry).

David Crouch recommends:

Crouch, D. (1998) expert evidence for: *Report of the Enquiry into the Future of Allotments in England and Wales*, London: House of Commons.

Crouch, D. (2006) *Report of Survey into Allotments in England*, Department of Communities and Local Government (with University of Derby).

Crouch, D. (2010) *Flirting with space: Journeys and creativity*, Farnham: Ashgate.

Crouch, D. (2012) *You and Yours*, BBC Radio Four, 6 April 2012.

Richard Wiltshire recommends:

APSE Association for Public Services Excellence (2012) *Local Authority Allotment Services,* Manchester: Association for Public Services Excellence, briefing 12/08.

Campbell, C. and Campbell, I. (2011) *Allotment Waiting Lists In England,* West Kirby: Transition Town West Kirby and the National Society of Allotment and Leisure Gardeners.

Crouch, D. and Wiltshire, R. (2005) *Designs on the Plot: The Future for Allotments in Urban Landscapes*, in: Viljoen, A. (ed) *Continuous Productive Urban Landscapes*, London: Architectural Press, pp. 124–131.

Crouch, D., Sempik, J. and Wiltshire, R. (2001) *Growing in the Community: A Good Practice Guide for the Management of Allotments,* London: Local Government Association.

Mares, T.M. and Pena, D.G. (2011) *Environmental and Food Justice: Toward Local, Slow, and Deep Food Systems*, in: Hope Alkon, A. and Agyeman, J. (eds) (2011) *Cultivating Food Justice: Race, Class and Sustainability,* London: MIT Press, pp. 197-219.

Martinez, M. (2010) *Power at the Roots: Gentrification, Community Gardens, and the Puerto Ricans of the Lower East Side,* Lanham: Lexington Books.

Wiltshire, R. (2010) *A Place to Grow,* London: Local Government Association.

Wiltshire, R. and Burn, D. (2008) *Growing in the Community,* 2nd Edition, London: Local Government Association.

Wiltshire, R. and Geoghegan, L. (2012) *Growing Alone, Growing Together, Growing Apart? Reflections on the Social Organisation of Voluntary Urban Food Production in Britain*, in: Viljoen, A. and Wiskerke, J.S.C. (eds) *Sustainable Food Planning: Evolving Theory and Practice,* Wageningen: Wageningen Academic Publishers, pp. 335–346.

Graeme Sherriff recommends:

Lang, T. and Heasman M. (2004) *Food Wars: The Global Battle for Mouths, Minds and Markets,* London: Earthscan.

McKay, G. (2011) *Radical Gardening: Politics, Idealism and Rebellion in the Garden,* London: Frances Lincoln Ltd.

Pearson, L.J., Pearson, L. and Pearson, C.J. (2010) *Sustainable Urban Agriculture: Stocktake and Opportunities*, in: *International Journal of Agricultural Sustainability*, no. 8 (1–2), pp. 7–19.

Sherriff, G. (2009) *Towards Healthy Local Food: Issues in Achieving Just Sustainability*, in: *Local Environment,* no. 14 (1), pp. 73–92.

Ken Elkes recommends:

Community Land Advisory Service (CLAS) (no date) *Welcome to CLAS,* Available online: <www.communitylandadvice.org.uk> (accessed 16 May 2012).

Federation of City Farms and Community Gardens (2005) *Community Garden Starter Pack*, Bristol: FCFCG.

Federation of City Farms and Community Gardens (2007) *Chillies and Roses: Inspiring Multi-ethnic Involvement at Community Gardens and Farms*, Bristol: FCFCG.

Federation of City Farms and Community Gardens (2008) *True Value of Community Farms & Gardens*, Bristol: FCFCG.

Federation of City Farms and Community Gardens (2010) *Growing Trends Research*, Available online: <http://www.farmgarden. org.uk/home/local-food-project/growing-trends-research> (accessed 16 May 2012).

The CPUL Repository

A listing of all references used in this book

● Abdulla, F.A. and Al-Shareef, A.W. (2009) *Roof rainwater harvesting systems for household water*, in: *Desalination*, vol. 243, pp. 195–207. **> 240–243**

● Ackerman, K. (2011) *The Potential for Urban Agriculture in New York City: Growing capacity, food security, and green infrastructure*, New York: Columbia University. **> 138–145**

● Adler, P.R., Summerfelt, S.T., Glenn, D.M. and Takeda, F. (2003) *Mechanistic approach to phytoremediation of water*, in: *Ecological Engineering*, vol. 20, pp. 251–264. **> 240–243**

● AECOM (2011) *The Detroit Works Project. Phase One: Research and Priorities: Policy Audit Topic: Urban Agriculture and Food Security*, Available online: <http://detroitworksproject.com/policy-audit-urban-agriculture-and-food-security> (accessed 20 Apr 2012). **> 155–161**

● Aenis, T. (2012) *Urban Gardening in Berlin: Qualifizierung, Netzwerkbildung und modellhafte Umsetzung im Garten- und Landbau*, Available online: <http://www.hu-berlin.de/pr/pressemitteilungen/pm1201/pm_120124_00> (accessed 16 May 2012). **> 155–161**

● AESOP Association of European Schools of Planning (no date) *Sustainable Food Planning Group*, Available online: <http://www.aesop-planning.eu/blogs/en_GB/sustainable-food-planning> (accessed 16 Dec 2012). **> 6–11, 12–17**

● AG Kleinstwirtschaft (no date) *Arbeitsgruppe Kleinstlandwirtschaft und Gärten in Stadt und Land*, Available online: <http://userpage.fu-berlin.de/~garten> (accessed 16 May 2012). **> 92–99, 146–153**

● Agrarbörse Deutschland Ost e.V. (2011) *StadtLandWirtschaft Berlin*, Available online: <http://www.landwirtschaft-berlin.de> (accessed 16 May 2012). **> 155–161**

● Agrarbörse Deutschland Ost e.V. (no date a) *Agrarbörse Deutschland Ost e.V.*, Available online: <http://www.agrar-boerse-ev.de/agrarboerse.php> (accessed 16 May 2012). **> 40–47, 92–99**

● Agrarbörse Deutschland Ost e.V. (no date b) *Landschaftspark Herzberge*, Available online: <http://agrarboerse.wordpress.com/standorte/landschaftspark-herzberge> (accessed 16 May 2012). **> 92–99**

● Agropolis München (no date) *Die Wiederentdeckung des Erntens im urbanen Alltag*, Available online: <http://agropolis-mueAgrarbörsenchen.de> (accessed 16 May 2012). **> 92–99**

● Akkerman, T., Hajer, M. and Grin, J. (2004) *The Interactive State: Democratisation from above?*, in: *Political Studies*, vol. 52(1), pp. 82–95. **> 48–53**

● Allen, A. and Wilson, C. (2012) *The Good Food Revolution: Growing healthy food, people and communities*, New York: Gotham Books. **> 40–47**

● Allen, P. (2004) *Together at the Table: Sustainability and sustenance in the American agrifood system*, Pennsylvania: PSU Press. **> 18–23**

● Allmende-Kontor (no date) *Das Allmende-Kontor*, Available online: <http://www.allmende-kontor.de:81> (accessed 16 May 2012). **> 92–99**

● Altieri, M. and Rosset, P. (1999) *Ten reasons why biotechnology will not ensure food security, protect the environment and reduce poverty in the developing world*, in: *Agricultural Biological Forum*, no. 2, pp. 155-162. **> 60–67**

● Alton, K. and Patterson, M. (2013) *Are there enough flowers to support London's bees?*, in: *BBKA News incorporating The British Bee Journal*, no. 6. **> 84–91**

● Alward, S., Alward, R. and Rybczynski, W. (1976) *Rooftop Wastelands*, Montréal: Minimum Cost Housing Group, McGill University, Available online: <http://www.mcgill.ca/mchg/past-project/rooftop> (accessed 5 Apr 2012). **> 68–75**

● Amt für Statistik Berlin Brandenburg (2012) *Höchste Quote der Empfänger sozialer Mindestsicherung in 2010 im Land Berlin*, Pressemitteilung 341 vom 16. Nov 2012, Available online: <https://www.statistik-berlin-brandenburg.de/pms/2012/12-11-16d.pdf> (accessed 2 Dec 2012). **> 146–153**

● Andernach Stadtverwaltung (no date) *Essbare Stadt*, Available online: <http://www.andernach.de/de/leben_in_andernach/essbare_stadt.html> (accessed 16 May 2012). **> 6–11, 92–99**

● Angold, P.G., Sadler, J.P., Hill, M.O., Pullin, A., Rushton, S., Austin, K., Small, E., Wood, B., Wadsworth, R., Sanderson, R. and Thompson, K. (2006) *Biodiversity in urban habitat patches*, in: *Urban Environmental Research in the UK:*

The Urban Regeneration and the Environment (NERC URGENT) Programme and associated studies, no. 360, pp. 196–204. **> 84–91**

● Anonymous (2009) *Horticultural engineering,* in: *Biosystems Engineering,* vol. 103, pp. 90–101. **> 240–243**

● anstiftung & ertomis Stiftungsgemeinschaft (no date a) *Interkulturelle Gärten,* Available online: <http://www.stiftung-interkultur. de/berlin> (accessed 14 Nov 2012). **> 92–99, 146–153**

● anstiftung & ertomis Stiftungsgemeinschaft (no date b) *Stiftung Interkultur,* Available online: <http://www.anstiftung-ertomis. de/die-stiftung/stiftung-interkultur> (accessed 16 May 2012). **> 92–99**

● anstiftung & ertomis Stiftungsgemeinschaft (no date c) *Urbane Gärten,* Available online: <http://www.anstiftung-ertomis.de/ urbane-gaerten> (accessed 7 Jun 2012). **> 108–113**

● APA American Planning Association (2007) *Policy Guide on Community and Regional Food Planning,* Available online: <https://www. planning.org/policy/guides/ adopted/food.htm> (accessed 16 May 2012). **> 1–5, 6–11, 18–23**

● Artscape (no date) *Wychwood Barns,* Available online: <http://torontoartscape.org/ artscape-wychwood-barns> (accessed 16 May 2012). **> 24–31**

● Atelier d'Architecture Autogérée (2012a) *Local/ Trans-local Acting,* in: *R-Urban Commons Files,* Available online: <http:// rurbancommons.wikispot. org/Catalogue_of_Commons> (accessed 16 May 2012). **> 108–113**

● Atelier d'Architecture Autogérée (2012b) *RUrban,* Available online: <http://r-urban.net> (accessed 7 Jun 2012). **> 108–113**

● ATTRA (2011) *Market Gardening,* Available online: <https://attra.ncat.org/ attrapub/PDF/market-gardening.pdf> (accessed 16 May 2012). **> 76–83**

● Audsley, E., Brander, M., Chatterton, J., Murphy-Bokern, D., Webster, C. and Williams, A. (2009) *How low can we go?: An assessment of greenhouse gas emissions from the UK food system and the scope to reduce them by 2050,* UK: WWF World Wide Fund for Nature. **> 76–83**

● Awan, N., Schneider, T. and Till, J. (2011) *Spatial Agency: Other ways of doing architecture,* London: Routledge. **> 108–113**

● Baguian, H. (2013) *Green mosaic planning in Bobo Dioulasso: An example of how a city integrated urban agroforestry in its climate change strategies,* Available online: <http:// resilient-cities.iclei.org/file-admin/sites/resilient-cities/ files/Resilient_Cities_2013/ Presentations/D5_ Baguian_RC2013_RUFS. pdf> (accessed 20 Jul 2013). **> 32–39**

● Bakker, N., Dubbeling, M., Gündel, S., Sabel Koschella, U. and Zeeuw, H. de (eds) (2000) *Growing Cities, Growing Food: Urban Agriculture on the policy agenda: a Reader on Urban Agriculture,* Feldafing GER: Deutsche Stiftung für Internationale Entwicklung (DSE), Zentralstelle für Ernährung und Landwirtschaft. **> 92–99, 146–153**

● Balmer, K., Gill, J., Kaplinger, H., Miller, J., Peterson, M., Rhoads, A., Rosenbloom, P. and Wall, T. (2005) *The Diggable City: Making Urban Agriculture a Planning Priority,* Available online: <http://www. portlandoregon.gov/ bps/42793> (accessed 16 May 2012). **> 12–17, 155–161**

● Barad, K. (2007) *Meeting the Universe Halfway,* Durham NC: Duke University Press. **> 108–113**

● Bates, A.J., Sadler, J.P., Fairbrass, A.J., Falk, S.J., Hale, J.D. and Matthews, T.J. (2011) *Changing bee and hoverfly pollinator assemblages along an urban-rural gradient,* *PloS One,* 6(8): e23459. **> 84–91**

● Bauer, M. (2009) *Park Genossenschaft Gleisdreieck,* Available online: <http:// www.berlin-gleisdreieck.de> (accessed 16 May 2012). **> 146–153**

● Bauer, M. (no date) *gleisdreieck-blog.de,* Available online: <http://gleisdreieck-blog.de/2011/08/06/ chronik-des-gemeinschaftlichen-gartnerns-auf-dem-gleisdreieck>* (accessed 16 May 2012). **> 146–153**

● BBC Bell Book & Candle Restaurant New York (2012) *About Bell Book & Candle,* Available online: <http:// bbandcnyc.com/about> (accessed 16 May 2012). **> 138–145**

● BBM Brandenburg + Berlin GmbH (no date) *VON HIER,* Available online: <http://www. vonhier.com/webseite/index. php?modul=ModulUeber_ von_hier> (accessed 16 May 2012). **> 92–99**

● Bechstein, F. and Kabbert, R. (2004) *Die Wertschöpfung soll in der Region bleiben: Aufbau eines regionalen Obstverarbeitungsbetriebes in Werder,* in: *Bauernzeitung Brandenburg,* no. 24. **> 12–17**

● Bee Collective (2012) *The Bee Collective* London, Available online: <https://sites. google.com/a/bee-collective. co.uk/beecollective/home> (accessed 8 Aug 2012). **> 84–91**

● Bee Urban (2012) *Bee Urban Keeper's Lodge,* Available online: <http:// projectdirt.com/group/ keeperslodge> (accessed 9 Aug 2012). **> 84–91**

● Beecraft (2011) *St. Ermin's Bees,* Available online: <http://www.bee-craft. com/information-database/ st-ermin's-bees> (accessed 1 Aug 2011). **> 84–91**

● Beecroft, M., Lyons, G. and Chatterjee, K. (2003) *Freight and Logistics: The seventh of eight reports from the Transport Visions Network,*

Transportation Research Group, University of Southampton, London: Landor Publishing. **> 76–83**

● Beinhocker, E.D. (2006) *The Origin of Wealth: Evolution, complexity, and the radical remaking of economics,* Cambridge MA: Harvard Business School Press. **> 48–53**

● Bellows, A.C., Robinson, V., Gutherie, J., Meyer, T., Peric, N. and Hamm, M.W. (2000) *Urban livestock agriculture in the State of New Jersey, USA,* in: *Urban Agriculture magazine,* Leusden NL: RUAF Foundation. **> 84–91**

● Benbow, S. (2012) *The Urban Beekeeper: A year of bees in the city,* London: Square Peg. **> 84–91**

● Benjamin, A. and McCallum, B. (2011) *Bees in the City: The urban beekeepers' handbook,* London: Guardian Books. **> 84–91**

● Berlin Das offizielle Hauptstadtportal (no date) *Bio- und Ökowochenmärkte,* Available online: <http://www.berlin.de/special/shopping/biomarkt> (accessed 16 May 2012). **> 92–99**

● Berliner GALK und Agrarbörse (2006) *Neue Felder für die Stadt: Urbane Landwirtschaft als Instrument der Stadtentwicklung?,* Available online: <http://www.stadtentwicklung.berlin.de/umwelt/landschaftsplanung/stadtland/download/workshopdoku_neue_felder.pdf> (accessed 12 Jan 2011). **> 12–17**

● Berman, L. (2012) *Urban Farming Idea Slowly Sprouts in Detroit,* in: *The Detroit News,* issue 20 Mar 2012, Available online: <http://www.detroitnews.com/article/20120320/OPINION03/203200352> (accessed 16 May 2012). **> 130–137**

● Bethanien Kunstraum (2012) *Hungry City,* Available online: <http://www.kunstraumkreuzberg.de/prog_3.html> (accessed 16 Nov 2012). **> 12–17**

● BFA Bee Farmers' Association (2011) *Migratory Beekeeping in the UK,* Available online: <http://www.beefarmers.co.uk/articles/p2_articleid/8> (accessed Nov 2011). **> 84–91**

● BFM Bath Farmers' Market (2009) *Bath Farmers' Market,* Available online: <http://www.bathfarmersmarket.co.uk/about> (accessed 16 May 2012). **> 6–11**

● BHCC Brighton & Hove City Council (2013) *The Brighton & Hove Local Biodiversity Action Plan,* Brighton: Environment and Sustainability Committee. **> 60–67**

● BHFP Brighton & Hove Food Partnership (2006) *Spade to Spoon: Making the Connections,* Brighton: Brighton & Hove Food Partnership. **> 18–23**

● BHFP Brighton & Hove Food Partnership (2012) *Brighton & Hove Food Partnership,* Available online: <http://www.bhfood.org.uk/about-us> (accessed 16 May 2012). **> 6–11**

● Biopilzfarm (no date) *Biopilze Berlin,* Available online: <http://www.biopilze-berlin.de/konzept_philosophie.html> (accessed 16 May 2012). **> 92–99**

● Blachman, E. (ed) (2010) *Agency Rules: Parks and recreation,* in: *The City Record: Official journal of The City of New York,* vol. CXXXVII, no. 176, 13 Sep 2010, Available online: <http://www.nyc.gov/html/dcas/downloads/pdf/cityrecord/cityrecord-9-13-10.pdf> (accessed 16 May 2012). **> 138–145**

● Blay-Palmer, A. (2009) *The Canadian Pioneer: The genesis of urban food policy in Toronto,* in: *International Planning Studies,* vol. 14/4, pp. 401–416. **> 18–23**

● Bohn, K. and Tomkins, M. (2009) *Keep on the grass: The idea of 'Embodied Desire' in the establishment of Continuous Productive Urban Landscapes,* paper at: *CAPPE's 4th Annual Conference 'The Politics of Space and Place',* Brighton: University of Brighton. **> 252–255**

● Bohn, K. and Viljoen, A. (2001) *Response to Theme 4: Synthesis and shape: Designs on the city,* in: Hewitt, M. and Hagan, S. (eds) (2001) *City Fights: Debates on urban sustainability,* London: James and James, pp. 112–121. **> 60–67**

● Bohn, K. and Viljoen, A. (2005) *More city with less space,* in: Viljoen, A. (ed) (2005) *Continuous Productive Urban Landscapes: Designing urban agriculture for sustainable cities,* Oxford: Architectural Press, pp. 251–264. **> 122–129**

● Bohn, K. and Viljoen, A. (2010a) *Continuous Productive Urban Landscape (CPUL): Designing essential infrastructure,* in: *Landscape Architecture China,* vol. 9, no. 1, pp. 24–30. **> 12–17**

● Bohn, K. and Viljoen, A. (2010b) *The CPUL City Toolkit: Planning productive urban landscapes for European cities* in: Viljoen, A. and Wiskerke J. (eds) (2012) *Sustainable Food Planning: Evolving theory and practice,* Wageningen: Wageningen Academic Press. **> 155–161**

● BÖLW Bund Ökologische Lebensmittelwirtschaft (2012) *Zahlen – Daten – Fakten: Die Bio-Branche 2012,* Available online: <http://www.boelw.de/uploads/pics/ZDF/ZDF_Endversion_120110.pdf> (accessed 16 May 2012). **> 92–99**

● Bonaiuti, M. (ed) (2011) *From Bioeconomics to Degrowth: Georgescu-Roegen's 'New Economics' in eight essays,* London: Routledge. **> 48–53**

● Boomgaarden, H. (no date) *Die grüne Stadt Andernach,* Available online: <http://www.heike-boomgaarden.de/projekte/projekt-andernach-unsere-stadt-blueht-auf/index.php> (accessed 16 May 2012). **> 92–99**

● Borasi, G. and Zardini, M. (eds) (2008) *Actions: What you can do with the city,*

Amsterdam: Sun Publishers.
> 12–17

● BOST (2011) *Bankside Open Space Trust*, Available online: <http://www.bost.org.uk> (accessed 18 Oct 2011). **> 155–161**

● Bradbear, N. (2003) *Beekeeping and sustainable livelihoods*, Rome: Agricultural Support Systems Division, Food and Agriculture Organization of the United Nations. **> 84–91**

● Brand, S. (ed) (1968–1972) *Whole Earth Catalog*, Menlo Park CA: Portola Institute. **> 108–113**

● Brand, S. (ed) (no date) *Whole Earth Catalog: Access to Tools and Ideas*, Available online: <http://www.wholeearth.com> (accessed 7 Jun 2012). **> 108–113**

● Braungart, M. and McDonough, W. (2002) *Cradle to Cradle: Remaking the way we make things*, New York: North Point Press. **> 60–67**

● Breeze, T.D., Roberts, S. and Potts, S.G. (2012) *The decline of England's bees*, Reading: University of Reading. **> 84–91**

● Briar, S.S., Miller, S.A., Stinner, D. and Kleinhenz, M.D. (2011) *Effects of organic transition strategies for peri-urban vegetable production on soil properties, nematode community and tomato yield*, in: *Applied Soil Ecology*, vol. 47(2), pp. 84–91. **> 240–243**

● Bright Farms (no date) *Healthy people – healthy community – healthy planet*, Available online: <http://www.brightfarms.com> (accessed 16 May 2012). **> 24–31**

● Bristol Food Network (2010) *Bristol local food update*, Available online: <http://www.bristolfoodnetwork.org/about> (accessed 16 May 2012). **> 6–11**

● The Brixton Pound (no date) *Key Facts*, Available online: <http://brixton-pound.org/about/keyfacts> (accessed 4 Nov 2012). **> 100–107**

● Broder, J. (2011) *Eastern Market heats up*, in: *The Metro Times*, issue Jun 15 2011, Available online: <http://www.detroiteasternmarket.com/news_page.php?id=131&p=7&s=> (accessed 17 Sep 2011). **> 130–137**

● Brodowin Ökodorf (2011) *2. Platz beim DKB-Landwirtschaftspreis 2011*, Available online: <http://www.brodowin.de/__dkb_landwirtschaftspreis_2011.html#.UjwDa389XQ8> (accessed 16 May 2012). **> 92–99**

● Brodowin Ökodorf (no date) *Unser Betrieb*, Available online: <http://www.brodowin.de/__unser_betrieb.html#.UjwGzX89XQ8> (accessed 16 May 2012). **> 92–99**

● Brooklyn Grange (2012) *About our farm*, Available online: <http://www.brooklyngrangefarm.com/ aboutthegrange> (accessed 6 Oct 2012). **> 24–31, 122–129, 138–145**

● Brown, J. (2010) *Growing Communities: Manifesto for feeding the city: Taking our food system back*, Available online: <http://www.transitiontownbrixton.org/wordpress/wp-content/uploads/2010/01/manifesto.pdf> (accessed 16 May 2012). **> 240–243**

● Brückenschlag e.V. (no date) *Bunte Gärten Leipzig: Die Gärtnerei*, Available online: <http://www.bunte-gaerten.de/gaert.html> (accessed 16 May 2012). **> 92–99**

● Brunori, G. and Rossi, A. (2000) *Synergy and coherence through collective action: Some insights from wine routes in Tuscany*, in: *Sociologia Ruralis*, vol. 40(4), pp. 409–423. **> 244–251**

Brunori, G., Rossi, A. and Guidi, F. (2012) *On the new social relations around and beyond food: Analysing consumers' role and action in Gruppi di Acquisto Solidale (Solidarity Purchasing Groups)*, in: *Sociologia Ruralis*, vol. 52(1), pp. 1–30. **> 244–251**

● Buck, C. (2009) *Invisible Food*, Available online: <http://www.artangel.org.uk//projects/2008/taz/invisible_food/invisible_food (accessed 4 Nov 2012). **> 100–107**

The Building Centre (2009) *London Yields: Urban Agriculture*, Available online: <http://www.buildingcentre. co.uk/urbanagriculture.html> (accessed 16 May 2012). **> 12–17**

Bürger für Leipzig Stiftung (no date) *Flächen für Leipzig*, Available online: <http://www.flaechen-in-leipzig.de/brachen/index.asp> (accessed 16 May 2012). **> 92–99**

● Campbell, L. and Wiesen, A. (eds) (2009) *Restorative Commons: Creating health and well-being through urban landscapes*, Newtown Square PA: U.S. Department of Agriculture Forest Service. **> 12–17, 40–47, 122–129, 146–153**

● Canning, P., Charles, A., Huang, S., Polenske, K.R. and Waters, A. (2010) *Energy use in the U.S. food system*, Economic Research Report no. 94, Washington: United States Department of Agriculture, Economic Research Service. **> 60–67**

● Cantliffe, D.J., Secker, I. and Karchi, Z. (2001) *Passive ventilated high-roof greenhouse production of vegetables in a humid, mild winter climate*, in: *Acta Horticulturae*, pp. 195–201. **> 240–243**

● Capital Growth (no date a) *Capital Growth Space Finder*, Available online: <http://www.capitalgrowth.org/spaces> (accessed 16 May 2012). **> 155–161**

● Capital Growth (no date b) *London's food growing network*, Available online: <http://www.capitalgrowth.org/big_idea> (accessed 4 Oct 2011). **> 24–31, 108–113, 155–161**

Capital Growth (no date c) *Frequently Asked Questions*, Available online: <http://www.capitalgrowth.org/big_idea/faqs/ (accessed 4 Nov 2012). **> 100–107**

Carbon Trust (2006) *The carbon emissions generated in all that we consume,* London: The Carbon Trust. **> 60–67**

Carey, J. (2011) *Who Feeds Bristol?: Towards a resilient food plan*, Bristol: Bristol City Council. **> 18–23**

Caridad Cruz, M. and Sánchez Medina, R. (2003) *Agriculture in the city: A key to sustainability in Havana, Cuba*, Kingston JAM: Ian Randle Publishers and International Development Research Centre. **> 12–17, 60–67**

Carrot City Ryerson (2012a) *Rooftop Gardens at Fairmont Hotels*, Available online: <http://www.ryerson.ca/carrotcity/board_pages/rooftops/fairmont.html> (accessed 16 May 2012). **> 24–31**

Carrot City Ryerson (2012b) *Mole Hill Community Garden*, Available online: <http://www.ryerson.ca/carrotcity/board_pages/housing/mole_hill.html> (accessed 16 May 2012). **> 24–31**

Carrot City Ryerson (2012c) *Southeast False Creek*, Available online: <http://www.ryerson.ca/carrotcity/board_pages/city/SEFC.html> (accessed 16 May 2012). **> 24–31**

Carter, C. (2011) *Global warming potential of produce grown on an allotment using a life cycle assessment approach, case study: Wellesbourne Allotment*, MSc Thesis, Guildford: University of Surrey. **> 76–83**

Cassman, K.G. (1999) *Ecological intensification of cereal production systems: Yield potential, soil quality, and precision agriculture*, in: *Proceedings of the National Academy of Sciences of the USA*, vol. 96(11), pp. 5952–5959. **> 60–67**

Castoriadis, C. (1991) *Philosophy, Politics, Autonomy: Essays in political philosophy*, Oxford: Oxford University Press. **> 48–53**

Cather, A. (2003) *Urban Grower's Manual*, Available online: <http://thefoodproject.org/sites/default/files/FoodProject_UrbanAgManual.pdf> (accessed 16 May 2012). **> 155–161**

CertCost (2009) *The Organic Rules and Certification database*, Available online: <http://organicrules.org/information.html> (accessed 16 May 2012). **> 68–75**

CGR Carrot Green Roof (no date) *Grow Together at the CGR!*, Available online: <http://carrotgreenroof.wordpress.com/about> (accessed 16 May 2012). **> 24–31**

Chiffoleau, Y. (2009) *From Politics to Co-operation: The dynamics of embeddedness in alternative food supply chains*, in: *Sociologia Ruralis,* vol. 49(3), pp. 218–235. **> 244–251**

Chossudovsky, M. (1997) *Globalisation of poverty, impacts of IMF and World Bank Reforms*, London: Zed Books. **> 146–153**

City Farmer (no date) *Urban Agriculture Notes*, Available online: <http://www.cityfarmer.org> (accessed 16 May 2012). **> 6–11, 12–17**

CKC Cultivate Kansas City (2011) *Urban Agriculture and Urban Planning & Design*, Available online: <http://www.cultivatekc.org/community/planning-design.html> (accessed 11 May 2011). **> 12–17**

Clausen, M. and Müller-Frank, S. (2012) *Prinzessinengärten: Anders gärtnern in der Stadt*, Köln: DuMont Buchverlag. **> 32–39**

Cohen, N. and Ackerman, K. (2011) *Breaking New Ground*, in: *The New York Times, The Opinion Pages, Mark Bittman Blog*, Available online: <http://bittman.blogs.nytimes.com/2011/11/21/breaking-new-ground> (accessed 24 Mar 2012). **> 138–145**

Cohen, N. and Reynolds, K. (2012) *Policy and research networks and collaborations to strengthen Urban Agriculture in New York City*, paper presented at: *Agriculture in an Urbanizing Society* conference April 2012, Wageningen: Wageningen University. **> 138–145**

Cohen, N., Reynolds, K. and Sanghvi, R. (2012) *Five Borough Farm: Seeding the future of Urban Agriculture in New York City*, New York: Design Trust for Public Space. **> 138–145**

Colasanti, K.J.A. and Hamm, M.W. (2010) *Assessing the local food supply capacity of Detroit, Michigan*, in: *Journal of Agriculture, Food Systems, and Community Development*, 1(2). **> 138–145**

Colding, J. (2007) 'Ecological land-use complementation' for building resilience in urban ecosystems, in: *Landscape and Urban Planning*, no. 81, pp. 46–55. **> 84–91**

Corelli Academy (2011) *The Corelli Bee Colony*, Available online: <http://corellifarmacademy.blogspot.co.uk/2012/05/corelli-bee-colony.html> (accessed 1 Aug 2012). **> 84–91**

COST and European Science Foundation (no date) *COST Action Urban Agriculture Europe*, Available online: <http://www.urbanagricultureeurope.la.rwth-aachen.de> (accessed 16 May 2012). **> 92–99**

COT Committee on Toxicity (2004) *Fish consumption in the UK (Annex 1)*, Available online: <http://cot.food.gov.uk/pdfs/fishreport200404.pdf> (accessed 16 May 2012). **> 240–243**

Crouch, D. and Ward, C. (1998) *The Allotment*, London: Faber and Faber. **> 60–67**

Dahlberg, K.A. (2002) *What are Local Food Systems?*, Available online: <http://homepages.wmich.edu/~dahlberg/F14.pdf>, in: Clancy, K., Wilson, R.L. and O'Donnell, J. (2002) *Strategies, policy approaches, and resources for local food system planning and organizing: a resource guide*, Available online: <http://homepages.wmich.edu/~dahlberg/Resource-Guide.html> (accessed 16 May 2012). **> 6–11**

Dahlberg, K.A. and Koc, M. (1999) *The restructuring of food systems: Trends, research, and policy issues*, in: *Agriculture and Human Values*, vol. 16(2), pp. 109–116, Available online: <http://link.springer.com/article/10.1023%2FA%3A1007541226426> (accessed 16 May 2012). **> 6–11**

Dahlberg, K.A., Clancy, K., Wilson, R.L. and O'Donnell, J. (1997) *Strategies, Policy approaches, and Resources for local food system planning and organizing: A Resource Guide*, Available online: <http://homepages.wmich.edu/~dahlberg/Resource-Guide.html> (accessed 16 May 2012). **> 6–11**

● Daniels (no date) *One Park Place*, Available online: <http://www.danielshomes.ca/images/news/oneparkplace.pdf> (accessed 16 May 2012). **> 24–31**

● Davis, M. (2006) *Planet of Slums*, London and New York: Verso. **> 146–153**

● Deacon, T.W. (1997) *The Symbolic Species: The co-evolution of language and the brain*, New York: Norton. **> 48–53**

● Defra (2008) *Risks to honeybees from home-garden use of pesticides*, York: HM Government, Department for Environment, Food and Rural Affairs. **> 84–91**

Defra (2010a) *Food 2030*, London: HM Government, Department for Environment, Food and Rural Affairs, pp. 81. **> 60–67**

● Defra Department for Environment, Food and Rural Affairs (2010b) *Produce Importing Practices*, Available online: <http://ww2.defra.gov.uk/food-farm/crops> (accessed 16 May 2012). **> 76–83**

● Defra (2011a) *Purchased quantities of household food and drink by Government Office Region and Country*, in: *Living Costs and Food Survey, updated: 12/13/2011*, London: Food Statistics Branch, HM Government, Department for Environment, Food and Rural Affairs, Available online: <http://www.defra.gov.uk/statistics/foodfarm/food/familyfood/datasets/> (accessed 16 May 2012). **> 76–83**

Defra (2011b) *The Natural Choice: Securing the value of nature*, London: HM Government, Department for Environment, Food and Rural Affairs. **> 60–67**

● Defra (2011c) *UK National Ecosystem Assessment*, London: HM Government, Department for Environment, Food and Rural Affairs. **> 84–91**

● Delaplane, K.S. and Mayer, D.F. (2000) *Crop pollination by bees*, Wallingford: CABI Publication. **> 84–91**

● Denny, G. (2012) *Reducing fresh produce CO_2 emissions through urban agriculture, seasonality, and procurement dependency: life cycle analysis for tomato, potato, and apple consumption in East Anglia and Greater London*, PhD Thesis, Cambridge: University of Cambridge. **> 76–83**

Derkzen, P. and Morgan, K. (2012) *Food and the City: The challenge of urban food governance*, in Viljoen, A. and Wiskerke, J. (eds) *Sustainable Food Planning: Evolving theory and practice*, Wageningen: Wageningen Academic Publishers. **> 18–23**

● Design Council (2008) *Dott07: Urban Farming*, Available online: <http://www.designcouncil.org.uk/Case-studies/Urban-Farming> (accessed 16 May 2012). **> 12–17**

Despommier, D. (2010) *The vertical farm: Feeding the world in the 21st century*, New York: St Martin's Press. **> 12–17, 24–31, 122–129**

DETR, Vale, R. and Vale, B. (1998) *Building a Sustainable Future: Homes for an Autonomous Community*, General Information Report no. 53, London: Department of the Environment, Transport and the Regions, BRECSU. **> 60–67**

Detroit Works Project (no date) *Long-term Planning: Planning for a Future City*, Available online: <http://detroitworksproject.com/about-us-2> (accessed 16 May 2012). **> 6–11, 138–145**

Devereux, C. (2012) *Urban Food Policies*, keynote speech at: *4th AESOP Sustainable Food Planning Conference Berlin 2012*. **> 6–11**

DFC Detroit Future City (2013) *The Land Use Element: The image of the city*, Available online: <http://detroitworksproject.com/wp-content/uploads/2013/01/DFC_Plan_Land-Use.pdf> (accessed 8 Feb 2013). **> 138–145**

● DfT Department for Transport (2002) *Transport Statistics Great Britain*, London: Department for Transport. **> 76–83**

● Domäne Dahlem Stiftung (no date) *Domäne Dahlem: Landgut und Museum*, Available online: <http://www.domaene-dahlem.de/> (accessed 16 May 2012). **> 92–99**

● Druckman, A. and Jackson, T. (2010) *Mapping our carbon responsibilities: More key results from the Survey of environmental lifestyle mapping (selma) framework*, RESOLVE Working Paper no. 02-09, Guildford: Research Group on Lifestyles, Values and the Environment, Centre for Environmental Strategy, University of Surrey. **> 60–67**

Duany, A. and Duany Plater-Zyberk & Co. (2011) *Garden Cities: Theory and practice of Agrarian Urbanism*, London: The Princes Foundation for the Built Environment. > **24–31**

Dubbeling, M. (2011) *Agromere: Integrating urban agriculture in the urban landscape*, in: *Urban Agriculture Magazine*, no. 25, pp. 43–46. > **32–39**

Dyke, C. (1988) *The evolutionary dynamics of complex systems: A study in biosocial complexity*, New York: Oxford University Press. > **48–53**

Eagle Street Rooftop Farm (no date) *About*, Available online: <http://rooftopfarms.org> (accessed 16 May 2012). > **24–31, 122–129, 138–145**

ECF Efficient City Farming GmbH (no date a) *EFC Cityfarm*, Available online: <http://www.ecf-center.de/en/ecf-cityfarm> (accessed 11 Jun 2012). > **40–47**

ECF Efficient City Farming GmbH (no date b) *Planung und Bau von Aquaponik-Farm-Systemen zur Gemüse- und Fischproduktion*, Available online: <http://www.ecf-center.de/en/> (accessed 16 May 2012). > **92–99**

EFCF European Federation of City Farms (no date) *A network of city farms*, Available online: <http://www.cityfarms.org> (accessed 16 May 2012). > **146–153**

Egziabher, A., Lee-Smith, D., Maxwell, D., Mernon, P., Mougeot, L. and Sawio, C.

(1994) *Cities Feeding People: An examination of urban agriculture in East Africa*, Ottawa: International Development Research Centre. > **12–17**

Ehrig, C. (1992) *Eignung von Laubkompost als Mittel zur Bodenverbesserung auf landwirtschaftlichen Flächen*, in: *Bodenökologie & Bodengenese*, no. 5, pp. 1–219. > **68–75**

Eli Zabar (no date) *New York's neighbourhood grocer, baker, caterer*, Available online: <http://www.elizabar.com> (accessed 16 May 2012). > **40–47, 138–145**

The European Commission (2011) *Our life insurance, our natural capital: An EU biodiversity strategy to 2020*, Brussels: The European Commission. > **60–67**

Exit Art (2009) *Vertical Gardens*, Available online: <http://www.exitart.org/sea/vertical_gardens.html> (accessed 16 May 2012). > **12–17, 155–161**

Eyck, A. van (1962) *The Child, the City and the Artist: An essay on architecture; the in-between realm*, Amsterdam: SUN Publishers, pp. 90–93. > **122–129**

FAD Fisheries and Aquaculture Department (2012) *Cultured Aquatic Species Information Programme*, Available online: <http://www.fao.org/fishery/culturedspecies/Cyprinus_carpio/en> (accessed 13 Apr 2012). > **240–243**

FAO Food and Agriculture Organization of the United

Nations (2011) *Food, Agriculture and Cities*, Rome: FAO. > **18–23**

Farming Concrete (2012) *Farming concrete: Reports*, Available online: <http://farmingconcrete.org> (accessed 16 May 2012). > **40–47**

Farming Concrete (no date) *About*, Available online: <http://farmingconcrete.org/about> (accessed 16 May 2012). > **138–145**

FCFCG The Federation of City Farms and Community Gardens (no date) *About City Farms and Community Gardens*, Available online: <http://www.farmgarden.org.uk/farms-gardens> (accessed 16 May 2012). > **32–29**

Feierstein, M. (2012) *Planet Ponzi*, London: Bantam Press. > **48–53**

Ferguson, S. (1999) *A brief history of grassroots greening on the Lower East Side*, in: Lamborn Wilson, P. and Weinberg, B. (eds) (1999) *Avant Gardening: Ecological struggle in the city and the world*, Brooklyn NY: Autonomedia, pp. 80–90. > **146–153**

FGCAT Fortis Green Community Allotments Trust (2010) *Fortis Green Allotments*, Available online:<http://www.fortisgreenallotments.co.uk> (accessed 16 May 2012). > **155–161**

Finster, M.E., Gray, K.A. and Binns, H.J. (2004) *Lead levels of edibles grown in contaminated residential soils: A*

field survey, in: *Science of the Total Environment*, no. 320, pp. 245–257. > **68–75**

FLL Forschungsgesellschaft Landschaftsentwicklung Landschaftsbau e.V. (2008) *Dachbegrünungsrichtlinie*, Tab. 3. Percentage of water retention in relation to depth of substrate, Bonn: FLL. > **68–75**

FoE Friends of the Earth (2012) *The Bee Cause*, Available online: <http://www.foe.co.uk/what_we_do/the_bee_cause_35033.html> (accessed 9 Aug 2012). > **84–91**

FÖL Fördergemeinschaft Ökologischer Landbau Berlin-Brandenburg e.V. (no date) *Abokisten*, Available online: <http://www.bio-berlin-brandenburg.de/nc/bioadressen/?tx_bioekfonline_pi1[category]=abokisten> (accessed 16 May 2012). > **92–99**

FoodShare Toronto (no date) *FoodShare: Good Healthy Food for All!*, Available online: <http://www.foodshare.net/about-us> (accessed 16 May 2012). > **257–259**

Freibauer, A., Rounsevell, M.D.A., Smith, P. and Verhagen, J. (2004) *Carbon sequestration in the agricultural soils of Europe*, in: *Geoderma*, vol. 122, pp. 1–23. > **60–67**

Gallagher, J. (2010) *Reimagining Detroit: Opportunities for redefining an American city*, Detroit: Wayne State University Press. > **130–137, 155–161**

Garnett, T. (2008) *Cooking up a Storm: Food, Greenhouse Gas Emissions and our Changing Climate*, Guildford: Food Climate Research Network, Centre for Environmental Strategy, University of Surrey. **> 76–83**

Geels, F.W. (2002) *Technological transitions as evolutionary reconfiguration processes: A multi-level perspective and a case-study*, in: *Research Policy*, vol. 31(8), pp. 1257–1274. **> 244–251**

Georgescu-Roegen, N. (1971) *The entropy law and the economic process*, Cambridge MA: Harvard University Press. **> 48–53**

Giampietro, M. and Mayumi, K. (2009) *The Biofuel Delusion: The fallacy of large-scale agro-biofuel production*, London: Earthscan. **> 48–53**

Gittleman, M., Librizzi, L. and Stone, E. (2010) *Community Garden Survey New York City: Results 2009/2010*, Available online: <http://www.greenthumbnyc.org/pdf/GrowNYC_community_garden_report.pdf> (accessed 16 Nov 2012). **> 146–153**

Global Generation (2012) *There's been a lot of buzz about our Honey Club!*, Available online: <http://www.globalgeneration.org.uk> (accessed 1 Aug 2012). **> 84–91**

Goodbun, J. (2011) *The Production of Value*, in: *SCIBE Working Paper 2*, Available online: <http://www.scibe.eu/publications> (accessed 7 Jun 2012). **> 108–113**

Goodbun, J., Till, J. and Iossifova, D. (2012) *Themes of Scarcity*, in: Goodbun, J., Till, J. and Iossifova, D. (eds) (2012) *Architectural Design: Scarcity: Architecture in an age of depleting resources*, London: John Wiley & Sons. **> 12–17**

Goodman, D., Goodman, M. and DuPuis, M. (2011) *Alternative food networks: Knowledge, place and politics*, London: Sage. **> 244–251**

Gorgolewski, M., Komisar, J. and Nasr, J. (2010) *Carrot City: Designing for Urban Agriculture*, Available online: <http://www.carrotcity.org> (accessed 20 Jan 2012). **> 24–31**

Gorgolewski, M., Komisar, J. and Nasr, J. (2011) *Carrot City: Creating places for Urban Agriculture*, New York: Monacelli Press. **> 12–17, 24–31, 40–47, 155–161**

Gotham Greens Farms LLC (no date a) *Gotham Greens: Local Produce*, Available online: <http://gothamgreens.com> (accessed 16 May 2012). **> 24–31**

Gotham Greens Farms LLC (no date b) *Our Approach to Sustainable Agriculture*, Available online: <http://gothamgreens.com/our-farm> (accessed 2 Jul 2012). **> 40–47**

Graaf, P.A. de (2012) *Room for urban agriculture in Rotterdam: Defining the spatial opportunities for urban agriculture within the industrialised city*, in: Viljoen, A. and Wiskerke, S.C. (eds) *Sustainable Food Planning: Evolving theory and practice*, Wageningen: Wageningen Academic Publishers, pp. 533–546. **> 40–47**

Graber, A. and Junge, R. (2009) *Aquaponic Systems: Nutrient recycling from fish wastewater*, in: *Desalination*, vol. 246, pp. 147–156. **> 240–243**

Grafenstein, M. von (no date) *Bauerngarten: Wir pflanzen – Sie ernten*, Available online: <http://www.bauerngarten.net> (accessed 16 May 2012). **> 92–99, 155–161**

GreenHomeNYC (no date) *Arbor House*, Available online: <http://greenhomenyc.org/building/arbor-house> (accessed 16 May 2012). **> 138–145**

Greenmuseum.org (2010) *Agnes Denes*, Available online: <http://greenmuseum.org/content/artist_index/artist_id-63.html> (accessed 12 Nov 2012). **> 122–129**

The Green Social Network (2009) *Project Dirt: Blenheim Gardens Edible Estate*, Available online: <http://www.projectdirt.com/project/7145/> (accessed 4 Nov 2012). **> 100–107**

Gröning, G. (1997) *Zur Entwicklung der urbanen Gartenkultur in Nordamerika: Ein Bericht über die 17. Tagung der American Community Gardening Association (ACGA)*, in: *Stadt und Grün*, vol. 46(8), pp. 563–572. **> 146–153**

Gröning, G. (2002) *Gemeinschaftsgärten in Nordamerika*, in: Meyer-Renschhausen, E., Müller R. and Becker, P. (eds) (2002) *Die Gärten der Frauen: Zur sozialen Bedeutung von Kleinstlandwirtschaft in Stadt und Land weltweit*, Herbolzheim: Centaurus, pp. 298–312. **> 146–153**

Gröning, G. and Wolschke-Bulmahn, J. (1995) *Von Ackermann bis Ziegelhütte: Ein Jahrhundert Kleingartenkultur in Frankfurt am Main*, Frankfurt a. M.: Frankfurter Verein für Geschichte und Landeskunde. **> 146–153**

grow to learn nyc (no date) *Registered School Gardens*, Available online: <http://www.growtolearn.org/view/RegisteredSchoolGardens> (accessed 16 May 2012). **> 138–145**

Growing Communities (2008) *Transforming food and farming through community-led trade*, Available online: <http://www.growingcommunities.org> (accessed 16 May 2012). **> 155–161**

Growing Communities (2009) *Annual Report 2008/9*, Available online: <http://www.growingcommunities.org> (accessed 16 May 2012). **> 40–47**

Growing Communities (no date a) *Our market gardens*, Available online: <http://www.growingcommunities.org/food-growing/market-gardens> (accessed 14 Apr 2012). **> 40–47**

Growing Communities (no date b) *Explore the Food Zones: Growing communities'* food zones towards a sustainable and resilient food & farming system, Available online: <http://www.growingcommunities.org/start-ups/what-is-gc/manifesto-feeding-cities/explore-food-zones> (accessed 2 Jul 2012). > **40–47**

● Growing Power, Inc. (2011) *Growing Power, Inc.*, Available online: <http://www.growingpower.org/index.htm> (accessed 14 Apr 2012). > **155–161, 240–243**

● Growing Power, Inc. (no date a) *Our Community Food Center,* Available online: <http://www.growingpower.org/headquarters.htm> (accessed 14 Apr 2012). > **68–75**

● Growing Power, Inc. (no date b) *Our history,* Available online: <http://www.growingpower.org/our_history.htm> (accessed 14 Apr 2012). > **40–47**

● GrowNYC (no date) *Garden – Teach – Recycle – Greenmarket,* Available online: <http://www.grownyc.org/about> (accessed 16 May 2012). > **138–145**

● Grünsteidel, I. (2000) *Community Gardens - Grüne Oasen in den Ghettos von New York,* in: Meyer-Renschhausen, E. and Holl, A. (eds) (2000) *Die Wiederkehr der Gärten: Kleinlandwirtschaft im Zeitalter der Globalisierung,* Innsbruck: Studienverlag, pp. 125–139. > **146–153**

● Grünsteidel, I. and Schneider-Sliwa, R. (1999)

Community Garden Bewegung in New York City, in: *Geographische Rundschau,* vol. 51(4), pp. 203–209. > **146–153**

○ Gussow, J.D. (1991) *Chicken Little, Tomato Sauce and Agriculture: Who will produce tomorrow's food?,* New York: The Bootstrap Press. > **60–67**

● Guyer, J.I. (2010) *Introduction: Number as Inventive Frontier,* in: *Anthropological Theory,* no. 10, pp. 36–61. > **108–113**

● Haeg, F. (2010) *Edible estates: Attack on the front lawn,* 2nd expanded edition, New York: Metropolis Books. > **100–107**

● Haeg, F. and Au, M. (2007) *Olympic Farming 2012,* Available online: <http://www.fritzhaeg.com/garden/initiatives/edibleestates/olympic-farming.html> (accessed 04 Aug 2012). > **24–31**

● Haide, E. von der (2012) *Urbane Gärten in München,* Available online: <http://maps.muenchen.de/rgu/urbane_gaerten> (accessed 16 May 2012). > **92–99**

● Haila, Y. (2012) *Genealogy of nature conservation: A political perspective,* in: *Nature Conservation,* vol. 1(1), pp. 27–52. > **48–53**

● Haila, Y. and Dyke, C. (2006) *What to say about Nature's 'Speech'?,* in: Haila, Y. and Dyke, C. (eds) *How nature speaks: The dynamics of the human ecological condition,* Durham NC: Duke University Press, pp. 1–48. > **48–53**

● Haney, D. (2010) *When Modern was Green: Life and work of landscape architect Leberecht Migge,* Abingdon Oxfordshire: Routledge. > **60–67, 92–99**

● Hantz Farms (2011) *Hantz Farms,* Available online: <http://www.hantzfarmsdetroit.com> (accessed 16 May 2012). > **155–161**

● Hardt, M. and Negri, A. (2009) *Common Wealth,* Cambridge MA: Belknap Press. > **108–113**

● Harper, D. (2001–2012) *'To produce': Online Etymology Dictionary,* Available online: <http://www.etymonline.com> (accessed 7 Jun 2012). > **108–113**

○ Hartling, E. and Urban Partners (2007) *Farming in Philadelphia: Feasibility Analysis and Next Steps,* Philadelphia: Institute for Innovations in Local Farming. > **155–161**

● Hartmann, K. (1998) *Gartenstadtbewegung,* in: Krebs, D. and Reulecke, J. (1998) *Handbuch der deutschen Reformbewegungen,* Wuppertal: Peter Hammer Verlag, pp. 289–300. > **146–153**

● Häußermann, H. and Siebel, W. (eds) (1993) *New York: Strukturen einer Metropole,* Frankfurt a. M.: Suhrkamp. > **146–153**

● Haygrove Ltd (2012) *Haygrove: Polytunnels for Gardeners,* Online: <http://www.gardentunnels.co.uk> (accessed 30 Jan 2012). > **240–243**

● Heaf, D. (2011) *Bee-friendly Beekeeper,* Reprint 2011 edition, Hohenwarsleben GER: NBB. > **84–91**

○ Hennecke, S. (ed) (2012) *Die Produktive Stadt: Katalog zur Ausstellung,* München: Technische Universität München. > **92–99**

● Hernandez, J.L., Frankie, G.W. and Thorp, R.W. (2009) *Ecology of Urban Bees: A review of current knowledge and directions for future study,* in: *Cities and the Environment,* no. 2, pp. 3–15. > **84–91**

○ Hester, R.T. (2006) *Design for ecological democracy,* Cambridge MA: The MIT Press. > **60–67**

○ HM Government (2006) *Climate change, the UK programme,* London: HM Government. > **76–83**

○ Hodgson, K., Caton Campbell, M. and Bailkey, M. (2011) *Urban agriculture: Growing healthy, sustainable places,* Planning Advisory Service Report no. 563, Chicago: American Planning Association. > **12–17, 138–145**

● Hopkins, R. (2006) *Review of CPULs – Continuous Productive Urban Landscapes,* Available online: <http://transitionculture.org/essential-info/book-reviews/cpuls> (accessed 12 Jan 2011). > **12–17**

● Hopkins, R. (2008) *The Transition Handbook: From Oil Dependency to Local Resilience,* Vermont: Chelsea Green Publishing. > **6–11**

Howard, E. (1902) *Garden Cities of To-Morrow*, 2nd edition, London: S. Sonnenschein & Co. > **24–31, 146–153**

HUB Humboldt Universität Berlin (2000) *Grüne Lungen für die Stadt*, Available online: <http://www2. hu-berlin.de/presse/zeitung/ archiv/00_01/num_2/14. html> (accessed 16 May 2012). > **92–99**

Hughes, C. (2010) *Urban beekeeping*, Preston: The Good Life Press Ltd. > **84–91**

Hynes, P. (1996) *A Patch of Eden: America's inner-city gardeners*, Vermont: Chelsea Green Publishing Company. > **146–153**

IFZS Initiative für Zeitgenössische Stadtentwicklung (no date) *Garten Annalinde*, Available online: <http://ifzs.de/annalinde> (accessed 16 May 2012). > **92–99**

IGG Internationale Gärten Göttingen (no date) *Internationale Gärten e.V. Göttingen*, Available online: <http://www.internationale-gaerten.de> (accessed 16 May 2012). > **92–99**

Ilbery, B. and Maye, D. (2005) *Food supply chains and sustainability: Evidence from specialist food producers in the Scottish/English borders*, in: *Land Use Policy*, vol. 22(4), pp. 331–344. > **244–251**

In Vitro Report (2008) *Commercial Aeroponics: The Grow Anywhere story*, in: *Research News: In Vitro Report – An Official Publication of the Society In Vitro Biology*, vol. 42(2), April–June 2008, Available online: <http://www.sivb. org/InVitroReport/42-2/ research.htm> (accessed 16 May 2012). > **76–83**

ISHS International Society for Horticultural Science (no date) *The world's leading independent organization of horticultural scientists*, Available online: <http://www. ishs.org> (accessed 16 May 2012). > **6–11**

James, P.T., Leach, R., Kalamara, E. and Shayeghi, M. (2001) *The Worldwide Obesity Epidemic*, in: *Obesity Research*, no. 9, pp. s228–s233. > **108–113**

Janik, E. (2009–2010) *Food will win the war: Food conservation in World War I Wisconsin*, in: *Wisconsin Magazine of History*, vol. 93(3). > **24–31**

Jansma, J. E. und Visser, A.J. (2011) *Agromere: Integrating urban agriculture in the development of the city of Almere*, in: *Urban Agriculture Magazine*, no. 25, pp. 28–31. > **12–17, 32–39**

Janun Göttingen e.V. (no date) *Göttinger Nährboden: Urbane Gärten in Göttingen*, Available online: <http://www.naehrboden-goettingen.de> (accessed 16 Dec 2012). > **92–99**

Jones, R. (2004) *European beekeeping in the 21st century: Strengths, weaknesses, opportunities, threats*, in: *Bee World*, no. 85, pp. 77–88. > **84–91**

Just Food (2010) *Food Justice: Legalize Beekeeping in NYC!*, Available online: <http://justfood. org/food-justice/food-justice-archive#beekeeping> (accessed 16 May 2012). > **138–145**

Kalish, J. (2011) *Farming Detroit*, in: *Make Magazine*, blog, 9 Oct 2011, Available online: <http:// blog.makezine.com/ archive/2011/09/farming-detroit.html> (accessed 25 Oct 2011). > **130–137**

Kampffmeyer, H. (1913) *Die Gartenstadtbewegung*, Leipzig: Teubner. > **146–153**

Karakatsouli, N., Papoutsoglou, E.S., Sotiropoulos, N., Mourtikas, D., Stigen-Martinsen, T. and Papoutsoglou, S.E. (2010) *Effects of light spectrum, rearing density and light intensity on growth*, in: *Aquacultural Engineering*, vol. 42, pp. 121–127. > **240–243**

Karlsdottir, S., Homme, J. and Bjornsdottir, R. (2012) *Aquaponics – Grønn vekst*, report no. 510–072, Nordisk Atlantsamarbejde (NORA). > **68–75**

Kerkhof, A.C., Benders, R.M.J. and Moll, H.C. (2009) *Determinants of variation in household CO_2 emissions between and within countries*, in: *Energy Policy*, no. 37, pp. 1509–1517. > **60–67**

Klein, A.-M., Vaissiere, B., Cane, J., Steffan-Dewenter, I., Cunningham, S., Kremen, C. and Tscharntke, T. (2007) *Importance of pollinators in changing landscapes for world crops*, in: *Proceedings of the Royal Society B: Biological Sciences*, no. 274, pp. 303–313. > **84–91**

Klein, N. (2008) *The Shock Doctrine: The rise of disaster capitalism*, New York: Metropolitan Books. > **146–153**

Klinger, D. and Naylor, R. (2012) *Searching for Solutions in Aquaculture: Charting a sustainable course*, in: *Annual Review of Environment and Resources*, vol. 37, pp. 247–276. > **68–75**

Koc, M., MacRae, R. Mougeot, L. and Welsh, J. (eds) (1999) *For Hunger-Proof Cities: Sustainable urban food systems*, Toronto: International Development Research Centre. > **12–17**

Koohakan, P., Ikeda, H., Jeanaksorn, T., Tojo, M., Kusakari, S.-I., Okada, K. and Sato, S. (2004) *Evaluation of the indigenous microorganisms*, in: *Scientia Horticulturae*, vol. 101, pp. 179–188. > **240–243**

Kotanyi, C. (2007) *AG Gleisdreieck*, in: AAA Atelier D'Architecture Autogérée (ed) (2007) *Urban Act*, pp. 16–21. > **146–153**

Kramer, K.J., Moll, H.C., Nonhebel, S. and Wilting, H.C. (1999) *Greenhouse gas emissions related to Dutch food consumption*, in: *Energy Policy*, no. 27, pp. 203–206. > **60–67**

Krasny, E. (2012) *Common Ground*, Venice: Biennale Architettura, p. 98. > **146–153**

Krugman, P. (2003) *The Great Unravelling: Losing our way in the new century*, New York: Norton & Company. **> 146–153**

Lamborn Wilson, P. and Weinberg, B. (eds) (1999) *Avant Gardening, Ecological struggle in the city and the world*, Brooklyn NY: Autonomedia. **> 146–153**

Lang, T., Barlin, D. and Caraher, M. (2009) *Food Policy: Integrating health, environment and society*, Oxford: Oxford University Press. **> 18–23**

Latour, B. (1993) *We have never been modern*, Cambridge MA: Harvard University Press. **> 108–113**

Lawton, J.H., Brotherton, P.N.M., Brown, V.K., Elphick, C., Fitter, A.H., Forshaw, J., Haddow, R.W., Hilborne, S., Leafe, R.N., Mace, G.M., Southgate, M.P., Sutherland, W.J., Tew, T.E., Varley, J. and Wynne, G.R. (2010) *Making Space for Nature: A review of England's wildlife sites and ecological network*, Report to DEFRA, York: HM Government, Department for Environment, Food and Rural Affairs. **> 60–67**

Leach, G. (1976) *Energy and Food Production*, Guildford: IPC Science and Technology Press for the International Institute for Environment and Development. **> 60–67**

Lee, H. (2010) *How food secure can British cities become?* in: Viljoen, A. and Wiskerke, J. (eds) (2012)

Sustainable Food Planning: Evolving theory and practice, Wageningen: Wageningen Academic Publishers, pp. 453–466. **> 60–67, 240–243**

Leeds Permaculture Network (no date) *Leeds Permaculture Network*, Available online: <http://www.leedspermaculturenetwork.org> (accessed 16 May 2012). **> 6–11**

Lefebvre, H. (1976) *The Survival of Capitalism: Reproduction of the relations of production*, London: Allison and Busby Ltd. **> x–xi, 68–75**

Levenston, M. (no date) *City Farmer News: New stories from 'Urban Agriculture Notes'*, Available online: <http://www.cityfarmer.info/about/> (accessed 16 May 2012). **> 6–11**

LFM London Farmers' Markets (no date) *Markets*, Available online: <http://www.lfm.org.uk/markets-home> (accessed 16 May 2012). **> 92–99**

Lim, C. and Liu, E. (2010) *Smartcities + eco-warriors*. Oxford: Routledge. **> 12–17**

Linn, K. (1999) *Reclaiming the sacred commons*, in: *New Village*, no. I, p. 45. **> 146–153**

Linn, K. (2007) *Building commons and community*, Oakland Cal: New Village Press. **> 146–153**

LMU Leeds Metropolitan University (no date) *Case Study: TRUG*, Available online: <http://www.

leedsmet.ac.uk/research/alderney-project.htm> (accessed 16 May 2012). **> 6–11**

The London Assembly (2010) *Cultivating the Capital: Food growing and the planning system in London*, London: The London Assembly. **> 6–11, 12–17**

Long, K. (2005) *Muf: A park in the Broadway Estate*, in: *Icon*, Available online: <http://www.iconeye.com/read-previous-issues/icon-022-|-april-2005/muf-|-icon-022-|-april-2005> (accessed 7 Jun 2012). **> 108–113**

Lovelidgge, B. (2011) *Polytunnels and Sundries: Stronger structures*, in: *Horticulture Week*, 2 Dec, pp. 32–36. **> 240–243**

Lufa Farms (no date a) *Ethics and Environment*, Available online: <http://montreal.lufa.com/en/about-the-farm> (accessed 23 May 2012). **> 40–47**

Lufa Farms (no date b) *Fresh – Local – Responsible*, Available online: <www.montreal.lufa.com> (accessed 16 May 2012). **> 24–31**

Lummel, P. (2009) *Domäne Dahlem: Beständig leben*, Available online: http://www.domaene-dahlem.de> (accessed 16 May 2012). **> 155–161**

Lynch, D.H., MacRae, R. and Martin R.C. (2011) *The carbon and global warming potential impacts of organic farming: Does it have a significant role in an*

energy constrained world?*, in: *Sustainability* 2011, no. 3, pp. 322–362, Available online: <http://www.mdpi.com/20711050/3/2/322> (accessed 16 May 2012). **> 76–83**

Madlener, N. (2009) *Grüne Lernorte: Gemeinschaftsgärten in Berlin*, Würzburg: Ergon Verlag. **> 146–153**

Malato, S., Fernandez-Ibanez, P., Maldonado, M.I., Blanco, J. and Gernjak, W. (2009) *Decontamination and disinfection of water by solar photocatalysis*, in: *Catalysis Today*, vol. 147, pp. 1–59. **> 240–243**

Malmö City (2010) *Policy for sustainable development and food*, Malmö: The City of Malmö. **> 18–23**

Marcuse, P. (1998) *Ethnische Enklaven und rassische Ghettos in der postfordistischen Stadt*, in: Heitmeyer, W., Dollase, R. and Backes, O. (eds) (1998) *Die Krise der Städte*, Frankfurt a. M.: Suhrkamp, pp. 176–193. **> 146–153**

Markthalle Neun GmbH (no date) *Über uns*, Available online: <http://markthalleneun.de/konzept> (accessed 16 May 2012). **> 92–99**

Massa, D., Incrocci, L., Maggini, R., Bibbiani, C., Carmassi, G., Malorgio, F. and Pardossi, A. (2011) *Simulation of crop water and mineral relations in greenhouse soilless culture*, in: *Environmental Modelling & Software*, vol. 26, pp. 711–722. **> 240–243**

● Matteson, K.C. and Lang-ellotto, G.A. (2009) *Bumble Bee Abundance in New York City Community Gardens: Implications for Urban Agriculture*, in: *Cities and the Environment*, no. 2, pp. 12. **> 84–91**

● Mattsson, E. (2006) *Contamination, pollution, highways – SE KRAV Standards 2006*, Available online: <http://organicrules.org/1069> (accessed 3 Feb 2012). **> 68–75**

● Mayor of London (no date) *What is the London Food Board?*, Available online: <https://www.london.gov.uk/priorities/business-economy/working-in-partnership/london-food-board/london-food-board> (accessed 16 May 2012). **> 100–107**

● McCullum, C., Desjardins, E., Kraak, V.I., Ladipo, P. and Costello, H. (2005) *Evidence-based strategies to build community food*, in: *Journal of the American Dietetic Association*, vol. Feb, pp. 278–283. **> 240–243**

● McFrederick, Q.S. and Lebuhn, G. (2006) *Are urban parks refuges for bumble bees Bombus spp. (Hymenoptera: Apidae)?*, in: *Biological Conservation*, no. 129, pp. 372–382. **> 84–91**

● McNeil, M.E.A. (2009) *The rise of the rooftop apiary*, in: *American Bee Journal*, no. 149. **> 84–91**

● Mees, C. and Stone, E. (2010) *Food, homes and gardens: Public community gardens potential for contributing to a more sustainable city*, in: Viljoen, A. and Wiskerke, J. (eds) (2012) *Sustainable Food Planning: Evolving theory and practice*, Wageningen: Wageningen Academic Publishers, pp. 431–452. **> 122–129**

● meine ernte Ganders und Kirchbaumer GbR (no date) *Gemüsegärten zum Mieten*, Available online: <http://www.meine-ernte.de/so-funktioniert.html> (accessed 16 May 2012). **> 92–99**

● Memmott, J. (2011) *Urban pollinators: Ecology and conservation*, Available online: <http://www.bbsrc.ac.uk/web/FILES/PreviousAwards/pollinators-memmott.pdf> (accessed 1 Aug 2012). **> 84–91**

● Mendes, W. (2008) *Implementing social and environmental policies in cities: The case of food policy in Vancouver, Canada*, in: *International Journal of Urban and Regional Research*. **> 18–23**

● Mendes, W., Balmer, K., Kaethler, T., and Rhodas, A. (2008) *Using Land Inventories to plan for Urban Agriculture: Experiences from Portland and Vancouver*, in: *Journal of the American Planning Association*, vol. 74(4), pp. 435–449. **> 138–145**

● Mesner, S. and Gowdy, J.M. (1999) *Georgescu-Roegen's evolutionary economics*, in: Mayumi, K. and Gowdy, J. M. (eds) *Bioeconomics and Sustainability: Essays in honor of Nicholas Georgescu-Roegen*, Cheltenham UK: Edward Elgar, pp. 51–68. **> 48–53**

● Metz, R., Böken, H. and Hoffmann, C. (2000) *Schwermetalle in der Nahrungskette, im Pfad Boden-Pflanze-Tier-Mensch*, in: *Arbeitstagung: Mengen- und Spurenelemente*, Tagungsband 20, Jena: Friedrich-Schiller-Universität Jena. **> 68–75**

● Meyer-Renschhausen, E. (2004a) *Das 'Geschlecht' des Gartens zwischen 'Haus und Hof': Gärten im sozialen Diskurs um das gute Leben, Selbsthilfe und sozialen Frieden*, in: Schneider, U. and Wolschke-Bulmahn, J. (eds) (2004) *Gegen den Strom: Gert Gröning zum 60. Geburtstag*, Universität Hannover: Beiträge zur räumlichen Planung 76, pp. 187–208. **> 146–153**

● Meyer-Renschhausen, E. (2004b) *Unter dem Müll der Acker: Community Gardens in New York City*, Königstein im Taunus: Ulrike Helmer Verlag. **> 146–153**

● Meyer-Renschhausen, E. (2008) *Die geraubte Utopie: Henny Rosenthals Immenhof*, in: Fischer, H. and Wolschke-Bulmahn, J. (eds) *Gärten und Parks im Leben der jüdischen Bevölkerung nach 1933*, München: Martin Meidenbauer Verlag, pp. 287–308. **> 146–153**

● Meyer-Renschhausen, E. (2011a) *Von Pflanzerkolonien zum nomadisierenden Junggemüse*, in: Müller, C. (ed) *Urban Gardening: Über die Rückkehr der Gärten in die Stadt*, München: Oekom Verlag. **> 146–153**

● Meyer-Renschhausen, E. (2011b) *Gemeinschaftlich betriebene Gemüsegärten in Berlin – eine Studie*, Available online: <http://issuu.com/anstiftungundertomiss/docs/studie_urbanagriculture_in_berlin_e_meyer-renschha> (accessed 1 Nov 2012). **> 146–153**

● Meyer-Renschhausen, E. (2012) *Urbane Landwirtschaft, Interkulturelle Gärten, Community Gardening in Berlin*, in: Bohn, K. *et al.* (2012) *Spiel/Feld Urbane Landwirtschaft*, Berlin: Technische Universität Berlin, pp. 30–37. **> 92–99**

● Meyer-Renschhausen, E. and Holl, A. (eds) (2000) *Die Wiederkehr der Gärten: Kleinlandwirtschaft im Zeitalter der Globalisierung*, Innsbruck: Studienverlag. **> 146–153**

● Meyer-Renschhausen, E., Müller R. and Becker, P. (eds) (2002) *Die Gärten der Frauen: Zur sozialen Bedeutung von Kleinstlandwirtschaft in Stadt und Land weltweit*, Herbolzheim: Centaurus. **> 12–17, 146–153**

● Miller, M. (2010) *English Garden Cities: An introduction*, Swindon: Letchworth Garden City Heritage Foundation. **> 146–153**

● Minneapolis Official Website of the City (2011) *Urban Agriculture Policy Plan*, Available online: <http://www.minneapolismn.gov/cped/planning/plans/cped_urban_ag_plan> (accessed 16 May 2012). **> 138–145**

● Mokyr, J. (1990) *The Lever of Riches: Technological creativity and economic progress*,

Oxford: Oxford University Press. **> 48–53**

● Moore Lappé, F. (1971) *Diet for a small planet*, New York: Ballantine. **> 146–153**

Morgan, K. (2009) *Feeding the City: The challenge of urban food planning*, in: *International Planning Studies*, no. 14/4, pp. 429–436. **> 18–23**

● Morgan, K. and Price, A. (2011) *The Collective Entrepreneur: Social enterprise and the smart state*, Tonbridge: The Charity Bank. **> 18–23**

Morgan, K. and Sonnino, R. (2010) *The Urban Foodscape: World cities and the new food equation*, in: *Cambridge Journal of Regions, Economy and Society*, no. 3(2), pp. 209–224. **> 18–23**

Morgan, K., Marsden, T. and Murdoch, J. (2006) *Worlds of Food: Place, power and provenance in the food chain*, Oxford: Oxford University Press. **> 18–23**

Morgan, K.J. and Morley, A. (2004) *Creating Sustainable Food Chains: Tapping the potential of positive public procurement*, in: Thomas, M. and Rhisart, M. (eds) (2004) *Sustainable regions*, Cardiff: Aureus Publishing. **> 12–17**

● Mougeot, L.J.A. (2001) *Urban Agriculture: Definitions, presence, potentials and risks*, in: Bakker, N. *et al.* (eds) (2001) *Growing Cities, Growing Food: Urban agriculture on the policy agenda: A reader on urban agriculture*, Feldafing

GER: German Foundation for International Development (DSE), pp. 1–42. **> 6–11**

● Mougeot, L.J.A. (2005a) *Agropolis: The social, political and environmental dimensions of urban agriculture*, London: Earthscan and Ottawa: International Development Research Centre. **> 12–17**

● Mougeot, L.J.A. (2005b) *Introduction*, in: Mougeot, L.J.A. (ed) *Agropolis: The social, political and environmental dimensions of Urban Agriculture*, London: Earthscan. **> 12–17**

● Müller, C. (ed) (2011) *Urban Gardening: Über die Rückkehr der Gärten in die Stadt*, München: Oekom Verlag. **> 6–11, 12–17**

● München Referat für Stadtplanung und Bauordnung (2012a) *Münchner Krautgärten*, Available online: <http://www.muenchen.de/rathaus/Stadtverwaltung/Kommunalreferat/stadtgueter/krautgaerten.html> (accessed 16 May 2012). **> 92–99**

München Referat für Stadtplanung und Bauordnung (2012b) *Münchner Grüngürtel*, Available online: <http://www.muenchen.de/rathaus/Stadtverwaltung/Referat-fuer-Stadtplanung-und-Bauordnung/Stadt-und-Bebauungsplanung/Gruenplanung/Muenchner-Gruenguertel.html> (accessed 16 May 2012). **> 92–99**

● S München Referat für Stadtplanung und

Bauordnung (2012c) *Landwirtschaft im Münchner Grüngürtel*, Available online: <http://www.muenchen.de/rathaus/Stadtverwaltung/Referat-fuer-Stadtplanung-und-Bauordnung/Stadt-und-Bebauungsplanung/Gruenplanung/Landwirte_im_Muenchner_Gruenguertel.html> (accessed 16 May 2012). **> 92–99**

● Münnich, G. and AG IKG (2010) *Interkulturelle Gärten in Berlin und Brandenburg*, Available online: <http://www.interkulturelle-gaerten-berlin.de> (accessed 12 Jan 2011). **> 155–161**

● Murray, H., Pinchin, T. and Macfie, S.M. (2011) *Compost application affects metal uptake in plants grown in urban garden soils and potential human health risk*, in: *Journal of Soils and Sediments*, no. 11, pp. 815–829. **> 68–75**

Murray, R. (2012) *The new wave of mutuality: Social innovation and public service reform*, London: Policy Network. **> 18–23**

● MVRDV (2001) *Pig City*, Available online: <http://www.mvrdv.nl/projects/181_pig_city/get.pdf.html> (accessed 16 May 2012). **> 24–31**

● myvillages.org (2011) *Vorratskammer* in: *Festival Über Lebenskunst*, Available online: <http://www.ueber-lebenskunst.org/downloads/uelk_festival_01_de.pdf> (accessed 16 May 2012). **> 155–161**

● Neighbour, A. (1866) *The Apiary; or Bees, Bee-hives and Bee Culture: Being a familiar account of the habits of bees etc.*, London: Kent and co. **> 84–91**

● Neori, A., Chopin, T., Troell, M., Buschmann, A.H. and Kraemer, G.P. (2004) *Integrated aquaculture: Rationale, evolution and state*, in: *Aquaculture*, vol. 231, pp. 361–391. **> 240–243**

● Neville, J. (2004) *The polytunnel companion*, Preston: Farming Books, pp. 95. **> 240–243**

● Nomadisch Grün gGmbH (no date) *Prinzessinnengärten: Urbane Landwirtschaft*, Available online: <http://prinzessinnengarten.net> (accessed 14 July 2012). **> 92–99**

Noy, M. (2009) *Abundance Report Oct 08*, Available online: <http://www.transitiontownbrixton.org/2009/12/abundance-report-oct-08/> (accessed 4 Nov 2012). **> 100–107**

Noy, P. and the Transition Town Food and Growing Group (2010) *Grower's Pack: How to get a community garden growing*, Available online: <http://www.transitiontownbrixton.org/groups-and-projects/foodgrowing-group> (accessed 16 May 2012). **> 155–161**

Nuvege (2011) *Vertical Farming Environments*, Available online: <http://www.nuvege.com> (accessed 16 May 2012). **> 24–31**

NYC Department of Health and Mental Hygiene (2010) *Rules of the City of New York: Title 24: New York City Health Code*, New York: 24 RCNY Health Code § 161.01. **> 138–145**

NYC Department of Parks & Recreation (2010) *Green Thumb: The largest community gardening program in the nation*, Available online: <http://www.greenthumbnyc.org> (accessed 16 May 2012). **> 155–161**

NYC The City of New York (2009) *Zoning Resolution (web version): Article II: Residence District Regulations: Chapter 2 – Use Regulations*, Section 22–14, New York: Department of City Planning. **> 138–145**

NYC The City of New York (no date) *PlaNYC*, Available online: <http://www.nyc.gov/html/planyc2030/html/home/home.shtml> (accessed 16 May 2012). **> 40–47, 138–145**

NYCCGC New York City Community Gardening Coalition (2010) *Recap: NYCCGC Rally & Parks Dept. Public Hearing Regarding Proposed New Rules*, Available online: <http://nyccgc.org/2010/08/recap-nyccgc-rally-parks-dept-public-hearing-regarding-proposed-new-rules> (accessed 16 May 2012). **> 138–145**

NYCDCP New York City Department of City Planning (1993) *A greenway plan for New York City*, Available online: <http://www.nyc.gov/html/dcp/html/

bike/gp.shtml#overview> (accessed 30 Aug 2011). **> 32–39**

NYCDCP New York City Department of City Planning (2012) *Zone Green: Text Amendment – Approved!*, Available online: <http://www.nyc.gov/html/dcp/html/greenbuildings/index.shtml> (accessed 16 May 2012). **> 138–145**

NYCDEP Department of Environmental Protection (no date) *Using Green Infrastructure to Manage Stormwater*, Available online: <http://www.nyc.gov/html/dep/html/stormwater/using_green_infra_to_manage_stormwater.shtml> (accessed 16 May 2012). **> 138–145**

NYCHPD New York City Department of Housing Preservation and Development (2006) *New Housing New York: Legacy Project: Request for Proposals*, issue 12 Jun 2006, Available online: <http://www.aiany.org/NHNY/rfp/index.php> (accessed 20 Jan 2012). **> 138–145**

Obama, M. (2012) *American Grown: The story of the White House kitchen garden and gardens across America*, New York: Crown. **> 24–31**

Oldroyd, E., Summers, R., Clavin, A. and Andrews, J. (2011) *Back to Front: Manual for growing food in front gardens*, Leeds: Infrapress. **> 155–161**

Oppenheimer, L.Y. (ed) (1964) *Franz Oppenheimer: Erlebtes, Erstrebtes, Erreichtes

- Lebenserinnerungen*, Düsseldorf: Joseph Melzer. **> 146–153**

Oudolf, P. and Kingsbury, N. (2010) *Landscapes in Landscapes*, New York: Monacelli Press. **> 32–39**

Parham, S. (2011) *Get Midtown buzzing*, Hatfield: University of Hertfordshire. **> 84–91**

Pavitt, J.J. (2005) *National Association of Farmers' Markets*, Available online: <http://www.northernruralnetwork.co.uk/uploads/articles/04janjamespavitt.pdf> (accessed 16 May 2012). **> 6–11**

Perez-Vazquez, A. (2002) *The role of allotments in food production as a component of urban agriculture in England*, London: Imperial College Wye, University of London. **> 84–91**

Petcou, C. and Petrescu, D. (2012) *R-Urban Resilience*, in: Tyszczuk, R. *et al.* (eds) *ATLAS: Geography, Architecture and Change in an Interdependent World*, London: Black Dog. **> 108–113**

Petts, J. (2001a) *Economic Costs and Benefits of Urban Agriculture in East London*, Available online: <http://www.cityfarmer.org/eastlondon.html> (accessed 12 Jan 2011). **> 12–17, 155–161**

Petts, J. (2001b) *Urban Agriculture in London*, Copenhagen: World Health Organization Regional Office for Europe. **> 12–17, 155–161**

Pinkerton, T. and Hopkins, R. (2009) *Local Food: How to make it happen in your community*, Totnes: Green Books. **> 155–161**

Plakolm, G. and Fromm, E. (2006) *Contamination, buffer zones, highways, herbs: AT Bio Austria General Standard 2006*, Available online: <http://organicrules.org/861> (accessed 3 Feb 2012). **> 68–75**

Plantagon (no date) *Feeding the city*, Available online: <http://www.plantagon.com> (accessed 16 May 2012). **> 24–31**

PlantLab (no date) *Welcome to the next generation of growing*, Available online: <http://www.plantlab.nl/4.0> (accessed 11 Mar 2012). **> 68–75**

Ploeg, J. D. van der, Renting, H., Brunori, G., Knickel, K., Mannion, J., Marsden, T., De Roest, K., Sevilla-Guzmán, E. and Ventura, F. (2000) *Rural development: From practices and policies towards theory*, in: *Sociologia Ruralis*, vol. 40(4), pp. 391–408. **> 244–251**

Ploeg, J. D. van der, Jingzhong, Y. and Schneider, S. (2012) *Rural development through the construction of new, nested, markets: Comparative perspectives from China, Brazil and the European Union*, in: *Journal of Peasant Studies*, vol. 39(1), pp. 133–173. **> 244–251**

Polimeni, J.M., Mayumi, K., Giampietro, M. and Alcott, B. (2008) *The Myth of

Resource Efficiency: The Jevons Paradox, London: Earthscan. **> 48–53**

Porritt, J., Manacorda, F. and Demos, T. (2009) *Radical Nature: Art and architecture for a changing planet, 1969–2009,* Köln: Buchhandlung Walther König. **> 12–17**

Pothukuchi, K. (2011) *The Detroit Food System Report 2009–2010,* Detroit: Detroit Food Policy Council. **> 130–137**

Pothukuchi, K. and Kaufman, J. L. (1999) *Placing the food system on the urban agenda: The role of municipal institutions in food systems planning,* in: *Agriculture and Human Values,* vol. 16(2), pp. 213–224, Available online: <http://link.springer.com/article/10.1023%2FA%3A1007558805953> (accessed 16 May 2012). **> 18–23**

Pothukuchi, K. and Kaufman, J.L. (2000) *The food system: A stranger to the planning field,* in: *Journal of the American Planning Association,* vol. 66(2), pp. 112–24. **> 6–11, 244–251**

Potts, S., Roberts, S., Dean, R., Marris, G., Brown, M., Jones, R., Neumann, P. and Settele, J. (2010) *Declines of managed honey bees and beekeepers in Europe,* in: *Journal of Apicultural Research,* no. 49, p. 15. **> 84–91**

Prairie Crossing (no date) *The Prairie Crossing Organic Farm,* Available online:

<http://prairiecrossing.com/farm/index.php> (accessed 16 May 2012). **> 24–31**

Produktif design studio (no date) *Maison Productive House,* Available online: <http://www.productive-house.com> (accessed 16 May 2012). **> 24–31**

Pure Food (2011) *Pure Food Produces Regents Park Honey,* Available online: <http://www.purefood.co.uk/index.php> (accessed 1 Aug 2012). **> 84–91**

Pure Hydroponics (no date) *Why Hydroponics,* Available online: <http://purehydroponics.com/why-hydroponics> (accessed 16 May 2012). **> 68–75**

Raiswell, C. and Cox, C. (2012) *Food Futures: A potted history,* Manchester: Manchester City Council. **> 18–23**

Ramirez, J.A. (2000) *The beehive metaphor: From Gaudi to Le Corbusier,* London: Reaktion Books. **> 84–91**

Rath, N. (1996) *Zweite Natur: Konzepte einer Vermittlung von Natur und Kultur in Anthropologie und Ästhetik um 1800,* Münster: Waxmann. **> x–xi**

Ray, C. (1999) *Towards a meta-framework of endogenous development: Repertoires, paths, democracy and rights,* in: *Sociologia Ruralis,* vol. 39(4), pp. 522–537. **> 244–251**

Recovery Park (no date) *Recovery Park FAQ,* Available online: <http://recoverypark.

org/faq> (accessed 3 Nov 2011). **> 130–137**

Redmond, M.Q. (2010) *Feeding the Future: A new view of providing lands,* in: *Building Metropolitan Atlanta: Past, present & future,* 18th Congress for the New Urbanism, pp. 74–77. **> 24–31**

Reeds, J. (2011) *Smart Growth: From sprawl to sustainability,* London: Green Books. **> 76–83**

REOS Partners (2011) *Food Projects,* Available online: <http://www.reospartners.com/themes/Food> (accessed 16 May 2012). **> 6–11**

Resh, H.M. (2004) *Hydroponic Food Production: A definitive guidebook for the advanced home gardener and the commercial hydroponic grower,* 6th ed, New Jersey: New Concept Press. **> 68–75**

RIBA President's Medals Student Awards (2008) *Adventure Farm by Robert Hankey,* Available online: <http://www.presidentsmedals.com/Entry-22861> (accessed 16 May 2012). **> 12–17**

Richter, J., Schnitzler, W.H. and Gura, S. (1995) *Vegetable production in periurban areas in the tropics and subtropics: Food, income and quality of life,* Feldafing GER: Deutsche Stiftung für Internationale Entwicklung (DSE)/ Council for Tropical and Subtropical Agricultural Research (ATSAF). **> 92–99**

Roberts, W. (2001) *The way to a city's heart is through its stomach,* Toronto: TFPC. **> 18–23**

Römkens, P.F.A.M. and Rietra, R.P.J.J. (2012) *Lead in soils and crops in urban agricultural growing areas in Leiden. Site-specific investigation of the risk of soil pollution for crop quality and human exposure,* report no. 2255, Wageningen: Alterra, Wageningen UR. **> 68–75**

Rosol, M. (2006) *Gemeinschaftsgärten in Berlin: Eine qualitative Untersuchung zu Potenzialen und Risiken bürgerschaftlichen Engagements im Grünflächenbereich vor dem Hintergrund des Wandels von Staat und Planung,* Berlin: Mensch & Buch Verlag. **> 6–11, 12–17, 146–153**

Ross, A. (2011) *Bird on Fire: Lessons from the world's least sustainable city,* New York: Oxford University Press. **> 18–23**

Rouphael, Y. and Colla, G. (2005) *Growth, yield, fruit quality and nutrient uptake,* in: *Scientia Horticulturae,* vol. 105, pp. 177–195. **> 240–243**

Roy, R. (2012) *Case studies in low-carbon living,* in: Herring, H. (ed) *Living in a low-carbon society in 2050,* Basingstoke: Palgrave Macmillan, pp. 95–120. **> 60–67**

Ryerson University Toronto (2009) *Carrot City: Designing for Urban Agriculture,* Available online: <http://www.ryerson.ca/carrotcity/> (accessed 16 May 2012). **> 155–161**

Rykwert, J. (1988) *The Idea of a Town: The anthropology of urban form in Rome, Italy and* the Ancient World, Cambridge MA: The MIT Press. **> 48–53**

Salle, J. de la and Holland, M. (eds) (2010) Agricultural Urbanism: Handbook for building sustainable food and agriculture systems in 21st-century cities, Winnipeg, Manitoba: Green Frigate Books. **> 24–31**

Salt, B. (1999) Gardening under plastic, London: Batsford, pp. 127. **> 240–243**

San Francisco Public Utilities Commission (no date) Installing Your Cistern for irrigation, Available online: <http://sfwater.org/modules/showdocument.aspx?documentid=239> (accessed 6 Apr 2012). **> 68–75**

Satzewich, W. and Christensen, R. (2011) SPIN farming basics: How to grow commercially on under an acre, self-published by authors. **> 24–31**

Sauerbeck, D. and Styperek, P. (1988) Schadstoffe in Böden, insbesondere Schwermetalle und organische Schadstoffe aus langjähriger Anwendung von Siedlungsabfällen, in: Teilbericht: Schwermetalle, UBA-Texte, vol. 16(88), pp. 1–207. **> 68–75**

Säumel, I., Kotsyuka, I., Hölscher, M., Lenkereit, C., Weber, F. and Kowarik, I. (2012) How healthy is urban horticulture in high traffic areas?: Trace metal concentrations in vegetable crops from plantings within inner-city neighbourhoods in Berlin, Germany, in:

Environmental Pollution, no. 165, pp. 124–132. **> 68–75**

Schlosser, E. (2012) Forward, in: Allen, W. and Wilson, C. The Good Food Revolution: Growing healthy food, people and communities, New York: Gotham Books, pp. XI-XIV. **> 40–47**

Schumacher, E. (1973) Small is Beautiful: Economics as if people mattered, London: Blond & Briggs Ltd. **> 40–47**

Schumpeter, J. (1994) History of economic analysis, London: Routledge (original 1954). **> 48–53**

Schumpeter, J. (2005) Capitalism, socialism and democracy, London: Routledge (original 1943). **> 48–53**

Seattle Department of Neighborhoods (no date) P-Patch Community Gardens, Available online: <http://www.seattle.gov/neighborhoods/ppatch> (accessed 16 May 2012). **> 138–145**

Seeds To Feed (no date) Georgia's Place community rooftop farm for formerly homeless adults, Available online: <http://seedstofeedrooftopfarm.tumblr.com/background> (accessed 16 May 2012). **> 138–145**

Seeing Green (no date) Seeing Green: The Value of Urban Agriculture, Available online: <http://www.seeingreen.com> (accessed 16 May 2012). **> 40–47**

SenStadt Senatsverwaltung für Stadtentwicklung

und Umwelt Berlin (2012) Strategie Stadtlandschaft Berlin: natürlich – urban – produktiv, Available online: <http://www.stadtentwicklung.berlin.de/umwelt/landschaftsplanung/strategie_stadtlandschaft/download/Strategie-Stadtlandschaft-Berlin.pdf> (accessed 12 Jul 2012). **> 6–11, 92–99**

Seyfang, G. and Smith, A. (2007) Grassroots innovations for sustainable development: Towards a new research and policy agenda, in: Environmental Politics, vol. 16(4). **> 244–253**

Shiva, V. (2006) Earth Democracy: Justice, sustainability and peace, London: Ed Books. **> 146–153**

Sites, W. (2003) Remaking New York: Primitive globalization and the politics of urban community, Minneapolis; London: University of Minnesota Press. **> 146–153**

Sky Vegetables, Inc. (no date) Sky Vegetables: The sky is the limit, Available online: <http://www.skyvegetables.com/about.html> (accessed 16 May 2012). **> 138–145**

Slobodkin, L. and Rapoport, A. (1974) An optimal strategy of evolution, in: The Quarterly Review of Biology, no. 49, pp. 181–200. **> 48–53**

Slow Food Convivium Berlin (no date) Gut, sauber und fair!, Available online: <http://www.slowfood-berlin.de/index.php> (accessed 16 May 2012). **> 92–99**

Smil, V. (2002) The earth's biosphere: Evolution, dynamics, and change, Cambridge MA: The MIT Press. **> 48–53**

Smit, J. (1996) Cities that feed themselves, in: Smit J., Ratta, A. and Nasr, J. (1996) Urban Agriculture: Food, jobs and sustainable cities, 2nd edition 2001, New York: United Nations Development Programme (UNDP) Publication, pp. 1–29. **> 146–153**

Smit, J. (2005) The Ethics of Urban Agriculture: Farming within the human settlement, Available online: <http://www.sustainableunh.unh.edu/fas/sidore_docs/JSmit.pdf> (accessed 18 Feb 2005). **> 12–17**

Smit, J., Ratta, A. and Nasr, J. (1996) Urban Agriculture: Food, jobs and sustainable cities, New York: United Nations Development Programme (UNDP) Publication. **> 6–11, 12–17, 146–153**

Smith, A., Watkiss, P., Tweddle, G., McKinnon, A., Browne, M. and Hunt, A. (2005) The validity of food miles as an indicator of sustainable development, Report ED50254-103, Oxon UK: Department of Environment, Food, and Rural Affairs, Available online: <http://statistics.defra.gov.uk/esg/reports/foodmiles/execsumm.pdf> (accessed 16 May 2012). **> 76–83**

Smith, C. (2010) London: Garden City?, in: London Wildlife Trust, Greenspace Information for Greater London, London: Greater London Authority. **> 84–91**

● Smith, E. (2010) *Brave Thinkers,* in: *Atlantic Magazine,* Available online: <http://www. theatlantic.com/magazine/ archive/2010/11/john-hantz/8277> (accessed 26 Oct 2011). **> 130–137**

● Smith, N. (1993) *Gentrification in New York City,* in: Häußermann, H. and Siebel, W. (eds) (1993) *New York: Strukturen einer Metropole,* Frankfurt a. M.: Suhrkamp, pp. 182–204. **> 146–153**

● SoCal Aquaponics (no date) *FAQ Hydroponics,* Available online: <http:// www.socalfishfarm.com/fish/ index.php?option=com_cont ent&view=article&id=54&It emid=112> (accessed 16 May 2012). **> 68–75**

● SoLawi Solidarische Landwirtschaft (no date) *... sich die Ernte teilen,* Available online: <http://www. solidarische-landwirtschaft. org/angebot> (accessed 16 May 2012). **> 92–99**

● Solomon, D. (2007) *The Edible City,* Available online: <http://culiblog. org/2007/02/the-edible-city> (accessed 16 May 2012). **> 6–11, 12–17**

● Something & Son LLP (no date a) *FARM:shop – Eat, drink, grow, work, play,* Available online: <http:// farmlondon.weebly.com/ farmshop.html> (accessed 16 May 2012). **> 155–161**

● Something & Son LLP (no date b) *FARM:,* Available online: <http://farmlondon. weebly.com> (accessed 16 May 2012). **> 68–75**

● Sonnino, R. (2007) *The power of place: Embeddedness and local food systems in Italy and the UK,* in: *Anthropology of food (S2),* Available online: <http://aof.revues.org/ index454.html> (accessed 16 May 2012). **> 244–251**

● Sorkin, M. (2012) *New York City (Steady) State,* in: *Scarcity: Architecture in an age of depleting resources,* Architectural Design Special Issue, vol. 82(4), pp. 102–109. **> 6–11, 122–129**

● SPUR (2012) *Public Harvest: Expanding the use of public land for Urban Agriculture in San Francisco,* San Francisco: SPUR. **> 138–145**

● Stanhill, G. (1977) *An Urban Agro-Ecosystem: The example of 19th-century Paris,* in: *Agro-Ecosystems,* no. 3, pp. 269–284. **> 60–67**

● Steel, C. (2008) *Hungry city: How food shapes our lives,* London: Chatto & Windus. **> 12–17**

● Stefanelli, D., Goodwin, I. and Jones, R. (2010) *Minimal nitrogen and water use in horticulture: Effects on quality,* in: *Food Research International,* vol. 43, pp. 1833–1843. **> 240–243**

● Steinhart, J. and Steinhart, C. (1974) *Energy use in the U.S. food system,* in: *Science,* vol. 184, pp. 307–316. **> 60–67**

● Stierand, P. (no date) *speiseräume: stadt/ernährung,* Available online: <http:// speiseraeume.de> (accessed 16 May 2012). **> 92–99**

● Stone, E. (2000) *Community Gardening in New York City becomes a political movement,* presentation at: *Perspectives of Small-Scale Farming in Urban and Rural Areas: About the Social and Ecological Necessity of Gardens and Informal Agriculture,* July 2000, Berlin, Germany. **> 146–153**

● Stone, E. (2002) *Community Gardening in New York City wird zur politischen Bewegung,* in: Meyer-Renschhausen, E., Müller R. and Becker, P. (eds) (2002) *Die Gärten der Frauen: Zur sozialen Bedeutung von Kleinstlandwirtschaft in Stadt und Land weltweit,* Herbolzheim: Centaurus, pp. 159–177. **> 146–153**

● Stone, E. (2009) *The Benefits of Community Managed Open Spaces: Community gardening in New York City,* in: Campbell, L. and Wiesen, A. (eds) (2009) *Restorative Commons,* Newton Square PA: U.S. Department of Agriculture Forest Service, pp. 122–137. **> 146–153**

● Stringer, S.M. (2010) *FoodNYC: A Blueprint for a Sustainable Food System,* Available online: <http:// www.mbpo.org/uploads/ policy_reports/mbp/ FoodNYC.pdf> (accessed 16 May 2012). **> 138–145**

● Stroom Den Haag (2009) *Foodprint. Voedsel voor de stad,* Available online: <http://stroom.typepad. com/foodprint/symposium1. html> (accessed 16 May 2012). **> 12–17**

● Sukkel, W., Geel, W. van and Haan, J.J. de (2008) *Carbon sequestration in organic and conventional managed soils in the Netherlands,* in: *Proceedings of the 16th IFOAM Organic World Congress, Modena, Italy, 2008,* pp. 550–553, Available online: <http://orgprints.org/view/ projects/conference.html> (accessed 15 Sep 2012). **> 60–67**

● Summerfelt, S.T. (2003) *Ozonation and UV irradiation: An introduction and examples of current applications,* in: *Aquacultural Engineering,* vol. 28, pp. 21–36. **> 240–243**

● Sun Works Inc. (2010) *New York Sun Works,* Available online: <http://www. nysunworks.org> (accessed 16 May 2012). **> 155–161**

● Sustain (2011) *Our purpose,* Available online: <http://www.sustainweb. org/about> (accessed 16 May 2012). **> 100–107**

● Sustain (2012) *Capital Bee: Campaigning for bees, forage and a pesticide free city,* Available online: <http:// www.capitalgrowth.org/ bees> (accessed 9 Aug 2012). **> 84–91**

● Sustain (no date) *London Food Link,* Available online: <http://www.sustainweb. org/londonfoodlink> (accessed 12 Jan 2011). **> 6–11**

● Sustainable Cities (2012) *Urban Agriculture: Star attraction at World Habitat Day in Dar es Salaam,* Available online: <http://blog.

sustainablecities.net/
category/dar-es-salaam-2>
(accessed 26 Oct 2012).
> **12–17**

Svendsen, E.S. (2009)
*Cultivating Resilience: Urban
stewardship as a means
to improving health and
well-being*, in: Campbell,
L. and Wiesen, A. (eds)
(2009) *Restorative Commons*,
Newton Square PA: U.S.
Department of Agriculture
Forest Service, pp. 59–87.
> **146–153**

Sweet Water (no date a)
*There grows the neighbour-
hood*, Available online:
<http://sweetwater-organic.
com> (accessed 16 May
2012). > **240–253**

Sweet Water (no date b)
Our mission, Available online:
<http://sweetwater-organic.
com/about> (accessed 16
May 2012). > **68–75**

Swyngedouw, E. and
Heynen, N.C. (2003) *Urban
political ecology, justice and the
politics of scale*, in: *Antipode
Special Issue*, vol. 35(5),
pp. 898–918. > **x–xi**

Tainter, J.A. (1988) *The
Collapse of Complex Societies:
Rethinking symbolism*, Cam-
bridge: Cambridge University
Press. > **48–53**

Tautz, J. (2008) *The buzz
about bees: Biology of a super-
organism*, Berlin; London:
Springer. > **84–91**

Taylor Lovell, S. (2010)
*Multifunctional Urban Agri-
culture for sustainable land use
planning in the United States*,
in: *Sustainability*, no. 2,
pp. 2499–2522. > **84–91**

Taylor Lovell, S. and Johnston, D.M. (2009) *Designing
landscapes for performance
based on emerging principles in
landscape ecology*, in: *Ecology
and Society*, vol. 14(1), Available online: <http://www.
ecologyandsociety.org/vol14/
iss1/art44/> (accessed 4 Dec
2010). > **12–17**

Tempelhofer Freiheit
(no date) *Allmende-Kontor*,
Available online: <http://
www.tempelhoferfreiheit.
de/en/get-involved/pioneer-
projects/allmende-kontor>
(accessed 16 May 2012).
> **92–99**

Terra Concordia gUG
Deutschland (no date)
*Mundraub: Freies Obst für
freie Bürger*, Available online:
<http://www.mundraub.org>
(accessed 16 May 2012).
> **92–99**

Thabit, W. (2003) *How East
New York became a ghetto*,
New York and London: New
York University Press. > **1–5,
6–11, 12–17**

Tittonell, P., and Giller,
K.E. (2012) *When yield gaps
are poverty traps: The para-
digm of ecological intensification in African smallholder
agriculture*, in: *Field Crops
Research*, vol. 143(2013),
pp.76–90. > **60–67**

Todd, N.J. (2005)
*The Promise of Ecological
Design*, 25th Annual E.F.
Schumacher Lectures,
Amherst, Massachusetts,
Available online: <http://
neweconomicsinstitute.org/
publications/lectures/todd/
nancy-jack/the-promise-of-
ecological-design> (accessed
7 Jun 2012). > **108–113**

Tokuyama, T., Mine, A.,
Kamiyama, K., Yabe, R.,
Satoh, K., Matsumoto, H.,
Takahashi, R. and Itonaga,
K. (2004) *Nitrosomonas
communis Strain YNSRA, an
Ammonia-Oxidizing Bacte-
rium*, in: *Journal of Bioscience
and Engineering*, vol. 98(4),
pp. 309–312. > **240–243**

Tomkins, M. (2009) *The
Elephant and the Castle:
Towards a London Edible
Landscape*, in: *The Urban
Agriculture Magazine*, no. 22,
pp. 37–38. > **6–11, 32–39,
155–161**

Toor, R.K., Savage, G.P.
and Lister, C.E. (2006)
*Seasonal variations in the
antioxidant composition of
greenhouse grown tomatoes*,
in: *Journal of Food Composition and Analysis*, vol. 19,
pp. 1–10. > **240–243**

Torrellas, M., Anton, A.,
Ruijs, M., Victoria, N.G.,
Stanghellini, C. and Montero,
J.I. (2012) *Environmental
and economic assessment of
protected crops in four European scenarios*, in: *Journal of
Cleaner Production*, volume in
press, pp. 1–11. > **240–243**

TPH Toronto Public
Health (2010) *Cultivating
Food Connections: Toward a
healthy and sustainable food
system for Toronto*, Toronto:
TPH. > **18–2**3

Tracey, D. (2011) *Urban
agriculture: Ideas and designs
for the new food revolution*,
Gabriola Island CAN: New
Society Publishers. > **68–75**

TSO and DfT The Sta-
tionery Office and Depart-
ment for Transport (2005)
National Travel Survey, in:
Focus on Personal Travel,
London: The Stationery
Office and Department for
Transport. > **76–83**

Transition Network (2012)
About transition network,
Available online: <http://
www.transitionnetwork.org/
about (accessed 4 Nov 2012).
> **100–107**

TT Transition Town
Brixton (2012) *About TTB:
Our aims and structures*,
Available online: <http://
www.transitiontownbrixton.
org/about-ttb/our-aims-and-
structure/ (accessed 4 Nov
2012). > **100–107**

TT Transition Town
Witzenhausen (no date) *Stadt
und Menschen im Wandel*,
Available online: <http://
www.ttwitzenhausen.de/wer-
wir-sind.html> (accessed 16
May 2012). > **92–99**

TUAN The Urban Agricul-
ture Network (2009) *Jac's
Journal: Board Announces
Upcoming Merger of TUAN
and MetroAg*, Available
online: <http://jacsmit.com/
jacsjournal.html> (accessed
16 May 2005). > **257–259**

TUB Technische
Universität Berlin
Architekturmuseum (2011)
*Die Produktive Stadt / Carrot
City*, Available online:
<http://architekturmuseum.
ub.tu-berlin.de/index.
php?set=1&p=524>
(accessed 16 May 2012).
> **6–11, 155–161**

TUB Technische Uni-
versität Berlin, Fachgebiet
Stadt & Ernährung (2011)
Stadtbaue/r/n, proceedings

of the symposium, unpublished. **> 40–47**

● TUB Technische Universität Berlin, Chair of Landscape Architecture and Open Space Planning (no date) *Urban Agriculture Casablanca: Urban Agriculture as an Integrative Factor of Climate-Optimised Urban Development, Casablanca / Morocco*, Available online: <http://www.uac-m.org/> (accessed 16 May 2012). **> 92–99**

● Tuomisto, H.L., Hodge, I.D., Riordan, P. and Macdonald, D.W. (2012) *Does organic farming reduce environmental impacts?: A meta-analysis of European research*, in: *Journal of Environmental Management*, vol. 112, pp. 309–320. **> 60–67**

● Turner, A.H. (2009) *Urban Agriculture and Soil Contamination: An introduction to urban gardening*, Available online: <http://cepm.louisville.edu/Pubs_WPapers/practiceguides/PG25.pdf> (accessed 30 Jan 2012). **> 240–243**

● Turner, J.S. (2000) *The Extended Organism: The physiology of animal-built structures*, Cambridge MA: Harvard University Press. **> 48–53**

● UCL Development Planning Unit (2007) *Harvesting locally grown food in Brixton!* at: open launch event for *ABUNDANCE*, London: DPU. **> 100–107**

○ UN United Nations (1993) *Convention on Biodiversity*, Available online: <http://www.cbd.int/history> (accessed 16 May 2012). **> 60–67**

○ UNUIAS United Nations University Institute for Advanced Studies (2010) *Cities, Biodiversity and Governance: Perspectives and Challenges of the Implementation of the Convention on Biological Diversity at the City Level*, Policy Report, Yokohama: UNUIAS. **> 60–67**

● UoB University of Brighton, Faculty of Arts (2006) *Utilitarian Dreams relocates to Havana*, Available online: <http://arts.brighton.ac.uk/whats-on/news-and-events/2006/news/utilitarian-dreams> (accessed 16 May 2012). **> 1–5**

● UoB University of Brighton, Faculty of Arts (2011) *Edible Campus 2011*, Available online: <http://arts.brighton.ac.uk/faculty-of-arts-brighton/extension-studies/edible-campus2/2011-edible-campus> (accessed 14 Jul 2012). **> 40–47**

○ Urban Design Lab (2011a) *Infrastructure > Health: Modelling production, processing and distribution infrastructure for a resilient regional food system*, New York City: The Earth Institute, Columbia University. **> 40–47**

○ Urban Design Lab (2011b) *The Potential for Urban Agriculture in New York City: Growing capacity, food security, and green infrastructure*, New York City: The Earth Institute, Columbia University. **> 122–129**

○ The Urban Task Force (1999) *Towards an Urban Renaissance*, London: Routledge. **> 12–17**

○ Vancouver: City of Vancouver Planning (2005) *Policy Report – Hobby Beekeeping (Urban Apiculture) in Vancouver*, Available online: <http://vancouver.ca/ctyclerk/cclerk/20050721/documents/pe3.pdfhttp://vancouver.ca/ctyclerk/cclerk/20050721/documents/pe3.pdf> (accessed 1 Aug 2012). **> 84–91**

● Veenhuizen, R.V. (ed) (2006) *Cities Farming for the Future: Urban Agriculture for green and productive cities*: Leusden NL: IDRC and RUAF Foundation. **> 84–91**

● Verran, H. (2010) *Number as an inventive frontier in knowing and working Australia's water resources*, in: *Anthropological Theory*, no. 10, pp. 171–178. **> 108–113**

● La Via Campesina (no date) *The international peasant's voice*, Available online: <http://viacampesina.org/en/index.php/organisation-mainmenu-44> (accessed 16 May 2012). **> 6–11**

● Via Verde Homes LLC (no date) *The building*, Available online: <http://viaverdenyc.com/the_building> (accessed 16 Dec 2012). **> 138–145**

○ Viljoen, A. (ed) (2005) *Continuous Productive Urban Landscape: Designing Urban Agriculture for sustainable cities*, Oxford: The Architectural Press. **> 1–5, 6–11, 12–17, 32–39, 60–67, 84–91, 155–161, 257–259**

● Viljoen, A. and Bohn, K. (2000) *Urban intensification and the integration of productive landscape*, in: *Proceedings of the World Renewable Energy Congress VI, Part 1*, Oxford: Pergamon Press, pp. 483–488. **> 12–17, 122–129**

○ Viljoen, A. and Bohn, K. (2005) *Continuous Productive Urban Landscapes: Urban Agriculture as an essential infrastructure*, in: *The Urban Agriculture Magazine*, no. 15, pp. 34–36. **> 12–17**

○ Viljoen, A. and Bohn, K. (2009) *Continuous Productive Urban Landscape (CPUL): Essential Infrastructure and Edible Ornament*, in: *Open House International: Designing edible landscapes*, vol. 34(2), pp. 50–60. **> 32–29**

● Viljoen, A. and Bohn, K. (2012) *Scarcity and Abundance: Urban Agriculture in Cuba and the US*, in: *Architectural Design Special Issue Scarcity: Architecture in an Age of Depleting Resources*, vol. 82(4), pp. 16–21. **> 40–47**

○ Viljoen, A. and Howe, J. (2005) *Cuba: Laboratory for Urban Agriculture*, in: Viljoen, A. (ed) (2005) *Continuous Productive Urban Landscapes: Designing Urban Agriculture for sustainable cities*, Oxford: Architectural Press, pp. 146–191. **> 122–129**

○ Viljoen, A. and Wiskerke, S.C. (eds) (2012) *Sustainable Food Planning: Evolving theory and practice*. Wageningen: Wageningen Academic Publishers. **> 6–11**

Viljoen, A., Bohn, K. and Pena Diaz, J. (2004) *London Thames Gateway: Proposals for implementing CPULs in London Riverside and the Lower Lea Valley*, Brighton: University of Brighton publication. **> 6–11, 12–17, 32–39**

Viljoen, A., Bohn, K., Tomkins, M. and Denny, G. (2009) *Spaces for people, Spaces for plants: Evolving thoughts on Continuous Productive Urban Landscape*, in: *Proceedings of the 2nd International Conference on Landscape and Urban Horticulture, Bologna, June 2009.* Leuven: Acta Horticulturae, no. 1, pp. 57–65. **> 40–47**

VOEN Vöhringer GmbH & Co. KG (2012) *Voen: Covering Systems,* Available online: <http://voen.eu/tunnel> (accessed 30 Jan 2012). **> 240–243**

VROM (2008) *NOBO: Normstelling en bodemkwaliteitsbeoordeling,* The Hague: Ministry of Housing, Spatial Planning and Environment (VROM). **> 68–75**

Wageningen University and Research Centre (2011) *Agromere,* Available online: <http://www.wageningenur.nl/en/Research-Results/Projects-and-programmes/Agromere.htm> (accessed 16 May 2012). **> 12–17**

Wagner, D. (1999) *Assessment of the probability of extreme weather events and their potential effects in large conurbations,* in: *Atmospheric Environment*, vol. 33, pp. 4151–4155. **> 240–243**

Waldheim, C. (ed) (2006) *The Landscape Urbanism Reader,* New York: Princeton Architectural Press. **> 6–11**

Waldheim, C. (2010) *Notes toward a History of Agrarian Urbanism,* in: White, M. and Przybylski, M. (eds) (2010) *On Farming: Bracket 1,* Barcelona: Actar, pp. 18–24. **> 6–11**

Warnecke, P., Gröning, G. and Friedrich, J. (2001) *Ein starkes Stück Berlin 1901–2001: 100 Jahre organisiertes Berliner Kleingartenwesen,* Berlin: Landesverband der Gartenfreunde e.V. **> 146–153**

Weber, C.H. and Scott Matthews, H. (2008) *Food Miles and the relative climate impacts of food choices in the United States,* in: *Environment Science & Technology,* vol. 42 (10), pp. 3508–3513. **> 60–67**

Weiss, A. (2011) *Food Works: A Vision to Improve NYC's Food System,* Available online: <http://council.nyc.gov/downloads/pdf/foodworks1.pdf> (accessed 16 May 2012). **> 138–145**

Welzel, K. (2010) *Urban Agriculture and Ecosystem Services: Pollination by Native Bee Communities in Berkeley, California,* Available online: <http://escholarship.org/uc/item/90m7f314> (accessed 27 Mar 2012). **> 84–91**

Wezenbeek, J.M. (2007) *Know the quality of your soil or aquatic sediment: Clarifying the risks,* Report reference no. 3BODM0704, SenterNovem. **> 68–75**

What if: projects Ltd. (no date) *Vacant Lot,* Available online: <http://www.what-if.info/Vacant_Lot_allotment_programme.html> (accessed 16 May 2012). **> 24–31**

White, H. and Natelson, S. (2011) *Good Planning for Good Food,* London: Sustain. **> 18–23**

WHO World Health Organization and FAO Food and Agriculture Organization of the United Nations (2005) *Fruit and vegetables for health: Report of a Joint FAO/WHO Workshop, 1–3 September, 2004, Kobe, Japan,* Rome: WHO. **> 92–99**

WHO World Health Organization (2009) *10 facts about water scarcity,* Available online: <http://who.int/features/factfiles/water/en> (accessed 4 Aug 2012). **> 68–75**

WHO World Health Organisation (2012) *Global Health Observatory: Urban population growth,* Available online: <http://www.who.int/gho/urban_health/situation_trends/urban_population_growth_text/en> (accessed 16 May 2012). **> 1–5**

Williams, A.G., Audsley, E. and Sandars, D.L. (2006) *Determining the environmental burdens and resource use in the production of agricultural and horticultural commodities,* Main Report DEFRA Research Project IS0205, Bedford: Cranfield University and DEFRA. **> 76–83**

Williams, A.G., Audsley, E., Pell, E., Moorehouse, E. and Webb, J. (2009) *Comparative Life Cycle Assessment of Food Commodities Procured for UK Consumption through a Diversity of Supply Chains,* Main Report DEFRA Research Project FO0103, Bedford: Cranfield University and DEFRA. **> 76–83**

Wiltshire, J., Tucker, G., Williams, A.G., Foster, C., Wynn, S., Thorn, R. and Chadwick, D. (2009) *Scenario building to test and inform the development of a BSI method for assessing GHG emissions from food,* Research Report FO0404, London: DEFRA, Available online: <http://randd.defra.gov.uk/Default.aspx?Menu=Menu&Module=More&Location=None&Completed=0&ProjectID=15650> (accessed 16 May 2012). **> 76–83**

Winne, M. (2008) *Closing the food gap,* Boston: Beacon Press. **> 18–23**

Winston, M.L. (1998) *From where I sit: Essays on bees, beekeeping, and science,* Ithaca NY; London: Comstock Pub. Associates. **> 84–91**

Wood, H. (2012) *White paper: Sustainable design teaching and practice,* in: *The Architects Journal,* no. 8, Available online: <http://www.architects-journal.co.uk/footprint/footprint-blog/-white-paper-sustainable-design-teaching-and-practice/8634451.article#> (accessed 30 Aug 2012). **> 12–17**

● Woods, J. (no date) *The Urban Aquaculture Manual*, Available online: <http://www.webofcreation.org/BuildingGrounds/aqua/Chap4.html> (accessed 16 May 2012). **> 240–243**

● Worcester University (2010) *Honey bees find richer diversity of pollen in urban areas,* Available online: <http://www.worcester.ac.uk/discover/honey-bees-find-richer-diversity-of-pollen-in-urban-areas.html> (accessed 1 Aug 2012). **> 84–91**

● Wrigley, E.A. (1988) *Continuity, Chance and Change: The character of the industrial revolution in England*, Cambridge: Cambridge University Press. **> 48–53**

● Wuhlegarten (no date) *wu'hпêgárteň: Interkultureller Garten Berlin-Köpenick e.V.*, Available online: <http://wuhlegarten.de/history> (accessed 16 May 2012). **> 92–99**

● ZALF Leibnitz-Institut für Agrarlandforschung e.V. (2011) *ZFarm: Städtische Landwirtschaft der Zukunft: Innovations- und Technikanalyse Zero Acreage Farming*, Available online: <http://www.zfarm.de/> (accessed 16 May 12). **> 155–161**

● Zeveloff, J. (2011) *Tour the hi-tech farm that's growing 100 tons of greens on the roof of a Brooklyn warehouse*, Available online: <http://www.businessinsider.com/gotham-greens-2011-7> (accessed 23 May 2012). **> 40–47**

● Ziesemer, J. (2007) *Energy use in organic food systems*, Rome: Natural Resources Management and Environment Department, Food and Agriculture Organization of the United Nations, Available online: <http://www.fbae.org/2009/FBAE/website/images/pdf/imporatant-publication/fao-organic-report.pdf> (accessed 16 May 2012). **> 76–83**

● 596 Acres (no date) *596 Acres*, Available online: <http://596acres.org> (accessed 16 May 2012). **> 138–145**

Notes on contributors

KATRIN BOHN

Katrin Bohn is an architect and visiting professor at the Technical University of Berlin. For the past 12 years, she has also taught architecture and urban design, mainly as a senior lecturer at the University of Brighton. Together with André Viljoen, she runs *Bohn&Viljoen Architects*, a small architectural practice and environmental consultancy based in London. Bohn&Viljoen have taught, lectured, published and exhibited widely on the design concept of *CPUL City (Continuous Productive Urban Landscape)* which they contributed to the international urban design discourse in 2004. Katrin's projects on productive urban landscapes include feasibility and design studies as well as food growing installations and public events, mainly for UK and German clients.

ANDRÉ VILJOEN

André Viljoen is an architect and principal lecturer at the University of Brighton and, with Katrin Bohn, contributes to the work of *Bohn&Viljoen Architects*. The publication, in 2005, of Bohn&Viljoen's book *CPULs Continuous Productive Urban Landscapes: Designing urban agriculture for sustainable cities* consolidated a body of research making the case for urban agriculture as an essential element of sustainable urban infrastructure. This book and the associated design concept had a significant international impact, resulting in invitations to consult, exhibit and lecture widely. In 2012, André jointly edited the book *Sustainable Food Planning: Evolving theory and practice*. This collection was the first of its kind to bring the disciplines of planning, design, public health and governance into dialogue to address the global challenge of food security.

NISHAT AWAN

Nishat Awan is a writer and spatial practitioner whose research interests include the production and representation of migratory spaces, enquiries into the topological as method and alternative modes of architectural practice. She is co-author of *Spatial Agency*, published by Routledge in 2011, and co-editor of *Trans-Local-Act*, published by aaa-peprav in 2011. She is a founding member of the art/architecture collective OPENkhana and is a Lecturer in Architecture at the University of Sheffield, UK.

GIANLUCA BRUNORI

Gianluca Brunori is full professor at Pisa University, Department of Agriculture, Food and Environment. His research activities focus on rural development strategies and on marketing of local food. Gianluca has been coordinator of the EU research project *Transforming Rural Communication (TRUC)* and has participated as leader of local research teams in several EU projects such as *Support of Learning and Innovation Networks for Sustainable Agriculture (SOLINSA), Knowledge brokerage to promote sustainable food consumption and production: Linking scientists, policy makers and civil society organisations (FOOD-LINKS)* and *Strengthening Innovation Processes for Growth and Development (IN-SIGHT)*.

NEVIN COHEN

Dr Nevin Cohen is Assistant Professor of Environmental Studies at The New School in New York, where he teaches courses in urban food systems and environmental planning and policy. His current research focuses on the development of urban food policy, the use of urban space for food production, and planning for ecologically sound urban food systems. Nevin is currently working on two book projects: a study of food policy-making in US and Canadian cities and an analysis of urban agriculture projects that focus on social justice. He has a PhD in Planning from Rutgers University, a Masters in Urban Planning from Berkeley, and a BA from Cornell.

VICTOR COLEMAN

Victor Coleman's professional training and early career as a Chartered Surveyor in local government focused on the repair and maintenance of public buildings. He is a fellow of the *Royal Institution of Chartered Surveyors* and *The Association of Building Engineers*. Victor managed his own practice for eight years and then sold the business to Lloyds Banking Group, remaining with Lloyds as a management surveyor. The recent recession provided an opportunity to undertake international voluntary work and research. In 2012, Victor graduated with a first class honours degree in Commercial Horticulture from Hadlow College, University of Greenwich.

DAVID CROUCH

David Crouch is one of the expert authors contributing to *CPUL 1*.

GILLEAN DENNY

A Philadelphia native, Gillean Denny obtained a Bachelors in Architecture from The Pennsylvania State University before pursuing an MPhil and PhD at the University of Cambridge as member of the *Gates-Cambridge Scholars*. Gillean has been involved with a number of design-build projects, dedicated to using local resources for the development of sustainable communities. Interested in the historical developments of urbanisation and the integration of sustainable practices in modern society, she has since examined the role of the urban plan in the reduction of environmental degradation. Outside of her research, Gillean pursues interests in a variety of diverse fields from architectural history to theatrical design.

FRANCESCO DI IACOVO

Francesco Di Iacovo is Professor in Agricultural Economics at Pisa University. His research activities are focused on multifunctional and peri-urban agriculture, land planning, social farming and social development in rural areas, and food issues. A member

of several EU projects (*SoFar, COST 866, Food-link, TRUC*), he is local coordinator of the *IMRD-EU-Erasmus Mundus*.

KEN ELKES

Ken Elkes represents Jeremy Iles who is one of the expert authors contributing to *CPUL 1*.

JAMES GODSIL

James Godsil is co-founder of *Sweet Water Organics* and the *Sweet Water Foundation*. He is now the president of the *Sweet Water Foundation (SWF)* and *Community Roofing & Restoration (CRR)* and is a past president of *ESHAC Inc*. He is also the co-founder of *Milwaukee Preservation Alliance, Milwaukee-Renaissance.com* and the *Indo American Aquaponics Institute (IAAI)*, a global coalition of development professionals and experts in their own fields of work. Between 2005 and 2010, James served on the *Growing Power* board. He was Milwaukee Entrepreneur of the Year 2010 and Mandi Award Navigator Finalist in 2013. In 2011, he took part in the *State Department American Speakers Program* in India. For his work in the *Bonobo Congo*

Biodiversity Initiative, he received the Milwaukee Zoological Society Award in 2008. James holds an MA from St Louis University Center for Urban Programs and is a Fulbright Fellow.

MARK GORGOLEWSKI

Dr Mark Gorgolewski is Professor and Program Director for the graduate program in the building science at Ryerson University in Toronto. He has worked for many years as an architect, researcher and sustainable building consultant in Canada and the UK. He is a director of the *Canada Green Building Council* and past chair of the *Association for Environment Conscious Building* (in the UK). He is co-author and curator of the *Carrot City* book and exhibit and has written several other books and many papers. Mark has received several awards for his teaching and research and participated in various sustainable building projects, including a winning design for the *CMHC Equilibrium (net zero energy) Housing Competition*.

YRJÖ HAILA

Yrjö Haila is Professor of Environmental Policy at the University of Tampere since 1995. He studied ecological zoology, with philosophy as secondary subject, at the University of Helsinki and defended his PhD thesis in 1983. Later he focused on ecological changes in environments intensively modified by humans, such as cities and commercially managed forests, and more theoretically on the nature–society interface. Yrjö has published *Humanity and Nature* with Richard Levins, published by Pluto Press in 1992, and *How Nature Speaks: The Dynamics of the Human Ecological Condition* which he co-edited with Chuck Dyke, published by Duke University Press in 2006, and several books in Finnish.

STEFAN JORDAN

Stefan Jordan has been a professional grower since 1984. He started in the UK as a YTS horticultural trainee taken on full-time in field-grown nursery stock. He moved to Poland for two years with the Institute of Pomology and Floriculture in Skierniewice. Back to the UK, Stefan studied for an HND in commercial horticulture at Writtle College to then take up a sandwich placement in France on organic top fruit farm and nursery stock with *Pépinières Bordet*. He worked there for many years before returning to the UK and lecturing in horticulture, forestry and arboriculture at Hadlow College in Kent. In this latest time, he had the opportunity to grow various crops in as many growing systems, and was equally fortunate to get his students involved with a variety of national and local food growing initiatives.

JUNE KOMISAR

June Komisar is an architect and an associate professor in the Department of Architectural Science at Ryerson University in Toronto. She has a professional degree in architecture from Yale University and a doctorate from the University of Michigan. She is a member of the *Toronto Food Policy Council* and an associate of the *Ryerson Centre for Studies in Food Security*. Her research interests include Brazilian architecture, historic preservation and adaptive reuse, as well as socially responsible design. June is a co-author of *Carrot City: Creating Places for Urban Agriculture,* with Mark Gorgolewski and Joe Nasr, as well as co-curator of the exhibit *Carrot City*.

HOWARD LEE

Dr Howard Lee trained initially as an ecologist (MSc ecology), but then moved into agriculture as a government potato breeder, combined with lecturing at Queen's University Belfast. In 1990, he took a Senior Lectureship at Wye College (University of London) and subsequently at Imperial College where he initiated, directed and taught on Britain's first MSc in sustainable agriculture and rural development (SARD). He moved to Hadlow College in 2004 and has lectured there until now. In 2006, he started Britain's first Foundation Degree in sustainable land management and continues to lead and teach on various aspects of sustainable agriculture to a range of degrees. Howard helped initiate the *HadLOW CARBON Community* and facilitated a community allotment on College land, which continues to be managed by village families and assisted by College staff and students.

ELISABETH MEYER-RENSCHHAUSEN

Elisabeth Meyer-Renschhausen is a freelance researcher and author on urban agriculture as well as a garden activist. After her doctorate, a study about the first women's movement in Germany, she became an associate professor/lecturer at the Department for Political Sciences and Sociology at the Free University of Berlin. She teaches at various universities in Germany and abroad. Her research addresses issues such as food cultures, globalisation, small-scale agriculture and community gardening, subject areas on which she has written and co-edited a number of books. Elisabeth is a co-founder of the *Allmende-Kontor* community garden on the former airport of Berlin-Tempelhof and recently founded three 'intercultural gardens' in Oldenburg.

KEVIN MORGAN

Kevin Morgan is Professor of Governance and Development in the School of Planning and Geography at Cardiff University. His food research interests cover public food provisioning, community food enterprises and urban food strategies. He is the co-author of *The School Food Revolution: Public Food and the Challenge of Sustainable Development*, published by Earthscan, and *Worlds of Food: Place, Power and Provenance in the Food Chain*, published by Oxford University Press. In addition to his academic research, he is actively involved in food policy activity in his capacity as a member of the *Food Ethics Council*, the chair of the *Bristol Food Policy Council* and coordinator of the *AESOP* sustainable food planning group.

JOE NASR

Dr Joe Nasr is an independent scholar, lecturer and consultant based in Toronto. He co-curated the travelling exhibit *Carrot City*, now adapted into a book and website repository. Joe has taught and held postdoctoral fellowships at a number of universities in several countries. He is a regular lecturer at Ryerson University and an Associate at its Centre for Studies in Food Security. He coordinated a training course on urban agriculture in the Middle East and North Africa. Joe is co-author or co-editor of four books, including the

seminal *Urban Agriculture: Food, Jobs and Sustainable Cities,* and author of dozens of articles.

PHILIPP OSWALT

Philipp Oswalt is an architect and writer. From 1988 to 1994 he worked as editor for the architectural journal *Arch+* and, in 1996/97, as architect for the Office for Metropolitan Architecture/Rem Koolhaas in Rotterdam. He taught as Visiting Professor for Design at the Technical University Cottbus (2000–2002) and, since 2006, has been Professor for Architecture Theory and Design at Kassel University. Philipp was the initiator and coordinator of the European Research project *Urban Catalysts* (2001–2003) on temporality in urban space, financed by the European Commission programme *City of Tomorrow*. He was also chief curator of the international research and exhibition project *Shrinking Cities* for the German Cultural Foundation (2002–2008) and co-curator of *Volkspalast* (2004), on the cultural use of the former *Palast der Republik* in Berlin. Since 2009 he has been director of the Bauhaus Dessau Foundation.

JORGE PEÑA DIAZ

Jorge Peña Diaz is one of the expert authors contributing to *CPUL 1*.

MARIT ROSOL

Marit Rosol has worked since 2006 as lecturer and researcher at the Department of Human Geography in Frankfurt/Main. She received her PhD from the Geographical Institute at the Humboldt-Universität zu Berlin in the same year. Prior to that, she studied Urban and Regional Planning in Berlin and Madrid, Spain. In 2012, she finished her habilitation research project on the question of 'governing through participation', based in parts on her empirical work in Vancouver, Canada. Her main focus in research and teaching consists in connecting processes of urban development with social theory. She also specialises in urban and landscape planning, urban gardening as well as participation studies. She has been working on the topic of community gardening since 2002.

GRAEME SHERRIFF

Graeme Sherriff is one of the expert authors contributing to *CPUL 1*.

MIKEY TOMKINS

Mikey Tomkins is a PhD student at the University of Brighton. His research looks at community food growing as an everyday practice and its potential contribution to concepts of urban agriculture. He is also a beekeeper, having kept bees in central London since 2000. In 2010, Mikey became project officer at *Sustain*, running the *Capital Bee* campaign for two years. The campaign facilitated apiaries in 50 communities through a dedicated training programme. Latterly it campaigned for a pesticide-free London. *Capital Bee* formed part of the overall *Capital Growth* campaign to support community food-growing in London.

URBANIAHOEVE

In the style of naming one's land and landscapes, from 'Walden' to 'Farm', places inspired by self-reliance and conviviality, Urbaniahoeve in Dutch means 'the city (as a) farmyard', indicating the ready-built city as the place where we might 'get ourselves back to the garden'. *Urbaniahoeve*, Social Design Lab for Urban Agriculture is artist Debra Solomon (art director), art historian Mariska van den Berg (writer/researcher of bottom-up public space infrastructure), and historian Annet van Otterloo (producer and project coordinator of artist-initiated urban regeneration). Their critical spatial practice comprises action research, creating spatial planning visioning for municipalities, and working with communities to build an edible ecological framework into our urban neighbourhoods.

YUNEIKYS VILLALONGA

Yuneikys Villalonga holds a BA in Art History from the University of Havana (2000) and is a curator and art critic working with Lehman College Art Gallery/ CUNY, New York. She is a contributor to the magazine *Art Experience: New York* and part of the curatorial team of the project *Artist Pension Trust*. Yuneikys worked as a curator at the Ludwig Foundation of Cuba (2000–2004) and as a lecturer at the Higher Institute of Art (2000–2004) and the

Behavior Art Workshop, led by artist Tania Bruguera (2005–2006) in Havana. In 2004, she won the National Prize of Curatorship from the National Union of Cuban Writers and Artists.

SABINE VOGGENREITER

Sabine Voggenreiter, MA, studied literature, philosophy and the history of art in Marburg. In the 1980s she was in charge of the *Pentagon Gallery* in Cologne. In 1989, she founded the *PASSAGEN* design festival, which takes place each year and has become the largest design event in Germany. In 1999, together with Kay von Keitz, she established the architecture forum *plan – Architektur Biennale Köln*, a flagship project that is part of the building culture initiative of the Ministry of Housing and Urban Development of the land North Rhine-Westphalia. In 2008, she won the EU competition Create NRW concerning the development of a creative neighbourhood in Cologne, *Design Quartier Ehrenfeld – DQE*. Sabine organises and curates exhibitions and arranges competitions, workshops and symposia in the fields of design, architecture

and art. She is the editor of numerous publications. In 2012, she was awarded Cultural Manager of the Year of the City of Cologne.

RICHARD WILTSHIRE

Richard Wiltshire is one of the expert authors contributing to *CPUL 1*.

Image credits

All images are copyright to the respective authors of the chapters in which they appear, except where stated otherwise within that chapter. For images in Bohn&Viljoen authored chapters we would like to acknowledge the following contributors or collaborators who generated these images with or for us, usually as part of fruitful design research processes:

CPUL City Theory

CHAPTER:
The *CPUL City* concept
Fig 1: B&V with Eva Benito Benito
Fig 2: B&V with Eva Benito Benito and Áine Moriarty

CHAPTER:
Productive life in the city
Fig 1: B&V with Thomas Müller

CPUL City Actions

CHAPTER:
An introduction
Fig 1: B&V with Nishat Awan, Department City & Nutrition Technical University of Berlin

CHAPTER:
The Urban Agriculture Curtain
Fig 2 and Fig 6: B&V with Marcel Croxson and Jack Wates

CHAPTER:
London Thames Gateway
Fig 1 and Fig 7: B&V with Mike Aling
Fig 2: B&V with Katja Schäfer and Jorge Peña Diaz
Fig 6 and Fig 8: B&V with Kabage Karanja

CHAPTER:
The Urban Farming Project
Fig 2: B&V with Nishat Awan, Department City & Nutrition Technical University of Berlin
Fig 9: B&V with Victoria Ridge

CHAPTER:
Urban Nature Shoreditch
Fig 3 and Fig 4: B&V with Eva Benito Benito
Fig 5: B&V with Eva Benito Benito and Lucy Taussig
Fig 6: B&V with Jonathan Gales and John Hibbett
Fig 7: B&V with Lucy Taussig
Fig 8: B&V with Áine Moriarty

CHAPTER:
The Continuous Picnic
Fig 2, Fig 6 and Fig 7: Jonathan Gales
Fig 3: B&V with Studio Columba
Fig 5: B&V with Nishat Awan, Department City & Nutrition Technical University of Berlin
Fig 8 and Fig 9: B&V with Christoph Holz

CHAPTER:
Urbane Agrikultur in Köln-Ehrenfeld
Fig 8: B&V with Nishat Awan, Department City & Nutrition Technical University of Berlin

CHAPTER:
Unlocking Spaces
Fig 2: B&V with Vaida Morkunaite, School of Architecture & Design University of Brighton
Fig 4 and Fig 7: Jonathan Gales
Fig 6: B&V with Studio Columba

CHAPTER:
Growing Balconies
Fig 3: B&V with Nishat Awan, Department City & Nutrition Technical University of Berlin

CPUL Repository

CHAPTER:
An introduction
Fig 1: B&V with Susanne Hausstein

Cover

Cover design: B&V with Susanne Hausstein
Cover image: B&V with Victoria Ridge

Index

Acknowledgements

As editors and authors we have a great number of people whose input, criticism, inspiration and support we wish to acknowledge. It is impossible to credit everyone individually, but many are named in the book's chapters. We owe a profound gratitude to all our contributing authors whose expertise allows for deeper insights into the *CPUL City* concept. It was also especially rewarding for us to be able to include reflections on developments in the field from contributors to the original 2005 *CPUL* book.

We would like to make a special acknowledgement to Nishat Awan, and to Susanne Hausstein and Stephen Moylan for their contribution to the book's graphic design and layout. A thank you also to Colin Priest and Amir Djalali for their critical eye and thumbs up at the beginning of the layouting process. Finally, to Routledge, our publishers, in particular Alex Hollingsworth and graphic designer Alex Lazarou for their creative inputs overall, as well as for bearing with us …

The University of Brighton and The Technical University of Berlin where we hold academic posts have enabled much of our work to advance, in general with their supportive research frameworks and in particular through funding research opportunities. Our work has also been enriched through our participation in the annual Sustainable Food Planning Conferences initiated by the Association of European Schools of Planning (AESOP) and being part of this wide multidisciplinary community of researchers, practitioners, activists and academics.

We would also like to thank all of those collaborators, amongst them many former students, who worked with us within *Bohn&Viljoen Architects* on the projects presented here, and thank you to Tom Phillips for welcoming us in his wonderful studio.

Katrin would like to thank Undine Giseke for the help and guidance received during her guest professorship at the Technical University in Berlin, as well as the staff at the Institute for Landscape Architecture and Environmental Planning for their ongoing support. She would also like to acknowledge, as chair of the Institute's department City and Nutrition, the enjoyable work with colleagues Nishat Awan and Kristian Ritzmann, which, amongst others, lead to the 'process diagrams' used in this book.

André would like to acknowledge the University of Brighton Sabbatical Award that enabled his 2011 field trip to the USA. There, Anastasia Cole Plakias, Jerry Caldari, Mara Gittleman, Kelli Jordan, Nevin Cohen, Jordan Bracket, Jo Foster, Yuni Villalonga, Pavel Acosta, Kami Pothukuchi, Sam Molnar, Dan Carmody, Ashley Atkinson, Gary Wozniack, John Gallagher, Shane Bernardo, Daryl Pierson, Malik Yakini, Dan Pitera, Charles Cross, Martin Bailkey, Will Allen, Jerry Kaufman, Marcia Caton Campbell, Heather Stouder, Mat Tucker, Rocky Marcoux, Tom Kubala, James Godsil and their colleagues all made time to meet and share knowledge.

Last, but not least, we would like to thank our families and friends in Germany, the UK, Ireland, South Africa and elsewhere in the world for their joy, stories and support. Especially, we would like to thank Thomas for innumerable delicious meals made with innumerable local or organic ingredients – as well as listening to CPUL chatter between a lot of other wonderful things.

Alma, Bertie and Lilo are some of those special people for whom we are doing this work and who have the freedom to twitch their small noses when being offered organic or local or ecological food. We would like to thank them for their presence and patience during many weekends in fields, at urban farms, installations or exhibitions, sometimes in the sun, sometimes in the rain.

Katrin Bohn & André Viljoen

Starting a productive urban landscape is the most important
action. It might then become continuous in a multitude of senses...
(image: Spiel/Feld Marzahn, Berlin, Germany, 2011– ongoing)